Jerusalem

Paul Hellander
Andrew Humphreys

LONELY PLANET PUBLICATIONS
Melbourne • Oakland • London • Paris

Jerusalem
2nd edition – October 1999
First published – March 1997

Published by
Lonely Planet Publications Pty Ltd A.C.N. 005 607 983
192 Burwood Rd, Hawthorn, Victoria 3122, Australia

Lonely Planet Offices
Australia PO Box 617, Hawthorn, Victoria 3122
USA 150 Linden St, Oakland, CA 94607
UK 10a Spring Place, London NW5 3BH
France 1 rue du Dahomey, 75011 Paris

Photographs
Many of the images in this guide are available for licensing from
Lonely Planet Images.
email: lpi@lonelyplanet.com.au

Front cover photograph
Panoramic view of Jerusalem (Alon Reininger, PNI)

ISBN 0 86442 784 0

text & maps © Lonely Planet 1999
photos © photographers as indicated 1999

Printed by Colorcraft Ltd, Hong Kong

Contents – Text

THE AUTHORS   3

THIS BOOK   4

FOREWORD   5

INTRODUCTION   9

FACTS ABOUT JERUSALEM   10

History 10
Geography 18
Climate 18
Ecology & Environment 18
Government & Politics 19
Economy 19
Population & People 20
Arts 21
Society & Conduct 25
Religion 27
Language 34

FACTS FOR THE VISITOR   36

When to Go 36
Orientation 36
Maps 37
Responsible Tourism 37
Tourist Offices 37
Documents 38
Embassies & Consulates 40
Customs 42
Money 42
Post & Communications 45
Books 48
CD ROMs 49
Newspapers & Magazines 49
Radio & TV 49
Photography & Video 50
Time 50
Electricity 50
Weights & Measures 50
Laundry 50
Health 50
Women Travellers 51
Gay & Lesbian Travellers 52
Disabled Travellers 52
Jerusalem For Children 52
Useful Organisations 53
Libraries 53
Cultural Centres 53
Dangers & Annoyances 53
Business Hours 54
Public Holidays 54
Special Events 56
Doing Business 57
Work 57

JEWISH FESTIVALS   58

GETTING THERE & AWAY   63

Air 63
Boat 67
Land 68
Warning 72

GETTING AROUND   73

To/From the Airport 73
Bus 73
Car & Motorcycle 74
Taxi 75
Bicycle 76
Organised Tours 76

THINGS TO SEE & DO   78

The Old City 78
Mt Zion 102
Kidron Valley 105
Mount of Olives 107
Mt Scopus 109
East Jerusalem 110
The New City Centre 113
Mea She'arim & The
Bukharan Quarter 116
Rehavia & Talbiyeh 119
Mamilla 119
The German Colony 122
Talpiot 122
Givat Ram & Museum Row ..123
Israel Museum 124
West of the New City 131
Activities 134
Courses 135

PLACES TO STAY
136

Places to Stay – Budget 137   Places to Stay – Top End 144
Places to Stay –
Mid-Range 140

PLACES TO EAT
146

Vegetarian & Health Food ..146   Ashkenazi 151   South American 153
Felafel, Shwarma &   Arabic 151   Asian 153
Humous 147   Armenian 152   Other Restaurants 154
Cafés 148   Greek 152   Places To Eat – Top End 154
Burgers & Pizza 150   Italian 152
Oriental (Sephardic) 150   Kurdish & Persian 153

ENTERTAINMENT
156

Bars & Clubs 156   Classical Music 158   Theatre 159
Folk/Traditional Music 158   Cinemas 158   Spectator Sports 159

SHOPPING
160

What To Buy 160

EXCURSIONS
163

Around Jerusalem 163   Jericho 167   Tel Aviv 170
Bethlehem 166   The Dead Sea 168

LANGUAGE
173

Hebrew 173   Arabic 174

GLOSSARY
176

Hebrew, Yiddish & Aramaic ..176   Arabic 178   Food Glossary 180

INDEX
188

Text 188   Boxed Text 192

METRIC CONVERSION
inside back cover

Contents – Maps

THINGS TO SEE & DO

Haram ash-Sharif/   Via Dolorosa 95   Yad Vashem 133
Temple Mount 85   Church of the Holy Sepulchre ..99

EXCURSIONS

Around Jerusalem 163

COLOUR MAPS
see back pages

MAP LEGEND
see back page

The Authors

Paul Hellander

Paul has never really stopped travelling since he was born in England to a Norwegian father and English mother. He graduated with a degree in Ancient, Byzantine and Modern Greek before arriving in Australia in 1977, via Greece and 30 other countries. He subsequently taught Modern Greek and trained interpreters and translators for thirteen years before throwing it all away for a life as a travel writer. Paul joined Lonely Planet in 1994 and wrote LP's *Greek Phrasebook* before being assigned to Greece and Eastern Europe where he covered Albania, Bulgaria, FYROM and Yugoslavia. Paul has also updated *Singapore* and covered Singapore in LP's *Malaysia, Singapore & Brunei* and *South-East Asia* guides. He can usually be found in cyberspace at paul@planetmail.net. When not travelling, he resides in Adelaide, South Australia, where he has a predilection for cooking Asian food and growing hot chillies. He was last seen heading for Greece and Cyprus.

Andrew Humphreys

Andrew has been living, travelling and working in the Middle East on and off since 1988 when he first went to Cairo on holiday and took three years to leave. Originally trained in London as an architect, while in Egypt he slid over into writing through a growing fascination with Islamic buildings. Following a spell in mainstream journalism based for several years in the Baltic States, Andrew hooked up with Lonely Planet for a return to the Middle East and has since authored guides to Central Asia, Egypt, Middle East, Syria, Jerusalem and Cairo.

FROM PAUL

During a busy and invigorating stay in Jerusalem many people offered invaluable assistance as I tried to juggle and filter a mind-numbing amount of information. Andrew Humphreys' meticulous work on the first edition made my task immeasurably easier. Thanks to David Beirman of the Sydney office of the Israel Government Tourist Office for the wealth of printed material and leads. A big 'todah' to fellow-author Daniel Robinson of Tel Aviv for his selfless assistance with background data; to Ohad & Einav Sharav for their invaluable contributions to the glossary; to David Martin of the British Council in East Jerusalem and his team; to Deborah Lipson for being an erudite guide and adviser; to Vincent Simmons for last-minute information; to Danny Flax for the tips and trips around the city; to Chaim Rockman for giving me pedal power; to the people of Jerusalem for their patience and understanding of my often seemingly trivial questions and for their enduring tenacity and resilience while sometimes living 'on the edge'.

Without Stella's blessing these assignments and long absences from home would not happen – todah! Byron & Marcus, here's another one to remember your old man by.

This Book

Andrew Humphreys researched and wrote the 1st edition of *Jerusalem*. Paul Hellander updated and expanded this 2nd edition.

From the Publisher
This book was edited and proofed by Ada Cheung, Katie Cody and Susan Holtham. Anna Judd coordinated the mapping and design; Mark Griffiths completed the layout and design of the book. Guillaume Roux designed the cover. Thanks to Kate Nolan for the illustrations and Quentin Frayne for putting together the Language chapter.

Acknowledgments
Many thanks to the travellers who used the last edition and wrote to us with helpful hints, useful advice, and interesting anecdotes:

Alberto Sigismondi, Anton Stonor, Arvid Leyman, Astrid Padberg, Ben Yehuda, Christina Helms, Crystal Cheng, D & B Schenfeld, Deniz Altayli, Dennis Riffel, Dorothy C Wertz, George Bond, Hanneke Fialka, Harry van Breen, Hugh Finsten, Jemgard Nissen, Jne Pieters, Julie Vowles, Kevin Kluetz, Mark Jarrett, Marvin Feldman, Mary Sunderland, Micah Maidenberg,'Philip Lim, Rees Cameron, Renata Cervenkova, Roger Butler, Sagie, Steve Dungey, Ted Bloomfield, The Supreme Court of Israel – Public Affairs Dept, UJ Hashem, Yoland & Rich Bodine, Zachary from Viamare.

Foreword

ABOUT LONELY PLANET GUIDEBOOKS

The story begins with a classic travel adventure: Tony and Maureen Wheeler's 1972 journey across Europe and Asia to Australia. Useful information about the overland trail did not exist at that time, so Tony and Maureen published the first Lonely Planet guidebook to meet a growing need.

From a kitchen table, then from a tiny office in Melbourne (Australia), Lonely Planet has become the largest independent travel publisher in the world, an international company with offices in Melbourne, Oakland (USA), London (UK) and Paris (France).

Today Lonely Planet guidebooks cover the globe. There is an ever-growing list of books and there's information in a variety of forms and media. Some things haven't changed. The main aim is still to help make it possible for adventurous travellers to get out there – to explore and better understand the world.

At Lonely Planet we believe travellers can make a positive contribution to the countries they visit – if they respect their host communities and spend their money wisely. Since 1986 a percentage of the income from each book has been donated to aid projects and human rights campaigns.

Updates Lonely Planet thoroughly updates each guidebook as often as possible. This usually means there are around two years between editions, although for more unusual or more stable destinations the gap can be longer. Check the imprint page (following the colour map at the beginning of the book) for publication dates.

Between editions up-to-date information is available in two free newsletters – the paper *Planet Talk* and email *Comet* (to subscribe, contact any Lonely Planet office) – and on our Web site at www.lonelyplanet.com. The *Upgrades* section of the Web site covers a number of important and volatile destinations and is regularly updated by Lonely Planet authors. *Scoop* covers news and current affairs relevant to travellers. And, lastly, the *Thorn Tree* bulletin board and *Postcards* section of the site carry unverified, but fascinating, reports from travellers.

Correspondence The process of creating new editions begins with the letters, postcards and emails received from travellers. This correspondence often includes suggestions, criticisms and comments about the current editions. Interesting excerpts are immediately passed on via newsletters and the Web site, and everything goes to our authors to be verified when they're researching on the road. We're keen to get more feedback from organisations or individuals who represent communities visited by travellers.

Lonely Planet gathers information for everyone who's curious about the planet – and especially for those who explore it first-hand. Through guidebooks, phrasebooks, activity guides, maps, literature, newsletters, image library, TV series and Web site we act as an information exchange for a worldwide community of travellers.

Research Authors aim to gather sufficient practical information to enable travellers to make informed choices and to make the mechanics of a journey run smoothly. They also research historical and cultural background to help enrich the travel experience and allow travellers to understand and respond appropriately to cultural and environmental issues.

Authors don't stay in every hotel because that would mean spending a couple of months in each medium-sized city and, no, they don't eat at every restaurant because that would mean stretching belts beyond capacity. They do visit hotels and restaurants to check standards and prices, but feedback based on readers' direct experiences can be very helpful.

Many of our authors work undercover, others aren't so secretive. None of them accept freebies in exchange for positive write-ups. And none of our guidebooks contain any advertising.

Production Authors submit their raw manuscripts and maps to offices in Australia, USA, UK or France. Editors and cartographers – all experienced travellers themselves – then begin the process of assembling the pieces. When the book finally hits the shops, some things are already out of date, we start getting feedback from readers and the process begins again ...

WARNING & REQUEST

Things change – prices go up, schedules change, good places go bad and bad places go bankrupt – nothing stays the same. So, if you find things better or worse, recently opened or long since closed, please tell us and help make the next edition even more accurate and useful. We genuinely value all the feedback we receive. Julie Young coordinates a well travelled team that reads and acknowledges every letter, postcard and email and ensures that every morsel of information finds its way to the appropriate authors, editors and cartographers for verification.

Everyone who writes to us will find their name in the next edition of the appropriate guidebook. They will also receive the latest issue of *Planet Talk*, our quarterly printed newsletter, or *Comet*, our monthly email newsletter. Subscriptions to both newsletters are free. The very best contributions will be rewarded with a free guidebook.

Excerpts from your correspondence may appear in new editions of Lonely Planet guidebooks, the Lonely Planet Web site, *Planet Talk* or *Comet*, so please let us know if you *don't* want your letter published or your name acknowledged.

Send all correspondence to the Lonely Planet office closest to you:

Australia: PO Box 617, Hawthorn, Victoria 3122
USA: 150 Linden St, Oakland, CA 94607
UK: 10A Spring Place, London NW5 3BH
France: 1 rue du Dahomey, 75011 Paris

Or email us at: talk2us@lonelyplanet.com.au

For news, views and updates see our Web site: www.lonelyplanet.com

HOW TO USE A LONELY PLANET GUIDEBOOK

The best way to use a Lonely Planet guidebook is any way you choose. At Lonely Planet we believe the most memorable travel experiences are often those that are unexpected, and the finest discoveries are those you make yourself. Guidebooks are not intended to be used as if they provide a detailed set of infallible instructions!

Contents All Lonely Planet guidebooks follow roughly the same format. The Facts about the Destination chapters or sections give background information ranging from history to weather. Facts for the Visitor gives practical information on issues like visas and health. Getting There & Away gives a brief starting point for researching travel to and from the destination. Getting Around gives an overview of the transport options when you arrive.

The peculiar demands of each destination determine how subsequent chapters are broken up, but some things remain constant. We always start with background, then proceed to sights, places to stay, places to eat, entertainment, getting there and away, and getting around information – in that order.

Heading Hierarchy Lonely Planet headings are used in a strict hierarchical structure that can be visualised as a set of Russian dolls. Each heading (and its following text) is encompassed by any preceding heading that is higher on the hierarchical ladder.

Entry Points We do not assume guidebooks will be read from beginning to end, but that people will dip into them. The traditional entry points are the list of contents and the index. In addition, however, some books have a complete list of maps and an index map illustrating map coverage.

There may also be a colour map that shows highlights. These highlights are dealt with in greater detail in the Facts for the Visitor chapter, along with planning questions and suggested itineraries. Each chapter covering a geographical region usually begins with a locator map and another list of highlights. Once you find something of interest in a list of highlights, turn to the index.

Maps Maps play a crucial role in Lonely Planet guidebooks and include a huge amount of information. A legend is printed on the back page. We seek to have complete consistency between maps and text, and to have every important place in the text captured on a map. Map key numbers usually start in the top left corner.

> Although inclusion in a guidebook usually implies a recommendation we cannot list every good place. Exclusion does not necessarily imply criticism. In fact there are a number of reasons why we might exclude a place – sometimes it is simply inappropriate to encourage an influx of travellers.

Introduction

Jerusalem is as much a concept as a physical city filled with people of flesh and blood. The site of David's kingdom and of the Jewish temple, of the crucifixion of Jesus, and of Mohammed's ascent to heaven, it's a place born of biblical tales and childhood wonder. For most young children Jerusalem is as fabled as Mt Olympus or Valhalla, if a little less exciting – no thunderbolts or battles with giants. It's a city that appears remarkably different to each pair of eyes; individual interpretation is shaped by faith and beliefs, (and the degree to which they're held), by received history, and by nationality.

It's also a city in which little tolerance has ever been shown for the opinion of one's fellow man. It is reckoned that, over the ages, more people have given up their lives for some particular vision of Jerusalem than has been the case for any other city. The conflict continues today, inexhaustibly fuelled by events that took place not just years ago but centuries and even millenia ago. History is relentlessly evoked every day to justify actions that to the outsider seem unfathomable and unpardonable.

But Jerusalem is also very much a city of the moment – history here is also something that is happening now. Anyone wanting a crash course in the modern Middle East should start by spending 10 minutes at Jerusalem's central bus station. Black-garbed haredim press shoulders with teenage conscripts, male and female, fooling around and only a little encumbered by their rifles. Yemenite music plays somewhere, competing with a Russian immigrant violinist busking Yiddish folk tunes; and there will be one or two Palestinian Arabs. All of these peoples and their respective societies combine in Jerusalem, and all are actively trying to shape the modern city in their own image. While McDonald's and Tower Records have opened stores in secular Jerusalem, the number of *yeshivot* (Jewish seminaries) increases elsewhere; a Palestinian college is founded in East Jerusalem; another Russian-language newspaper appears. The richness and variety of contemporary Jerusalem is every bit equal to its more celebrated collection of often overly revered monuments.

Of course, it is precisely because of those monuments, and to gorge themselves on that history, that most visitors do come. The important thing is not to let the concept of Jerusalem get in the way of the city.

Facts about Jerusalem

HISTORY
David's City

Situated in the cradle of civilisation, the Land of Israel was destined to play a role in human history out of all proportion to its size, due to the fact that over 3000 years ago, a people settled on this Land with the conviction that it had been divinely assigned to them. Ever since, and even during 2000 years of exile, Jews have completely identified with Israel as their homeland, and with Jerusalem as their capital. Jerusalem subsequently acquired spiritual importance for Christianity due to its association with the life and death of Jesus; and for Islam, for which it became the third holiest city, and for whose followers Jerusalem is the place from where Mohammed ascended to heaven.

The first references to Jerusalem appear in the so-called 'Execration' texts from Egypt that date from the 20th to the 19th century BC. These two texts, thought to contain information for putting a curse over the pharaoh's enemies, both mention Jerusalem. A clearer historical record of Jerusalem, as a Canaanite city-state, appears in the archive of Tel el-Amarna (from 14th century BC Egypt), where a number of letters sent by the ruler of the city, Abdi-Hepa, to the pharaoh were found.

A more tangible history of Jerusalem begins in the Chalcolithic period (4th millennium BC) where graves and pottery from the early Bronze Age (4000 BC to early 3000 BC) have been found within the limits of the city, making this area one of the oldest settlements in the world.

However, the best-known historical story of Jerusalem begins in 1000 BC with David, king of the Israelites and slayer of Goliath. At the time of David, Jerusalem was held by the Jebusites and took the form of a small citadel on the Ophel Ridge, the area immediately south-east of the modern Jewish Quarter. Its unassuming location sat astride no trade routes, upon no high hill, next to no ocean nor river, yet because of its neutrality, it was an ideal site for David to make his capital city and thereby unite the disparate tribes.

The 'City of David' became the first unified Jewish capital, serving to tie together the previously disparate 12 tribes of Israelites. To his city the king brought the Ark of the Covenant, reputedly the chest built to contain the stone tablets on which the Ten Commandments were written. David died before his plans to build a house for the Ark saw fruition but the mission was taken up by his son and appointed successor, Solomon.

On a hill just to the north of the city, Solomon oversaw the construction of a vast temple (referred to by historians as the First Temple) which, when dedicated in approximately 950 BC, ensured Jerusalem's status as the focus of Jewish religious life. Solomon had chosen this particular hill, known as Mt Moriah, deliberately. According to Jewish tradition, it was the foundation stone of the world and was also the place where Abraham had been prepared to sacrifice his son Isaac to God and where he received God's covenant that the Land was 'promised to Abraham and his seed forever'. For Muslims, this story is one of the near-sacrifice of Ishmael, Abraham's son by his concubine Hagar, who was sent out into the desert and, it is said, became the forefather of the Arab peoples.

Despite this, the kingdom failed to survive the death of Solomon 17 years later, and split in two. Jerusalem remained as the capital of Judah, the kingdom comprising the three tribes that remained loyal to the lineage of David.

Fall of the First Temple Weakened by the split, first the 10 rogue tribes and then the Kingdom of Judah fell to the conquest of the Assyrians in 734 BC. Jerusalem survived intact by submitting to the suzerainty

Jerusalem Time Line

period	duration	major events	existing monuments
Canaanite	pre-1000 BC	City of Ursalim mentioned in Egyptian texts of 2000 BC.	
First Temple	1000 to 586 BC	David conquers Jerusalem. Solomon builds First Temple. Conquest and destruction by Nebuchadnezzar.	David's City archaeological excavations and Hezekiah's Tunnel
Second Temple	538 BC to 70 AD	Persian rule, then conquest by Alexander and Greek rule. Romans arrive in 63 BC. Reign of Herod the Great. Birth of Jesus.	Western Wall and Kidron Valley tombs
Roman	66 and 132	Jewish revolts, resulting in destruction of Second Temple (70 AD) and Jerusalem (135 AD). Building of Aelia Capitolina.	The Cardo in the Jewish Quarter of the Old City
Byzantine	324 to 638	Spate of biblical building led by Queen Helena, mother of Emperor Constantine.	Original parts of the Church of the Holy Sepulchre
Early Muslim	638 to 1099	Islamic conquest of Jerusalem led by Umayyad Caliph Omar.	Dome of the Rock and Al-Aqsa Mosque
Crusader	1099 to 1187	Massacre of Jews and Muslims.	St Anne's Church and most of the Church of the Holy Sepulchre
Ayyubid & Mamluk	1187 to 1517	Saladin conquers Jerusalem. Islamification of the city under Mamluks.	Many of the secondary structures on the Haram ash-Sharif
Ottoman	1517 to 1917	Jerusalem falls off the map for 300 years. First waves of Jewish immigration. First settlement outside the city walls in 1860s.	Suleyman's city walls, Mea She'arim and foundations of the New City
British Mandate	1917 to 1948	Jerusalem enters the 20th century. Palestinian Arab riots and uprisings.	Much of the central New City
Divided Jerusalem	1948 to 1967	State of Israel proclaimed, immediately triggering war. Jerusalem partitioned.	Divided Jerusalem is commemorated in the Tourjeman Post Museum and Artillery Hill Park
Unified Jerusalem	1967 to present	Israeli troops recapture Old City in Six Day War and annex East Jerusalem.	Western Wall plaza and Jewish Quarter of the Old City

Psalm 137

By the rivers of Babylon, there we sat down, yea, we wept, when we remembered Zion.
We hanged our harps upon the willows in the midst thereof.
For there they that carried us away captive required of us a song; and they that wasted us required of us mirth, saying,
Sing us one of the songs of Zion.
How shall we sing the Lord's song in a strange land?
If I forget thee, O Jerusalem, let my right hand forget her cunning.
If I do not remember thee, let my tongue cleave to the roof of my mouth; if I prefer not Jerusalem above my chief joy.

Extract from King James version

of the Assyrians until it became caught in the middle of a conflict between the Babylonians and Egyptians. The Jewish king, Zedekiah, backed the wrong side with the result that in 586 BC Jerusalem fell to Nebuchadnezzar, the King of Babylon. The Temple was destroyed (2 Kings 25, 2 Chronicles 36) and the Jews were driven from the city into exile. The bitterness of exile is encapsulated in Psalm 137, arguably the first literary evocation of Jerusalem. (See the boxed text 'Psalm 137'.)

Second Temple The period of exile lasted from 586 to 538 BC until the Babylonian empire fell to King Cyrus of Persia, who allowed the Jews to go home. He even donated money with which the Jerusalemites set about rebuilding their city, including the Temple. The Second Temple was completed around 515 BC. City walls were also added under the direction of the very able Persian-appointed governor, Nehemiah.

In 331 BC the unstoppable army of Alexander the Great rolled up on the scene and although he did not physically attack the city, the inhabitants of the area peacefully surrendered to him. Alexander's rule was benevolent, as initially was that of his successors, the Syrian-based Seleucids, but later attempts forcibly to Hellenise the Jewish population and Jerusalem itself – including the re-dedication of the Jewish

Temple to Zeus with the highly provocative sacrifice of a pig – triggered a revolt. The revolt was initiated by five brothers from the Hasmonean house, led by the eldest, Judah the Maccabee. The fight for religious freedom became a successful bid for political independence and an independent kingdom was established under a Hasmonean dynasty.

Fall of the Second Temple The victorious Hasmoneans were undermined by ideological rifts and the Jewish kingdom was easily swallowed by Pompey the Great's Roman armies. Herod the Great, whose parents were Nabateans (Arab traders) converted to Judaism, was installed by the Romans as king. A man of excesses, he built a great palatial fortress for his residence (on the site now occupied by the Citadel and stretching well into the Armenian Quarter). However, his major endeavour was to set 10,000 workmen to reconstruct and expand the Temple, so transforming it into 'the most wonderful edifice ever seen or spoken of', according to the historian Flavius Josephus, writing in the 1st century AD. At the time of Herod it is estimated that Jerusalem's population was around 100,000 – an enormous city for this period. At the beginning of the 19th century, the city's population was only 9000, and it did not regain the proportions it had in Herod's time until 1948.

Following the death of Herod, the Romans governed through military procurators. The most famous of these was Pontius Pilate, the man who ordered the crucifixion of Jesus of Nazareth. The Romans, with no religious or sentimental attachment to Jerusalem, governed from Caesarea.

Jesus was one of many orators critical of the materialism and decadence of the wealthy Jerusalemites, and contemptuous of Roman authority. Though his views represented those of many Jews, among whom religious and political upheaval was fermenting, he had very little impact while he was alive and it wasn't until some 300 or more years after his death, with the conversion of the Roman emperor Constantine to Christianity, that the ministry of the Nazarene began to spread.

In 40 AD the deranged emperor Gaius Caligula tried to erect his own image in the Temple; only his fortuitous assassination averted a revolt. Extremist elements urged the more moderate Jews into open revolt (the First Revolt of 66 AD). It took four years for the Romans to quell the uprising and it was only after a prolonged siege that, in 70 AD, the Roman general Titus breached the walls of Jerusalem. In retaliation the Temple was completely destroyed and the Jews were sold into slavery or exiled.

After the Roman destruction of the Second Temple and Jerusalem, in which they left standing only part of the four walls surrounding the Temple Mount and the towers that had guarded Herod's palace, the area remained largely uninhabited. The only exceptions were soldiers of the Roman Tenth Legion, many of whom probably lived in the ruins of the city.

Aelia Capitolina While Jerusalem remained standing it acted as a focus for renewed Jewish nationalist aspirations, and this prompted the emperor Hadrian to have the city razed to the ground. This action provoked the Second Revolt (132-35 AD), led by Simon Bar Kochba. It took three years, but the Romans prevailed again. As a precaution against further rebellion they executed Jewish leaders and elders, broke up communities and built their own Roman city of Aelia Capitolina on the levelled ruins of Jerusalem. The centre of this newly named province of Palestine was named after Hadrian's family and the three Capitolian Roman gods.

Hadrian's city has set the street pattern for the streets in the Old City until today, with four quarters divided by two intersecting main streets, known as the Cardo and the Decumanus. The Cardo still exists as Habad St/Souk Khan as-Zeit, while the Decumanus is now David St/Bab as-Silsila. The city in fact had two Cardines (plural of Cardo), and probably two Decumani too. The second Cardo is today Hagay St/ Share' al-Wad.

The Christian City
In 330 AD, Constantine was the first emperor to permit Christianity as a recognised religion of the newly decreed Holy Roman (Byzantine) empire, marking the beginning of more than 300 years of uninterrupted Christian rule in Jerusalem. The emperor's intensely religious mother, Helena, initiated a wave of biblical building which resulted in structures like the Church of the Holy Sepulchre and the Church of the Nativity in nearby Bethlehem.

The emperor Justinian ruled in the 6th century. He was a great builder in general, and in Jerusalem in particular, and was responsible for the construction of the Nea Church and repairs made to the city's walls and markets.

The Rise of Islam
Change came again in the 7th century. After weathering an invasion by the Persians, abetted by the Jews, the Byzantines were bundled out of Palestine by the sudden onslaught of a hitherto unknown force: the armies of Islam. Led by Caliph Omar ibn Khattab, the Muslims captured Jerusalem in 638 AD. The adherents of this new religion claimed Jerusalem as a sacred city because they believed the Prophet Mohammed had ascended to heaven from within its walls.

Yiddish

Yiddish is the language of the Ashkenazi Jews of Eastern and Central Europe. Written in the Hebrew script, it became one of the world's most widespread languages by the 19th century in places where Jewish communities were established. It, along with Hebrew and Aramaic, is one of the three major literary languages in Jewish history.

Yiddish probably originated in the 9th century, though the earliest written documents date back only to the 12th. It emerged as an adaptation of Middle High German and later gained a strong Slavic component. It was originally called Judisch-Deutsch (Jewish-German), but this term eventually gave way to the term Yiddish.

Yiddish-speakers simply call it 'Mama loschen', the mother tongue. This reflects the traditional split between the genders, with the men educated in the Hebrew and Aramaic of the Torah and the Talmud, and the women speaking Yiddish, the vernacular, in the home. A remnant of this attitude remains, with some ultra-orthodox continuing to object to the use of Hebrew as the national language of Israel on the grounds that the language in which Torah is written is itself holy and should be therefore be reserved for religious purposes only.

For several centuries after its appearance, Yiddish was considered a vulgar, or common, language not to be used by scholars or respectable writers. It was a dialect of the poor. Teachers and writers of 'literature' still used Hebrew. Early works in Yiddish were both religious and secular. Religious books included translations from the Bible, prayer books, and religious poems. Secular books were mainly adaptations from German or Italian: stories sung by roving minstrels or tales of knights and their daring exploits that were quite similar to other popular stories of the Middle Ages. One of the best known of these works was *Bove-Buch*, written in 1507 by Elijah Bachur (also known as Elijah Levita). It was based on an Italian version of the medieval French epic *Sir Bevis of Hamtoun*.

The turbulence of the Thirty Years' War from 1618 to 1648 and the expulsion from Germany of the German Jews drove secular Yiddish literature out of existence for more than a century. Religious writing in Yiddish, however, survived. The most durable is a paraphrased version of the first five books of the Bible by Jacob Ben Isaac Ashkenazi. Entitled *Tzeno Ureno*, it was published in 1608 and is still read today.

By the late 18th century the Jews of Central Europe were distracted by a variety of philosophical and religious movements within Judaism. Religious traditionalists urged the Ashkenazi to maintain their ancient heritage, while others – students of the Enlightenment – sought to bring Jews into the mainstream of European life.

One of the traditionalists, Rabbi Nahman of Bratslav, assembled one of the best collections of Yiddish folklore. Of the modernists, Israel Axenfeld used his stories to satirise the superstitions of Eastern European Jews and to criticise their reluctance to accept modern education. Probably the most influential of the Enlightenment figures was the philosopher Moses Mendelssohn (grandfather of the composer Felix Mendelssohn), who produced a voluminous amount of literature in both Yiddish and Hebrew.

Yiddish literature also migrated to the New World and persisted into the 20th century. Isaac Bashevis Singer's popular novels and short stories, such as *In My Father's Court* and *Yentel* were all originally written in Yiddish, then translated into English for wider consumption. Yiddish is, though, declining; in Israel *sabras* are brought up with Hebrew as their native language, and few of the younger generations of the Diaspora communities understand the language of their grandparents.

The caliph identified the site of the ascent as the plateau on which the Temple had stood. At that time, after centuries of neglect, the place was serving as a rubbish tip. Though Omar had the plateau cleared and re-dedicated as a Muslim place of worship, it was a later caliph, Abd al-Malik, who crowned the Islamic precinct with the magnificent Dome of the Rock in 691 AD.

The first centuries of Muslim rule were marked by tolerance towards Jews and Christians, but later Islamic dynasties were not so benevolent. In the latter part of the 11th century pilgrims were returning to Europe with stories of persecution and Muslim desecration of Jerusalem's holy sites. In 1071 the gates were closed on the stream of pilgrims altogether. Rallied by the appeal of Pope Urban II in Rome, Christians throughout Western Europe responded by embarking on a crusade to liberate the holy places, thus setting in motion one of the most appalling episodes in the entire history of Jerusalem.

The Crusades
On 15 July 1099 the First Crusaders breached the northern walls of the city. Under the banner of Christendom they proceeded to massacre an estimated 40,000 Muslim and Jewish inhabitants. Records state that, six months later, the streets still reeked of rotting bodies. Jerusalem was proclaimed the capital of the Latin Kingdom and Christian pilgrims poured in to settle the recently de-populated quarters of the city.

The bloody victory was short-lived. In 1187 Saladin (Salah ad-Din), ruler of Egypt, routed the Crusaders and reinstated Islam in Jerusalem. There followed a series of increasingly ill-fated campaigns by Christian forces to recapture the city, but these finally gave out in the face of the Mamluks, a Cairo-based dynasty of former slaves that had superseded Saladin and his successors.

The Islamic City
Under the Mamluks, Jerusalem underwent a process of Islamification with the construction of large numbers of mosques and theological schools, all executed in a distinctive architectural style. Many of these buildings remain today and add much to the character of the Muslim Quarter of the Old City. The most distinctive of Jerusalem's attributes, however, was not constructed until the reign of Suleyman the Magnificent (1520-66), sultan of the Ottoman empire (which defeated the Mamluks in 1517).

It was Suleyman the Magnificent, Jerusalem's greatest builder since Herod the Great, who built the massive wall that still surrounds the Old City. His solid rule returned the city to prosperity, but his death left it in the hands of petty officials who were remarkable only for their corrupt and violent brand of administration.

Decline & Stagnation Off the major trade routes and of little strategic value, Jerusalem was largely ignored by the ruling powers in Constantinople, and for three centuries seemed to have fallen off the map. Local warlords and Bedouins took advantage of the lack of law and order to carve out independent domains, while the physical face of the city suffered as buildings, streets and infrastructure fell into disrepair. An English visitor of 1842 described the city thus:

> Nothing can be more devoid of interest than her gloomy half-ruinous streets and poverty-ridden bazaars ... there is certainly no city in the world that the traveller will sooner want to leave than Jerusalem.

Despite the city's decrepit state, the 18th and 19th centuries saw an increase in Jewish immigration as Jews sought to escape persecution in the Diaspora. However, in the former city of David the Jews found themselves very much at the bottom of the religious pecking order. While all were obliged to defer to the Muslims, the Jews were also to a great extent at the mercy of the Christians. In 1848 a Jew who strayed into the Church of the Holy Sepulchre was almost torn apart by an enraged mob – the Greek Patriarchate claimed an official document existed that gave them the right to beat any Jews entering or even passing by the church.

Most Jews who came to Jerusalem at this time were desperately poor and came with three aims in mind: to pray, to die and to be buried in the Holy City.

The New City
Up until the mid-19th century, no one lived outside the city walls for fear of attacks by bandits and wild animals. Each evening at sunset the six great city gates were swung closed and they stayed that way until sunrise. It was the pressure of overcrowding in the tiny cramped confines of the existing city (exacerbated by continued immigration) that finally forced the Jews to colonise the surrounding hills and valleys.

The settlement outside the city's walls began with Mishkenot Sha'ananim, a small development across the valley from Jaffa Gate, inspired and financed by an English philanthropist, Sir Moses Montefiore. However, the first residents were so afraid of attack that they would return each night to the security of their former quarters in the crowded Old City. Nevertheless, other experimental communities were rapidly established beyond the safety of the ramparts (Mea She'arim, Yemin Moshe and Nahalat Shiv'a), laying the foundations of what was to become the New City.

By this time it was apparent that the decrepit Ottoman empire was becoming frail and vulnerable, and the major European powers began jockeying for a share of the inheritance. The first British consulate had opened in Jerusalem in 1838, proclaiming itself a protector of the Jewish elements in Syria and Palestine, and the establishment of diplomatic representations of other European powers were not far behind. As well as embassies and consulates, Jerusalem also attracted many grandiose 'Christian missions', whose evangelistic activities, ostensibly involving the custody of the various holy shrines, often looked suspiciously like the distinctly secular machinations of international politics.

By the 1840s, the Jews were the largest single group in the city; by the 1880s they were the absolute majority.

David Ben-Gurion, Israel's first prime minister

The Divided City
The rivalry between Europe's great powers within Jerusalem was effectively brought to an end when British forces, led by General Allenby, captured the city from the Turks in 1917. In 1920 the San Remo Peace Conference assigned to Britain the Mandate of Palestine, including Jerusalem, which was to operate until 1947.

In November 1917, Arthur Balfour, then British foreign secretary, sent to Baron Lionel Rothschild a letter known as the Balfour Declaration, which detailed official British support for the Zionist claims for 'the establishment in Palestine of a national home for the Jewish people'. Belfour, however, made it clear that 'nothing shall be done to prejudice the civil and religious rights of existing non-Jewish communities', and this was underlined in the League of Nations Palestinian Mandate of 1922, which also provided for the preservation of existing rights and free access to 'Holy Places'.

This met the fate of many such idealistic endeavours, and the British administrators, based in Jerusalem, found themselves caught in the middle, the target of Jewish terrorist attacks and equally vilified Arabs.

JERUSALEM'S HIGHLIGHTS

Any list of highlights is a completely subjective matter, doubly so with Jerusalem, a city which has always managed to inflame passions while dividing opinions with an equal intensity.

The **Old City** viewed in early morning light from the **Mount of Olives** (photo by Lee Foster).

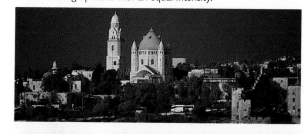

Left: Drinking mint tea at one of the cafés just inside **Damascus Gate** and watching the cinematic crush passing by (photo by Gadi Farfour).
Right: The sobering quality of the **Yad Vashem** Holocaust Memorial complex (photo by Eddie Gerald).

Left: The **Western Wall**
Right: **Dome of the Rock** (both photos by Andrew Humphreys)

The early evening colour, smells and sounds of **Mahane Yehuda** market as traders try to make their last sales of the day (photo by Christine Osborne).

Strong on late 19th/ early 20th century works, the **Israel Museum** art collection comes with a few surprises (photo © The Israel Museum Jerusalem/ Adam Bartos).

Jerusalem – holy to Judaism, Christianity and Islam – attracts pilgrims from around the world.

Serious unrest led the British to decide in 1939 that an independent state was required. The original white paper called for joint Arab and Jewish participation, but by 1947 the idea formed of Jerusalem as a separate entity administered by the United Nations.

At the end of November 1947, UN Resolution 181 was passed, terminating the British Mandate and partitioning Palestine into separate Arab and Jewish states, with Jerusalem having the legal status of a *corpus separatum* under a Trustee Council responsible to the UN.

The Jewish State partioned by the UN was considerably slimmer than that existing today. The Palestinian West Bank would have been broader than its present borders, extending west to enclose the current 'Jerusalem Corridor'. A large portion of modern northern Israel from Akko to the Lebanese border and from the Lebanese border to just before Safed would have come under Palestinian control, linked to the West Bank by a narrow strip in the Jezreel valley. The partition plan also made provision for an elongated Gaza Territory running south along the Egyptian border. The Palestinian rejection of the UN partition led directly to the War of Independence.

In 1948 the British withdrew, and the next day the proclamation of the State of Israel triggered a war which left Jerusalem split in two. The Jordanians held the Old City and the areas immediately north and east, while the Jews held the west, the New City, which Ben-Gurion declared to be 'an inseparable part of Israel, and her eternal capital'.

This schismatic state of affairs remained for 19 years with the city split present-day HaShalom Rd. The scarred no-man's-land was heavily mined and guarded by snipers on both sides. The sole official point of crossing, for the few who were permitted to pass from one side to the other, was the Mandelbaum Gate. This checkpoint passed into history with the Six Day War, when the whole of Jerusalem was captured by the Israelis. (The Mandelbaum Gate is remembered in the Tourjeman Post Museum and also celebrated in a novel by Muriel Spark.)

The Schismatic City

The Six Day War officially 'reunified' the city under Israeli control, but in reality this is something of a misnomer. The respective Jewish and Palestinian communities live and work separate from each other, with their own central districts, their own schools, police and fire departments, their own electricity grids, their own newspapers, and two completely opposing and mutually exclusive views on the rights to ownership of the city. Israeli control over East Jerusalem is still unrecognised by the UN, reflected by the fact that most countries have not moved their embassies from Tel Aviv.

The Palestinians, supported by most Arab states, hope to have East Jerusalem as the capital of their future state. The Israelis, on the other hand, consider Jerusalem to be their 'eternal and indivisible capital'. The Arab-Jewish struggle for Jerusalem continues, but the weapons employed are no longer guns and grenades: they are bricks, breeze blocks and bulldozers.

In what one housing minister referred to as 'the battle for Jerusalem', the Israelis have dedicated the last 30 years to a massive settlement program, ringing the core of the city with many large, new Jewish neighbourhoods. They hope that these will forestall any future suggestion of repartitioning. Most controversially, there have been large seizures of Arab land in East Jerusalem, and Jews now outnumber Palestinians in this sector.

Final Status

The final status of Jerusalem is one of the key issues in the ongoing peace process. The issue was re-ignited in early 1999 when the European Union publicly challenged Israel's jurisdiction and continued to meet with Palestinian officials at Orient House, the PLO's unofficial headquarters in East Jerusalem. Then Prime Minister Netanyahu, facing a general election, ordered the closure of Orient House, and two other Palestinian Authority offices in Jerusalem. To complicate matters further, the Holy See, which also has never recognised Israel's claim to East Jerusalem, claims a 'right and duty' to help to resolve the matter.

Until the two sides come to an agreement over this sacred and much contested city, it is unlikely that there will ever be a lasting peace in the Middle East.

GEOGRAPHY

Jerusalem is located high in the Judean Hills – a fact that often surprises first-time visitors. The approach from the west is gradual, through rolling plains with cultivated fields and olive groves marking the approach to the Judean foothills. Forests once covered much of the hills surrounding Jerusalem and they are still evident on the foothills themselves, but Jerusalem itself is built on the bare, craggy limestone summit of the hills in a fairly exposed position. All new buildings in the city are required by law to be built from the local limestone and it is this feature above all else that distinguishes Jerusalem from other Israeli cities.

To the east the land drops away sharply into the Judean Desert and eventually into the Dead Sea. On a fine day the views can be stunning. The intensity of the light, coupled with the harsh stone of its location, give Jerusalem its special ethereal quality.

CLIMATE

Jerusalem's climate is temperate, with two distinct seasons: winter, when it's cold and rainy, and summer, which tends to be long, hot and dry. You can expect July and August temperatures to range between 25°C and 30°C (74 to 86°F), though low humidity makes the heat easier to bear. The city's high altitude means that by September evening temperatures have already dropped to a level where a light jacket or jumper (sweater) is a good idea. Rainfall kicks in around November and usually carries on through to sometime around March. The winters can be surprisingly severe, and most years see snow. That said, even deepest winter is punctuated by many bright, sunny days and the skies tend to remain quite clear.

ECOLOGY & ENVIRONMENT

Israel generally has not had a good track record when to comes to issues pertaining to ecology and the environment. A devil-may-care attitude prevails among many Israelis, born perhaps out of the original need to develop the nation rapidly and exploit what resources were available. Litter is discarded wantonly and water courses are thoughtlessly polluted by industrial and agricultural effluent.

Visitors to Mea She'arim in particular will be shocked by the enormous amount of litter covering the streets and, while the problem is less pronounced elsewhere, littering is a big problem throughout the city. This is as much to do with haredi attitudes towards litter as it is to the limited financial resources allocated for street cleaning.

The Jordan River is a prime example of a fundamental resource being exploited for agriculture. In fairness, the Jordanians, who share the river with the Israelis, are as culpable for its current state of neglect. The overuse of water from the Jordan River basin has resulted in a considerable drop in the water level of both the Sea of Galilee (Kinneret) and the Dead Sea.

Israeli agriculturalists have, to their credit, made extensive use of drip irrigation, which has greened large tracts of previously unusable land using the minimum amount of water needed. This is still, however, too great an amount for the fragile Jordan River ecosystem to support.

The Society for the Preservation of Nature in Israel (SPNI), established in 1953, supports and promotes ecologically sustainable

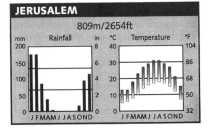

JERUSALEM

809m/2654ft

| mm | Rainfall | in | °C | Temperature | °F |

development. SPNI also runs tours for visitors and maintains a network of field stations around the country. In Jerusalem its office and bookstore (☎ 622 2357) is at 13 Heleni HaMalka St, PO Box 930, Jerusalem 91008.

GOVERNMENT & POLITICS

Although Jerusalem houses the Israeli parliament, the Knesset, the real face of city politics is the mayor. The present incumbent is Ehud Olmert, but in the minds of most Jerusalemites the post will always be associated with its previous occupant, Teddy Kollek.

Holding office from 1965 to 1993, the popular Kollek was devoted to the city and worked tirelessly on its behalf. The Israel Museum, the restoration of the Old City ramparts and Damascus Gate, the new City Hall complex – all stand as testaments to the tenacity of the former mayor. When the Israeli government wouldn't come up with the funds, he successfully rallied international Jewry and built with their donations. Kollek earned great respect across the board for his even-handed treatment of the Arab population and refusal to bow to the demands of the more extreme political factions.

The Knesset is in the southern Jerusalem suburb of Kiryat Ben-Gurion and is open to visitors. (See the Givet Ram & Museum Row section of the Things to See & Do chapter for details).

ECONOMY

In the years immediately after independence the Israeli economy was a triumph of skill and initiative over lack of natural resources. The rapid growth of population and constant cash injections from abroad in the form of aid and investment stimulated steady expansion and development. Roads were built, vast tracts of desert were reclaimed and cultivated, swamps were drained and a modern well-trained and well-equipped army was put together from scratch. However, the burden of military spending along with antiquated state restrictions on private enterprise, began to show in the economy as chronic inflation, which by 1985 was running at around 500%.

The currency was changed from lirot to shekels to new shekels in the struggle to control its devaluation. After a series of severe cuts in the government budget and in food subsidies, followed by a freeze on prices, wages and taxes, the Israeli government eventually managed to reduce the inflation rate to around 20%. It now stands at around 4 to 4.5% annually.

While the Israeli economy is apparently buoyant and healthy it has in recent times become troubled and is currently growing at a mere 1.9%, the lowest annual quarterly increase since 1989. Unemployment and inflation have made life increasingly difficult for the average Israeli while hotel prices have increased anywhere from between 50 and 100% since the last edition of this guide. Even a trip to the supermarket can mean a major capital outlay for weekly groceries, and Israelis – already great lovers of 'plastic fantastic' – can be seen contributing more and more to their ballooning credit card debt at the supermarket checkout.

While Jerusalem kowtows in many respects to the country's economic powerhouse, Tel Aviv, its economy is to a large degree dependent on the pilgrim and tourist trade. In this area Jerusalem attracts far more visitors than its secular-leaning sister city on the coast.

A crippling 60% of the national budget is still eaten up by defence spending and foreign debt – the annual trade deficit in 1995 hit an all-time high of US$9.2 billion – but as long as the peace process stays on course prospects look generally good. A lasting peace with the Palestinians may even lead to a lifting of the Arab boycott on all foreign companies that do business with Israel and result in increased investment from abroad. Additionally, since the signing of the Oslo Accords, tourism to Israel has risen from 1.5 million visitors in the late 1980s to over 2.5 million in 1998. Predictions are that all being well, this could hit a figure of five million by the end of the 20th century.

FACTS ABOUT JERUSALEM

POPULATION & PEOPLE

Although it has the feel of a small provincial town, its population of 622,100 makes Jerusalem Israel's largest city. The majority of the population are Israeli Jews (429,100), with Palestinian Arabs numbering around 170,000.

In 1948, when the State of Israel was created, there were approximately 100,000 Jews in Jerusalem. The phenomenal growth rate since then has been achieved largely through the mass immigration of Jews from abroad ('making *aliyah*', which translates literally as 'stepping up'). The most conspicuous of the *olim* (new immigrants) are the Russians, who began arriving in Israel in huge numbers following the reform and collapse of the Soviet Union in the late 1980s and the socio-economic chaos there in the 1990s. Their presence in Jerusalem isn't as high profile as in Tel Aviv or the desert towns, but frequently on Ben Yehuda St you'll hear mournful Slavic melodies wheezed out by busking accordionists.

Boys, Girls & Guns

Israel is still technically at war with more than a few of its fellow Middle Eastern countries. It's also enmeshed in battles with Palestinian terrorist groups and struggling to contain the sporadically violent extremist factions within its own society. Consequently, wherever you go you'll see armed soldiers. Bus stations, in particular, are filled with soldiers in olive green uniforms either arriving home on leave or heading off back to base. Having on occasion to ask, 'Excuse me, could you move your gun so I can sit down there', is an accepted part of bus travel.

What takes more getting used to is the pre-pubescent appearance of some of the soldiers. Unlike most standing armies, the Israeli Defence Force (IDF) is a citizens' army made up of conscripts – both men and women – plucked from civilian life at age 18, fresh from high school. With the conscripts barely out of adolescence, it's an army where fatigues are supplemented by RayBans, and M16 rifles double as crucial fashion accessories.

Nor is it always necessary to wear a uniform to carry a gun. Any soldier who loses their weapon (though rarely are women assigned to the weapon-carrying infantry units) is liable to seven years imprisonment; off-duty, jeans and T-shirt-clad soldiers sometimes haul their rifles around if there's no secure place to leave them. Once we even spotted two young men attempting to groove on a Jerusalem dance floor encumbered by machine guns slung across their backs! (We suspect that this had a lot more to do with narcissism than security, however.)

The initial spell of compulsory service in the IDF is three years for men and 18 months for women. Once this has been completed, every male is assigned to a reserve unit to which they are recalled for about 30 days service each year until they reach the age of 35. Single women are also liable for reserve service up until the age of 34, but in practice they're exempt once they're about 25 years old.

It remains a point of increasing friction that all *yeshiva* students – young men studying in ultra-orthodox seminaries – are exempt from the draft. (The blanket exemption previously enjoyed by the haredim was only revoked in 1998.) The ultra-orthodox communities explain that this is because their continual study of the Torah and their prayers are as valuable to the security of Israel as are soldiers. Secular Israelis fume that those who are often the most vocal concerning the 'holy' territory of Israel aren't forced to fight for it. Arab Israelis are also exempt from the draft, but there are volunteer Bedouin and Druze companies in the IDF.

It is a sobering thought that since 1947 nearly 19,000 IDF officers and soldiers have been killed; most deaths in action now occur in Lebanon.

Another perhaps surprising element in the melange of Jerusalem's faces are the dark-skinned Jewish Ethiopians. They were airlifted to Israel from their famine-struck country in two massive operations in 1985 and 1991, but many Jews, especially Ashkenazim (those of European background), have found this hard to accept. In what amounts to racial prejudice, aspersions were cast on the Ethiopians' Jewishness and it was suggested that they should go through religious conversion, including ritual immersion.

ARTS

Israelis have a great enthusiasm for the arts in all forms – the country sustains several world-class orchestras, the cities and towns are crowded with art galleries, theatre performances are well attended, and bookshops are plentiful and well-stocked. By no means is it all great art, but that's not the point – the arts in Israel serve to stimulate and provoke discussion, and on that level they succeed completely.

Music

Classical Israel has long been associated with excellence in classical music. This really started in the 1930s when Jewish musicians, including the best of Europe's composers, performers and teachers, fled to Palestine to escape Nazism. The Israeli musical pedigree was further boosted by the waves of Soviet Jews who arrived during the 1980s – a popular joke is that a Soviet Jew who arrives at Ben-Gurion airport without a violin must be a pianist. Less amusingly, many accomplished musicians who had been guaranteed employment in the former Soviet state orchestras must often find other work in Israel; sometimes they are heartbreakingly reduced to busking.

The Israel Philharmonic Orchestra (whose home is the Binyanei Ha'Umah Conference Centre) and violinist Yitzhak Perlman are world-renowned, and there are many other musicians and groups worthy of note. Major orchestras and groups perform regularly from October to July, though visitors

will not always find it easy to get tickets as these are mainly sold by subscription.

In 1986 the Nuyha/Al-Hakawati Theatre in East Jerusalem produced the first-known Arabic operetta. The music department of this theatre teaches the use of traditional Arab instruments and incorporates a recording studio.

Klezmer This is the traditional Yiddish dance music created in the Ashkenazi Jewish communities of Eastern and Central Europe – think *Fiddler on the Roof*. Centred on the core trio of accordion, clarinet and violin, the sound can range from weeping melancholy through to wild thigh-slapping, high-kicking exuberance. In the past 20 years klezmer has experienced something of a revival and it's no longer confined to wizened old men turning out hoary standards at wedding parties. Modern bands such as the New York-based Klezmatics, who draw large audiences wherever they perform, have extended the boundaries with eclectic fusions and new compositions. The classical violinist Yitzhak Perlman's klezmer album *In The Fiddler's House* was also extremely well received.

Popular Listening to Israeli pop music is to be transported to a world of permed blonde hair, white pressed trousers, hand-holding and wistful smiles. How bad is it? Well, gaining a Eurovision song contest nomination is still considered a mark of success. It's little wonder that the last (and, as far as we can remember, only) impact that Israeli pop had on the international scene was back in the late 1980s when Ofra Haza made it big with her much-sampled *Im Nin' Alu* (from her album *Yemenite Songs*).

Connoisseurs of kitsch might want to look out for *Umpatampa* by Dana International, a lollipop sucking, transsexual disco queen. See the boxed text 'Dana International – Israel's Pride or Shame?'.

Those with other tastes might look out for Noa (Achinoam Nini), a sprite-like Yemeni singer with a wistful, soaring voice who sings in both Hebrew and English. Her 1994

Dana International – Israel's Pride or Shame?

When transsexual singer Dana International won the Eurovision song contest in 1998 with a catchy sugar-pop hit called *Diva*, divisions between Israelis and Palestinians were briefly put on hold as the ultra-orthodox took on the secular over an issue that divided a nation as much as the politics of Islamic extremists Hamas.

Dana International was formerly a man known as Yaran Cohen, who gained fame in Israel as a female impersonator in Tel Aviv night clubs before undergoing a sex-change operation in 1993. She was selected to represent Israel at the annual schmalzy music fest. Her unprecedented win sparked spontaneous demonstrations of joy in Tel Aviv, Israel's secular capital, with people waving flags and dancing in the street.

On the other hand, religious Jews were horrified that Dana International, who was born a man, represented Israel. Her win drew flack from Israel's influential *haredi* (ultra-orthodox) lobby, with the Sephardic religious party Shas declaring that the win 'symbolised the sickness of secular Israel'.

Both secular and religious Jews see Dana's victory as a battle in the constant cultural civil war they are fighting against each other. Israelis are every bit as divided about religion and culture as they are about peace with the Palestinians, which is, at least, the subject of negotiations. There is no real dialogue between secular and religious Israelis, and Dana's victory is another sign that the gulf between them is growing wider. Despite continuing haredi opposition, Israel won the right to host the 1999 Eurovision song contest in Jerusalem.

---

album *Noa* is considered by many to be her best. Israeli jazz is best represented by the silky voice and smooth piano playing of Nurit Galron, who sings laid-back jazz numbers in Hebrew. Check out her self-titled album *Nurit Galron* for a sample of some of her best work.

Literature

Hebrew as a modern language only came into being at the very end of the 19th century, largely through the championing of one man, Eliezer Ben Yehuda. In the relatively short time since then, Israelis have created a mountain of national literature that has made its entry into libraries the world over. For details on Yiddish literature see the boxed text 'Yiddish' earlier in this chapter.

The best represented contemporary Israeli author available in translation these days is the Jerusalem-born 'Peace Now' activist Amos Oz, whose books have been published in 22 languages. Many of his novels and stories are set in his home city and almost anything he's written is worth reading, though one book in particular is a must for any serious visitor to this city – *Jerusalem City of Mirrors* is a lyrical and historical tour of the city he loves and lives in. Almost rivalling Oz in his collection of international accolades is life-long Jerusalem resident novelist David Grossman. This author of *The Smile of the Lamb*, *See Under Love* and, most recently, *The Book of Intimate Grammar*, has had his work compared favourably with Günter Grass and Gabriel García Márquez.

Much less well known abroad but enormously popular at home is the Sephardic poet Yehuda Amichai. While the writings of Oz and Grossman often employ Jerusalem as a backdrop, in the work of life-long resident Amichai the Holy City frequently takes centre stage. He's probably the city's foremost spokesperson.

Israeli control over Jerusalem and the subsequent hounding of any Palestinian writer whose works manifested even a hint of political involvement has led to Beirut becoming the centre of Palestinian literary life.

The most internationally prominent Palestinian author and academic is Edward Said, born in Jerusalem in 1936 into a Christian Arab family which fled to Egypt in 1948; the family home became for a while the offices of the Zionist International Christian Embassy. As a result, Said went against the prevailing trend of literary criticism to become a formidable advocate of the intellectual's social responsibility, writing works of political and cultural criticism such as *Orientalism*, *Culture and Imperialism*, and *Peace and its Discontents*, a volume of essays on the peace process. Formerly a member of the Palestinian National Council (he resigned in 1991 in protest at Arafat's support of Saddam Hussein), Said continues to advocate the replacement of Israel by a jointly Arab and Jewish, wholly secular, democratic state.

Another Jerusalem-born Palestinian author whose works are readily available in English translation is Liana Badr, who fled to Beirut via Jordan in 1967. In recent years she has returned to live in Ramallah, just north of Jerusalem, but her first-hand experience of social and political upheaval forms the basis of much of her work; *The Eye of the Mirror* and the short story collection *A Balcony over the Fakihani* are both available in English language editions.

Architecture

It's only in the 20th century that Jerusalem has developed anything that could be thought of as an indigenous style of architecture. Through its millennia-long history, Jerusalem's architecture has reflected and conformed to the tastes of whatever dynasty or empire was in occupation at the time. Solomon's city was in essence Phoenician; and the Jerusalem of Herod the Great was Hellenistic; the reconstructed Aelia Capitolina was Roman, which was then reshaped by the Byzantines and Crusaders.

Jerusalem in Print

Although the Bible, in its more than 700 references to the city, heralds Jerusalem variously as 'the golden', 'the sacred' and 'the holy', few writers since have shown much sympathy for the place. One early Muslim scribe did define happiness as 'eating a banana in the shadow of the Dome of the Rock', but the 10th century Arab geographer Ibn Muqaddasi probably spoke more representatively when he described Jerusalem as 'a golden basin filled with scorpions'.

If anything, the image of the place had fallen even further when the grand tourists from Europe and America began to discover Palestine in the mid-19th century. The French poet, essayist and philosopher Gustave Flaubert, visiting in 1850, was of the view that Jerusalem was 'a charnel house surrounded by walls'; roughly 100 years later this sentiment was echoed by Aldous Huxley, who referred to the city as 'the great slaughterhouse of the religions'. *Moby Dick* author Herman Melville spent eight days in the city and was profoundly depressed by the 'stony tombs, stony hills and stony hearts'.

Mark Twain, though finding Jerusalem 'mournful and dreary and lifeless', at least found a wealth of targets to satirise in his *Innocents Abroad* – 'there will not be a second coming', he quipped, 'Christ had been in Jerusalem once and would not deign to come again'. Twain's mocking scepticism was shared by George Bernard Shaw, who, when visiting in the 1930s, advised the early Zionists to erect notices at every holy site reading 'do not trouble to stop here, it isn't genuine'.

With a succinctness that, again, might have appealed to Twain, Selma Lagerlof, Nobel prize-winning author of the international bestseller *To Jerusalem*, pinpointed a sad truth to the effect that in Jerusalem 'one hates one's fellow man to the glory of God'.

Islamic *sabil* (drinking fountain)

Later, an Islamic spin was put on the whole thing, most notably by the Mamluks (responsible for some of the most attractive structures in the Old City today), followed up by the introduction of Ottoman Turkish elements, including the Old City walls.

Towards the end of the 19th century, a whole new series of architectural references were introduced as the great powers of Europe embarked on an unrestrained building spree, vying for political influence in the Holy City. The ostentatious churches, hospices and missions they threw up were all executed in their own national styles. (The author Amos Elon describes them as being 'like flags planted in the ground'.) So it is that Jerusalem has an Italianate hospital straight out of a Canaletto painting, an Oxford quadrangle on Nablus Rd, a cluster of Muscovite onion-domes on the Mount of Olives and a Rhineland Gothic castle on Mt Scopus.

The one mitigating factor in this Euro-Disneyfication of the city was the predominant use of Jerusalem stone, which did at least ensure some degree of uniformity. The white stone, quarried locally, has been the one constant element throughout the city's entire history of building. In 1917 the stone's use was even made obligatory in a law introduced by the British military governor, Sir Ronald Storrs – this bit of enlightened legislation has stuck.

It was also during the British Mandate that the first steps towards formulating a concept of 'Jerusalem architecture' were made. The International Style, then coming into vogue in Europe, was imported into Palestine by Jewish architects fleeing the rise of Nazism in the 1930s. The functional, unadorned lines of this new architectural style were adapted to local conditions and combined with local motifs such as the dome and arch. This is seen to best effect at Hadassah Hospital on Mt Scopus, designed in the 1930s by famed German architect Erich Mendelsohn, and at St Andrew's Church (1930), which although very modernist in design, manages to echo Crusader structures such as the Church of St Anne in the Old City.

Another innovation at this time – seen in Hadassah Hospital – was the attempt to break down monolithic masses into smaller units, often of different heights, echoing the hillside tumble of traditional Arab villages. It's a technique that has since been much employed, most notably in the design of the Israel Museum complex (1965).

This very flexible design vocabulary has continued to serve as the blueprint for local architecture. With a few unfortunate exceptions (the Knesset building and some of the tower-block hotels come to mind), the result is an extremely cohesive cityscape with a strong awareness of historical tradition and a harmonious relation with the surrounding topography.

Painting

Painting in Jerusalem got its first real shot in the arm through the founding of the Bezalel Art School when Boris Schatz collected paintings and objects in order to teach his students to create a 'Hebrew style' of painting. In time other paintings and objects were added and eventually came to constitute the Bezalel Art Museum contained within the larger Israel Museum. The Israel Museum itself is an important cultural institution which houses a wide-ranging art collection reflecting current Israeli art as envisaged by Boris Schatz. See the Israel Museum section on pp 124-30.

Ticho House (Beit Ticho) near the centre of the New City is another focus for local art. The previous owner of the house, Anna Ticho, was an excellent landscape artist and upon her death bequeathed over 2000 drawings to the collection that is now on display in this small museum. There are often temporary exhibitions and the house also serves as a venue for cultural events such as concert and lectures. See the New City Centre section of the Things to See & Do chapter.

Apart from the Israel Museum and Ticho House, art exhibitions are held in the Artists' House, Hutzot ha-Yotzer (the Craftsmen's Centre), the International Cultural Centre for Youth, and in private galleries. Concerts and theatre performances are given at Binyane Ha'Uma (the Convention Centre), the Khan (housed in a restored 18th-century building), and the Wise Auditorium at Hebrew University.

SOCIETY & CONDUCT

There are three distinct social elements in Jerusalem: the secular Israelis, the haredi (ultra-orthodox) communities and the Palestinian Arabs. Few, if any, concessions need to be made by tourists in the secular areas of town (which include the New City centre and areas south and west), where the inhabitants lead a lifestyle similar to that enjoyed in much of Europe or the US. Elsewhere in Jerusalem, however, large parts of society revolve around religion, which means that many of the dos and don'ts you should consider have a religious basis (see the Religion section later in this chapter).

The most obvious thing to be aware of is dress. In predominantly orthodox Jewish areas of town (the Jewish Quarter of the Old City and New City districts like Mea She'arim) very strict attention has to be paid to what you wear, with modesty being the keyword. This means that women should be covered from neck to ankle, with no bare shoulders or upper arms exposed, and that legs must be hidden beneath a loose-fitting skirt – trousers won't do.

Sorry for What?

Two recent immigrants, one from Russia and one from America, and a native Israeli are at the supermarket where they come across a sign reading 'We're sorry, but due to shortages we have no meat'. The Russian turns to the other two and asks, 'What is meat?'. The American shrugs, 'What do they mean by shortages?'. The Israeli shakes his head and looks perplexed, 'What do they mean by this sorry?'.

Israelis tell this joke among themselves, and any visitor who's been in the country for more than five minutes will nod despairingly at the punch line. The Israelis, as they'll readily agree, are not exactly hot on the niceties of social intercourse. No official or sales assistant will acknowledge your existence until addressed directly. If you're dining out, a waitress will flick a menu at the table, then indicate she's ready to take your order with an uninterested, 'Yeah?'. Likely looking places to ask for directions or timetables ward off all potential inquiries with prominently displayed 'No Information' notices.

It's not that Israelis are bad-mannered, explains travel writer Stephen Brook, but rather that they have no manners at all. Faced with a waiter who shrugs aside your complaints of cold food with 'People don't like it if it's too hot', you might feel that such distinctions are irrelevant. But one thing to remember is never to lose your temper and start shouting, because there's nothing that Israelis love more than a good row.

Clashes between haredim and secular Jews are frequent, and the gulf between the two seems to be widening. Some observers have even suggested that if there was no 'Palestinian problem' to pre-occupy Jews there would be an equally serious 'Jewish problem'. A win in the 1998 Eurovision song contest by a transsexual Israeli singer (see the boxed text 'Dana International – Israel's Pride or Shame?' earlier in this chapter) was seen by many as a rallying call for increased secularism and openness in Israeli society but by the more conservative of the religious spectrum it was seen as an abomination.

Generally speaking, the Palestinians, though they are themselves quite conservative, are far more accepting of foreigners' ways – jeans and T-shirts are acceptable for women visiting East Jerusalem, although shorts and revealing tops are definitely not a good idea. In the Old City, most religious sites (the Haram ash-Sharif/Temple Mount and the Church of the Holy Sepulchre included) will refuse entrance to anyone improperly dressed.

Jewish Society

The assassination of Yitzhak Rabin by Yigal Amir in November 1995 dispelled any lingering image of Israeli Jews as a monolithic bloc. The truth is that they are a deeply divided nation. Nowhere is this more evident than in Jerusalem, where 'two Jews equals three opinions' is more than an amusing aphorism. Divisions between the secular vs religious, orthodox vs reform, hawks vs doves, Sephardim (Oriental Jews) vs Ashkenazim (European and American Jews), *sabras* (native-born Israelis) vs recent African or Russia immigrants – everything is an issue here to be debated and argued in cafes and newspaper columns, on TV talk shows and over dining room tables.

Unfortunately, in Jerusalem differences of opinion have a nasty habit of going beyond verbal arguments, especially where the city's ultra-orthodox communities are concerned. There is a real attempt by the haredim to force their strict ideology on the less observant majority of society. In recent years haredim have burnt down bus stops for carrying lewd advertising, invaded football pitches hosting matches on Shabbat, assaulted 'improperly dressed' women, and picketed shops that open on Shabbat. Somewhat ironically, ultra-orthodox elements called for the banning of Stephen Spielberg's *Schindler's List* on the grounds that it contained nudity, and objected to photographs in Vad Yashem holocaust memorial complex for the same reason.

An indication of the depth of these divisions came when the left-wing, secular Tel Aviv daily newspaper *Ha'aretz* marked the 1999 Independence Day with a feature about the alienation felt by the secular, humanist Zionist Israelis who made aliyah in the 1950s and 60s, but describe the contemporary state as 'becoming corrupt, Levantine and fundamentalist'.

This cultural collision intensified with the ultra-orthodox influence that characterised Netanyahu's coalition government, voted out of power in 1999. The fundamental dilemma of religion and government came to a head in 1999 when Aryeh Deri, the political leader of Shas, the haredi Sephardic party which held the balance of power in the Likud-led coalition government, was convicted by the Supreme Court of receiving bribes and misuse of government funds. His supporters claimed ethnic and religious persecution, and refused to recognise the authority of the secular court; secular Israelis fume that the delaying tactics of Deri's defence team dragged the trial out for five years, during which time Deri was allowed to remain politically active, wielding extraordinary power.

In addition, the increasing numbers of very large families that result from religious opposition to birth control means that the haredi element is expected to be in the majority in Jerusalem within the decade. It's a state of affairs that genuinely frightens the city's secular population, who fear a descent into a darkened, religiously oppressive state along the lines of fundamentalist Islamic states. Anti-haredim protests are common.

Orthodox & Gay – Oxymoron or Personal Paradox?

It is almost inconceivable for outsiders to reconcile the black-suited image of haredi Jewry with the world of homosexuality. Yet the few haredim who have spoken out on this always controversial topic confirm that gays and lesbians do exist, if not exactly flourish, in a closeted religious community.

The research of sociologist Alfred Kinsey in the 1940s and 50s suggested that at least 10% of humanity has homosexual preferences. While this figure is disputed, it is evident that an increasing number of ultra-orthodox Jews are confessing to having sexual preferences for their own gender. In an interview given in 1998 to the *Jerusalem Post* a young haredi man complained that the ultra-orthodox rabbis pretend that 'homosexual orthodox' is an oxymoron and that all gays must be secular.

Previously, most declared orthodox gays and lesbians either abandoned their orthodoxy altogether or left Israel to seek freedom in gay-tolerant Jewish communities in the US or Europe. Progressive congregations such as the Reform or Conservative movements accept openly gay members and many orthodox gays and lesbians simply swapped allegiance to these more tolerant groups.

The revulsion felt by the haredim against homosexuality is legendary. First and foremost it is considered a biblical sin – and the lives of the ultra-orthodox are ruled completely by the Torah. Shlomo Benziri, then deputy health minister and a member of the Shas party, claims that homosexuality is 'an illness and an abomination', not a legitimate lifestyle.

Palestinian Society

Up until the Six Day War in 1967 Palestinians effectively controlled and ran all of East Jerusalem. They still live in East Jerusalem but their tenure in the eastern half of the city is tenuous at best, with a growing barrage of petty restrictions and bureaucratic hurdles being imposed upon them almost daily. Many West Bank Palestinians may not enter Jerusalem without first obtaining a hard-to-get permit.

Palestinians effectively constitute the majority of residents of the Old City, as a walk down the crowded streets will easily and visually testify. Although about 5% of Palestinians are Christian rather than Muslim (Mrs Arafat is a notable example), there doesn't appear to be the same split along religious lines as is apparent among the Jewish population – yet.

Palestinian society is a patriarchal, extended family social network and members of the same family from across generations often live in close proximity to one another.

RELIGION

Sacred to Judaism, Christianity and Islam, Jerusalem has more religious significance than any other city in the world.

Judaism

Judaism is Israel's dominant faith. The haredim spend entire lifetimes studying Judaism, so don't expect to find all your questions answered below.

Fundamentals Judaism has a good claim to being the first monotheistic faith, coupled with the belief that the Jews are, individually and collectively, God's chosen people. These tenets are encapsulated in the opening line of the *Shema*, the great declaration of faith which the ultra-orthodox say each morning and evening: 'Hear, O Israel, the Lord [is] your God, the Lord is One!'.

'God' is in fact never actually named as such by religious Jews, who use various euphemisms such as HaShem (the Name) and Adonai (my Lord); in English, it is written as G-d. This is because the Tetragrammaton, the 4-letter Hebrew name of God, is considered too holy to pronounce. The High Priest alone would say it, once a year, when he blessed the people on Yom Kippur. After the destruction of the Temple in 70 AD, the vowels that go between the consonants Y-H-W-H have been lost. ('Jehovah' was created by using the vowels from the word 'Adonai'.)

Taken from the Torah – the first five books of the Bible – the 613 *mitzvot* (commandments) affect all aspects of life, from the ritual circumcision of boys eight days after birth, to dietary regulations, the observance of Shabbat and festivals, the ethical treatment of Jews and Gentiles, to burial practices.

Although the highly prescriptive nature of Judaic law may appear highly intrusive and sometimes inexplicably irrelevant, there is a pragmatic streak running throughout – in matters of life and death, religious laws are automatically suspended.

After biblical texts, the next most revered works are known collectively as the Talmud, which is the compilation of teaching and commentary on Judaic law, written in a mixutre of Hebrew and Aramaic. There are in fact two versions of the Talmud: the Palestinian Talmud which originated around 500 AD, and the Babylonian Talmud, which was completed in the region of present-day Iraq about 100 years later. The longer Babylonian Talmud is the one generally referred to. Both versions consist of *Mishnah*, the actual laws, and *Gemara*, the commentaries. Gemara also includes *aggadah*: witticisms, legends and nonhalachic teachings. Perhaps the most famous of these is Hillel's Golden Rule: 'That which is hateful to you, do not do to another person'.

Shabbat As any visitor cannot help but notice, the Biblical injunction to 'remember the Sabbath and keep it holy' is taken very seriously in Israel. Between sunset on Friday and sunset on Saturday, observant Jews neither work nor employ others. Public transport stops, and the ultra-orthodox

have been known to block roads and stone passing cars that contravene their very strict interpretation of Shabbat prohibitions.

It is illegal in Israel to force a Jew to work on Shabbat; although this ban does not apply to Christian or Islamic employees, the Jerusalem haredim in particular take a very dim view of establishments that open on Shabbat. A seven day supermarket which opened in early 1999 has become a cause célèbre, attracting each week both demonstrating haredim and secular shoppers determined not to be forced to observe Shabbat.

Within the home, fires (extended to include electrical appliances) may neither be lit nor extinguished, so a light left on stays on – and observant Jewish smokers go cold-turkey every week.

The same restrictions on work and travel apply during festivals such as the first and last days of Pesah, and on Yom Kippur (see the Jewish Festivals section on pp 58-62).

Kashrut This is the system of Jewish dietary laws (*kosher* is the adjective). Basically, kosher restaurants will not serve pork, or any fish that does not have fins and scales in its natural state (no shellfish, crustaceans, shark, eels, or – sob! – sturgeon caviar). If meat is served it must come from a mammal which both chews the cud and has cloven hooves (so no rabbit or horse meat). All poultry (except birds of prey) are kosher. Blood may not be eaten, and part of the kosher slaughtering process involves lightly salting meat to remove any leftover traces of blood.

Dairy products may not be mixed with meat; as well as obvious things like cheeseburgers, a kosher restaurant will also not serve you a dairy dessert or white tea or coffee after a meat meal (although some may permit nondairy coffee whiteners). A meat sandwich will be 'buttered' with margarine. Kosher cheese is made without using rennet, which is extracted from calves' stomachs, and desserts are made with agar-agar instead of gelatine. The full English breakfast of bacon, eggs, black pudding and buttered toast fails on all counts.

Observance of kashrut ranges from the haredim, who will only eat meat slaughtered under intensely strict rabbinic supervision and after consuming meat wait six hours before eating dairy products, to the 'so long as it's not on the same fork' quasi-secular view of others. Any restaurant or product labelled as kosher will have rabbinic certification.

Dress The most distinctive dress belongs to the haredim. The men are easily identifiable by their black hats (often replaced on Shabbat with grand fur hats known as *streimels*), long black coats, white shirts worn without ties, beards and cropped hair with *peyot* (side curls). Some groups include more modern permutations of this clothing code, but it is always in black. Women's clothing is not as distinctive, but they do wear long coats and skirts to ensure that as little flesh as possible is visible. After marriage they are obliged to cover their hair with a hat, scarf or wig.

For morning prayers haredi men (and some Reform or Conservative women) wear a *tallit*, a prayer shawl made of white wool or silk, often with black or blue bands; it is worn all day on Yom Kippur. On each of the four corners of the tallit are *tzitzit*, ritual fringes. The ultra-orthodox also wear a *tallit katan* under their clothes, often with the fringes hanging out.

The most common sign of a religious Jewish man is the *kippah* (skullcap) known in Yiddish as a *yarmulke*. Wearing a kippah is not actually a *mitzvah* (commandment) but is essentially a tradition, recalling the ancient practice of covering one's head as a sign of respect. The ultra-orthodox wear kippot at all times, others only in the synagogue and for prayer. Secular Jews and Gentiles are expected to don a kippah as a courtesy on appropriate occasions.

At the Western Wall, and perhaps in some of the bus stations, you may notice Jewish men wearing a leather strap wrapped around their right arm and a small box strapped to their head. These are *tefillin* (boxes which enclose a parchment inscribed with a stipulated portion of the Torah).

Kippot

The most common sign of a religious Jew is the *kippah* (skullcap) known in Yiddish as a *yarmulke*. There is no universally recognised size for kippot (generally, those with enough hair wear smaller ones secured with bobby-pins) and you will see various styles, colours and materials.

You can very often tell the religious and political affiliation of a man by the kind of kippah he is wearing. All men don a kippah at synagogues and at places such as the Western Wall; the observant wear one all the time. Some Reform and Conservative women also wear kippot in the synagogue.

Ultra-orthodox men usually wear black velvet kippot under their hats (and, on Shabbat and certain holidays, under their *streimels*, fur hats).

Zionists, including right-wing settlers, wear medium-sized crocheted kippot with colourful designs around the edge. The newer models have a design that goes all the way to the middle of the kippah. If a man is wearing such a crocheted kippah (probably knitted by his wife or girlfriend), has *tzitzit* (tassels) flying from his hips and an M16 slung over his shoulder, he's almost certainly a settler. A huge crocheted kippah, often in white, is a sign that the wearer is a Messianist of some sort, perhaps an extreme right-wing settler.

Political moderates often wear knitted kippot of a single, unostentatious colour, often brown or tan. Tiny knitted kippot are sometimes worn by traditional (but not necessarily orthodox) Mizrahi men so that passers-by don't mistake them for Arabs.

Since the murder of Yitzhak Rabin, Conservative and Reform men and women have increasingly tried to find a style of kippah that doesn't make the wearer look like an opponent of the peace process. Some have adopted the Bucharian kippah, a large, round embroidered cap, while others have chosen kippot crocheted with thick (rather than thin) yarn.

Daniel Robinson

Tefillin shel yad is worn around the arm and hand, and *tefillin shel rosh* is placed around the head. The shel yad binds the arm, therefore the body; the shel rosh binds the mind. The purpose is to remind Jews that the mind, heart and body are to be used for good and not evil. Tefillin are traditionally worn during the morning service except on Shabbat and festivals.

Mezuzoth, the small containers attached to doorframes, similarly contain parchments inscribed with the appropriate biblical verses. Observant households have at least one *mezuzah* for the front door; the haredim also have them throughout the house. They're attached on an angle because the early rabbis couldn't agree on whether mezuzoth should be horizontal or vertical.

Synagogues Unlike Christian churches, the synagogue's function isn't limited to that of a prayer hall. Diaspora synagogues almost always function as community centres, whereas in Israel, where Jewish culture is reflected throughout the society, most synagogues are almost exclusively places to pray (though some are used for study).

Synagogue architecture is so unprepossessing because originally neither Christian rulers in Europe nor Muslim overlords elsewhere allowed Jews the ostentatiousness that their own churches and mosques were allowed to have. There are no domes or minarets, flying buttresses or spires; in fact from the outside it's very often quite difficult to identify a synagogue. You have to look for small indicators such as a *menorah* (the seven-branched candelabra), or the six-pointed Star of David.

The focal point of the interior of a synagogue, normally set in the eastern wall, is the *Aron Hakodesh*, the Ark containing one or more copies of the Torah. These are handwritten by a specialist scribe in Hebrew on parchment scrolls with a quill pen. The Ark is usually screened with a curtain. A light is kept burning continually in front of the Ark, in remembrance of the continual light in the Temple and as a mark of respect to the holiness of the Scrolls.

The seven-branched menorah is one of the universal symbols of Judaism.

In the centre of the synagogue (or in more modern structures, at the front) is the reading desk, normally on a raised *bimah* (platform). On Shabbat and during festivals, readings from the Torah are made from here. The Torah is also read on Monday and Thursday morning.

As in the Temple, the sexes are traditionally seated separately, often with a gallery for women. Mixed seating is allowed in Reform and Conservative synagogues.

Heads must be covered at all times in a synagogue but otherwise the apparent lack of decorum during services often surprises first-time visitors. Children play and people talk to each other and wander in and out of the synagogue.

Burial Customs Physical resurrection is one of the Jewish beliefs, so cremation is out of the question, as generally are autopsies. There is a special rabbinical unit with the grisly task of recovering all body parts for burial after a catastrophe such as a plane crash or a terrorist bomb. The body is buried within 24 hours of death – without a coffin in Israel.

Visitors to Jewish graves place stones rather than flowers on the grave because this is a more permanent way of showing that a visit has been made. It also involves the mourner in the mitzvah of burying the deceased, thus helping to return them to God.

Graves are sacrosanct, which has serious implications for archaeology. Sites and even archaeologists are increasingly attacked by flying squads of haredi (whom archaeologists contemptuously call the 'bone chasers'), who take it upon themselves to rebury all human remains before anybody has had a chance to excavate or study them properly. They do this on the off chance that they might be Jewish, regardless of any evidence to the contrary. This clash between secular scholarship and Judaic law is seriously damaging archaeology in Israel. The political influence of the haredi parties has also resulted in the budget of the Israel Antiquities Authority being slashed to the point that existing sites cannot be maintained, never mind excavating the new sites that are discovered practically every time someone digs a ditch or sinks foundations.

Who is a Jew? This is a continually vexed question which often exercises *Jerusalem Post* columnists. As far as the haredim are concerned, the answer is simple: Reform and Conservative doesn't count, and the secular Jews are merely Hebrew-speaking *goyim* (Gentiles).

As far as the State of Israel is concerned, Jewish identity is passed on by matrilineal descent, so if your mother is Jewish, you are, too. Many people, are uncomfortable with this assumption that Jewishness is biological, preferring to determine the matter on grounds of personal religious belief. This, however, has direct bearing on the Law of Return (passed in 1950), which states that any person recognised as a Jew has the inalienable right to live in Israel. According to the Law of Return, a Jew is defined as any person whose mother was Jewish, or who has converted to Judaism. A Jew who has converted to another religion is not eligible for the Law of Return.

The matter of conversion is another vexed point. Since the destruction of the Second Temple, there has been a tradition of actively discouraging converts on the grounds that few people would want to share the fate

of the Jewish people. A modern convert is still ritually discouraged three times. Wanting to marry a Jewish person is, for the ultra-orthodox, a very good reason *not* to accept a prospective convert. At the present time, only haredi conversions are recognised by the Chief Rabbinate of Israel as eligible for the Law of Return.

Islam

The Arabic word *Islam* means 'voluntary surrender to the will of Allah (God) and obedience to his commands'. The youngest of the three monotheistic religions which revere Jerusalem, Islam was born when Mohammed was inspired in a series of revelations that were documented as the text of the Quran. The establishment of the first Muslim community in 622 AD is marked as the starting point of the Islamic calendar.

There are two main schools of Islam: Shi'ia and Sunni. The Palestinians, like the neighbouring Jordanians and Egyptians (and unlike the Iranians, Iraqis and the other Gulf States), are Sunni. The main difference is that Shi'ia tradition has a much greater emphasis on the role of the *imam*, the religious teacher of the mosque.

Fundamentals Islam recognises both Judaism and Christianity, regarding Mohammed as the last in a line of Prophets that includes Moses and Jesus. The Torah and the Gospels are accepted, but Muslims believe that the Quran supersedes them.

The Quran consists of 114 *suras* (chapters), arranged in order of length; sura 96, begins 'Recite! In the name of your Lord' and is thought to be the first in chronological order. The Quran is the main source of Islamic law, covering everything from times of worship to inheritance, with explanations provided by the *hadith* (tradition), which consists of *matn*, the text, and *sanad*, the chain of authorities that leads all the way back to the Prophet.

The 'Five Pillars of Islam' are: the belief that there is no God but Allah, and that Mohammed is his Prophet; *salat*, prayer, which is performed five times a day; *siyam*, fasting during the month of Ramadan; *zakat*, an income tax-like charity expected from the rich; and *Haj*, the pilgrimage to Mecca, which Muslims are expected to make at least once in a lifetime if they are physically and financially able to do so.

Dietary Laws Islamic dietary laws are not as complex as the Jewish kashrut, although they share some points of similarity. Alcohol is forbidden, as is the consumption of pork, birds of prey, other carnivores and blood. Muslims are only allowed to eat *halal* meat, ie from animals that are slaughtered in the Quranically prescribed manner.

Behaviour Islam strictly forbids the free mixing of the sexes after puberty, a rule that applies to all socialising, not just premarital sex (hence the often unwelcome interest many Muslim males show towards western women).

Marriages are generally arranged by parents with the couple's consent. Islam does not condone sexual discrimination; the husband and wife are equal partners in the family, playing their role in respective fields. Divorce is permitted but is regarded as the most abominable of legal acts. Although extramarital sex is forbidden, Islam permits polygamy (polygamy is illegal under Israeli law, though this law doesn't apply to Muslims in the Palestinian Territories, most of whom have only one wife anyway).

Dress Simplicity and modesty are encouraged. Muslims are required to cover their bodies properly and decently. Men must be covered from navel to knees, and must not wear pure silk or gold. Women must cover the whole body except the face and hands. A woman's outfit must not arouse a man's 'base' feelings, so tight-fitting, transparent or revealing styles are out. Most Palestinian women wear the *hejab* (headscarf); the *kufeyya* (chequered scarf) worn by men is a cultural rather than a religious item.

Non-Muslims should be aware of these dress codes and, out of respect, adhere to them when in predominantly Muslim areas.

The Palestinian *thob* (basic dress) often features densely patterned embroidery.

Mosques The word 'mosque' comes from the Arabic word *mesjid*, meaning a place of adoration. Most mosques have .s and minarets (from where the call to prayer is made or, these days, broadcast), making them easy to recognise. Inside, facing the holy city of Mecca in Saudi Arabia, is the *mihrab* (prayer niche), normally an arched alcove about 1.5m high. The *minbar*, a freestanding pulpit, is usually nearby, and it's from here that the imam (religious teacher) gives the Friday sermon. Also at the front of the mosque is the *khatib*, a low, railed wooden platform where a reader sits to recite the Quran to the worshippers.

There are no professional priests attached to a mosque. The imam who gives the weekly sermon normally has a regular fulltime job. Once every mosque would have had a *muezzin* to cry the call to prayer five times a day from atop the minaret; these days he's largely been replaced by taped recordings.

Not all mosques welcome curious sightseers. Sometimes they'll be a sign saying 'For Prayers Only' posted prominently by the entrance. If you're unsure then ask. You must always remove your shoes before entering a mosque.

ISRAELI MINISTRY OF TOURISM

TOWER OF DAVID MUSEUM OF THE HISTORY OF JERUSALEM/DAHLIA AMOTZ

TOWER OF DAVID MUSEUM OF THE HISTORY OF JERUSALEM/TAL GLICK

Top Left: Snowy Mt Zion just outside the wall of Jerusalem's Old City
Top Right: Tower of David courtyard with poppies
Bottom: Night view of the Citadel

Clockwise from Top: Dome of the Rock; Tomb of Zechariah; Shrine of the Book; Russian Orthodox Church of the Holy Trinity

LEE FOSTER

ANDREW HUMPHREYS

PAUL HELLANDER

ANDREW HUMPHREYS

Christianity

The relative standing of Christian denominations elsewhere in the world counts for little in Jerusalem. While the Vatican-based Roman Catholic Church may be the world's richest and highest profile branch of Christianity, as a relative newcomer to the Holy Land (established only during the Crusades in the 12th century AD), it has very little authority in Jerusalem. The Protestants have even less.

The most powerful Christian church in Israel is the Greek Orthodox Church, which has jurisdiction over more than half of Jerusalem's Church of the Holy Sepulchre and has a bigger portion of the Church of the Nativity in Bethlehem than any other denomination. The Greek Orthodox patriarchate has seniority in the Christian hierarchy of Israel, despite the fact that this church represents only a fraction of the world's Christian population and is geographically confined mainly to Greece and the Slavic countries. Similarly, by dint of being one of the first into Palestine, the Armenian Church, with a world congregation of only six million, owns a third of Jerusalem's holy sites. Obscure in the church councils of the world, the Copts and Assyrians are also highly visible in Jerusalem.

There are, of course, age-old disputes over who owns what. In an attempt to settle the issue, in 1757 the Turkish authorities drew up the rights of possession for nine of the most important shrines. Known as the Status Quo, this ruling is still applicable today. However, it has done nothing to end the intense rivalry in the Holy City between the various Christian factions, and these occasionally erupt in fisticuffs in the aisles of the sacred sites (see the boxed text 'Rites & Wrongs' in the Things to See & Do chapter).

Christian Orthodox The Greek Orthodox Church is the oldest ecclesiastical body in Jerusalem and is probably the closest successor to the original Judaeo-Christian community of St James. A Greek-speaking Christian community emerged here in the mid-2nd century, gaining importance during the rule of Constantine, when most of the holy sites were rediscovered.

The modern Greek Orthodox community in Jerusalem is predominantly Arabic-speaking but is led by an almost exclusively Greek-speaking priesthood. The Orthodox patriarchate of Jerusalem is the only autonomous church in the country, with all the others being dependent to various degrees on a head office abroad. Jerusalem is also the home of two Russian Orthodox missions and a small Romanian Orthodox community and church.

Armenian An ancient kingdom which spent most of the 20th century as a small province of the Soviet Union, Armenia is represented by one of the Holy Land's more powerful Christian communities. Much of Mt Zion is the property of the Armenian Church and it also shares the churches of the Holy Sepulchre and the Nativity with the Orthodox and Latin patriarchates. During the Mandate, the Armenians were a prosperous community of some 5000 people, with their own churches, schools and culture, but due to emigration they number only about 2500 today.

Syrian Orthodox & Coptic There has been a Syrian bishop in Jerusalem since 1140, the Copts since 1236. Also called the Jacobites, the Syrian Orthodox Church is headed by an archbishop whose residence is the monastery of St Mark. The Copts, who are from Egypt, have a monastery upstairs at the back of the Church of the Holy Sepulchre. Both of these groups celebrate Christmas at the Armenian altars in the Church of the Nativity, but otherwise they use their own small chapels in the Church of the Holy Sepulchre.

Ethiopian From the Middle Ages until the 16th century, the Ethiopians owned chapels and altars in various holy places. Today in Jerusalem they are confined to a ramshackle monastery on the roof of the Church of the Holy Sepulchre.

Catholic The western, Latin patriarchate of Jerusalem was established by the Crusaders in 1099, ceased to exist in 1291, and was re-established in 1847. Most Catholic religious groups were established here over the past 130 years, except the Franciscans, who for more than 500 years were the sole body in charge of Catholic interests in Palestine and the Middle East.

Protestant Anglican and Prussian Lutherans arrived in Jerusalem 160 years ago. Their aim was missionary work among Jews and Muslims, but the Greek Orthodox Church proved the source of most of their converts. Today, the Evangelical Episcopal Church is mostly Arab-speaking, and the Anglican archbishop in Jerusalem presides over a synod made up of Egyptian, Libyan, Sudanese, Iranian and Jordanian bishops.

The Anglicans have no rights in the Church of the Holy Sepulchre, but an arrangement with the Greek Orthodox Church allows them to occasionally celebrate Mass in the nearby Chapel of St Abraham. The Anglican cathedral is St George's in East Jerusalem.

The German Lutherans established hospitals, schools, and hospices in Palestine, including the Hospice of the Order of St John in Jerusalem and the Augusta Victoria Hospice (now a hospital) on Mt Scopus. There are some non-German Lutheran institutions in Israel, including the Swedish Theological Institute and the Finnish Missionary School in Jerusalem, the Swedish school and hospital in Bethlehem, and the Scandinavian Seamen's churches in Haifa and Ashdod. There are also several minor Protestant groups representing reformed Christianity, including Presbyterians, Baptists, Pentecostalists, Quakers and Adventists.

Christian Zionism & the International Christian Embassy In 1980, when the Israeli government claimed Jerusalem as the capital of the Jewish State, 13 countries closed their embassies in the city in protest and transferred them to Tel Aviv. Reacting to what they saw as unfair treatment of the Israelis, a group of Christians already living in Israel set up the International Christian Embassy in Jerusalem (ICEJ).

The ICEJ does not claim to represent all Christians, rather it represents a 'nation' of Christian Zionists who interpret the Bible as supporting the Jewish people and the modern State of Israel. In fact, one suspects that the pro-Jewish stand of the ICEJ is grounded in a fear of Islam. The Christian Zionists believe that Israel's borders should rightly include present-day Jordan; they also dispute the claim that Jerusalem is Islam's third holiest site.

LANGUAGE
Israel's national language is Hebrew. It's the most spoken language, followed by Arabic. English is also widely spoken and you'll almost always be able to find someone who understands it. Most of the important road and street signs are in all three languages. With the influx of worldwide Jewry in Jerusalem, many other languages are commonly understood too – French, German and Yiddish are the main ones, but Spanish and j are also common. See the Language Guide at the back of the book.

The Hebrew Alphabet
Written from right to left, Hebrew has 22 basic characters – but from there it starts to get very complicated. Like English, not all these characters have fixed phonetic values and their sound can vary from word to word. You just have to *know* that, for instance, Yair is pronounced 'Ya-ear' and doesn't rhyme with 'hare' or 'fire'.

Other letters change their sound value with the addition of diacritical marks but these diacritical marks are quite often left out. Like Arabic, the same sound can also be represented by what seem like different characters but are in fact the same character but in different forms, depending on where it falls in a word. Also there is a second 'handwritten' alphabet often used for fancy ad copy, shopfront signs and poster text, in which many of the characters are dissimilar to their 'standard' forms.

Ben Yehuda & the Revival of Hebrew

Part of the foundation process of the modern Israeli state was the unprecedented linguistic feat of reviving a long-defunct biblical tongue, and turning Hebrew into a living, modern language. Even before the rise of Yiddish in the Middle Ages, Hebrew had ceased to be the Jewish lingua franca – the Greek Old Testament was produced in the 2nd century BC for the benefit of Hellenistic Jews who could no longer read Hebrew, and the language of Roman-occupied Judaea was Aramaic.

The man responsible for the remarkable achievement of reviving the Hebrew lanaguage was Eliezer ben Yehuda, a Lithuanian Jew born on 7 January 1858. Like most of his peers he was introduced to biblical Hebrew through a thoroughly religious upbringing. Ben Yehuda came to the nascent state of Israel in 1881 imbued with the idea of making the previously biblical language a secular tool that would enable Jews of Palestine and the Diaspora to communicate in one unified tongue.

While the Hebrew language had survived essentially intact, it had remained static from biblical times and was not spoken as a living language. Consequently it did not have words for such modernities as 'electricity' or 'car' and new terms had to be coined from scratch. It is believed that Ben Yehuda spoke – rather than recited – Hebrew for the first time at a cafe in Montmartre in Paris prior to departing for Palestine. Upon arrival he took it upon himself to speak only Hebrew to anyone he met, and his first-born son was the first exclusively Hebrew-speaking child in modern history.

His persistence and proselytising paid off and his teachings took hold among an enthusiastic group of would-be Hebrew speakers. Part of Ben Yehuda's legacy is the 17-volume *Complete Dictionary of Ancient and Modern Hebrew*. Hebrew is now the native language of choice for just under six million Israelis.

It is worth noting that transliteration from Hebrew script into English is at best an approximate science. The presence of sounds unknown in English and the fact that the script is incomplete (most vowels are not written in modern Hebrew) combine to make it nearly impossible to settle on one agreed method of transliteration. A wide variety of spellings of Hebrew words is therefore possible when they appear in Latin script and that goes for place names and people's names as well. We take comfort in the knowledge that the Israelis themselves are no better at this inexact science than we are – one street we found in Haifa was labelled 'Hayim' at one end and 'Chaim' at the other, both are transliterations of the same Hebrew name.

Facts for the Visitor

WHEN TO GO

There are few seasonal factors which will drastically affect your visit. Jerusalem's climate (see the Facts about Jerusalem chapter) is not so extreme that there's any specific time to make a point of avoiding, but to miss the worst of the summer heat it's probably best to skip July and August – although it does still cool off considerably in the evenings at this time.

It's also worth being aware of the various Jewish festivals. The major festivals are the Israeli high season with a corresponding hike in hotel rates of up to 25%. In addition, all Jewish shops and business completely close down (you'll have difficulty finding anything to eat), and public transport grinds to a halt. The ones to avoid are Rosh HaShanah and Yom Kippur, Sukkot and Pesach (see Public Holidays later in this chapter). They are, however, usually mercifully brief.

Easters in Jerusalem are extremely colourful, especially the Orthodox which comes a week after the western Christian celebrations, but accommodation may be hard to come by as the city fills up with pilgrims – booking is recommended.

ORIENTATION

As cities go, Jerusalem is actually quite small, but finding your way around is made confusing by the hide-and-seek topography. The city is also quite hilly which means that traversing the city for any distance means frequent ascents and descents – a point worth taking into account if you are a keen pedestrian or cyclist. The first thing to know is that the city is broken into three distinct areas: the Old City, East Jerusalem and the New City (also referred to as West Jerusalem).

Old City

For many visitors this is Jerusalem. Encircled by fortified walls, the Old City is a single tightly bound square kilometre containing 20,000 people and 3000 years of history. The Western Wall is in here, as is the Dome of the Rock and the Church of the Holy Sepulchre, built over the site of the biblical Golgotha. Navigation is difficult without a map, as the narrow, gully-like alleys twist and turn, leaving the uninitiated visitor without any sense of direction.

Of the seven gates to the Old City, the most important are likely to be the Jaffa Gate, which is the main access from the New City, the New Gate at the northwestern tip of the Old City leading into the Christian Quarter and the Damascus Gate, which faces East Jerusalem and leads directly into the heart of the commercial section of the Muslim Quarter.

New City

This is the predominantly Jewish commercial and administrative district, embracing a diversity of lifestyles from the 19th century orthodoxy of the Mea She'arim neighbourhood to the Baywatch babes round the pool at the Paradise Hotel.

The New City is roughly centred on the triangle formed by King George V St, Jaffa Rd and pedestrianised Ben Yehuda St. The latter two converge at Zion Square, a cramped plaza which serves as a popular gathering point. Most of the middle and top-end hotels and eating places are around here, along with the most popular cafes and bars.

Mahane Yehuda, the New City's cheap produce market, is just to the west of the central area, while further out and to the south west are the Knesset building, the Israel Museum and the Vad Yashem Holocaust memorial complex.

East Jerusalem

This is the Palestinian part of Jerusalem, east of HaShalom Rd (the former 'Green Line' which divided Jerusalem between 1948 and 1967). It is a district made up of small businesses, shops, travel agencies, moneychangers, hotels and restaurants, mainly centred on the two main streets of Nablus Rd (Derekh Shchem in Hebrew) and Salah ad-Din St. These form a triangle with congested Sultan Suleyman St, which runs in the shadow of the Old City's north wall.

It's the only part of Jerusalem that stays open during Shabbat and other religious holidays – worth noting if you are hanging out for a bite to eat during these times. (See the Jewish Festivals special section on pp 58-62.)

MAPS

A very worthwhile investment is *Carta's Map of Jerusalem* (24 NIS). Alternatively, a company called Map produces a pocket-sized 50-page *Jerusalem The New Street Atlas* (65 NIS). This is far more comprehensive than the Carta map but, for those new to the city, doesn't really give a good impression of how it all fits together. There is also an A4 sized version of this street atlas (approximately 80 NIS), which is easier on the eye but more unwieldy to cart around. There's also an excellent 1:2500 map, *Jerusalem – The Old City*, produced by the Survey of Israel (20 NIS).

More a memento than an on-the-hoof aid, Steimatzky, the bookseller, does a very attractive panoramic 3D map of the Old City (15 NIS). All of these maps are locally produced and should be available from any branch of Steimatzky or from the Society for the Protection of Nature in Israel (SPNI) shop – see the Shopping chapter for details.

The SPNI also offers a series of excellent 1:50,000 Hiking & Touring maps. The only catch is they are all in Hebrew with the lone exception of the Eilat Mountains map, which is in English. This map costs 52 NIS from the SPNI. You can also get hold of a very good pair of 1:250,000 maps produced by the Survey of Israel Cartography Department (☎ 03-623 1923, fax 03-562 0988) at 1 Lincoln St, Tel Aviv, for 30 NIS. Both these maps cover the whole country, but are due for an update, since the last (partial) revision was carried out in 1997.

A free but very poor city map is also handed out at the Safra Square tourist information office.

RESPONSIBLE TOURISM

Israel is a small country and receives a large number of visitors – over 2.5 million each year. That's third more than the total population of Israel moving around the country visiting sites, using resources and placing increasing pressure on the infrastructure.

The greater majority of visitors move around the country in buses, coaches and cars adding considerably to the carbon monoxide and other pollutants soup that exhaust emissions create. It's a heavy burden for a geographically small nation.

Individual travellers will find it hard to avoid motorised transport, but might consider hiking or cycling tours of the country which are becoming more and more popular. The SPNI runs a wide range of ecologically sound tours catering for all tastes and budgets. A company in Jerusalem called Walk Ways (see Cycling in the Things to See & Do chapter for details) organises cycling tours of the Galilee, the Jordan Valley and the Negev and Sinai deserts. This is an excellent way to visit the country while minimising the impact on the environment.

Low-impact, low-polluting travel should be the aim of all responsible tourists. Choose your transport with forethought and take out of the environment whatever you take in. That way Israel will continue to cater for its visitors long into the future.

As with all countries which permit the export of antiquities, the purchase of these souvenirs come involve an ethical dimension – see the Shopping chapter.

TOURIST OFFICES
Local Tourist Offices

The main city tourist information office (Map 3, ☎ 625 8844) is in the City Hall Complex on Safra Square, at the eastern end of Jaffa Rd. It goes by the grand name of the Jerusalem Information & Tourism Centre and is open Sunday to Thursday from 8.30 am to 4.30 pm, and Friday from 8.30 am to noon, closed Saturday. There's also a second, now privately-run tourist information office at Jaffa Gate in the Old City, open the same hours.

Possibly also of use, the Christian Information Centre (☎ 627 2692, fax 628 6417) on Omar ibn al-Khattab Square, opposite the entrance to the Citadel (Map 6), is very good on everything pertaining to the city's Christian sites and also has a good selection of Jerusalem books. Catholics can apply here for tickets for Midnight Mass on Christmas Eve in the Church of the Nativity in Bethlehem. The centre is open Monday to Saturday from 8.30 am to 1 pm, closed Sunday.

The Jewish Student Information Centre (☎ 628 2643, fax 628 8338, email jseidel@jer1.co.il, 5 Beit El St) in the Jewish Quarter of the Old City (adjacent to the Hurva and Rambam synagogues, Map 6). It has a lounge with refreshments, a library and evening activities, and it provides assistance with accommodation, Shabbat dinners and free tours, as well as general information for the Jewish visitor.

Tourist Offices Abroad

Australia
(☎ 02-9326 1700, fax 9326 1676, email aicc@mpx.com.au, Web site www.wej.com.au/tourism) 395 New South Head Rd, Double Bay, Sydney 2028, NSW

Canada
(☎ 416-964 3784, fax 964 2420, email igto@indirect.com) 180 Bloor St West, Suit 700, Toronto, Ontario M5S-2V6

Denmark
(☎ 033-119 711, fax 914 801) Vesterbrogade 6D, DK-1620 Copenhagen V

France
(☎ 01 42 61 01 97, fax 01 49 27 09 46, email infos@otisrael.com) 22 Rue des Capucines, F-75002 Paris

Germany
(☎ 069-756 1920, fax 7561 9222, email igtofra@aol.com) Bettina Strasse 62, D-60325 Frankfurt-am-Main
(☎ 089-212 3860, fax 212 8630) Stollberg Str 6, D-80539 Munich
(☎ 030-203 9970, fax 2039 9730) Friedrichstrasse 95, D-10117 Berlin

Italy
(☎ 02-7602 1051, fax 7601 2477) Corso Europa 12, I-20122 Milano

Japan
(☎ 3-3238 9081, fax 3238 9077, email listman@clal-ns.or.jp) 22 Ichibancho, Chiyoda-Ku, Tokyo 102

Netherlands
(☎ 020-612 8850, fax 689 4288, email igto.adam@wxs.nl) Stadhouderskade 2, 1054 ES Amsterdam

South Africa
(☎ 011-788 1703, fax 447 3104, email igto@icon.co.za) 5th Floor, 33 Bath Avenue, Rosebank 2196

UK
(☎ 0171-299 1111, fax 299 1112; from April 22 2000 ☎ 020-7299-111, fax 7299 1112; email igto-uk@dircon.co.uk) 180 Oxford St, London W1N 9DJ

USA
(☎ 312-782-4306, fax 782-1243, email igtochicago@aol.com) 5 South Wabash Ave, Chicago, ILL 60603-3073
(☎ 972-991-9097, fax 392-3521, email igtotx@onramp.net) 5151 Belt Line Rd, Suite 1280, Dallas, TX 75240
(☎ 213-658 7462, fax 658 6543) 6380 Wilshire Blvd 1718, Los Angeles, CA 90048
(☎ 212-499-5660, fax 499-5655, info@goisrael.com) 800 Second Ave, New York, NY 10017

See also the Israel government tourist office's Web page at www.goisrael.com.

Society for the Protection of Nature in Israel

The Society for the Protection of Nature in Israel is an organisation devoted to environmental preservation. Much of the work is facilitated through 26 field study centres dotted throughout Israel; the head office is in Tel Aviv, with a branch office in Jerusalem (Map 3, ☎ 624 4605, 13 Helene HaMalka St) in what was originally a pilgrims' hospice built by the Russian Church. From here they offer tours in and around Jerusalem and also have the country's best shop for maps and hiking-related books and pamphlets. The office is open Sunday to Wednesday from 9 am to 4.45 pm, Thursday from 9 am to 5.45 pm, and Friday from 9 am to 12.30 pm.

DOCUMENTS
Visas

With all but a handful of exceptions, a tourist visa is not required to visit Israel; all you normally need is a passport, valid for at least six months from your date of entry.

The exceptions include holders of passports from most African and Central American countries, India, Singapore and some of the former Soviet republics.

Under normal conditions, tourists are allowed a three month visit, although visitors entering through the land borders with Egypt and Jordan are often initially only granted a month's stay. On your arrival, Israeli immigration officials will give you a duplicate entry permit to fill in. The second copy will be returned to you and you need to keep this until you leave the country. Do not lose this small piece of paper or you'll face a long delay in the already lengthy departure procedure.

If you appear to to the immigration officials to be 'undesirable', or are suspected of looking for illegal employment, the immigration officials may question the purpose of your visit and ask to see both a return flight/ferry ticket as well as evidence of financial support. Travellers found to have insufficient money to cover their proposed stay period have, in the past, been prevented from entering the country and put on the next flight home. More commonly, if unimpressed, immigration may only allow you a shorter stay, of for example, one month only.

Visa Extensions If you want to extend your stay beyond the initial three months, you need to apply for a visa. You can do this at the Ministry of the Interior office (Map 2, ☎ 622 8211 or 629 0231) at 1 Shlomzion St, in the central area of the New City.

The process of applying for an extension visa involves an early start to beat the long queues. The office opens at 8 am and by the time the doors open the queue is usually depressingly long. Once you've gained an audience, convincing the civil servants that you should be allowed to stay can be difficult; one crucial requirement is that you must have proof that you can support yourself without recourse to illegal employment.

If the petition is accepted your stay will be extended for typically three months, although sometimes it can be for one month only and sometimes for six.

One passport-sized photo is required, and the process costs 110 NIS. There is no fee for citizens of Belgium, Luxembourg or the Netherlands.

The maximum period a foreigner is allowed to stay in Israel varies according to which official you ask. It can be one month if they don't like the look of you or several years if they do. Usually, one year is the most you can stay without pulling strings.

FACTS FOR THE VISITOR

The Israeli Stamp Stigma

Israel is the venue for that popular Middle Eastern game, the Passport Shuffle. This involves getting in and out of the country without having your passport stamped with any incriminating evidence to tell that you were ever there.

This game was devised because those countries which do not officially recognise the existence of Israel (including Lebanon, Syria and the Gulf States) refuse to allow anyone across their borders whose passport is marred by evidence of a visit to the Jewish state. Israeli immigration officials will, if asked, stamp only your entry permit and not your passport. This is fine if you are flying both into and out of Israel, but if crossing by land into either Egypt or Jordan the Arab immigration officers are generally not so obliging, and their entry stamps will be a dead giveaway.

Another solution used by many Israelis and some lucky foreigners is to have a second passport acquired through having dual nationality. You can still ask for a stamp-less entry, but in the off-chance that your request is ignored your chances of visiting other Middle East countries won't be totally compromised.

Expired Visas The 64 shekel question is: what happens if you try to leave Israel after overstaying your visa, and without having obtained an extension? At Ben-Gurion airport, if the overstay is less than a month you may be let off, but then again you may be charged the cost of the visa renewal (110 NIS) *and* have a fine slapped on top; if the overstay is more than a month then you're definitely going to have to dig deep into your pockets.

It has also happened that those wildly over the mark have had their passports stamped to bar them from returning to Israel for a period of five years. Expired visa holders attempting to depart from Ovda airport or any land borders will almost certainly be turned away and sent to the Ministry of the Interior.

Travel Insurance

A collision with the Israeli medical system can cause severe injuries to your finances, and doctors and hospitals in Jerusalem often expect immediate cash payment. It's wise to come protected by good travel insurance. When looking for a policy, coverage for lost baggage, cancelled flights and minor medical bills may be nice, but what you're really looking for is coverage against a true catastrophe such as hospitalisation following a road accident or serious illness.

Many travel agents are now keen to sell insurance as part of the flight package and they should be able to advise on the options. Check the fine print as some policies exclude coverage for 'dangerous' occupations such as rock climbing, motorcycling or scuba diving. If you are likely to engage in anything like that, you don't want a policy which leaves you out in the cold. If you do require medical attention be sure to save all your documentation and invoices and put in a claim to your insurance company as soon as possible.

Hostel & Student Cards

Bring along your Hostelling International (HI) card and International Student Identity Card (ISIC) if you have them, as both of them can be useful. HI membership will save you money at their affiliated hostels – although they still tend to be way more expensive than the privately owned competition. An ISIC card entitles the holder to a 10% discount on all Egged bus fares over 10 NIS, and 20% off fares on Israel State Railways as well as substantial discounts at most museums and archaeological sites. Even if signs make no mention of student discounts, produce your card and inquire. Student cards issued by your individual university or college are often not recognised.

EMBASSIES & CONSULATES
Israeli Embassies & Consulates

These are some of the Israeli embassies and consulates abroad:

Argentina
    (☎ 01-342 1465, fax 342 5307, email cultura@israel-embassy.org.ar) Av De Mayo 701 Piso 10, Buenos Aires
Australia
    Embassy: (☎ 02-6273 1309, 6273 1300, fax 6273 4273, email IsrEmb.Canberra@u030.aone.net.au) 6 Turrana Ave, Yarralumla, Canberra, ACT 2600
    Consulate: (☎ 02-9264 7933, fax 9290 2259, email isconsyd@infinet.net.au) 37 York St, Sydney, NSW 2000
Belgium
    (☎ 02-373 5500, fax 373-5617, email isremb@online.be) Av De L'observatoire 40, Brussels 1180
Canada
    Embassy: (☎ 613-567 6450, fax 237 8865, email embisrott@cyberus.ca) 50 O'Conner St, Suite 1005, Ottawa, Ontario KIP 6L2
    Consulate: (☎ 514-393 9372, fax 393 8795, email cgisrmtl@videotron.net) 115 Blvd Rene Levesque Ouest, Suite 2620, Montreal, Quebec H3B 4S5
Cyprus
    (☎ 2-665196, fax 663486, email israel@cytanet.com.cy) 4 Grypari Street, PO Box 5049, Nicosia
Egypt
    Embassy: (☎ 2-3610528, 3610545, fax 3610 414, email isremcai@internetegypt.com) 6 Sharia Ibn el-Malek, Giza, Cairo
    Consulate: (☎ 3-5860492, 5863874, fax 5870 646, email consilx@alexnet.com.eg) 207 Ahmed Abdel Salem Aref St Laurent, PO Box 3060, Alexandria

France
Embassy: (☎ 01 40 76 55 00, fax 01 40 76 55 55) 3 rue Rabelais, F-75008 Paris
Consulate: (☎ 09 17 73 990, 09 15 33 987, fax 09 15 33 994, email isconsulat@aol.com) 146 rue Paradis, F-13006 Marseille

Germany
Embassy: (☎ 0228-934 6500, fax 934 6555, email Botschaft@israel.de) Simrockallee 2, PO Box 200230, Bonn D-53173
Consulate: (☎ 030-893 2203/2204/2205/2206, fax 8928908, email israel@berlin.snafu.de) Schinkelstrasse 10, PO Box 330531, Berlin D-14193

Ireland
(☎ 01-668 0303, fax 668 0418, email Embisrae@Iol.Ie) Carrisbrook House, 122 Pembroke Road, Ballsbridge, Dublin 4

Italy
(☎ 06-36 19 85 00, fax 36 19 85 55, email Israel .Roma@agora.stm.it) Via Michele Mercati 14, 00197 Rome

Jordan
(☎ 3272-507 215, 507 218, fax 506 283, email isrem@go.com.jo) 47 Maysaloun St Rabiya, PO Box 950866 Amman 111195-Jordan

Netherlands
(☎ 070-376 0500, fax 376 0555, email ambassade@israel.nl) 47 Buitenhoff, The Hague 2513 AH

New Zealand
(☎ 04-472 2362, 472 2368, fax 499 0632, email israel@central.co.nz) DB Tower, The Terrace 111, PO Box 2171, Wellington

South Africa
Embassy: (☎ 012-3422693, 3422697, fax 342 1442, email embofisr@iafrica.com) 339, Hilda St, Hatfield 0083, PO Box 3726, Pretoria 0001
Consulate: (☎ 021-457215, fax 4610075) Church Square House, 8th Floor 5 Spin St, PO Box 180, Cape Town

Turkey
Embassy: (☎ 312-446 3605, fax 426 1533, email dideme@dominet.in.com.tr) Mahatma Gandhi Sok 85 Gaziosmanpasa, Ankara
Consulate: (☎ 212-225/1040/1041/1042/1043, fax 225 1048, email isrcon@comnet.com.tr) Valikonag Caddesi No 73 Nisantas, İstanbul

UK (☎ 0171-957 9547, fax 957 9555; from April 22, 2000 ☎ 020-7957 9547, fax 7957 9555; email isr-info@dircon.co.uk) 2 Palace Green, London W8 4QB

USA
Embassy: (☎ 202-364-5500, fax 364-5607, email ask@israelemb.org) 3514 International Drive NW, Washington DC 20008
Consulate: (☎ 212-499-5300, fax 499-5555, email nycon@interport.net) 800 Second Ave, New York NY10017

There are eight other Israeli consulates in the USA; phone one of the above two for contact details.

Embassies & Consulates in Jerusalem

Although Israel claims Jerusalem as its capital, this is not recognised by most of the international community. Instead, most foreign embassies are in Tel Aviv, with just a handful of consulates in Jerusalem. Note that some countries maintain consulates in both East and West Jerusalem. All consulates are closed on Saturday and Sunday.

Denmark (☎ 625 8083, fax 624 7403, email adtalbar@mail.inter.net.il) 10 B'nei Brit St, West Jerusalem

France
(☎ 625 9481, fax 625 9178, email consulate@p-d.com) 5 Paul Emile Botta St, West Jerusalem, Map 3
(☎ 582 8387, 582 0032) Sheikh Jarrah, East Jerusalem, Map 4

UK (☎ 541 4100, fax 532 2368 or 523 5629, email britain@palnet.com, Web site www.britishconsulate.org) 19 Nashashibi St, Sheikh Jarrah, PO Box 19690, Map 9
East Jerusalem (☎ 671 7724) Tower House, Kikar Remez West Jerusalem, Map 3

USA
(☎ 628 2456, fax 628 2454, Web site www .usis-jerusalem.org) 27 Nablus Rd, East Jerusalem, Map 5 (for consular services, visas, American citizen services and public diplomacy) 16-18 Agron St, West Jerusalem, Map 3 (for political, economic, administrative and aid functions)

Your Own Embassy

It's important to realise what your own embassy – the embassy of the country of which you are a citizen – can and can't do to help you if you get into trouble.

In general, it won't be much help if the trouble you're in is even remotely your own fault. Remember that you are bound by local laws. Your embassy will not be sympathetic if you are jailed for committing a crime, even if such actions are legal in your own country.

In genuine emergencies you might get some assistance, but only if other channels have been exhausted. For example, if you need to get home urgently, a free ticket home is exceedingly unlikely – the embassy would expect you to have insurance. If you have all your money and documents stolen, it might assist with getting a new passport, but a loan for onward travel is out of the question.

Some embassies used to keep letters for travellers or have a small reading room with home newspapers, but these days the mail holding service has usually been stopped and even newspapers tend to be out of date.

CUSTOMS

You can bring duty-free into Israel up to 1L of spirits and 2L of wine for every person over 17 years of age, as well as up to 250g of tobacco or 250 cigarettes. Animals, firearms, plants, and fresh meat may not be brought into the country. Video equipment, personal computers and diving apparatus must be declared at customs and a deposit paid to be collected on departure (to prevent you bringing any of this stuff in and flogging it while here).

MONEY
Currency

The national currency is the new Israeli shekel (NIS). The correct plural in Hebrew is *shekelim,* but even Israelis tend to say 'shekels' when speaking in English. Expats call them 'sheks'. The 'old shekel' was dropped in 1985 as part of a rescue plan to reduce inflation. The new shekel is divided into 100 *agorot.* There are coins of 10 and 50 agorot and 1 and 5 NIS, and notes of 5, 10, 20, 50, 100 and 200 NIS.

Many Israelis talk in terms of US dollars, not shekels, a habit acquired in the days when the national currency was constantly being devalued. Upmarket hotels still quote their prices in dollars as do the HI hostels, most car hire companies and many airlines. At most places, payment in dollars is accepted and, for the customer, it's preferable because payments made in foreign currency are free of the 17% value added tax (VAT).

For this reason all mid-range and top-end accommodation rates will be given in US dollars, and not shekels in this book.

After the dollar one foreign currency is as good as any other and moneychangers and banks will take whatever you've got.

Exchange Rates

country	unit		NIS
Australia	A$1	=	2.69
Canada	C$1	=	2.78
Egypt	E£1	=	1.20
euro	€1	=	4.28
France	10FF	=	6.52
Germany	DM1	=	2.19
Japan	¥100	=	3.45
Jordan	JD1	=	5.74
New Zealand	NZ$1	=	2.17
UK	UK£1	=	6.55
USA	US$1	=	4.01

Exchanging Money

In the major towns and cities there is no shortage of places to change money – not only are there countless banks and exchange bureaux, but many Arab shopkeepers double as moneychangers and the reception at your hostel or hotel is probably quite likely to indulge in a little banknote barter too.

Generally speaking there is little variation in the rates of exchange on offer but you ought to check on the commission charged by the banks because sometimes this can be extremely voracious. The best deals are offered by the Arab moneychangers in Jerusalem and the exchange bureaux in Jerusalem and Tel Aviv, none of which charge any commission at all.

Although banking hours vary, generally they are Sunday to Tuesday and Thursday from 8.30 am to 12.30 pm and 4 to 5.30 pm, and Wednesday, Friday and eves of religious holidays from 8.30 am to noon.

Some bank branches also have currency exchange ATMs which accept several of the major international currencies and offer the convenience of 24 hour accessibility, seven days a week; the drawback is a whopping transaction charge.

At the end of your stay you can convert your shekels at the airport or at the port in Haifa. You are allowed to freely reconvert up to US$500 but for anything over that you must produce a bank receipt as proof of the original exchange.

Cash If you want the best deal when exchanging money, go to the legal moneychangers in the Old City and East Jerusalem. The two just inside the Damascus Gate seem to give a better price than those anywhere else. The moneychanger just inside the Petra Hostel near Jaffa Gate seems to be open when the others are closed. Other moneychangers can be found on David St, the Old City's main bazaar street going east from Jaffa Gate, and on Salah ad-Din St in East Jerusalem.

In the New City go to Change Point at 33 Jaffa Rd or 2 Ben Yehuda St (Map 3), neither of which charges commission. The Jaffa Rd branch is open daily from 9 am to 9 pm, but closed on Saturday. The one on Ben Yehuda St is open from 9.30 am to 7.45 pm Sunday to Thursday, from 9.30 am to 2 pm on Friday, and is closed on Saturday. Most banks are located on Jaffa Rd around Zion Square, and most are open from 8.30 am to 12.30 pm and 4 to 5.30 pm Sunday to Tuesday and on Thursday; from 8.30 am to noon on Wednesday and Friday; and are closed Saturday.

Travellers Cheques Travellers cheques are widely accepted and you'll have no trouble getting them cashed – Eurocheques can even be exchanged at post offices. Beware, though, that commission charges can be as high as 20 NIS *per cheque* regardless of the amount, so shop around. The best bet is to go to one of the commission-free exchange bureaux (see Exchanging Money) or, if you are carrying their cheques, to the American Express Travel service office (☎ 624 0830, fax 624 0950) at 19 Hillel St, two blocks south of the Ben Yehuda mall (Map 4). The staff will replace lost or stolen travellers cheques, hold mail etc. The office is open from 9 am to 5 pm Sunday to Thursday, closed on Friday and Saturday. The

local agent for Thomas Cook is Aweidah Tours (☎ 628 2365, fax 628 2366) at 23 Salah ad-Din St in East Jerusalem (Map 5); however, this office does not cash cheques.

ATMs Many bank foyers are equipped with cash-dispensing ATMs accepting all of the major international credit cards. Be aware that your home bank may be charging you hefty premiums for the use of an overseas ATM, so check the current rates before you leave.

If you don't have your PIN but are carrying a Visa card, Bank Leumi (Zion Square, Map 4) will give you a cash advance, subject to a credit status check. If you lose your plastic, call the Tel Aviv office of your credit card company:

American Express	☎ 03-524 2211
Diners Club	☎ 03-572 3572
Eurocard	☎ 03-576 4444
Visa	☎ 03-572 3572

Credit Cards Israelis live on credit and owe their freewheeling lifestyles to Visa, American Express, Diners Club and the like. To this end nearly every establishment takes credit cards because it wouldn't have any business if it didn't. It's not unusual for Jerusalemites to cover the cost of their cappuccino and croissant with a piece of plastic.

International Transfers For anyone unfortunate enough to run out of money, the Israeli post operates a Western Union international money transfer service. For details, go to any post office or call ☎ 177-022 2131, toll-free.

Security

Keeping your cash, plastic and travellers cheques in body pouches is of course a secure method of protecting you money, but if you retrieve it in public to pay for transactions, you may inadvertently be showing would-be thieves exactly where you keep your money. Better keep some cash handy in a secure inside pocket and dip into your security pouch only in the safety of your hostel or hotel room.

'Fanny packs' (bumbags), while enormously popular and convenient do scream 'Tourist!' and can easily be slashed or removed by accomplished thieves. It is probably better to avoid them. Keep your money in more than one location on your person (keep, for example, a spare US$50 in your shoe) and never keep more than one credit card in the same place.

Costs

You can bring an unlimited amount of foreign and local currency into Israel – which is lucky, because the cost of living in Jerusalem is high, though of course it depends on your requirements. You can stay in a budget hostel for between 25 NIS and 35 NIS (US$6.50 to US$8.50) per night. Accommodation aside, a reasonable daily budget allowing for a midday snack, an evening meal, and sundry sightseeing fees would perhaps be 100 NIS, or a little over US$25.

Alternatively, you can stay in some very impressive hotels from around US$250 for a single. These hotels often have international quality restaurants where a meal will cost in the region of US$50 to US$70 a head.

Tipping & Bargaining

Tipping Not so long ago, apparently, no-one tipped in Jerusalem. Now your bill arrives appended with a large handwritten 'Service is not included', delivered by a waiter wearing a steely smile that says '15%. No less'. You may frequently feel the extra money is undeserved but that's not the point – service industry staff salaries in Israel are customarily low and the system relies on tips from the customers to even up the balance. Therefore, when pricing a menu, always allow for that extra percentage on top.

Note that taxi drivers in Jerusalem do not expect to be tipped; they're usually content just to overcharge.

Bargaining There are few bargains to be had, though of course in the Old City bazaars you can try your luck at haggling. This is not always the fun it is made out to be. It can be time-consuming, frustrating and, in general, an unwelcome hassle.

The golden rules are: don't start bargaining unless you are really interested in buying; have a good idea of the item's value both locally and back home; and don't be intimidated – easier said than done. Also do not use large notes or travellers' cheques, as getting change can be a problem.

Basically, the bargaining game is played like this: the shopkeeper usually attracts your attention and gives you a price anywhere from two to 10 times above the realistic going rate. If you are genuinely interested, pull a face showing disgust or amusement at this quote and state your offer in a 'take it or leave it' manner. This should, of course, be substantially below the amount you are actually willing to pay. Stick to your guns and do not be bullied or cajoled into paying too much. Turning away from a bargaining session can often cut a price in half.

Traditionally, Arab shopkeepers sell their goods cheaper early in the day, as it is believed that a quick first sale means good business later. However, this line is often used to persuade customers to pay more, thinking that they are getting a bargain.

Taxes & Refunds

Israel has a value added tax (VAT) on a wide range of goods, but tourists are entitled to a refund on most items purchased with foreign currency in shops that are registered as such with the Ministry of Tourism (there'll be a sign in the window or at the till). The procedure for reclaiming your 17% seems to have been designed with the specific aim of deterring the faint-hearted.

The net figure on one invoice must be at least US$50, with the exception of electrical appliances, cameras, films, photographic accessories and computers. The purchases need to be wrapped in a sealed plastic bag, of which at least one side must be transparent with the original invoice displayed inside so that it can be read without opening the bag. The bag needs to remain sealed for the duration of your time in Israel.

When leaving from Ben-Gurion airport, go to the Bank Leumi counter in the departure lounge and present your sealed bag. The bank will stamp the invoice, identify the goods and refund in US dollars the VAT paid (less commission). At other departure points, customs officials will do the honours and the refund will be mailed to your home address.

POST & COMMUNICATIONS
Post
The main post office (☎ 624 4745) with poste restante is at 23 Jaffa Rd (Map 3). The main section is open Sunday to Thursday from 7 am to 7 pm, and Friday from 7 am to noon, but closed Saturday. After hours letters, telegrams and telexes can be sent from the information desk.

There are several post office branches. The one in Omar ibn al-Khattab Square inside Jaffa Gate in the Old City (Map 6) is open Sunday to Thursday from 7.30 am to 2.30 pm, and Friday from 8 am to noon. There's another in the Jewish Quarter, just off the Cardo by the Broad Wall (Map 9), which is open from 8 am to 12.30 pm and 4 to 6 pm on Sunday, Monday, Wednesday and Thursday; from 8 am to 1.30 pm on Tuesday; and 8 am to noon on Friday. It is closed Saturday.

East Jerusalem's main post office is on the corner of Salah ad-Din and Sultan Suleyman Sts (Map 5). It's open from 8.30 am to 2.30 pm and 4 to 6.30 pm on Sunday and Thursday; from 8.30 am to 12.30 pm on Monday, Wednesday and Friday; and from 8.30 am to 2.30 pm Tuesday. It's closed Saturday.

Postal Rates Letters posted in Jerusalem take between seven and 10 days to reach North America and Australia, and a little less to Europe. Incoming mail is fairly effecient, taking about three or four days from Europe and around a week from countries further afield. At the time of writing, a normal airmail letter to Europe cost 1.80 NIS, to the USA 2.20 NIS and to Australia 2.70 NIS.

Telephone
Jerusalem is included within Israel's state-of-the-art, card-operated public telephone system and international calls can be made from any public phone box. Telecards can be bought from lottery kiosks, newsagents, bookshops, vending machines or 24-hour kiosks; they're available in denominations of 20 units (11 NIS), 50 units (24 NIS) and 120 units (52 NIS).

The international access code is either ☎ 012, ☎ 013 or ☎ 001 – depending on which carrier you use (see the table on the next page) – followed by the country code, city code and then the number you wish to be connected with.

Standard rates apply between 8 am and 10 pm; from 10 pm to 1 am and all day Saturday and Sunday calls are 25% cheaper, while calls made between 1 am and 8 am are 50% cheaper all week.

You can also make discount international calls from Solan Telecom at 2 Luntz St (Map 3), which is a small pedestrianised street running between Jaffa Rd and Ben Yehuda St. Solan is open 24 hours, seven days a week.

The international country code for Israel is ☎ 972, and the telephone area code for Jerusalem is ☎ 02. Other useful numbers are: information ☎ 144; the time ☎ 155; police ☎ 100; first aid/ambulance ☎ 101 or ☎ 911; and fire service ☎ 102.

Calling Overseas The costs for calling overseas vary depending on which company you use and also on the time of day or night you make your call. Off-peak is usually between midnight and 7 am. The three companies offering overseas connections compete quite rigorously and their prices, while on the whole quite low for international calls, can differ quite considerably. Compare the sample charges in the table later, but be aware that these may have changed by the time you read this. Use the appropriate ISD prefix to select the company you wish to use, then dial the country code, city code and your phone number. Charges are per unit used.

FACTS FOR THE VISITOR

country called	Barak ☎ 013	Golden Lines ☎ 012	Bezeq ☎ 001
Australia	0.81 NIS	1.85 NIS	1.84 NIS
Canada	0.73 NIS	0.84 NIS	1.77 NIS
Egypt	2.09 NIS	1.85 NIS	4.62 NIS
France	0.98 NIS	1.04 NIS	0.98 NIS
Germany	0.62 NIS	1.04 NIS	1.19 NIS
Greece	0.76 NIS	1.04 NIS	0.19 NIS
Ireland	0.73 NIS	0.76 NIS	0.71 NIS
Italy	1.42 NIS	1.04 NIS	1.32 NIS
Jordan	1.13 NIS	1.28 NIS	3.23 NIS
Netherlands	1.31 NIS	1.04 NIS	0.98 NIS
South Africa	1.15 NIS	1.85 NIS	1.84 NIS
Sweden	1.22 NIS	1.04 NIS	0.98 NIS
UK	0.62 NIS	1.04 NIS	1.19 NIS
USA	0.73 NIS	0.84 NIS	0.71 NIS

Mobile Phones Mobile phones can be rented by the day from Quick-Phone (Map 2, ☎ 538 8848, 27 Strauss St), Shako Land (☎ 177 022 2554 toll-free, 18 King David St) or Video City (Map 3, ☎ 623 4539, 43 Jaffa Rd). Rates start at about US$1 per day.

The Israeli mobile network does not have reciprocal global roaming arrangements with many countries because of the different technical nature of their handsets. You should check with your mobile phone service if your phone can be used in Israel.

Introducing the eKno

There's a wide range of local and international phonecards. Lonely Planet's eKno Communication Card is aimed specifically at travellers and provides cheap international calls, a range of messaging services and free email – for local calls, you're usually better off with a local card.

You can register online at www.ekno. lonelyplanet.com, or by phone from Israel by dialling ☎ 1-800-945-9176. Once you have joined, to use eKno from Israel, dial ☎ 1-800-945-9177.

New countries are being added all the time. Check the Web site for updates.

Fax & Telex

To send a fax or telex, go to the main post office. Faxes cost 17 NIS for the first sheet and 9 NIS for any subsequent ones. Faxes can also be sent from Solan Telecom for 12 NIS per sheet, irrespective of the destination, and they'll receive faxes for you for a small fee.

The main post office also operates a 24 hour telegraph service, although you might have to wake up the person on duty. Alternatively, Solan Telecom will send telegrams at 25 NIS for the first seven words, address included, and 1.70 NIS for each additional word.

Email & Internet Access

Customers can send and receive email at the Strudel Internet café-wine bar (Map 3, ☎ 623 2101, fax 622 1445, email strudel@inter.net.il, 11 Monbaz St) near the Russian Compound. It has four computer stations linked to the Web; time online is charged at 6 NIS for 15 minutes. Printouts cost 1 NIS per sheet for black and white and 2 NIS for colour.

Nearby is the Netcafe (Map 3, ☎ 624 6327, email info@netcafe.co.il, 9 Helene HaMalka St) where you can surf and email for 14 NIS for 30 minutes or 25 NIS for one hour. It's open from about 10 am til late on weekdays, 10 am to 3 pm on Fridays and 9 pm till late on Saturdays. This place is great for nonsmokers, because smoking is banned. There are also snacks and drinks available if Net surfing whets your appetite.

Tmol Shilshom (Map 3, ☎ 623 2758, email info@tmol-shilshom.co.il, 5 Solomon St) is a little café-cum-bookshop that has the cheapest Internet access charges in town: 9 NIS for 30 minutes. There are only two terminals, so phone reservations are suggested. Internet access is limited to 10 am to 3 pm.

If you are in Jerusalem or Israel for any length of time and you have your own computer with you, you might want to take out your own Internet account. Of the number of providers, Netvision (☎ 04-856 0660, fax 04-855 0345, email admin@netvision.net.il)

Internet Resources

Israel is very much a computer-literate society and one that has been quick to seize upon the possibilities offered by the Internet. Point and click surfers can drop by Jerusalem's *Strudel* or *Netcafe* internet cafés, book domestic air tickets or even 'ask the rabbi'. There is also heaps of practical information on the Net that may be of use to anyone planning a visit to Israel, and the following are just a few suggestions of places to start:

www.birzeit.edu/index.html
   The Web site of Birzeit University 20km north of Jerusalem. A one-stop shop for all you could want to know about the Palestinian Territories, including a link to all the useful Palestinian Web sites.
www.bnb.co.il
   Good information on bed and breakfast accommodation options in Jerusalem.
www.cbs.gov.il
   For lovers of number crunching and statistics covering population data to the latest balance of payments figures, you can't go wrong with the Central Bureau of Statistics' homepage.
www.city.net/countries/israel
   More links specifically geared to the visitor, including categories such as travel and tourism, maps, museums and galleries and lodgings.
www.haaretzdaily.com
   The online, English-language edition (with back copies) of Ha'aretz, the daily newspaper based in Tel Aviv. Secular and distinctly more left-wing than the *Jerusalem Post*.
www1.huji.ac.il/jeru/jerusalem.html
   A virtual tour through the Old City of Jerusalem with links to information on other parts of the country.
www.iguide.co.il
   Bills itself as the Complete Guide (almost) to the World Wide Web in Israel and boasts over 950 links arranged in categories such as arts and reference.
www.infotour.co.il
   The Israel Government Tourist Office's Web page. Good for seeing what the IGTO wants you to know and has other useful links on the country.
www.israel.org
   The homepage of the Israeli Foreign Ministry, this includes biographies of ministers, a guide to the peace process, a weekly survey of the Israeli press and links to the Web sites of Israeli embassies worldwide.
www.israelhotels.org.il
   The homepage of the Israel Hotel Association. Good for getting an overview of hotels in Israel. Only members of the IHA are listed.
www.jpost.co.il
   The online edition of the English-language daily, the *Jerusalem Post*, which includes daily news, columns, features reviews and a tourism section – and there's no subscription fee.
www.lonelyplanet.com
   This is the Lonely Planet site homepage – follow the links to the Travellers' Reports for the latest postings on Israel.
www.travelmag.co.uk
   An independent Internet-published travel magazine – the contents change every month and there may not necessarily be anything on Israel, but there's always plenty else of interest and plenty of good links.
www.visit-palestine.com
   The official tourism Web site of the Palestinian Ministry of Tourism & Antiquities. Comprehensive data on the seven main Palestinian towns.

has been used with considerable success and lack of fuss. Visit its Web page (www .netvision.net.il/services) for full details. The company is based in Haifa but has local analogue and ISDN access numbers in each telephone region.

BOOKS

Few places can have inspired more wordage than Jerusalem. Our list covers just a few of the more interesting titles. All of the books should be available from most good English-language bookshops – including those belonging to the Steimatzky chain in Jerusalem (see the Shopping chapter for details).

Most books are published in different editions by different publishers in different countries. As a result, any given title might be a hardcover rarity in one country while it's readily available in paperback somewhere else. Fortunately, bookshops and libraries search by title or author, so your local bookshop or library is best placed to advise you on the availability of the following recommendations.

Lonely Planet

If you want to see more of the area around Jerusalem, Lonely Planet also publishes *Israel & the Palestinian Territories* and an accompanying *Israel & the Palestinian Territories Travel Atlas*, as well as the comprehensive, regional *Middle East* guide.

Guidebooks

Anyone whose visit to Jerusalem is primarily motivated by the city's biblical and ancient history should take a look at *The Holy Land from the Air* by Amos Elon. This book uses spectacular aerial photography to illustrate the many legendary and religious sites in the region. For anyone with a specific interest in the subject, *Jerusalem Architecture* (hardback only) by David Kroyanker is a beautifully produced, lavishly illustrated survey of building in the city from the time of King David right up to the 1990s.

The excellent *Illustrated Atlas of Jerusalem* by Dan Bahat & Chaim Rubinstein is a superb pictorial documentary of every facet of the history of this fascinating city. It is richly illustrated with detailed diagrams, photographs, drawings and revealing architectural cutaways of all the major and minor places of interests. At UK£60 it's not cheap, but this book a must for any serious historical scholar of Jerusalem.

Widening the field, the *Blue Guide to Jerusalem* is a supremely scholarly general reference to the art architecture, culture and history of the Holy City.

Travel

More autobiography than travelogue, *This Year in Jerusalem* by acclaimed novelist Mordechai Richler is a warm-hearted account of a Jewish childhood in Canada, throughout which the Holy City loomed large on the horizon. Richler's Jerusalem is in stark contrast to that described in *Roots Schmoots* by Howard Jacobson, a secular Jewish-English intellectual and author who visited the city as part of his investigation into what it means to be a modern-day Jew – he did not seem to like what he found.

Saul Bellow, the prolific essayist and novelist, describes in *To Jerusalem and Back – a Personal Account*, the trip he made to Israel in 1975, the year before he won the Nobel prize for literature.

History & Politics

If you are going to read one book during your visit, make it *Jerusalem: City of Mirrors* by Amos Elon. An essayist and historian by trade and longtime resident of the city, Elon has a great knack for bringing out the relevant in the ancient, darting backward and forward through history to illustrate his themes. Best of all, he is adept at lightening otherwise heavy topics with great anecdotes and a deflating wit.

For anyone struggling to understand the events that have led up to the current political impasse, the second volume of Martin Gilbert's companion studies on the history of Jerusalem, *Jerusalem in the 20th Century*, is both authoritative and readable. Even more accessible is Gilbert's *Jerusalem Illustrated History Atlas*.

General

To be enjoyed rather than believed at face value, *O Jerusalem* by Dominique Lapierre & Larry Collins is a novelisation of the events of the 1948 War. Moving forward several years, a partitioned Jerusalem forms the backdrop of *The Mandelbaum Gate*, Muriel Spark's mannered novel peopled with uptight expatriates. *Winter in Jerusalem* by Blanche d'Alpuget brings the city up to date, playing up the colour and romance of the place to provide a vivid backdrop to a young woman's quest for identity.

Two very different anthologies about Jerusalem are *Jerusalem Anthology*, edited by Reuven Hammer with a foreword by Teddy Kollek, and *Jerusalem: the Holy City in Literature*, edited by Miron Grindea, with a foreword by Graham Greene.

For literature by Jerusalem authors, see Arts in the Facts about Jerusalem chapter.

CD ROMS

The CD ROM *Jerusalem* is produced by Tyrell Multimedia and published by Simon & Schuster Interactive. It's a visual exploration of 3000 years of the city's history through animation, film clips and fancy graphics. There's also a similar Israeli-produced disk, *Jerusalem 3000*, which purports to do the same thing.

NEWSPAPERS & MAGAZINES

The *Jerusalem Post* is the country's only English-language daily (although there's no Saturday edition). Some find its right wing leanings disagreeable, but buy it on Friday for the extensive 'what's on' supplement. It also has regular tourism columns. You can also read the *Jerusalem Post* at www.jpost .co.il on the Web.

The secular, left-leaning Tel Aviv-based daily *Ha'aretz* is available in both English and Hebrew editions and enjoys the reputation of being the country's most intellectual paper. The Internet editions are available at www.haaretzdaily.com; but the site has been unstable recently.

The diametric opposite to the *Jerusalem Post* is the poorly funded, weekly publication *Biladi – the Jerusalem Times*, which reports purely on Palestinian issues. You'll normally only find the *Times* sold in East Jerusalem and on David St in the Old City.

The Jerusalem Report (www.jreport.virtual .co.il) is a fortnightly English-language current affairs magazine like *Time*, covering Israel, the Middle East and the Jewish World. It's a lively enough publication and delves into the political, religious and cultural aspects of Israeli life.

Look out in the hostels and bars for the freebie *Traveller*, a lively monthly aimed squarely at backpackers, with useful features such as a round-up of the city bar scene and ideas on cheap eating. *Your Jerusalem* is another monthly freebie (pick it up at the Safra Square tourist office), aimed at residents of the city; it's useful for its 'what's happening' listings, restaurant reviews and a good 'events for children' section.

Western newspapers are easily found in Jerusalem and they're usually only a day old – try the Steimatzky chain.

RADIO & TV

National Radio 1 (575, 1170 and 1458AM in Jerusalem) has English-language news bulletins at 7 am, 1 pm and 5 pm daily. The BBC World Service can be picked up on 1322AM with news at 2 pm, 5 pm and 8.15 pm, while Voice of America is on 1260AM.

Jerusalem has one all English radio station, Radio West which can be picked up on 102.8FM. The station broadcasts CNN news on the hour followed by local news.

Jerusalem viewers receive Israel's two state TV stations, both of which carry masses of English-language programs (news in Engliah on Channel 1 is at 6.15 pm during the week, 4.30 pm Friday and 5 pm Saturday). These are supplemented by Arabic-language Jordan TV and Middle East TV, the latter a Christian station administered by North Americans. Most nonorthodox Israelis also have cable, with its 32 channels including CNN, Sky, BBC World, Discovery and MTV.

For weekly TV and radio listings pick up the Friday edition of the *Jerusalem Post*.

PHOTOGRAPHY & VIDEO

Whatever you run out of or whatever needs replacing, you'll be able to find it in Jerusalem, but there's little doubt that it would have been way cheaper back home.

Photography presents no particular problems, although if you take it seriously then you might want to bring along a polarising filter to counter sun glare. Other than military installations there's little that can't be photographed – even IDF soldiers are happy to preen and pose for a visitor's camera. The exceptions are the orthodox Jews, who really dislike having their photograph taken. Arab women often react angrily, too, if they're snapped unawares, so ask first.

For good photography, the best time of the year to visit is between November and April, when the sky is clear of any high-temperature haze and the afternoon sun warms rather than bleaches.

There are a couple of quick processing places on Jaffa Rd, most conveniently, Kodak Express at No 36 (Map 3), but for more specialised needs such as slides and black and white prints, try Schwartz (Map 3, ☎ 625 5046) at 11 Hillel St. In East Jerusalem, try Photoshop (Map 2, ☎ 538 4451) in the courtyard of 74 HaNevi'im St, or Photo Zoom (Map 5, ☎ /fax 628 8750) at 27 Salah ad-Din St in East Jerusalem.

TIME

Jerusalem is two hours ahead of GMT/ UTC, eight hours behind Australian Eastern Standard Time and seven hours ahead of American Eastern Standard Time. So when it's noon in Jerusalem it's 5 am in New York, 10 am in London and Paris, and 8 pm in Sydney.

ELECTRICITY

Israel uses 220V, 50 cycles, alternating current. Standard wall plugs are a flat three-pronged type with the positive and negative prongs at a 45° angle.

The wall sockets will accept the two or three-pronged European plugs, but not the standard Australian ones. To be on the safe side, always bring an adaptor since it will be less hassle than finding one in Jerusalem.

WEIGHTS & MEASURES

Israel uses the metric system. Users of the imperial system should the conversion table inside the back cover of this book.

LAUNDRY

With only two espresso machines but plenty of charm, coffee and good home cooking while you wait, Tzipor Hanefesh (Map 3, ☎ 624 9890, 10 Rivlin St) is a friendly three storey café/laundromat. One machine load costs 11 NIS and a 45 minute drying cycle costs 5 NIS. It's in the trendy central area of Nahalat Shiv'a.

There's another good laundromat called Laundry Place (Map 3, ☎ 625 7714) close by at 12 Shamai St, one block south of Ben Yehuda St. It's open from 8.30 am to 12.30 am Sunday to Friday, and from 8.30 am to 3.30 pm on Friday. Star Laundry (Map 4 ☎ 566 9434, 25 Jabotinsky St) in Rehavia collects and delivers free of charge; it's open Sunday to Thursday 8.30 am to 7 pm, Friday 8.30 am to 2 pm, closed Saturday.

HEALTH

Jerusalem represents no major health hazards for the visitor. Probably the biggest health worries you can expect to face are

Everyday Health

Normal body temperature is up to 37°C (98.6°F); more than 2°C (4°F) higher indicates a high fever. The normal adult pulse rate is 60 to 100 per minute (children 80 to 100, babies 100 to 140). As a general rule the pulse increases about 20 beats per minute for each 1°C (2°F) rise in fever.

Respiration (breathing) rate is also an indicator of illness. Count the number of breaths per minute: between 12 and 20 is normal for adults and older children (up to 30 for younger children, 40 for babies). People with a high fever or serious respiratory illness breathe more quickly than normal. More than 40 shallow breaths a minute may indicate pneumonia.

Medical Kit Check List

Following is a list of items you should consider including in your medical kit – consult your pharmacist for brands available in your country.

☐ **Aspirin** or **paracetamol** (acetaminophen in the USA) – for pain or fever

☐ **Antihistamine** – for allergies, eg hay-fever; to ease the itch from insect bites or stings; and also to prevent motion sickness

☐ **Antibiotics** – consider including these if you're travelling well off the beaten track; see your doctor, as they must be prescribed, and carry the prescription with you

☐ **Loperamide** or **diphenoxylate** –'blockers' for diarrhoea; and **prochlorperazine** or **metaclopramide** for nausea and vomiting

☐ **Rehydration mixture** – to prevent dehydration, eg due to severe diarrhoea; particularly important when travelling with children

☐ **Insect repellent**, **sunscreen**, **lip balm** and **eye drops**

☐ **Calamine lotion**, **sting relief spray** or **aloe vera** – to ease irritation from sunburn and insect bites or stings

☐ **Antifungal cream** or **powder** – for fungal skin infections and thrush

☐ **Antiseptic** (such as povidone-iodine) – for cuts and grazes

☐ **Bandages**, **sticking plasters** and other wound dressings

☐ **Water purification tablets** or **iodine**

☐ **Scissors**, **tweezers** and a **thermometer** (note that mercury thermometers are prohibited by airlines)

☐ **Syringes** and **needles** – in case you need injections in a country with medical hygiene problems. Ask your doctor for a note explaining why you have·them.

☐ **Cold** and **flu tablets**, **throat lozenges** and **nasal decongestant**

☐ **Multivitamins** – consider for long trips, when dietary vitamin intake may be inadequate

over-exposure to the sun and possibly an upset stomach caused by the change in diet. No vaccinations are required; however we recommend you vaccinate yourself against hepatitis A. Polio, typhoid, rabies and hepatitis B all occur, and you should consider immunisation before leaving home, particularly if you will be travelling to rural areas.

Medical Attention

In emergencies call ☎ 101 (Hebrew) or ☎ 911 (English) or contact the Magen David Adom (Red Star of David; ☎ 523 133) – the Israeli equivalent of the Red Cross. There's also a special medical help line for tourists: ☎ 177-022 9110. Every day the *Jerusalem Post* carries a list of the city's late-opening pharmacies.

In the Old City, the Orthodox Society (Map 6, ☎ 627 1958), on Greek Orthodox Patriarchate St in the Christian Quarter, operates a low-cost clinic that, we're told, welcomes travellers. It also does dental surgery. The clinic is open from 8 am to 3 pm Monday to Saturday, closed Sunday.

A more expensive alternative is the Jerusalem Medical Centre (Map 2, ☎ 561 0297) on Diskin St in the Kiryat Wolfson district of the New City.

WOMEN TRAVELLERS

In certain areas of Jerusalem, sexual harassment is a constant problem for women travellers. The majority of problems will arise with Arab males, but Jewish men are not known for their respectful conduct towards women either. The harassment is rarely physical but even persistent verbal abuse can stop you enjoying your stay.

As far as Palestinian areas go, it is vital that you dress with great modesty. A *hejab* (headscarf) isn't necessary, but in general, think 'nun'. In places like East Jerusalem and the Old City everything from the throat down to the upper arms and calves needs to be covered. No tight-fitting clothes either – a long skirt and blouse or baggy T-shirt fits the bill and is also relatively comfortable.

However, even nuns – the genuine wimple-wearing articles – are not always exempt from the attentions of wandering hands. How you deal with unwanted attention is a matter of personal choice. In late 1995, The *Jerusalem Post* reported on three women tourists who resisted the physical advances of some Arab men with a little black-belt karate. The men were left needing hospital treatment. Not every woman has that kind of deterrent at her disposal, and often the best you can do is to politely but firmly turn down the whispered invitations and ignore any come-ons.

In one or two places the best advice, unfortunately, has to be for women not to walk alone; the Mount of Olives, in particular, has a bad reputation and Lonely Planet has also received letters from women who've had unpleasant encounters while walking on the ramparts of the Old City walls of Jerusalem and the narrow streets to and from some of the backpacker hostels in the Muslim quarter.

Jerusalem's rape crisis centre can be contacted on ☎ 625 5558.

GAY & LESBIAN TRAVELLERS

Homosexuality is legal in Israel but it's anathema to Jerusalem's large religious sector; as a result the city's gay and lesbian community is obliged to keep a low profile.

The Society for the Protection of Personal Rights (SPPR), which represents gays and lesbians in Israel, has successfully lobbied in recent years for legislative changes, and the Knesset now has a committee which deals with gay rights. All progress in this area may, however, have come to a halt following the rise to political prominence of ultra-orthodox and right wing elements.

There are very few bars and clubs around (Tel Aviv is a better bet), and all this author turned up was the Orion and the Yellow Submarine (see the Entertainment chapter). The Tmol Shilshom café/bookshop in Nahalat Shiv'a (Map 3) is also gay-run, but other than a shelf of second-hand gay fiction, that doesn't amount to much.

For further information about what's going on in Jerusalem, call the gay switch-board (☎ 03-629 2797) on Sunday, Tuesday, Wednesday and Thursday from 7.30 to 11.30 pm, and Monday 7 to 11 pm. The SPPR (☎ 03-620 4327, fax 525 2341), PO Box 37604, Tel Aviv 61375, also operates a gay hotline (☎ 03-629 3681) and publishes a newsletter in English, *Israel Update* – send a self-addressed envelope for a copy.

DISABLED TRAVELLERS

Many hotels and most public institutions in Jerusalem provide ramps, wheelchair-accessible toilets and other conveniences for the disabled. In particular, the HI-affiliated Beit Shmuel has rooms specially adapted for wheelchair users. If you have any specific concerns, try contacting Milbat – The Advisory Centre for the Disabled (☎ 03-530 3739) at the Sheba Medical Centre in Tel Aviv for information and advice.

The Yad Sarah Organisation (Map 2, ☎ 644 4444) 43 HaNevi'im St, also lends wheelchairs, crutches and other aids free of charge, but a small deposit is required. It's open to visitors Sunday to Thursday from 9 am to 7 pm, Friday from 9 am to noon.

The Museum of the History of Jerusalem at the Citadel has a signposted route around the museum designed especially for disabled people and the popular Israel Museum is well-adapted to cope with visitors in wheelchairs.

JERUSALEM FOR CHILDREN

Jerusalem is not particularly child-friendly. The congested roads of the New City mean children have to be kept on a tight (metaphorical) leash; similarly so on the packed alleyways of the Old City, where your offspring are in constant danger of being washed away by the relentless human undertow. There are, however, quite a few open, green spaces where the kids can run free – Liberty Bell Gardens (Map 4) has the added attraction of its train carriage puppet theatre (☎ 561 8514 for schedule details) and plenty of climbing frames, climbable sculptures and football fields.

Other good youngster-friendly places are the New Biblical Zoo (especially at feeding time – ☎ 643 0111 for details), which has a special children's zoo and creative play area, and the Bloomfield Science Museum (Map 1), stuffed with plenty of hands-on exhibits. The Israel Museum (Maps 1 & 2, ☎ 670 8935) has a full line-up of children's events each month, including song and play for pre-schoolers, and cartoon screenings (all in English). Older children might also enjoy the Citadel, a castle with lots of turrets, towers and battlements.

Kids' Jerusalem Adventures (☎/fax 536 3449, email kidsjlmadv@netmedia.co.il) is a company which specialises in custom tours of the city for families with children.

For further ideas look out for the gushingly named *Israel Loves Kids, Kids Love Israel* by Barbara Sofer – it should be available from branches of Steimatzky. For more general information, see Lonely Planet's *Travel With Children* by Maureen Wheeler.

USEFUL ORGANISATIONS

Jerusalem, the Alternative Information Centre (☎ 624 1159, fax 625 3151, 6 Koresh St) is a joint Israeli-Palestinian project which provides nongovernment information concerning developments within Palestinian society and the Israeli response. Specifically geared to assisting visiting journalists, the AIC will also help individual travellers interested in learning more about the complexities of local politics. It produces two publications, the weekly *The Other Front* and the monthly *News From Within*.

Having been in operation for over 20 years, the Volunteer Tourist Service has assisted hundreds of thousands of tourists visiting Israel. Staffed entirely by volunteers, this organisation helps visitors with various problems, answers queries, and even traces lost relatives and friends. It can also arrange a visit to an Israeli home, matching up the visitor's profession or hobby with that of the host. Volunteers can be found at Ben-Gurion airport between noon and 8 pm or in the lobbies of major hotels from 6 to 8.30 pm except on Shabbat and Jewish holidays.

LIBRARIES

Books on Jerusalem as well as other general nonfiction and fiction titles and English-language newspapers and magazines are available to the public at two British Council libraries: 4 Abu Obeida St (Map 5, ☎ 628 2545, fax 628 3021, Web site www.ej .britishcouncil.org/eastjerusalem) in East Jerusalem (turn right just past the Tombs of the Kings) and 3 Shimshon St (Map 3, ☎ 673 6733) in the south of the New City. Both are open Monday to Thursday from 10 am to 1 pm and 4 to 7 pm, and Friday from 10 am to 1 pm, closed Saturday and Sunday. There's another good library at the Hebrew Union College at 13 HaMelekh David St in the New City (Map 3). It's open Sunday to Thursday from 8 am to 5 pm.

CULTURAL CENTRES

In addition to the two British Councils (see above) there is also an American Cultural Center at 19 Keren HaYesod (Map 5, ☎ 625 5755), which is open Sunday to Thursday 10 am to 4 pm, Friday 9 am to noon; an Alliance Française (Map 3, ☎ 625 1204, 625 7167) on Agron St, opposite the Supersol supermarket, and a French Cultural Centre (Map 5, ☎ 628 2451) at 21 Salah ad-Din St in East Jerusalem.

DANGERS & ANNOYANCES

While security and safety in a wider sense are not matters which should concern the average visitor, petty theft is just as much of a problem in Jerusalem as it is anywhere else. The standard precautionary measures should be taken. Always keep valuables securely on your person or locked in a safe – never leave them in your room or in a car or bus (unhappily there are more than a few fellow travellers who make their money go further by helping themselves to other people's).

Use a money belt, a pouch under your clothes, a leather wallet attached to your belt, or extra internal pockets in your clothing. Do not use 'bumbags' (fanny packs) they scream 'Tourist!' and 'I have something valuable to steal!!'. Keep a separate record of your passport, credit card and travellers' cheque numbers. Crowded tourist spots and markets are an obvious hunting ground for pickpockets, so take extra care.

The narrow streets of the Old City have been the scene in the past of occasional violence. This in part accounts for the heavy presence of green-clad IDF soldiers replete with bulletproof vests and automatic rifles. While acts of violence are rare these days, trouble can flare up unexpectedly and visitors should be aware of possible ramifications. If a 'scene' seems to be brewing it is best to move away as quickly as possible and let the security forces handle it.

Crowded places like the Mahane Yehuda Market on Jaffa Road have been the scene of attempted and successful suicide bombing attacks. If you frequent this crowded and busy market, keep your wits about you, watch out for suspicious-looking characters and be prepared for frequent bomb scares, signalled when the phrase '*hefetz hashud*' (suspicious object) is passed around through the onlooking crowds.

Emergency In emergencies dial ☎ 100. Arab police seem to be responsible for basic duties in East Jerusalem and the Old City and their station is on Omar ibn al-Khattab Square, beside the Citadel (Map 6). However, they are most likely to refer you to the central police station in the Russian Compound in the New City (Map 3). The city's lost and found office is also here. It's open from 7.30 am to 4 pm on Sunday, Tuesday and Thursday, from 7.30 am to 2 pm on Monday and Wednesday, and from 9.30 am to 12.30 pm on Friday (closed Saturday). See the Health section in this chapter for medical services.

BUSINESS HOURS

The most important thing to know is that on Shabbat, most Jewish-run shops, offices and places of entertainment close down. It is in fact illegal for a Jewish employee to be forced to work during this period. Shabbat starts at sundown Friday and ends at sundown Saturday.

During this time you'll find it difficult to purchase anything to eat, you can't easily change money and your movements are restricted because most buses aren't running. The country kicks back into action on Saturday evening, when the cafés, bars and restaurants always experience a great post-Shabbat rush.

Predominantly Muslim areas such as East Jerusalem and the Muslim Quarter of the Old City remain open on Saturday but close early on Friday for afternoon prayers. Christian-owned businesses (concentrated in the relevant quarter of Jerusalem's Old City) close on Sunday.

Standard Israeli shopping hours are from 8 am to 1 pm and 4 to 7 pm or later Monday to Thursday, and from 8 am to 2 pm on Friday, with some places opening after sundown on Saturday, too.

PUBLIC HOLIDAYS

One patient researcher some years ago sat down to compile a list and discovered that between the various religions and their different denominations the people of Israel celebrate more festivals each year than there are days. Our list below describes just some of the more notable holidays in the annual calendar.

Israeli

For Jewish religious holidays, see the Jewish Festivals section on pp 58-62.

Holocaust Day (Yom HaShoah)

Periodically throughout the day air-raid sirens wail to signal two minutes of silence in remembrance of the six million victims of the Nazi Holocaust. It's an incredibly moving and eerie experience as everyone on the streets stops and puts their bags down; all traffic comes to a halt – engines are stopped and everybody gets out to stand in silence beside the car.

Independence Day (Yom HaAtzmaut)

On 14 May 1948 Israel became an independent state and since then the day has been celebrated by Jews worldwide (note that the date changes with the lunar calendar). In Jerusalem it's celebrated with parades, aerial flypasts, concerts, picnics and fireworks.

Public Holidays in 2000

Jewish holidays follow a lunar calendar and therefore fall on a different date each year according to the western Gregorian calendar. For example, Rosh HaShanah fell on 11 September in 1999, while in 2000, it is on 30 September.

However, it will always fall around this time, unlike the Muslim holidays which, following the Islamic calendar, move back a number of days each year. Therefore, Ramadan, which starts on or around 20 December in 1999, will begin again around 27 November the following year.

The Orthodox churches celebrate Easter and Christmas roughly two weeks after the western churches because they still adhere to the Julian, rather than the Gregorian calendar.

The following list is for 2000; consult an Israeli tourist information office for public holidays in 2001 and 2002.

January
Orthodox Christmas (5-6)
Armenian Christmas (19)
Tu B'Shevat (22)

February
Eid al-Fitr (10)
Black Hebrew Day of
Appreciation & Love

March
Eid al-Adha (15)
Purim (21)

April
Good Friday (2)
Ras E-Sana (Muslim New Year) (4)
Easter Sunday (4)
Pesah (20-26)
Armenian Holocaust Day (24)
Mimouna (27)
Orthodox and Armenian Good Friday (28)
Orthodox and Armenian
Easter Sunday (30)

May
Holocaust Day (Yom HaShoah) (4)
Independence Day (Yom HaAtzamaut) (10)
Lag B'Omer (23)

June
Liberation of Jerusalem Day (4)
Shavuot (9)
Mawled (Prophet's Birthday) (13)

August
Tisha B'Av (10)

September
Rosh HaShanah (30)

October
Yom Kippur (9)
Sukkot (14-20)
Simhat Torah (21)

November
Ramadan (27)

December
Hanukkah (22-28)
Christmas (25)

Muslim

Muslim holidays in Jerusalem are not as disruptive as the Jewish ones. Even during Ramadan, when Muslims fast during daylight hours, the heavy tourist presence in the Old City means that it is expedient for most Muslim-run cafes, restaurants and food stalls to remain open.

Prophet's Birthday (Mawled)
This is Mohammed's birthday, celebrated with much consumption of sticky and very sweet sweets and confectionery.

Lailatul Miraj
This commemorates the night Mohammed ascended to heaven from the Temple Mount in Jerusalem.

Ramadan
For non-Muslim visitors, the major effect of this month-long dawn-to-sunset fast is that the less commercial Muslim Arab areas are very quiet, with many businesses open for only limited hours.

Eid al-Fitr
This is the great feast to mark the end of Ramadan. Muslims express their joy at the end of their fast by offering a congregational

prayer, preferably in an open field. These express their gratitude to Allah for enabling them to observe the fast, thus fulfilling one of the fundamental duties of Islam. Special dishes are prepared and it is customary to visit relatives and friends, to go out for a day trip and to give presents to children. Everyone eats a great deal.

Eid al-Adha

This is the most important feast of the Muslim calendar. It commemorates the occasion when Allah asked Abraham to sacrifice his son, Ishmael. A lamb was sacrificed instead of the boy after Abraham had shown his readiness to obey. Today Muslims offer a congregational prayer on the day, followed by a ritual slaughter – mainly of sheep, but also goats or cows. The meat of the sacrificed animal is given to needy people and to older relatives. Clothes and money are sometimes given, too.

Christian

Many visitors with a western Christian background will find festivals in Jerusalem are celebrated very differently from the way they are used to. This is largely due to the domination of the Orthodox (eastern) Church, and also to the fact that Christianity is very much in third place in the religious stakes here. Christmas Day, for example (ignoring the fact that it is celebrated on three separate occasions by the various denominations), is just another day for most people.

Christmas Day

Apart from 25 December, Christmas is celebrated on 7 January by the Orthodox and on 19 January by the Armenians.

The event to attend is the midnight Mass on Christmas Eve (24 December), held at Bethlehem's Church of the Nativity. During the day a procession departs from Jerusalem for the church but, due to the popularity of the service, not everyone gets in. Pew space inside the church is reserved for ticket-holding observant Catholics only (the tickets, which are free, must be applied for in advance at the Terra Sancta office in the Christian Information Centre at Jaffa Gate). The rest of the crowd, along with an international massed choir, congregates outside the church in Manger Square where a large video screen relays the service being conducted inside. It can be an extremely cold night, so wrap up well if you're going. Buses back to Jerusalem run irregularly all night.

Easter

Celebrated first by the Roman Catholics and the Protestants and then about two weeks later by the Orthodox Church, Easter means absolute chaos in Jerusalem's Old City. The Via Dolorosa and the narrow streets around the Church of the Holy Sepulchre become clogged with pilgrims staking out their spots for the various services and processions. Note that at this time pilgrims fill many of the cheap hostels in Jerusalem's Old City and completely block-book everything in Bethlehem.

Armenian Holocaust Day

Every year on 24 April the Armenians commemorate their overlooked tragedy with a parade and service in the Old City.

SPECIAL EVENTS

Throughout the year, Jerusalem is a major venue for various special events in particular, national celebrations of Jewish festivals and the annual Israel Festival. Usually held sometime during May or June, the latter is a three week program of cultural events featuring music, theatre and dance performances which makes good use of some of the city's unique venues such as the Citadel, Sultan's Pool and the Mt Scopus amphitheatre.

Holy Fire

At a few minutes after 1 pm on Orthodox Easter Sunday the Church of the Holy Sepulchre is witness to the miracle of the Holy Fire. Observed by thousands of worshippers, the Greek Orthodox Patriarch enters the tomb and the doors are sealed behind him. After a pause, the lights go out, a peal of bells ring and the Patriarch reappears brandishing a torch blazing with the Holy Fire. The flame is immediately spread from one candle to the next to illuminate the whole church.

Those wishing to see this should get there very early – the devout begin arriving the day before and spend the previous night sleeping on the cold stone floors around the tomb.

February
Jerusalem Musical Encounters
March
International Festival of Poets
International Judaica Fair
May, June
Israel Festival
July
International Film Festival
August
International Puppet Theatre Festival
September
Early Music Workshop
October
Jerusalem Marathon

For further information, contact the events department of the Ministry of Tourism (☎ 625 8152, fax 625 9837).

DOING BUSINESS

While Jerusalem's glittering and secular twin Tel Aviv gets the lion's share of business in Israel, it may be possible to set up business contacts here. A good start would have to be the Israel Business & Government Directory or the Israel Marketing & Media Directory. The first publication lists government companies, major business associations and organisations as well as the biographies of the 120 Knesset members. The second publication gives valuable pointers to advertising, public relations, major Israeli advertisers and the broadcast and print media. Both retail for around 108 NIS and can be ordered from the *Jerusalem Post* (☎ 537 8377, fax 537 8372, email orders@jpost.co.il).

WORK

Israeli work permits are *very* hard to get unless you're with an international company, or a Jewish organisation. Instead, Israel seems to tolerate illegal workers (as long as they are otherwise law-abiding).

It's not difficult to find casual work in Jerusalem, it's just difficult to make it pay. In many cases employers are just out to exploit a plentiful supply of cheap, sometimes desperate, foreign labour.

As in other cities, the catering industry soaks up most illegal workers. It's unlikely, however, that you'll be waiting on tables (and thus benefiting from the heavy tipping) – instead you'll be washing dishes or cleaning, for around 10 to 15 NIS per hour.

There's a lot of labour-intensive work around, particularly in construction, an area that the South African travellers seem to have monopolised. Most hostels also employ people to work at the reception or bar – the pay is nothing great but you get your bed for free and maybe enough money to cover food and beer.

Women might find au pair work more appealing. There are a couple of reputable agencies that arrange short-term work and pay US$500 to US$700 a month, with accommodation and meals on top. The *Traveller* carries ads for these agencies, but the paper was in danger of closing down when we last checked.

For other work check out the notice boards and ask around at hostels (Petra, Al-Arab and Tabasco in Jerusalem) and bars.

JEWISH FESTIVALS

Beginning with the High Holy Days, the Jewish religious year is punctuated by festivals; some, such as Hanukkah and Purim, are joyful while others, Tisha B'Av in particular, are periods of profound mourning. The Jewish dates are given first, followed by the approximate western months in parentheses.

Rosh HaShanah   Tishri 1-2   (September/October)

The first of the 10 'Days of Awe' which end with Yom Kippur. In addition to general new year celebrations, Rosh HaShanah, as the anniversary of the Creation, also heralds a period of reflection concerning one's relationship with God and place in the world. The *shofar*, an ancient trumpet made out of a ram's horn, is blown at morning prayers as a call to contemplation. Festival lights are lit the night before.

New year foods include apple dipped in honey to symbolise the wish for a sweet year, as well as whole fish, which represent the blessings of many children. Other significant foods are carrot, cabbage, and pomegranate.

Yom Kippur   Tishri 10   (September/October)

The Day of Atonement comes at the end of the ten Days of Awe; the belief is that one's deeds are recorded on Rosh HaShanah, and the books sealed on Yom Kippur. The night before is marked by a festive meal (the last for the next 25 hours), and special charity plates are set out in the synagogues for the donations which have replaced the Temple sacrifices.

Top: Hanukkah dreidle, used for top games during Hanukkah
Left: Sounding the shofar during the Days of Awe

Preparing for Yom Kippur involves asking forgiveness from those whom one has wronged, in order to start the year with a clean slate concerning both God and one's fellows. White robes symbolising purity are worn in synagogue. The Ark containing the Torah scrolls remains open during the service because Moses returned with the second set of law tablets on Yom Kippur, and also as a reminder of the time when the High Priest would enter the Holy of Holies in the Temple on this one day and bless the people using the Name of God. The day ends with a final sounding of the shofar in the synagogues and at the packed Western Wall.

Not for nothing is Yom Kippur also known as the 'Shabbat of Shabbats'; in addition to the full fast (total abstention from food and drink), the observant also refrain from sex, bathing and using cosmetics (including soap and toothpaste), wearing leather, and, of course, all Jewish businesses close down completely from sunset of the previous day. Yom Kippur is respected even by secular Israelis, and no cars are to be seen in the streets.

Sukkot & Simhat Torah   Tishri 15-22 (September/October)

Originally a harvest festival, the most conspicuous aspect of Sukkot are the eponymous 'sukkot' (sukkah is the singular), the temporary booths built on balconies, in gardens, and even in hotels and restaurants to commemorate the 40 years that the Israelites spent in the wilderness after leaving Egypt. The first and last days of Sukkot are observed like Shabbat. The observant eat all their meals inside a sukkah, and some even sleep in them.

Right: Putting the finishing touches on a sukkah, the eponymous 'booth' of Sukkot

Left: Parading the Torah
scrolls for Simhat Torah

The last day of Sukkot is Simhat Torah, the 'Rejoicing of the Torah'.
This is the day on which the final portion of the Torah (Deuteronomy
33-34) is reached, at which point the cycle of readings begins again.
The Torah scrolls are removed from the Ark and are paraded seven times
around the *bimah*, the platform of the synagogue. The worshippers
dance ecstatically, with the scrolls, between each circuit of the binmah.
In Jerusalem, thousands of people carry the scrolls under a canopy to
the Western Wall in a mind-boggling mass of singing and dancing.

Hanukkah   Kislev 25-Tevet 2   (November/December)
Also known as the Festival of Lights, Hanukkah commemorates the
rededication of the Temple in 164 BC after the successful Maccabean
Revolt. A miracle was performed when the supply of ritually pure lamp
oil, enough for only one day, lasted for eight, until fresh supplies
arrived. Therefore, a candle is added to the menorah every evening

until all eight have been lit – the raised ninth candle is a 'helper' from which the others are lit, and isn't counted. These Hanukkah lamps are displayed in windows and doorways to publicise the miracle; in Mea She'arim they are often enchantingly hung outside the building.

Dairy products and fried food are features of Hanukkah, which means lots of cheesecakes, felafel, *latkes* (hash browns), and *sufganyiot* (jam donuts). In a nod towards Christmas, with which Hanukkah occasionally coincides, it's become customary to give children gifts. Children also expect to receive Hanukkah *gelt* (cash gifts), and dreidle games played with a specially marked top are another kiddie-friendly feature.

Tu B'Shevat   Shevat 15   (January/February)
The 'New Year for Trees' is a rabbinic rather than a biblical festival and was originally instituted to help calculate the agricultural tithe which was owed to the priests and the Temple as well as for the support of the poor.

Tu B'Shevat has been adopted as a festival of the literal Land of Israel and a celebration of the country's agricultural roots. Social responsibility is also part of the festival in that one plants for future generations. As well as planting fruit trees, it is also customary to eat particular foods of biblical significance: wheat, barley, grapes, figs, pomegranate, olives and dates, as well as almonds, citrus fruits, carob and apples.

Purim   Adar 14   (February/March)
Purim commemorates the salvation of the Jewish community in Persia from a plot by Haman, the prime minister, to eliminate them. They were saved by the courageous intervention of the king's Jewish wife, Esther, advised by her cousin Mordecai. The entire Megillah (Book of Esther) is read on the eve of the festival, and is repeated the following morning, with the children encouraged to exercise their rattles, fire cap guns, shout and boo every time Haman is named.

Purim has a distinctly carnival air. The schools are populated with Batmen, Teletubbies, and fairies. Gifts, usually of confectionary, are exchanged. *Hamantashen* or *oznei Haman* (Haman's ears), pastries filled with fruit, jam, or poppy seeds are eaten, as well as lentils and Persian dishes; and in the face of the usual abstemious ritual use of wine, it is a actually *mitzvah* (a religious obligation) to get so happily drunk that one cannot distinguish between 'blessed be Mordecai' and 'cursed be Haman'.

Pesach   Nisan 15-22   (March/April)
Along with Hanukkah, Passover is one of the great defining points of Jewish history and identity. The event commemorated is the Exodus, when Moses led the Israelites out of slavery in Egypt towards the Promised Land. The name of the festival comes from the fact that the angel of destruction ordered to kill all firstborn Egyptian animals and humans was instructed to pass over the Israelite homes which had the blood of a slaughtered lamb painted on the doorway. The Haggadah (story of the Exodus) is retold at the Seder (Pesach meal). Before the Temple was destroyed, Pesach was marked by the sacrifice of a lamb

or kid, which was then roasted whole and eaten at the Seder; now, as a reminder that the Temple no longer exists, roast meat must not be served. Pesach remains the pre-eminent pilgrimage festival – 'Next year in Jerusalem' is sung after the final blessing.

Because the Israelites left Egypt in such a hurry that the bread dough had no time to rise, *matzah* (unleavened bread) is eaten throughout Pesach, and all ordinary grain products are banned and must be removed from the house and sold to gentiles. Some haredi communities still bake their own matzah on the first night of Pesach; everyone else buys the commercially available brands. The Ashkenazim forbid beans, rice, peanuts and sweetcorn as well; Sephardic Jews don't follow this strict interpretation. The first and last days of Pesach are treated like Shabbat, with shops closed and no public transport.

Mimouna   Nisan 23   (February/March)
This festival takes place the day after the last day of Pesach, and has been celebrated by the North African Jewish communities for generations. The exact origins of Mimouna are unknown but one theory is that it's an Arabisation of the Hebrew *emunah*, meaning faith or belief in the coming of the Messiah. Street parties and open-house celebrations are organised; foreigners – Jewish and gentile alike – are warmly invited to join in. Check the Safra Square tourist information office for the local arrangements.

Lag B'Omer   Iyyar 18   (April/May)
Lag B'Omer is a spring festival, marking the end of a period of mourning for all 24,000 students of Rabbi Aikva who died in a plague, as well as the victims of later pogroms. Tradition has it that when the plague stopped, Akiva found five last students to whom he revealed the 'light of the Torah'; when one of these students, Rabbi Shimon bar Yochai, died on a subsequent Lag B'Omer, his disciples were similarly enlightened.

In memory of these rabbinic Sages, bonfires are lit across Israel, making Lag B'Omer a pyromaniac's delight, with children competing to build the biggest fire. Ultra-orthodox boys at the age of three are often given their first, ceremonial haircut on Lag B'Omer.

Tisha B'Av   Av 9   (July/August)
The Ninth of Av is traditionally the date of most of the great tragedies which affected the Jewish people, including the final defeat of Simon bar Kochba in 135, the expulsion from Spain in 1492 and the first deportations from the Warsaw Ghetto in 1942. Most important of the disasters collectively mourned on Tisha B'Av is the destruction of both the First Temple in 586 BC, and the Second Temple in 70 AD.

As with Yom Kippur, a full fast is observed from sunset to sunset and the Western Wall is crowded with people reciting from Lamentations and Kinnot, dirges which recall tragedies of Jewish history. It's also traditional to visit graves on Tisha B'Av.

Getting There & Away

Flying is the most common means of getting to Israel. Ben-Gurion airport, situated midway between Jerusalem and Tel Aviv, is the country's busy international gateway. There are also the options of sailing from Cyprus or Greece, or coming in overland via Jordan or Egypt (the borders with Syria and Lebanon are closed).

AIR

Jerusalem is served by Ben-Gurion airport; for details of getting to and from the airport, which is about 50km west of the city centre, see the Getting Around chapter. Jerusalem is also served by a smaller domestic airport to the north of the city, where you can catch flights to Eilat and the Galilee.

For airport information call ☎ 03-971 0000; for recorded English-language flight information call ☎ 03-971 2484.

Airline Offices

Airline offices are all in the New City unless otherwise stated.

Air France
  (☎ 625 2495) 3 Shlomzion HaMalka
  (☎ 628 2535) As-Zahra St, East Jerusalem
Alitalia
  (☎ 625 8653) 23 Hillel St
  (☎ 628 3515) 20 Salah ad-Din St
Arkia Airlines
  (☎ 625 5888) 97 Jaffa Rd
British Airways
  (☎ 625 6111) 33 Jaffa Rd
El Al
  (☎ 625 6934) 236 Jaffa Rd
KLM
  (☎ 625 1361) 33 Jaffa Rd
Lufthansa
  (☎ 624 4941) 16A King George V St
Olympic Airways
  (☎ 623 4538) 33 Jaffa Rd
Sabena
  (☎ 623 4971) 23 HaMelekh David St
SAS
  (☎ 628 3235) 14 El Zahara St, East Jerusalem

Swissair
  (☎ 623 1373) 31 HaNevi'im St
Tower Air
  (☎ 625 5137) 14 Hillel St
TWA
  (☎ 624 1576) 34 Ben Yehuda St

Other Parts of Israel

Arkia, the national domestic carrier, flies from the airport at Atarot, north of the city, direct to Eilat and Rosh Pina, with further connections to Haifa and Tel Aviv. There are no flights on Saturday. Arkia's office is in the city centre (☎ 625 5888, room 121, Klal building, 97 Jaffa Rd).

Other Countries

Airfares to Israel vary considerably according to the season. Much higher prices apply from July to September and during Jewish holidays in particular. Note that it can sometimes be difficult to get a flight out of Israel in a hurry, so think carefully before travelling to Israel on a one-way ticket. Bucket shops such as Mona Travel in Tel Aviv (see Travel Agents later in this chapter) can be a good place to get quick exit tickets.

USA & Canada New York offers the widest choice of carriers, but you can also fly from Los Angeles, Chicago, Miami, Atlanta and Toronto. Many North American travellers prefer to fly nonstop with El Al for security reasons. El Al also flies via London, Manchester and Paris. TWA flies nonstop and via Paris for less than El Al, and Delta started flying to Israel in 1991. All of these airlines have discounted fares from time to time. The Belgian carrier Sabena, which offers an overnight stay in Brussels, is often good value. Cheap fares to Ben-Gurion airport from New York cost around US$700 return.

Another option is to fly via Eastern Europe. The journey time is longer than a direct flight, and the Eastern European airlines'

Air Travel Glossary

Baggage Allowance This will be written on your ticket and usually includes one 20kg item to go in the hold, plus one item of hand luggage.

Bucket Shops These are unbonded travel agencies specialising in discounted airline tickets.

Bumped Just because you have a confirmed seat doesn't mean you're going to get on the plane (see Overbooking).

Cancellation Penalties If you have to cancel or change a discounted ticket, there are often heavy penalties involved; insurance can sometimes be taken out against these penalties. Some airlines impose penalties on regular tickets as well, particularly against 'no-show' passengers.

Check-In Airlines ask you to check in a certain time ahead of the flight departure (usually one to two hours on international flights). If you fail to check in on time and the flight is overbooked, the airline can cancel your booking and give your seat to somebody else.

Confirmation Having a ticket written out with the flight and date you want doesn't mean you have a seat until the agent has checked with the airline that your status is 'OK' or confirmed. Meanwhile you could just be 'on request'.

Courier Fares Businesses often need to send urgent documents or freight securely and quickly. Courier companies hire people to accompany the package through customs and, in return, offer a discount ticket which is sometimes a phenomenal bargain. In effect, what the companies do is ship their freight as your luggage on regular commercial flights. This is a legitimate operation, but there are two shortcomings – the short turnaround time of the ticket (usually not longer than a month) and the limitation on your luggage allowance. You may have to surrender all your allowance and take only carry-on luggage.

Full Fares Airlines traditionally offer 1st class (coded F), business class (coded J) and economy class (coded Y) tickets. These days there are so many promotional and discounted fares available that few passengers pay full economy fare.

ITX An ITX, or 'independent inclusive tour excursion', is often available on tickets to popular holiday destinations. Officially it's a package deal combined with hotel accommodation, but many agents will sell you one of these for the flight only and give you phoney hotel vouchers in the unlikely event that you're challenged at the airport.

Lost Tickets If you lose your airline ticket an airline will usually treat it like a travellers cheque and, after inquiries, issue you with another one. Legally, however, an airline is entitled to treat it like cash and if you lose it then it's gone forever. Take good care of your tickets.

MCO An MCO, or 'miscellaneous charge order', is a voucher that looks like an airline ticket but carries no destination or date. It can be exchanged through any International Association of Travel Agents (IATA) airline for a ticket on a specific flight. It's a useful alternative to an onward ticket in those countries that demand one, and is more flexible than an ordinary ticket if you're unsure of your route.

No-Shows No-shows are passengers who fail to show up for their flight. Full-fare passengers who fail to turn up are sometimes entitled to travel on a later flight. The rest are penalised (see Cancellation Penalties).

On Request This is an unconfirmed booking for a flight.

Air Travel Glossary

Onward Tickets An entry requirement for many countries is that you have a ticket out of the country. If you're unsure of your next move, the easiest solution is to buy the cheapest onward ticket to a neighbouring country or a ticket from a reliable airline which can later be refunded if you do not use it.

Open Jaw Tickets These are return tickets where you fly out to one place but return from another. If available, this can save you backtracking to your arrival point.

Overbooking Airlines hate to fly empty seats and since every flight has some passengers who fail to show up, airlines often book more passengers than they have seats. Usually excess passengers make up for the no-shows, but occasionally somebody gets 'bumped' onto the next available flight. Guess who it is most likely to be? The passengers who check in late.

Point-to-Point Tickets These are discount tickets that can be bought on some routes in return for passengers waiving their rights to a stopover.

Promotional Fares These are officially discounted fares, available from travel agencies or direct from the airline.

Reconfirmation If you don't reconfirm your flight at least 72 hours prior to departure, the airline may delete your name from the passenger list. Ring to find out if your airline requires reconfirmation.

Restrictions Discounted tickets often have various restrictions on them – such as needing to be paid for in advance and incurring a penalty to be altered. Others are restrictions on the minimum and maximum period you must be away, such as a minimum of 14 days or a maximum of one year.

Round-the-World Tickets RTW tickets give you a limited period (usually a year) in which to circumnavigate the globe. You can go anywhere the carrying airlines go, as long as you don't backtrack. The number of stopovers or total number of separate flights is decided before you set off and they usually cost a bit more than a basic return flight.

Stand-by This is a discounted ticket where you only fly if there is a seat free at the last moment. Stand-by fares are usually available only on domestic routes.

Transferred Tickets Airline tickets cannot be transferred from one person to another. Travellers sometimes try to sell the return half of their ticket, but officials can ask you to prove that you are the person named on the ticket. This is less likely to happen on domestic flights, but on international flight tickets are compared with passports.

Travel Agencies Travel agencies vary widely and you should choose one that suits your needs. Some simply handle tours, while full-service agencies handle everything from tours and tickets to car rental and hotel bookings. If all you want is a ticket at the lowest possible price, then go to an agency specialising in discounted fares.

Travel Periods Ticket prices vary with the time of year. There is a low (off-peak) season and a high (peak) season, and often a low-shoulder season and a high-shoulder season as well. Usually the fare depends on your outward flight – if you depart in the high season and return in the low season, you pay the high-season fare.

reputation for awful service and delays is pretty much deserved, but the low fares offered by Romanian (Tarom Airlines), Hungarian and Czechoslovak airlines can be tempting.

The *New York Times*, *LA Times*, *Chicago Tribune* and *San Francisco Examiner* all produce weekly travel sections in which you'll find travel agents' ads. Council Travel and STA have offices in major cities nationwide. The magazine *Travel Unlimited* (PO Box 1058, Allston, Mass 02134) publishes details of the cheapest air fares and courier possibilities from the USA to destinations all over the world.

In Canada, Travel CUTS has offices in all major cities. The *Toronto Globe & Mail* and *Vancouver Sun* carry travel agents' ads. The magazine *Great Expeditions* (PO Box 8000-411, Abbotsford BC V2S 6H1) is useful.

Australia & New Zealand There are no direct flights from Australia/New Zealand to Israel; however a number of carriers fly via Asia or Europe. One-way tickets range from about A$1100 to A$1400 in low season, (A$100 to A$300 more in high season). Return tickets cost between A$1750 and A$2250 in low season (A$150 to A$500 more in high season). Some of the cheaper airlines flying to Israel are Olympic via Athens, Alitalia via Rome, Egypt Air/Air Sinai via Cairo, and Korean Airlines via Seoul. Thai and Ansett fly to Bangkok and Hong Kong and their flights link with El Al flights. Lufthansa, Air France and Qantas team up with a deal that starts from A$2300 – good if you are on a frequent flyer program. At the top end of the price range are British Airways, South African Airways and KLM. Another option is to buy a round-the-world ticket with, say, Qantas or British Airways, or a cheaper one with Alitalia, combined with United Airlines. Fares are about A$2300 (low season) and A$2800 (high season).

STA Travel and Flight Centres International are major dealers in cheap air fares. Check the travel agents' ads in the Yellow Pages. The Axis Travel Centre in Adelaide (axistravel@email.msn.com) is gaining a good reputation in the industry and may be worth contacting for any good deals going.

UK Some charter flights to Ben-Gurion from the UK continue to offer the best deals at around UK£220 for a 12 month open return. This can come down to as little as UK£180 for a one to four week return. A one-way charter ticket averages about UK£140. To secure a cheap fare for summer and Christmas flights, however, you must book well in advance.

It is worth shopping around cheap flight specialists in London and Manchester. STA, with branches throughout the UK, is regularly among the cheapest, as are Trailfinders and the various Earls Court Rd cheap ticket specialists. It may also be worth contacting Israel Travel Service (☎ 0161-839 1111) in Manchester, a private and extremely helpful outfit with extensive experience.

Check out the ads in the *Times* and the Sunday newspaper travel supplements, and in London look in free magazines such as *TNT*, which are distributed outside many of the central tube stations.

Continental Europe Charter flights to Ben-Gurion leave from most European countries with considerable savings on scheduled fares; the cheapest are found in Germany, France, Belgium, the Netherlands and Scandinavia. Prices are slightly higher than those departing from the UK.

A less expensive option is to fly with the various Eastern European airlines; these flights can be picked up in Western Europe (see USA & Canada earlier this section).

Asia Hong Kong is *the* discount air fare capital of the region, but you'll also find good value in Bangkok and Kuala Lumpur. The bucket shops in these cities are at least as unreliable as those of other cities. Ask the advice of other travellers before purchasing a ticket.

STA Travel is a reliable company with branches in Hong Kong, Tokyo, Osaka,

Singapore, Bangkok, Jakarta, Bali, Seoul, Taipei, Kuala Lumpur, Kathmandu and Delhi.

Egypt There are El Al and Air Sinai flights between Ben-Gurion airport and Egypt (Cairo and the Red Sea port of Hurghada), which will save you having an Egypt-Israel border stamp in your passport (see under Documents in the Facts for the Visitor chapter). These flights cost about US$165 one way, US$230 return.

Departure Tax
The tax for foreigners flying out of Ben-Gurion airport is around 41 NIS (US$13), but this is accounted for in the cost of your ticket. Information on sea and land departure taxes is contained in those sections following.

Travel Agents
The student travel agency ISSTA (Map 2, ☎ 625 7257, 31 HaNevi'im St), is open Sunday to Friday from 9 am to 6 pm, (closes at 1pm Wednesday and Friday), but is closed on Saturday.

Mona Tours (Map 3, ☎ 625 3002, 4 Hillel St) also specialises in discount flights for students and young travellers and claims to offer the cheapest air fares in Israel.

The Tel Aviv office of Mona Tours (☎ 03-621 1433, fax 528 3125, email miridave@netvision.net.il, 25 Bograshov St) is probably the best place to get a cheap ticket out of Israel in a hurry. Also in Tel Aviv, the Travel Centre (☎ 03-528 0955, 528 7307) specialises in discount fares to Europe. They will send tickets to Jerusalem at no extra charge.

BOAT
Routes & Fares
Israel is connected to mainland Europe by a regular ferry service between Haifa and Piraeus, (near Athens) in Greece. This service stops at Lemessos (Limassol) in Cyprus and usually again in Rhodes or Crete. Departures from Haifa are on Thursday and Sunday evenings, departures from Piraeus are

on Mondays and Thursdays; these are subject to frequent seasonal change and you should check with a travel agent in good time before making concrete travel plans.

The cheapest tickets to Piraeus are US$96 for deck class, US$106 for a Pullman seat and from US$125 per person in a four-berth cabin. Students and those under 26 get a discount of about 20%. These prices are for one-way voyages in the low season; in the high season, (varying slightly between companies but roughly from mid-June to mid-September), prices go up by between 11% and 15%. For return voyages, 20% reductions are made on tickets (although not from the already discounted student and under 26 prices).

Travellers with campervans can sleep in their van on the deck and avoid expensive cabin costs when travelling on Poseidon Lines' *FB Sea Symphony*.

If you stop over at any port along the way (ie get off and resume your journey on another ferry), a disembarkation fee of US$22 per person, US$44 per vehicle is charged for *each* stopover en route. Passengers from Rhodes to Haifa are charged US$44. If you bring a vehicle into Lemesos or Piraeus, a municipal tax is also charged on top of the disembarkation fee; at Lemesos it's CY£30, at Piraeus it's 1400 dr.

The Haifa-Piraeus run takes about 58 hours, so take plenty of food and drink (or money) for the voyage.

Alternatively, it's possible to take the ferry only as far as Rhodes and change there for Marmaris in Turkey. Low season fares to Rhodes from Haifa are US$91 for deck class, US$101 for a Pullman seat and US$120 for a cabin berth (see comments on fares for the Haifa-Piraeus route earlier this section). From Rhodes the fare to Marmaris is 12,000 dr one way (19,000 dr return). Low season fares from Haifa to Lemesos only are US$58/68/87.

Buying Tickets
There are two major ferry companies: Poseidon Lines and Salamis Lines. The former is Greek-owned and run and the latter is

Cypriot-owned and run. Travellers' tales about the comfort level of both lines vary, so keep your ear to the ground for current opinions.

Passengers should note that on Fridays, or on the eve of Jewish public holidays the port closes down at 1 pm and access to the port and ferry is not possible, even though the ferry usually leaves at 8 pm in the evening. Check-in in this instance must take place before 1 pm. While no departures are currently scheduled for Fridays, this may change depending on the season.

Tickets can be bought at all ports of call as well as directly from the following port offices:

Poseidon Lines
Cyprus
(☎ 05-745 666, fax 745 666) Poseidon Lines (Cyprus) Ltd, 124 Franklin Roosevelt St, Lemesos

Greece
(☎ 01-965 8300, fax 965 8310, email poseidon.lines@ath.forthnet.gr) Poseidon Lines Shipping Co, Alkyonidon 32, 166 73 Voula, Athens

Israel
(☎ 04-867 4444, fax 866 1958) Caspi Travel, 76 Ha'Atzmaut St, Haifa

UK
(☎ 0171-431 4560, fax 431 5456, email ferries@viamare.com) Viamare Travel Ltd, 2 Sumatra Rd, London NW6 1PU

Salamis Lines
Cyprus
(☎ 05-355 555, fax 364 410) Salamis Tours, PO Box 351, Lemesos

Greece
(☎ 01-429 4325, fax 429 4557) Salamis Lines (Hellas), Fillelinon 9, 185 36 Piraeus

Israel
(☎ 04-861 3670, fax 04-861 3613) A Rosenfeld Shipping Ltd, 104 Ha'Atzmaut St, Haifa

UK
same as for Poseidon Lines above

LAND
Jerusalem can be reached by bus from Egypt or Jordan, both of which have open land borders with Israel; due to continuing political tensions, Lebanon and Syria currently do not.

To/From Egypt
Legalised by the signing of the 1979 Camp David Peace Accord, travel between Israel and Egypt is now a thriving part of the tourist scene. There are two border crossing points: Rafah (Rafiah) and Taba. Buses travel direct between Jerusalem and Cairo via the Rafah crossing; Taba is the border crossing to Egypt via Sinai.

Rafah Only one tour company in Jerusalem currently runs services via the Rafah route and that is Mazada Tours (Map 3, ☎ 623 5777, fax 625 5454, 9 Koresh St), two blocks south of Safra Square. Buses depart daily at 7 am and cost US$35 one way or US$50 return (12-14 hours). There are also overnight services on Sunday, Tuesday and Thursday, departing at 6.30 pm (US$40/60). Add to that an Israeli departure tax of US$32 (payable to the bus company) and an Egyptian entry tax of US$6. You can change money at the border, but you may only import or export a maximum of E£20 into and out of Egypt.

Alternatively, you can take public transport to Cairo from Tel Aviv. An Egged bus departs daily for Rafah (27NIS, 2 hours) at 9 am from the central bus station. After passing through Israeli immigration, catch the shuttle bus (about US$2) to the Egyptian hall. Once through procedures there you can catch a local Egyptian bus or service taxi for Cairo, some five hours away.

On the return leg, the bus departs from the Cairo Sheraton at 5.30 am on Sunday, Monday, Wednesday and Thursday. Tickets are bought at the hotel from Masr Travel. The fare is US$40 one way.

Taba Do not go to Egypt via Rafah if you want to go to Sinai without first visiting Cairo; instead, head for Eilat on Israel's Red Sea coast. Buses to Eilat run from Jerusalem's central bus station about four times a day. The Israeli-Egyptian border crossing is at Taba, just 4km south of central Eilat. While there are no organised buses from Eilat into Egypt, the crossing is simple enough and once over the border it's possible to pick up local Egyptian transport both for destinations in Sinai and for Cairo.

The border is officially open 24 hours but closes occasionally – you need to time your crossing to be able to find transport on the other side. Unlike Rafah, where you can be held up for three or four hours, it's normally possible to stroll through the formalities at Taba in around 30 minutes. There is a 61NIS (US$14.50) Israeli departure tax payable at Taba as well as a E£17 (US$5) Egyptian entry tax. Visitors to Taba only are exempt from these taxes as payment is made some way past the Taba Hilton compound at a small roadside booth. When leaving Egypt there is a E£2 departure tax, so make sure you retain some small change.

Once on the Egyptian side you can change money at the Taba Hilton, or in a small foreign exchange booth in the customs and passport control building, and then it's a further 1km walk to the small tourist village and the bus stop. Alternatively, shared minibuses to Nuweiba (E£30) await arrivals just past the customs area.

To/From Jordan

Unlike Egypt, which still maintains something of a 'you keep to your side of the fence and I'll keep to mine' peace with Israel, Jordan and the Jewish state have become best buddies, exchanging coach loads of visitors on a daily basis. The Allenby/King Hussein Bridge, which until very recently served as the only meeting point of the two neighbours, has been supplemented by two other crossings: Jordan River and Arava. Travellers no longer have to collude in the pretence that they suddenly materialised on King Hussein Bridge without ever stepping foot in anywhere called Israel. There is absolutely no problem entering Jordan with an Israeli visa in your passport. For more details see under Documents in the Facts for the Visitor chapter.

Allenby/King Hussein Bridge This crossing is only 30km from Jerusalem on one side and 40km from Amman on the other. You can easily get here by taking a service taxi (30NIS, 45 minutes) from opposite Damascus Gate in Jerusalem – ask for 'Jisr Al-Malek Hussein', not 'Allenby Bridge' since the Israeli name may not be understood. Remember, anyone turning up here without a valid visa will be sent back. However, the flip side is that the Jordanian officials here can be asked not to stamp visa holders' passports – this is the only crossing at which travellers looking to move on to Syria or Lebanon can avoid the incriminating evidence of a trip to Israel.

Note that if you are entering Jordan this way and intend to return to Israel, you must keep the entry form given to you by the Jordanians – they could well insist on you prolonging your stay in Jordan if you cannot present it on departure.

Crossing can take anything up to three hours depending on the traffic – try to avoid the busiest time between 11 am and 3 pm. The Israeli departure tax is a steep 140NIS, which is considerably higher than at the other land border crossings. The reasoning behind this high fee is that you are supposedly paying for the privilege of exiting both Palestinian *and* Israeli territory. Once through all the immigration procedures and out the other side look for the white service taxis to Amman (JD2 per person); the yellow cars are 'special' taxis that charge JD10 to JD12 for the same ride.

The bridge is open Sunday to Thursday from 8 am to midnight (avoid crossing during the Jewish Shabbat as it may be difficult to find onward transport). These times are subject to frequent change and it's advisable to check with the tourist information office in Jerusalem.

Jordan River The Jordanians call this the Jisr Sheikh Hussein (Sheikh Hussein Bridge). The least used of the three border crossings, it's 6km east of Beit She'an in the Galilee and though it is considerably closer to Jerusalem than the Arava crossing at Eilat it is not particularly convenient. However it is a modern border crossing with good facilities and if you don't already have your Jordanian visa you can get one here.

Take a Tiberias bus and change at Beit She'an for one of four daily buses to the border (6.60NIS). They leave Beit She'an at 8.40 am, 9.20 am, 3 pm and 6 pm, returning from the border back to Beit She'an some 15-20 minutes after the above departure times. Once across the border, however, you're in the middle of nowhere. Either take a minibus to Irbid or take a taxi to the main road some 3km away, from where you can try and hitch to somewhere more life supporting.

The border is open daily from 8 am to 8 pm, (closes 5pm Friday and Saturday). The Israeli departure tax here is a more reasonable 57NIS.

Arava Opened in August 1994 this crossing (known as Wadi Araba to the Jordanians) is just 4km from central Eilat. Once over the border, the carved stone city of Petra, arguably the Middle East's second greatest attraction after the Pyramids, is less than two hours' drive away. We do not, however, recommend that you try making a day trip of it – there's simply too much to see. Also, the huge volume of coach traffic at this crossing often means lengthy delays of up to three hours.

Border opening times are from 6.30 am to 10 pm Sunday to Thursday, and from 8 am to 8 pm Friday and Saturday. We strongly advise getting here before opening time to be ahead of the buses, which start rolling up soon after.

A direct and much needed bus service between Eilat and Aqaba has been on the cards ever since the border re-opened, but at the time of research nothing had happened. Enquire at Eilat's central bus station or tourist information office for the latest information.

The Israeli departure tax here is 61NIS and Jordanian visas are issued. These can be expensive ranging from JD6 for French passport holders to an outrageous JD38 for Canadian passport holders. Australians, New Zealanders, British, Irish and Americans all pay something between these two extremes. South Africans and Japanese get their visas free.

Both sides have money-changing facilities but the Jordanians offer far more favourable rates. Once across the border you have to take a taxi to the Aqaba bus station (JD5), from where buses can be caught to Petra (JD3), departing at 8.30 and 10 am and at noon, 2 and 3.30 pm. While we don't recommend this, if there are enough of you and if you are very short of time it may be worth sharing a taxi direct from Aqaba to Petra and back at a cost of JD40 (with two hours of driver's waiting time thrown in) or JD50 (with five hours waiting time). Rates are fixed.

Bus

Israel's bus network is dominated by Egged, the second largest bus company in the world after Greyhound. Although the inter-urban buses are always busy, those heading for the Dead Sea and in particular Eilat are the only ones for which you need to reserve seats in advance. Buses for the Dead Sea are always busy and seem to operate independently of official timetables. The simple rule is to make a start as early as possible.

Unless otherwise stated, buses run daily between about 5.30 am and 11 pm. On Shabbat, the last Friday buses leave at around 3 pm, and the first Saturday buses leave at about 6 pm. The central bus station is on Jaffa Rd, on the west side of town and may still be being rebuilt (Map 2). Call ☎ 530 4555 for intercity bus information.

The left-luggage office is at 195 Jaffa Rd, directly opposite the station. It's open Sunday to Thursday from 7 am to 7 pm, (closes at 1pm Friday), closed Saturday. The charge is 5NIS per item per day.

Buses leave from the central bus station for the following destinations:

Beersheba (25NIS, 1½ hours) every 30 minutes until 8.30 pm
Eilat (57NIS, 4½ hours) 7 and 10 am, 2 and 5 pm; book a day in advance
Ein Gedi (18NIS, 1½ hours) 8.40 am and 4, 7.45 and 9.40 pm; you can also take Eilat or Masada buses
Haifa (38NIS, 2 hours) every 45 minutes, last bus is at 7.15 pm

Masada via Ein Gedi (35.50 NIS, 1¾ hours) Sunday-Thursday 8:45 am, 9:40 am,11:00 am, 12:00 pm, 1:00 pm; Friday 8:45 am, 9:50 am, 1:00 pm. You can also take an Eilat bus
Safed (40NIS, 3 hours) only one or two a day, take a Tiberias bus and change
Tel Aviv (17NIS, 1 hour) every 10 to 15 minutes; bus No 405 goes to the central bus station, bus No 480 goes to the Arlosoroff terminal
Tiberias (39NIS, 2½ hours) every hour until 7 pm

Sherut (Service Taxi)

Sheruts are an affordable alternative to buses, and on Shabbat they are the only way of getting around in all but the Palestinian areas. In the New City, service taxi companies have regular services to the following destinations:

Haifa & Eilat
Yael Daroma (☎ 622 6985) Shamai St, next door to Kesher-Aviv; reservations a day in advance are normally necessary
Tel Aviv
HaBirah (☎ 623 2320) 1 Harav Kook St, opposite Zion Square
Kesher-Aviv (☎ 625 7366) 12 Shamai St, south of and parallel to Ben Yehuda St; 18NIS per person (25NIS Friday and Saturday)

Service taxis to all West Bank destinations as well as those to the Gaza Strip depart from a service taxi rank across from Damascus Gate in East Jerusalem (Map 5). They operate daily from about 5 am until about 5 pm, after which time the service becomes less dependable.

Car & Motorcycle

Egypt and Jordan both have open land borders with Israel; Lebanon and Syria do not. Private cars may cross the borders but not taxis or hire cars. Drivers and riders of motorbikes will need the vehicle's registration papers and liability insurance. For Israel an international driving permit is not necessary – your domestic licence will do.

Jerusalem is approached from the west side along a busy but well-engineered highway (Route No 1) from Tel Aviv and other destinations. The road narrows somewhat after the Sha'ar HaGai interchange and at peak times traffic can bank up for some distance on the approach into Jerusalem. It might be worth considering turning right onto Route No 38 from the Sha'ar HaGai interchange and then turning left after 5.5km onto the scenic Route No 395, which will lead you into Jerusalem via Ein Kerem.

Approaching from the east, drivers are faced with the long climb from below sea level along a winding approach that enters Jerusalem just north of Mt Scopus. This route gets busy during rush hours and there may be traffic queues before the Israeli control point just before Jerusalem. This approach will be made by drivers coming from Eilat or Tiberias.

Hitching

Hitching is never entirely safe in any country in the world, and Israel is no different. There have been incidents in which hitchhikers in Israel have been abducted and killed – and not all, it's thought, for political reasons. Travellers who decide to hitch should understand that they are taking a small but potentially serious risk. At least hitch in pairs and let someone know where you are planning to go. And, above all, women should never hitch without male company.

You will notice, however, a large number of soldiers soliciting lifts by the roadside. This is because it's traditional, and actively encouraged, for Israelis to give lifts to soldiers – so bear in mind that if you are hitching you will be last in line for a lift if there are any IDF uniforms to be seen. Note that even female soldiers are forbidden to hitch because of the potential danger.

Also, take note that sticking out your thumb is not the locally accepted way to hitch a lift. Here it means something more basic and impolite, although most locals recognise foreigners' intentions. The local way to hitch is to point down at the road with your index finger.

Hitching into Jerusalem off the motorway from the west may be tricky since you will have to position yourself on the approach roads, and merging traffic may be too preoccupied with surrounding traffic to be able to stop comfortably to pick up hitchers. It should in practice be easier coming from the east, though drivers may be less willing to pick you up because of security concerns in the West Bank areas.

WARNING

The information in this chapter is particularly vulnerable to change: prices for international travel are volatile, routes are introduced and cancelled, schedules change, special deals come and go, and rules and visa requirements are amended. Airlines and governments seem to take a perverse pleasure in making price structures and regulations as complicated as possible. You should check directly with the airline or a travel agent to make sure you understand how a fare (and ticket you may buy) works. In addition, the travel industry is highly competitive and there are many lurks and perks.

The upshot of this is that you should get opinions, quotes and advice from as many airlines and travel agents as possible before you part with your hard-earned cash. The details given in this chapter should be regarded as pointers and are not a substitute for your own careful, up-to-date research.

Getting Around

TO/FROM THE AIRPORT

The only cheap way into Jerusalem from Ben-Gurion airport is by Egged bus Nos 945 or 947, which depart every half-hour from just outside the arrivals terminal. The 30 minute trip to the central bus station costs 17NIS. This service is not very convenient for the Old City or East Jerusalem, especially if you're carrying heavy luggage and need to look for a place to stay.

The most convenient, but also more expensive, way to get to the Old City or East Jerusalem is to take a sherut (service taxi) from just outside the arrivals terminal. These run all night, departing whenever they're full; the fare is 40NIS (US$10). 'Special' (ie nonshared) taxis are available for all destinations, but are much more expensive. The fare to the city centre costs about 95NIS, and around 30% more between 9 pm and 5.30 am. To protect arrivals from rip-off tactics, the authorities have posted most fares on a massive sign. Check this carefully before you're hustled into a taxi (see the Special Taxi section later in this chapter).

To get to the airport call Nesher Taxis (Map 3) (☎ 623 1231, fax 624 1114, 21 King George V St) on the corner of Ben Yehuda St. They pick up from anywhere in the city, seven days a week, 24 hours a day, and the cost is 34NIS per person. Reserve one day ahead if possible, and definitely if you plan to travel on a Saturday.

BUS
Egged

Most urban buses in Jerusalem are operated by the Egged company. Within the city limits there's one flat fare whether you ride just one stop or 10. At the time of writing this fare was 4.30 NIS (no transfers); buy your ticket from the bus driver.

Despite the frequency of most bus services they do fill up, especially in the rush hours which occur roughly between 7 and 8 am and 4 and 6 pm Monday to Thursday, and most of Saturday evening. Most buses run from about 5.30 am to about midnight.

Remember that on Friday and on the eve of Jewish holidays, buses only run until 3 or 4 pm, and Saturday services don't resume until sunset.

Following are the major bus routes:

Bus No 1
From platform D of the central bus station to Mea She'arim, Jaffa Gate, Mt Zion and then to the Old City's Jewish Quarter
Bus No 7
From the bus station down Keren HaYesod, through Talpiot and out to Ramat Rachel
Bus No 9
From Jaffa Rd to the Knesset, the Israel Museum and the Givat Ram campus of the Hebrew University and then into Rehavia via Ramban St and down Keren Ha Yesod
Bus No 13
From Kiryat HaYovel via Jaffa Rd to Jaffa Gate
Bus No 17
To Ein Kerem
Bus No 18
Runs the length of Jaffa Rd, connecting the New City centre with the bus station
Bus No 20
From Yad Vashem via Jaffa Rd to Jaffa Gate
Bus No 23
From Yad Vashem via Jaffa Rd to Damascus Gate
Bus No 27
From Hadassah Medical Centre to Mt Herzl and Yad Vashem, along Jaffa Rd past the central bus station, left along HaNevi'im and via Strauss and Yezehekel Sts to the Nablus Rd bus station near Damascus Gate
Bus No 28
From Jaffa Rd to Mt Scopus and French Hill

For city bus information call ☎ 530 4555.

Monthly Pass A monthly discount bus pass called *hofshi hodshi*, which can be bought on the bus or at ticket offices at the central bus station, allows for unlimited travel within the city during that calendar month. The pass costs 160 NIS and is on sale only at the beginning of each month. This is only worth buying if you are planing to take a lot of buses.

Arab Buses

These serve East Jerusalem and outlying towns and villages such as Bethany and Bethlehem. While Jewish buses tend to be air-conditioned, clean, fast and modern, the Arab buses are virtual antiques, and not well-kept ones at that. If you have the choice use a sherut instead – they're only slightly more expensive but they're much faster. The Arab bus stations are on Nablus Rd and Suleyman St (Map 5).

CAR & MOTORCYCLE

Traffic in Jerusalem is horrendous and Israelis exhibit near-suicidal tendencies once behind the wheel. Unless you expect to be regularly criss-crossing town, a car may be more trouble than it's worth.

However, road transport authorities have built a series of fairly efficient freeways that can transport you around the city's perimeters quite efficiently.

When driving in Jerusalem itself try and avoid Jaffa Rd. Private cars may not use this busy thoroughfare when travelling east towards the city, but may travel west along it out of the city – that is if you can get onto it in the first place. This confusing regulation is not in force during Shabbat.

A car can be a great advantage for day trips to the Dead Sea or the Galilee. Unfortunately most of the car rental offices are in one of the busiest parts of the New City on King David St, so if you hire a car, you are not going to be able to completely avoid driving in the city. Just get your bearings on a map before you set off and beware of the Jaffa Rd trap.

Road Rules

In Israel you drive on the right-hand side of the road. Seat belts should be worn at all times by front seat occupants. The speed limit is 50km/h (31 mp/h) in built up areas and 90km/h (56mp/h) elsewhere unless

stated otherwise, but this is typically ignored. There seems to be a lack of regulatory road signs, but virtually all major cities, towns and places of interest are signposted in English.

Parking

With a rapid increase in private car ownership, parking is becoming a major problem in Jerusalem. Street parking is strictly regulated; to avoid a ticket or having your car towed, be sure to follow the rules.

Generally, there is no free street parking; parking cards can be purchased from the post office or at street kiosks. Each parking card has five hours worth of street parking and costs about 45 NIS. With a parking card affixed to the car's front window, you can park where the kerb is marked by blue and white stripes. You cannot legally park anywhere else.

Between the hours of 7 am and 5 pm, you can only park at a marked kerb for one hour. Between 5 and 10 pm you can park for longer, with a set of displayed parking cards indicating the number of hours parked. Overnight parking on areas marked with blue and white stripes is unregulated. If you need to park for a longer period during the day, use a public car park.

Car Rental

Local car hire firms generally offer lower rates than international companies like Avis, Budget and Hertz. Eldan, in particular, stands out, with good rates and offices nationwide. If you are planning to drive throughout the country, it is a good idea to use a company that has a few offices in case you need a replacement car. Note that you are not allowed to take hired vehicles over the border into Sinai or Jordan.

Prices do vary dramatically and shopping around is recommended. Based on three days' rental, you'll be spending around US$60 to US$80 per day for a Fiat Uno or similar, with air-con, insurance and unlimited mileage. July and August rates are substantially higher than the rest of the year. Be wary of initial quotes – check if insurance and unlimited mileage are included, and if there is a minimum rental period.

Most car rental companies require that drivers be over 21 years old and have an unblemished, valid drivers licence (an International Driving Permit is not necessary for most nationalities).

The major rental companies in Jerusalem are:

AutoRent
(☎ 624 4222) King David Hotel, HaMelekh David St
Avis
(☎ 624 9001) 22 HaMelekh David St
Best
(☎ 538 9226, fax 500 0859) 178 Jaffa Rd
Budget
(☎ 624 8991, fax 625 9456) 23 King David St
Eldan
(☎ 625 2151, fax 625 2154) 24 HaMelekh David St
Eurodollar & Europcar
(☎ 623 5467) 8 HaMelekh David St
Hertz
(☎ 623 1351) 18 HaMelekh David St
Reliable
(☎ 624 8204) 14 HaMelekh David St
Sa-Gal
(☎ 624 8003) same address as Reliable
Splendid
(☎ 624 2488, fax 242 557) same address as Reliable

An often overlooked alternative to the Jewish-owned companies are the Palestinian companies. In addition to any political reasons you may have for giving them your business, their cars are considered 'protected' in East Jerusalem and other Arab areas, including the West Bank, and should be spared the hostility and stones that on occasion are still targeted towards cars displaying yellow Israeli numberplates.

Holy City
(☎ 582 0223, fax 582 4329) East Jerusalem, behind the US Consulate
Orabi
(☎ 995 3521, fax 995 3521) Jerusalem St, Al-Bireh, near Ramallah
Petra
(☎ 582 0716, fax 582 2668) Main St, East Jerusalem

Road Orthodoxy

When death and disablement prove insufficient incentives to get drivers to slow down, the *haredi* road safety campaigners play on even greater fears. Signs in the Mea She'arim district display the macabre message, 'Drive Carefully: the Pathologist Awaits' – a reference to autopsies that they claim have been carried out indiscriminately in Jerusalem's hospitals in violation of strict religious law.

Perhaps of more immediate concern to would-be drivers is the possibility of being pelted by stones or other objects if you drive your vehicle in ultraorthodox areas on the Shabbat. Fortunately most main streets are blocked off to deter drivers anyway, but you could find yourself in hot water if you accidentally stray off the beaten path in your car. At this time your best bet is to walk anyway – when else do pedestrians get the chance to reclaim the streets from the automobile?

TAXI
Sherut (Service Taxi)

Sheruts are usually stretch-Mercedes, seating up to seven passengers, or larger 12-seater minivans, which operate on a fixed route for a fixed price just like a bus. If you are uncertain about the fare, just ask your fellow passengers. Regular rates are normally about 20% more than the bus, but are sometimes on a par.

With a sherut you can get out anywhere along the way, but you pay the same fare regardless of the distance actually travelled. After dropping off a passenger the sherut then picks up replacement passengers wherever possible.

On some routes, the sheruts operate as standins for Egged buses during Shabbat, providing the only transport while Egged is off the road. For details of service taxi companies see under Sherut in the Getting There & Away chapter.

GETTING AROUND

'Special' Taxi

Drivers of 'special' (that is, nonshared or regular) taxis have a terrible and richly deserved reputation with tourists and locals alike for overcharging and being generally unhelpful and impolite.

If a driver can possibly overcharge you, he most certainly will. Common ploys are 'my meter doesn't work' or 'for you my friend, special price'. Pay no attention to these diversions as they are preludes to a scam. Before setting off in a taxi, point to the meter and make sure the driver understands that you want it switched on.

Roughly speaking, a trip across town – say from the bus station to the Old City – should cost 15 to 20 NIS – no more. When you arrive at your destination, the taxi meter should spit out a little printed receipt. Take it.

If you think you are going to be ripped off, get out of the taxi. If you have been ripped off, take the taxi registration number and report it to the Controller of Road Transport (☎ 622 8456, fax 622 8452, 97 Jaffa Rd, 91008 Jerusalem) giving full details of the alleged rip-off. The driver will ultimately be fined for the transgression.

BICYCLE

There's just too much traffic in Jerusalem to make cycling a comfortable way of getting around. For anyone who is in less than perfect physical shape, there are also a good few too many hills – you will need a bike with a good range of gears. However, during Shabbat and on public holidays, cycling becomes an ideal way to see the city without traffic and exhaust fumes and somehow the hills don't seem to be such a bother at these times.

If you are in Jerusalem on Yom Kippur (a single day in October), that's the time to ride your bike (see under Public Holidays in the Facts for the Visitor chapter). Thousands of young and old cyclists take advantage of the dearth of motor traffic and take to the streets to enjoy this once-a-year bikefest. But beware – it's also a time when the casualty wards at the hospital are very busy

with not-so-experienced cyclists who come a cropper.

Walk Ways (☎ 533 6294, fax 533 2402, email rockman@netvision.net.il) rent and sell new or second-hand bikes and spare parts and will deliver to your hotel or hostel. You can also contact the Jerusalem Cycle Club (☎ 561 9416) for information on cycling in Jerusalem and possible organised cycling tours. See also under Cycling in the Activities section of the Things to See & Do chapter.

ORGANISED TOURS
Bus Tours

A good introduction to the city is the Egged Bus Tours Route 99, 'Circular Line'. This service takes you on a comfortable coach to 36 of the city's major sites, with basic commentary in English (sort of) provided by the driver. A ticket is 18 NIS, valid for a day's unlimited travel, enabling you to get off and back on wherever you wish. Bear in mind, however, the infrequency of the service: departures occur at 10 and 11 am, noon and 1, 2 and 4 pm Sunday to Thursday, and at 10 and 11 am and noon on Friday. The coach leaves from Ha'Emek St by Jaffa Gate but you can board at any of the stops on its continuous circular route (taking 1½ hours in total), which ends up where it started.

Egged also runs a half-day tour of Jerusalem's Old City (US$24) departing Sunday to Thursday at 9.30 am; a half-day tour of the Old City (US$32) including the Mount of Olives and the Hasmonean tunnel departing every Tuesday at 10 am; and a full-day tour (US$46) including Yad Vashem and Bethlehem, departing daily at 9.30 am. For further information visit the Egged Tours offices at 193 Jaffa Rd, (Map 2, ☎ 530 4879) or Shlomzion HaMalka St, (Map 3, ☎ 622 1999) which runs south off Jaffa Rd near Zion Square.

Walking Tours

Up-to-date details of the following and other walking tours are available at the tourist information office in the Safra Square complex north of Jaffa Rd (Map 3).

Free Walking Tours The Jaffa Rd tourist information office organises a free Saturday morning walking tour around a different part of the city each week. Meet at 10 am by the entrance to the Russian Compound at 32 Jaffa Rd (Map 3). Unfortunately, these free tours inevitably attract a large crowd so although the guides are well informed you'll often struggle to hear them.

The Sheraton Plaza Hotel (☎ 625 9111), on the corner of King George V and Agron Sts in the New City, also offer free walking tours most days of the week, and non-guests are welcome. Meet in the hotel lobby at 9 am.

The Jewish Student Information Centre (see under Tourist Offices in the Facts for the Visitor chapter), which is committed to giving young Jewish people a fresh awareness of their heritage, organises free walking tours of Jewish sites in the Old City's Jewish and Muslim quarters. Visit the centre (Map 9) or call ☎ 628 2643 for current schedules.

Zion Walking Tours Enjoying one of the best reputations for Old and New City tours, Zion (☎ 628 7866, fax 629 0774) has its office on Omar ibn al-Khattab Square, opposite the entrance to the Citadel (Map 6). Particularly good value is the three hour 'Four Quarters' tour of the Old City which departs at 9 and 11 am and 2 pm Sunday to Friday, costing US$10 (students US$9). A number of readers have recommended guide Stanley Ziring who guides the 11 am tours on Monday, Tuesday and Thursday.

Other tours themes include the 'Pre-Temple Period route', the 'Underground City of Jerusalem' and 'Mea She'arim'.

Zion also conducts a tour of the Judean Desert and Jericho costing US$45; bookings are essential for this tour.

Archaeological Seminars Walks Innovative walks are also offered by Archaeological Seminars (☎ 627 3515, fax 627 2660, email office@archesem.com) including a tour of the controversial Western Wall tunnel. This underground walk along the base of the Western Wall takes place on Sunday, Tuesday and Wednesday at 9.30 am (US$16) and again at 6 pm (US$14) on Wednesdays; bookings are essential.

They also offer a fanciful 'Raiders of the Lost Ark' walk which aims to trace the supposed path of the 1911 Parker Mission that searched for the Ark of the Covenant. This walk takes you to the City of David excavations, Warren's Shaft and Hezekiah's Tunnel and costs US$16. It leaves on Thursday mornings at 9.30 am.

Society for the Preservation of Nature in Israel (SPNI) SPNI mainly organises hikes and treks in the surrounding countryside but each Thursday, at 8 am, it runs a full-day tour of the Jewish parts of the Old City for 132 NIS. For contact details see Tourist Offices in the Facts for the Visitor chapter.

West Bank Tours

If you are concerned about visiting the West Bank on your own, you might consider taking a Palestinian-organised guided tour. The Jerusalem Hotel (☎ 627 7216, fax 628 3282, email raed@jrshotel.com) runs a series of tours to the West Bank lasting from five to six hours or a full day. Departing most mornings of the week, they take in visits to Hebron, Bethlehem, Ramallah, Nablus, Jericho and a Palestinian refugee camp.

These tours are very reasonably priced in comparison with Israeli-organised tours, starting from 30NIS to visit a refugee camp and 70NIS for a full-day visit to Bethlehem and Hebron. Ask for Abu Hassan.

Things to See & Do

THE OLD CITY

A bazaar of living history, the Old City is a densely packed labyrinth of more than 100 streets, 1000 shops and stalls, and 3000 years of human experience. As you walk along the Via Dolorosa you are treading on the paving stones that were there at the time of Christ – they were uncovered while new sewers were being dug in the 1970s. Rather than store them in a museum, the municipality had them re-laid. It is this perpetuation of the ancient in the 20th century that creates the appeal of the Old City.

The Old City is under administration of the Israelis, but is predominantly Palestinian Arab in make-up and appearance. The two do not as a rule mix (although in the past there were times when they cohabited quite peacefully), and instead the Old City is divided into four hazily defined quarters. At the same time, it's focused on three definite centres of gravity.

The Christian and Armenian quarters have developed in homage to the Church of the Holy Sepulchre, the site traditionally considered to be that of Jesus' crucifixion and subsequent burial and resurrection. The Muslim Quarter huddles in the shadow of the Haram ash-Sharif/Temple Mount, site of the Dome of the Rock, while the Jewish Quarter is oriented towards the Western Wall, the last vestige of the Second Temple.

Walls & Gates

The walls as they exist today, all 4.3km of them, are the legacy of Suleyman the Magnificent, who oversaw their construction between 1536 and 1541. The northern wall, including Damascus Gate, was built first and then extended south, at which point it was delayed by a dispute over whether or not Mt Zion and the Franciscans' monastery should stand within or without. To save time and expense the builders decided against looping around the monastery, leaving the Franciscans out in the cold. Popular legend has it that when news reached Suleyman of this miserly cost-cutting exercise he was furious and had the architects beheaded. Another version of the tale has it that they were put to death so they would never build another wall to challenge the magnificence of Jerusalem's wall.

There were seven gates in Suleyman's walls. An eighth was added in the late 19th century, which is still known as the New Gate. All but the Golden Gate on the eastern side of the Haram ash-Sharif/Temple Mount are accessible and, time permitting, you should try to make a point of entering or leaving the Old City by each of them.

Note that each of the gates has at least three names: Arabic, Hebrew, and a more internationally recognised anglicised name. While almost everybody recognises the names Damascus Gate and Jaffa Gate, if you wanted an Arab taxi driver to take you, for example, to Herod's Gate, you would have to ask for Bab as-Zahra.

The following description of the gates begins with the Damascus Gate and continues clockwise around the wall.

Damascus Gate (Maps 6 & 7) One of the most impressive structures of Islamic architecture in Jerusalem, Damascus Gate is also the busiest and most photogenic of the Old City gates. The amphitheatre-like plaza out the front was created in the early 1970s. It now serves as a makeshift marketplace and it's a great place to sit and observe the bustle.

The gate itself dates in its present form from the time of Suleyman the Magnificent, although there had been a gate here long before the arrival of the Turks. This was the main entrance to the city as early as the time of Herod Agrippa, who ruled in the 1st century AD. The gate was considerably enlarged during the reign of the emperor Hadrian.

The foundations of Hadrian's 'Great Gate' were uncovered during major renovations in 1967 and are now open to visitors.

Views of the City

The following is a rundown of the best places from which to view Jerusalem. See the individual sections in this chapter for opening times and admission costs:

Mount of Olives The Mount of Olives affords the classic panorama of Jerusalem with the golden dome rising above the city walls. Come early in the morning when the sun is behind you and the view is at its clearest.

Mt Scopus From here there are marvellous views of the city to the west and, from the amphitheatre, even better views to the east across the Judean Desert to the Dead Sea.

Dormition Monastery This monastery is on Mt Zion just outside the city walls.

Lutheran Church of the Redeemer Right in the middle of the Old City, the church tower offers photographers the best shots of the Haram ash-Sharif/Temple Mount.

Haas Promenade A favourite spot for strolling Jerusalemites, this attractive stepped terrace in the south of Jerusalem faces up the Hinnom Valley to the Old City.

City Tower In the New City on the corner of Ben Yehuda and King George V Sts, the City Tower is a multistorey shopping mall with a rooftop restaurant, the Jerusalem Delight, which offers 360° views over the city centre.

YMCA The belfry of the YMCA building on HaMelekh David St has great views across the Hinnom Valley to Mt Zion and the Old City.

Jerusalem Wings These aerial tours are unforgettable, see the Activities section at the end of this chapter for details.

Facing the outside of the gate, take the steps to your right which lead down to a small plaza; go through the door under the walkway and the old Roman gate is on your right at the foot of the wall. It's actually only one of two small entrances that flanked a much larger central gate; this is clearly illustrated on an adjacent copper wall plaque.

Inside, some of the old Roman gatehouse has been excavated, and its cavernous rooms now house a collection that illustrates the development of the gate area. It's worth a visit. The **Roman Square excavations**, as they're known, are open from 9 am, closing at 5 pm Saturday to Thursday, 2 pm Friday. Admission is 3.50 NIS. One of the entrances to the ramparts above is also through here.

In Arabic this gate is known as Bab al-Amud (Gate of the Column), after a Roman column erected by Hadrian, which once stood in a square just inside the gate. The column is shown on the **Madaba Map**, a 6th century Byzantine mosaic discovered in Jordan, a copy of which is on display in the Roman Square excavations. In Hebrew, the Damascus Gate is called Sha'ar Shechem (Leading to Schecham Road).

Herod's Gate (Map 7) The Crusaders breached the city walls on 15 July 1099 just 100m east of this gate . The name derives from a mistaken belief held by Renaissance pilgrims that one of the nearby buildings was once the palace of Herod the Great.

The Damascus Gate is depicted on the 'Madaba map' of Byzantine Jerusalem.

In Hebrew the gate is known as Sha'ar HaPerahim and in Arabic, Bab as-Zahra (Flower Gate).

St Stephen's Gate (Map 7) This is the gate that leads to the Mount of Olives and Gethsemane. From their positions on that biblically famed hillside, Israeli paratroopers fought their way through this gate during the Six Day War (on 7 June 1967) to capture the Old City.

Although Suleyman called it Bab al-Ghor (Gate to the Valley of Jordan), the name never stuck and it became known as St Stephen's Gate after the first Christian martyr, who was stoned to death nearby. The Hebrew name, Sha'ar Ha'Arayot (Lions Gate), is a reference to the two pairs of Mamluk lions carved on both sides of the archway.

Golden Gate (Map 7) Uncertainty surrounds this sealed entrance to the Haram ash-Sharif/Temple Mount. There are various mentions of the eastern gate to the Haram ash-Sharif/Temple Mount, but its exact location is unknown; there are, however, Herodian elements in this structure. The gate was probably sealed by the Muslims in the 7th century to stop non-Muslims entering.

Many traditions are associated with the eastern gate. Jewish belief is that this is the gate by which the just will enter Jerusalem on the Day of Judgement; many Christians believe that Jesus used this gate on Palm Sunday and Muslim legend has it that a Christian conqueror will enter here.

Dung Gate (Map 9) In Hebrew this gate is known as Sha'ar HaAshpot. The popular theory as to how these two unflattering appellations came about is that at one time the area around the gate was the local rubbish dump. Its Arabic name is Bab al-Maghariba (Gate of the Moors) due to the fact that North African immigrants lived nearby in the 16th century.

Presently the smallest of the city's gates, at one time it was even more diminutive. The Jordanians widened it during their tenure in the city in order to allow cars to pass through. You can still make out traces of the original, narrower Ottoman arch.

Zion Gate (Maps 8 & 9) This gate was punched through to give access to the Franciscan monastery left outside the walls by Suleyman's architects.

During the 1948 War of Independence, soldiers holding Mt Zion tried to burst through here in a desperate attempt to relieve the besieged Jewish Quarter. First they tried to dynamite the wall at a spot 100m east of the gate (it still bears the scar) and when that failed they launched an all-out assault which ended disastrously. A memorial plaque to the fallen is set within the gate, and the bullet-eaten façade gives some indication of how ferocious the fighting must have been.

In Hebrew the Zion Gate is known as Sha'ar Ziyyon and in Arabic as Bab Haret al-Yahud (Gate of the Jewish Quarter).

Jaffa Gate (Map 6) The actual gate is the small block through which the doglegged pedestrian tunnel passes (the dogleg was to slow down charging enemy forces; you'll find the same thing at Damascus and Zion gates); the breach in the wall through which the road now passes was only made in 1898 in order to permit the visiting Kaiser Wilhelm II and his party to ride with full pomp into the city.

Just inside the gate, on the left as you enter, are two graves said to be those of Suleyman's beheaded architects.

The Arabic name for the gate is Bab al-Khalil (Gate of the Friend), which refers to the holy city of Hebron ('Al-Khalil' in Arabic). In Hebrew it is known as Sha'ar Yafo because this was the start of the old road to the historical port of Jaffa (Yafo).

New Gate (Map 6) This is the most modern of the gates, it was opened in 1887 by Sultan Abdul Hamid to allow direct access from the newly built pilgrim hospices to the holy sites of the Old City's Christian Quarter. In Hebrew it is known as Sha'ar HeHadash, and in Arabic as Bab al-Jadid.

Ramparts Walk

One of the best ways to see the Old City and its surroundings is to walk around the top of the walls. Sections of the ramparts are as far as 15m above street level and the views across the Old City rooftops are superb. This walk will also enable you to make some kind of sense of the layout of the place.

It's not a good idea to make the walk after rain or snow as, despite new paving and guardrails, the stone can be slippery underfoot. In parts the walk is strenuous and steep and involves quite a bit of climbing up and down large stone steps. In addition, women should not walk unaccompanied here at any time because of the risk of sexual assault and mugging.

It isn't possible to make a complete circuit of the wall because the Haram ash-Sharif/Temple Mount stretch is sealed off for security reasons. Instead, the walk is in two sections: Jaffa Gate north to St Stephen's Gate (via New, Damascus and Herod's gates) and Jaffa Gate south to Dung Gate (via Zion Gate). Of the two walks the northern section is probably the longer and more interesting and offers the best views. The southern section passes some uninspiring, seemingly derelict sections of the Armenian Quarter, but does afford a good view over Mt Zion and its associated buildings. The Ramparts Walk can conveniently be combined with a couple of Old City walks (see the boxed text 'Walking Tours of the Old City).

While you can descend at any of the gates, getting up onto the walls is only pos-

sible at two of them. At Jaffa Gate the stairs for the Damascus Gate walk are on the left as you enter the Old City (through an arch in the facade of the Golden Gate jewellery shop). At Damascus Gate the ramparts are reached by going through the Roman Square excavations (see Damascus Gate at the beginning of this section). The stairs for the Dung Gate stretch are outside the walls, 100m south of Jaffa Gate.

The walls are open from 9 am, closing 4 pm Saturday to Thursday, 2 pm Friday and holiday eves. The section from the Citadel to Zion Gate is open Sunday to Thursday until 9.30 pm. Tickets cost 10 NIS and are valid for four admissions over two days (three at the weekend), allowing you to do the combined 3.5km walk gradually. Note that tickets cannot be purchased on Saturday.

Rooftop Promenade

For a different perspective on the Old City, climb the metal stairway on the corner of Habad St and St Mark's Rd (Map 9) or the steep stone stairs in the south-western corner of the Khan as-Sultan (Map 7), both of which lead onto the rooftops around the David St and Al-Wad markets. Come up in the day for a peek through the ventilation ducts at the bustle below, but also make a night-time visit to appreciate the Old City in moonlit silhouette.

The Citadel/Tower of David (Map 6)

This is both one of the country's most impressive restoration projects and a major museum complex, so it's worth paying a visit to the Citadel early in your stay for an excellent grounding in Jerusalem history.

The Citadel started life as the palace of Herod the Great in the 1st century BC. A megalomaniacal builder, Herod furnished his palace with three enormous towers, the largest of which was reputedly modelled on the Pharos lighthouse of Alexandria, one of the Seven Wonders of the ancient world. The chiselled-block remains of one of the lesser towers still serve as the base of the Citadel's main keep.

Walking Tours of the Old City

Jerusalem's Old City is a maze of narrow streets, souqs, plazas and alleyways that you can spend a lifetime there and never see all that it has to offer. Nevertheless, with only two days at your disposal, you can take a couple of do-it-yourself walks that allow you to see the best of all four quarters of this immensely varied city. The two walks suggested here combine the two legs of the ramparts walk with a meandering route that takes you to both the Christian and Muslim quarters and the Jewish and Armenian quarters.

Walk 1 – The Northern Ramparts and the Muslim and Christian Quarters
*   Allow about 1½ hours for this walk of contrasts and surprises
*   See Maps 6 and 7

Make an early start (9 am) from Jaffa Gate and climb up to the ramparts walkway and head north-westwards along the walls running parallel to Jaffa Rd. Every so often you can stop at buttresses along the wall for photo shots or just to take in the morning views of the New City. The wall runs for the first half of its course above the relatively quiet religious neighbourhoods of the Christian Quarter with occasional views into school classrooms and leafy courtyards.

It is a relatively easy walk as far as the Damascus Gate, where things can get a little strenuous. Two routes lead over Damascus Gate: the high or the low route. Take the high one for better photo opportunities, but watch your footing. The city looks quite different from the vantage point high on the wall here and the otherwise hidden contours are quite visible.

From Damascus Gate the wall runs eastward as far as Herod's Gate, past increasingly quiet and remote Arab neighbourhoods with several up and down climbs. The walk takes a sharp right at the north-eastern extreme of the Old City and meanders down to St Stephen's Gate where you must descend from the Rampart Walk. Watch out for young boys who may try to relieve you of a few shekels by claiming that the exit gate is stuck and then 'fixing' it.

St Stephen's Gate marks the introduction to the Stations of the Cross/Via Dolorosa route. This is a quiet part of the city and as you head back into the Old City you will see the Bab al Arbat entrance (for Muslims only) to the Haram ash-Sharif. Half-way along the Sh'ar Ha'Arayot you will come across on your left the first Station of the Cross, where Jesus was condemned to death by Pontius Pilate. From here the Via Dolorosa begins in earnest and you enter once more the tourist side of the Old City with shops selling wooden cribs, crosses, and other Christian memorabilia.

Follow the Via Dolorosa as far as the Church of the Holy Sepulchre (see the Via Dolorosa map on p 95) and visit the site of Jesus' crucifixion and burial. This most holy of Christianity's pilgrimage sites will either entrance or disappoint you. Linger as long as you feel necessary.

Following Herod's death in 4 BC the palace was used by the Roman procurators as their Jerusalem residence until it was largely destroyed by Jewish rebels in 66 AD. The Byzantines, who came along some 250 years later, mistook the mound of ruins for Mt Zion and presumed that this was King David's palace – hence the name 'Tower of David'. They constructed a new fortress on the site.

As Jerusalem changed hands, so too did possession of the Citadel, passing to the invading Muslim armies and then to the Crusaders, who added the moat. It took on much of its present form in 1310 under the Mamluk Sultan Malik an-Nasir, with

Walking Tours of the Old City

Upon exiting head right towards the Christian Quarter Rd with its many carpet and souvenir shops and turn left. Walk left down to where this road meets busy David St and turn right past more shops until you reach Jaffa Gate.

Walk 2 – The Southern Ramparts and the Jewish and Armenian Quarter
- Allow about 1¼ hours for this less strenuous and more moderate walk
- See Maps 8 and 9

Start your walk from the southern side of Jaffa Gate. The entrance is not obvious, so follow the sights. The first part of the walk takes you past the rather misnamed Armenian Garden. This rather derelict piece of the Old City is less an exotic botanical display than an overgrown wasteland used mainly for parking cars by the Armenian religious community.

The wall turns sharply left at the south-western extremity of the Old City where, had the original intentions been carried out, the wall would have swung out to encompass Mt Zion. The cost-cutting by the architects cost them their heads and Mt Zion remains to this day firmly outside the Old City. There are good views over the Church of the Dormition and the buildings containing King David's Tomb and the Coenaculum – the site of the Last Supper.

The walk then continues along an apparently treacherous section of wall which has only flimsy iron railings to save you from plunging into Armenian Patriarchate Rd below. Little is given away, even from this vantage point, of the small and rather mysterious Armenian Quarter to your left. Continue onwards and downwards until you reach your exit at the Dung Gate.

From the Dung Gate head straight for the Western Wall Plaza and the obligatory visit to Judaism's holiest site, the Western Wall. Take in the sights and sounds of this always vibrant part of the Old City. *Bar mitzvah* celebrations often take place here – sometimes several at the same time.

From the plaza head up the ramp and stairs to the left to enter the Jewish Quarter proper. Make for Hurva Square with its reconstructed synagogues, Jewish Quarter Rd and the Cardo, the main street of Roman Jerusalem.

Find Habad Rd and turn right into Or HaChaim St, wandering along the narrow, stone-clad streets of this residential part of the Jewish Quarter. Turn left onto Arafat St and skirt the closed and otherwise inaccessible main Armenian Quarter compound until you meet up with the only public road that traverses the Quarter, Armenian Patriarchate Rd. Follow this to the right and around, passing the Armenian Museum and St James' Cathedral along the way.

End your walk back at Jaffa Gate.

Suleyman the Magnificent making further additions between 1531 and 1538.

Suleyman was responsible for the gate by which the Citadel is now entered, and it was on the steps here that General Allenby accepted the surrender of the city on 9 December 1917, bringing to an end exactly 400 years of rule by the Ottoman Turks.

Fittingly for a site that represents a microcosm of the city through the ages, the Citadel also serves as the **Tower of David Museum of the History of Jerusalem** (☎ 627 4111, fax 628 3418, email tower@ netvision.net.il). Its numerous rooms contain some impressive dioramas, artefacts, holograms and videos that tell a version of the city's story. Visitors can follow one of four or five special signposted routes through the museum, including one for the disabled.

The entrance to the Citadel is just inside Jaffa Gate. From April to October it's open from 9 am, closing at 5 pm Sunday to Thursday, and 2 pm Friday, Saturday and holiday eves. From November to March the museum opens at 10 am and closes at 4 pm (10am to 2 pm Saturday). At 11 am daily there's a free guided tour in English.

One of the highlights is a detailed large-scale model of Jerusalem, made in the late 19th century and discovered almost 100 years later in a Geneva warehouse. It's displayed in an underground chamber reached from the central courtyard garden.

Every important historical site in Israel seems to feel the need to put on a sound and light show and the Citadel joins the club with a production of questionable quality. The show is presented in English at 9.30 pm on Monday and Wednesday and at 9 pm on Saturday. There are performances in French, German and Hebrew on other days of the week at differing times. Wrap up well if you are going because evenings are often surprisingly chilly, even in summer.

Admission to the sound and light show only is 24 NIS (students 17 NIS), or you can buy a combined ticket that includes the museum entry fee for 40 NIS (students 28 NIS).

If all of this is not enough, there is the 'Mystery in the Citadel' in which you become detective, judge and jury over a light-hearted historical murder. Four suspects lead the audience around part of the museum in search of the murderer of Aristobulus III, the high priest and brother-in-law of King Herod. For this pleasure expect to pay 28 NIS (students 24 NIS) or buy a combined ticket (including the museum entry fee) for 38 NIS (students 32 NIS). This is conducted at 10 pm in summer and 9 pm in winter.

Haram ash-Sharif/Temple Mount

Dominating not only the Old City but in some ways the whole country, this vast esplanade, known either as Haram ash-Sharif (The Noble Sanctuary) in Arabic or Har HaBayit (Temple Mount) in Hebrew, has become a spiritual keystone to the Jewish and Muslim faiths and something of an obstacle to peace between the two peoples.

Though all three great monotheistic faiths agree on the sanctity of this place, (which has been identified as ancient Mt Moriah on which Abraham was called to sacrifice his son in a test of his faith), in no way does a shared sense of holiness translate into any form of kinship.

Instead, the area (the closest spot on earth to paradise in Islamic belief) is surrounded by barbed wire and sharpshooters and is patrolled by watchful flak-jacketed soldiers. Religious Jews still bristle at the presence of the Muslims on the site of the First Temple, destroyed by Nebuchadnezzar, and the Second Temple, destroyed by the Romans. Muslims, who have worshipped at their mosque here for 1300 years, rebuff all demands for Jewish access, seeing these as attempts to further erode Palestinian rights.

Periodically there are clashes at the gates, tear gas mists the air and more blood is spilt. In 1999 a Jewish extremist was sentenced to jail for plotting to start a holy war by desecrating the area by throwing a pig's head into the Al-Aqsa Mosque. The angel may have stayed the hand of Abraham but he's done far less well since.

For the impartial visitor, the Haram ash-Sharif/Temple Mount provides a relaxing contrast to the noise and congestion of the surrounding narrow streets. An artificial plateau constructed by Herod the Great when he enlarged the Second Temple, it's a flat paved area the size of a couple of football fields. Its edges are fringed with some attractive Mamluk buildings and, at the south, the older Al-Aqsa Mosque; positioned at the centre is the Dome of the Rock.

Nine gates connect the enclosure to the surrounding narrow streets, and although you can leave the compound by any of them, non-Muslims are only allowed to enter through two: Gate of the Moors (Bab al-Maghariba), reached from the Western Wall plaza, and Chain Gate (Bab as-Silsila), at the eastern end of Bab as-Silsila St.

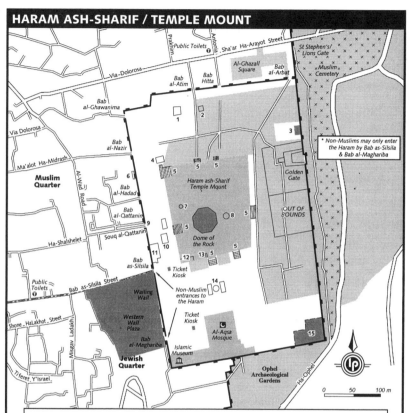

HARAM ASH-SHARIF / TEMPLE MOUNT

Map labels:
Public Toilets, Sha'ar Ha-Arayot Street, St Stephen's/Lions Gate, Praghim, Antonia
Via Dolorosa, Al-Ghazali Square, Bab al-Arbat, Muslim Cemetery
Bab al-Atim, Bab Hitta
Bab al-Ghawanima
Bab al-Nazir
Via Dolorosa
Ma'alot Ha-Midrash
Muslim Quarter
Al-Wad Road
Bab al-Hadad
Bab al-Qattanin
Ha-Shalshelet
Souq al-Qattanin
Bab as-Silsila
Public Toilets
Bab as-Silsila Street
Shone - HaLakhot Street
Misgav Ladakh
Wailing Wall
Western Wall Plaza
Tiferet Y'Israel
Bab al-Magharība
Islamic Museum
Jewish Quarter
Haram ash-Sharif Temple Mount
Golden Gate
OUT OF BOUNDS
Dome of the Rock
Ticket Kiosk
Non-Muslim entrances to the Haram
Ticket Kiosk
Al-Aqsa Mosque
Ophel Archaeological Gardens
Ha-Ophel

* Non-Muslims may only enter the Haram by Bab as-Silsila & Bab al-Magharība

0   50   100 m

---

1 **Dome of Suleyman Pasha**
2 **Sabil - Public Fountain**
3 **Solomon's Throne**
4 **Sabil of Sheikh Budir**
5 **The Stairs of Scales of Souls**
   Muslims believe that scales will be hung from the
   column-supported arches at the top of these stairs
   on Judgment Day to weigh the souls of the dead.
6 **Small Wall**
   A little visited northern extension of the Western Wall.
7 **Dome of the Ascension**
   According to Muslim tradition Mohammed prayed
   here before his ascent.
8 **Dome of the Chain**
   This is the smaller version of the Dome of the Rock,
   in the exact centre of the Haram. Mystery surrounds
   the reason for its construction. A popular theory is
   that it was a trial-run for the real thing; another is
   that it was the Haram's treasury. Its name comes from
   the legend that Solomon hung a chain from the dome
   and those who swore falsely whilst holding it were
   struck by lightning.
9 **Gate of the Cotton Merchants**
   This is the most imposing of the Haram's gates, make a
   point of departing through here into the Mamluk-era

arcaded market of the Cotton Merchants
(Souq al-Qattanin).
10 **Sabil of Qaitbay**
   Though overshadowed by its more illustrious neighbours,
   this is one of Jerusalem's most beautiful structures.
   It was built by Egyptians in 1482 as a charitable act to
   please Allah, and it features the only carved stone dome
   outside Cairo.
11 **Mamluk Arcade**
12 **Dome of Learning**
   Along with parts of the façade of the Al-Aqsa Mosque,
   this is one of the very few remaining Ayyubid
   (1187-1250) structures in Jerusalem. Note the
   very unusual entwined columns flanking the door.
13 **Summer Pulpit**
   Built by the Mamluks in the 14th century and renovated
   by the Ottomans, this was used to deliver outdoor sermons.
14 **Al-Kas Fountain**
   One of many ablutions fountains on the Haram
   for the ritual washing before prayers.
15 **Solomon's Stables**
   A cavernous vaulted hall under the Haram,
   constructed by the Crusaders to accommodate their horses.
   Unfortunately it's closed except by arrangement.
   This area is out of bounds.

Entrance to the Haram itself is free, but to visit the two mosques (highly recommended) and the museum, a ticket must be purchased for 22 NIS (students 12 NIS) from the ticket kiosk just inside the Bab al-Maghariba.

Visiting hours are slightly confusing as they are based around Muslim prayer schedules, which follow the lunar calendar. Basically, the Haram is open from 8 am to 3 pm Saturday to Thursday (closed Friday), although those inside by then are allowed to stay until 4 pm. During prayers (approximately from 11.30 am to 12.30 pm in winter and 12.30 to 1.30 pm in summer) the museum shuts and entry to the mosques is for Muslims only. Note also that during the month of Ramadan (see the boxed text 'Public Holidays' and the Public Holidays section in the Facts for the Visitor chapter) the Haram is only open from 7.30 to 10 am. It is completely closed on Muslim festivals such as the Eid.

Visitors must be suitably dressed. Long robes are available for those with bare legs and arms, but you should dress appropriately out of respect. As well as patrols of Israeli Defence Force (IDF) soldiers and Palestinian police to keep the peace there are plain-clothed Muslim guards monitoring decency (note that couples holding hands will be rebuked).

In addition, certain unmarked areas are strictly off-limits and if you stray, even unintentionally, you will be lectured and perhaps even arrested. Presumably Islamic authorities are loath to see casual visitors getting too close to the sensitive Golden Gate, though the out-of-bounds eastern end of the Haram ash-Sharif/Temple Mount is a rather scruffy and dry concrete plateau of olive trees. Stay away from the sides of the Al-Aqsa Mosque, the Solomon's Stables corner and the garden on the eastern side.

The self-appointed guides can also be a complete nuisance. They often approach with an official bearing and ask to see your ticket, then with it in hand they'll lead you over to one or other of the mosques while launching into a historical spiel; if you hadn't planned on taking a guide, then stop them fast. Their other trick is to fluster people by saying, 'Quick, quick the mosque is closing, you have to hurry to see it'; of course they attach themselves to explain everything 'quick, quick'. Simply don't hand over your ticket to anyone but the guy at the door, who is also the person to ask about closing times.

Note that in addition to removing your footwear to enter the mosques, all bags and cameras must be left outside, too – leave someone on watch, as Lonely Planet has received letters warning about thefts.

For best effect, visit the Islamic Museum and Al-Aqsa Mosque before you visit the spectacular Dome of the Rock.

Islamic Museum Although there are some interesting objects in here they are so badly displayed and labelled that most visitors have little incentive to linger for more than a few minutes. However, admission is included in the price of your ticket to the mosques, so you might as well take a look. Exhibits include ornate architectural pieces from various mosques, weaponry, textiles, ceramics, Qurans, glassware and coins.

Al-Aqsa Mosque While the Dome of the Rock serves more as a figurehead than a mosque, Al-Aqsa is a functioning house of worship, accommodating up to 5000 praying worshippers at a time.

Believed by some to be a converted 6th century Byzantine church, Muslims maintain that Al-Aqsa was built from scratch from 705 to 715 AD by the son of Abd al-Malik, patron of the Dome. Clarification of the issue is complicated because nothing much remains from the original structure, which was twice destroyed by earthquakes in its first 60 years. What is sure is that the mosque was largely rebuilt in the 10th century, while the facade was remodelled by the Ayyubids (1187-1250 AD).

The modern structure is a conglomeration of restorations and rebuilding, featuring columns donated, strangely enough, by Benito Mussolini, and elaborately painted ceilings courtesy of Egypt's King Farouk. The intricately carved *mihrab* (prayer niche indicating the direction of Mecca), however, does date from the time of Saladin, as did an equally magnificent carved wooden *minbar* (pulpit) which was lost in a 1969 fire started by a deranged Australian (see the boxed text 'Jerusalem Syndrome' later in this chapter).

Dome of the Rock Enclosing the sacred rock upon which Abraham prepared to sacrifice his son and from which, according to Islamic tradition, the Prophet Mohammed was accepted into heaven to pray with the other saints and Allah himself, the Dome was built between 688 and 691 AD, making it one of the oldest surviving Islamic monuments in existence. Its patron was the Umayyad Caliph Abd al-Malik. His motives were shrewd as well as pious: the caliph was concerned that the imposing Church of the Holy Sepulchre was seducing Arab minds.

In asserting the supremacy of Islam, Abd al-Malik had his Byzantine architects take as their model the rotunda of the Holy Sepulchre. But they didn't adopt the dark, gloomy interiors or austere stone facades of the Christian structures; instead, their mosque was covered, both inside and out, with bright mosaics and scrolled verses from the Quran, while the crowning dome was covered in solid gold that shone as a beacon for Islam.

A plaque was laid inside honouring Al-Malik and giving the date of construction. Two hundred years later the Abbasid Caliph al-Mamun altered this to claim credit for himself; he neglected, however, to amend the original date.

During the reign of Suleyman the Magnificent the original, badly deteriorated exterior mosaics were removed and replaced. They were renewed again in 1963. The gold dome also disappeared long ago, melted down to pay off some caliph's debts. The current convincingly 'golden' dome of anodised aluminium was financed by Gulf State nations. Essentially, however, what you see today is the building as conceived by Abd al-Malik; very little has changed since its completion.

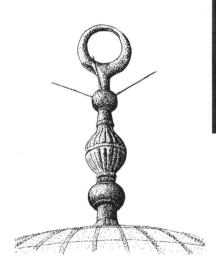

Decorative pinnacle on the Dome of the Rock

Inside, lying directly under the 20m-high dome and ringed by a wooden fence, is the rock from which Mohammed began his Night Journey to heaven (his footprint is apparently visible in a small glass encased area). Muslim tradition also has it that this is the foundation stone of the world.

Steps below the rock lead to a cave known as the 'Well of Souls' where the dead are said to meet twice a month to pray. If you descend into the cave you will more than likely find Muslim women praying and you may be ushered out by an anxious guard after only a few seconds.

Orthodox Jews may not enter the mosque because they might inadvertently trespass on the site of the Holy of Holies, the innermost sanctum of the Temple containing the Ark of the Covenent which only the High Priest is permitted to enter (and even then only on Yom Kippur).

Do not be surprised to see young Israeli army recruits – minus boots and weapons – being given a cultural tour of the mosque by an equally youthful female officer.

Mamluk Buildings You ought to make a point of strolling around the northern section of the Haram to admire the façades on the northern and western sides. Mainly religious schools, these buildings feature some delightfully ornate stonework. See Mamluk Buildings in the Muslim Quarter section later in this chapter.

Western Wall (Map 9)

In stark contrast to the ornate magnificence of the Muslim's Dome of the Rock, the Western Wall (HaKotel HaMa'aravi or just HaKotel) is actually nothing more than a bare stone wall. However, it still manages to be one of the most captivating places in all of Jerusalem.

It is part of the retaining wall built by Herod the Great in 20 BC to contain the landfill on which the Second Temple compound stood. The Temple was destroyed in 70 AD, but since the *Shehina* (Divine Presence) is believed never to have deserted the Wall, it's regarded as the most holy of all Jewish sites.

During the Ottoman period the Wall grew as a place of pilgrimage where Jews would come to mourn and lament their ancient loss – hence the name 'Wailing Wall'. At this time houses pressed right up to the wall, leaving just a narrow alley for prayer. In 1932 this scene was evocatively portrayed in a painting by the Russian Jewish artist Marc Chagall (now held by the Tel Aviv Museum of Art).

In 1948 the Jews lost access to the Wall when the whole of the Old City was taken by the Jordanians. Nineteen years later, when Israeli paratroopers stormed in during the Six Day War they fought their way directly to the Wall. Their first action on securing the Old City was to bulldoze the Arab neighbourhood to create the plaza that exists today.

The area immediately in front of the Wall now operates as a great open-air synagogue. It's divided into two areas: a small southern section for women, and a more active, larger northern section for men. Here the black-garbed *haredim* rock backwards and

---

God's Fax Line

Courtesy of Israel's national phone company, Bezek, the pious can now fax the Almighty. Messages received on fax 02-561 2222 are collected and taken once a day (Shabbat excepted) by telephone company employees down to the Western Wall to be wedged in-between the stones.

Bezek says that over 100 messages a day are received, and more during Jewish holidays. There is no fee charged for the service. If you don't want to send a fax, you can make a virtual visit to the Wall at its own Web site www.kotelkam.com complete with WebCam so that you can observe the comings and goings of the faithful *and* post an email message.

---

forwards on their heels, bobbing their heads in prayer and occasionally breaking off to press themselves against the Wall and kiss the stones. To celebrate the arrival of Shabbat there is always a large crowd at sunset on Friday and students from the nearby Yeshiva HaKotel shuffle down to dance and sing. The Wall is also a popular site for bar mitzvahs, held on Shabbat or on Monday and Thursday mornings.

The Wall's fascination extends beyond the Jewish world. Madonna visited, as did Michael Jackson one Saturday in 1993. His visit in particular raised the ire of the orthodox Jews because of the accompanying entourage of camera-clicking press corps (photography is forbidden on Shabbat). Nevertheless, non-Jewish visitors who dress modestly and, in the case of men, don the obligatory *kippah* (skullcap) are permitted to approach the Wall.

Note the different styles of stonework: the huge lower layers are the Herodian stones, identifiable by their carved edges, while the strata above that, which are chiselled slightly differently, date from the time of the construction of the Al-Aqsa Mosque. Also visible at close quarters are the wads of paper, from sticky notes to exercise books, stuffed into the cracks – it's believed that prayers inserted into the Wall have a better than average chance of being answered.

The Wall is accessible 24 hours a day, and admission is free. We highly recommend that you see the place bathed in moonlight.

Wilson's Arch Situated to the north of the men's prayer section, this arch (now inside a room) carries Bab as-Silsila St above to the Temple Mount across the former Tyropoieion (Cheesemaker's) Valley. It was once used by priests on their way to the Temple. Look down the two illuminated shafts to get an idea of the wall's original height. Possibly Hasmonean (150-40 BC) but at least Herodian, the room's function is unknown.

Women can reach this room via an archway west of the men's area, near the telephones. Theoretically, the arch room is open from 8.30 am to 3 pm on Sunday, Tuesday and Wednesday; from 12.30 to 3 pm on Monday and Thursday; and from 8.30 am to noon on Friday (closed Saturday).

The Western Wall Tunnel

This controversial tunnel runs from the plaza of the Western Wall along the base of the original Herodian wall to an exit on the Via Dolorosa in the Arab Quarter. It was dug by archaeologists who wished to explore the now hidden lower section of the original structure. Contrary to the hysteria whipped up in the media at the time, the tunnel runs outside the confines of the Temple Mount compound not under it, and offers a worthwhile excursion for the truly curious but non-claustrophobic (it is a fairly narrow passage).

Telephone bookings must be made beforehand and (perhaps to assuage Muslim sensitivities) visits are limited to certain times of the week. Archaeological Seminars charge US$16 for a morning tour and US$14 in the afternoon. For contact details see under Archaeological Digs in the Activities section at the end of this chapter.

There Goes the Neighbourhood

On Al-Wad Rd, a little south of the fork with Souq Khan as-Zeit St in the heart of the Muslim Quarter, a broad arch bridges the street, and from one of its windows hangs an Israeli flag the size of a bedsheet. This is the controversial home of the hawkish Israeli politician and war hero Ariel Sharon.

In a widely publicised move, Sharon purchased the property as a statement of his belief that Jews should be able to live anywhere within Israel. His lead inspired the formation of Ateret Kohanim, an organisation dedicated to 'Judaising' the Old City through purchasing property (often covertly) in predominantly Muslim areas.

The majority of less extremist Israelis regard this attempted settlement as needlessly aggressive and Ateret Kohanim do not enjoy widespread support. Nevertheless, Palestinians have little choice but to live with it, and a round-the-clock detachment of IDF soldiers lounges around the doorway of Beit Sharon to see that they do so quietly. Ironically, Sharon doesn't actually live here, underscoring the fact that his purchase of the property was nothing more than a political gesture.

It's also illuminating to note that prior to Sharon's 'occupation', the Israeli government had forbidden an Arab family to move into the Jewish Quarter of the Old City to reclaim an ancestral plot, citing as a reason the fact that it would disturb the homogeneity of the neighbourhood.

Jewish Quarter (Map 9)

Roughly defined as the area south of Bab as-Silsila St and east of Habad St, the Jewish Quarter is an area you'll recognise immediately by its scrubbed stone; neat, precise edges; and the air of no one being home.

Flattened during the fighting in 1948, the Jewish Quarter has been almost entirely reconstructed since its recapture by the Israelis in 1967. Though modern, the architecture of the quarter is traditional in style, designed to maintain the character of the Old City, though lacking a little in spirit.

There are few historic monuments above ground level but the digging that went on during construction unearthed a number of interesting archaeological finds, some of which date back to the time of the First Temple (c 1000-586 BC). Everything is well signposted, and while there's nothing unmissable, the area around the Quarter Cafe is very pleasant and there are great views of the Haram ash-Sharif/Temple Mount and Western Wall from the stairs beside the Church of St Maria.

The Cardo Cutting a broad north-south swath, this is the reconstructed Cardo Maximus, the main street of Roman and Byzantine Jerusalem. At one time it would have run the whole breadth of the city, up to what is now Damascus Gate, but in its present form it stops just south of David St, the tourist souq. It serves as the main entry into the Jewish Quarter from the Muslim and Christian areas.

As depicted on the 6th century **Madaba Map** of the Old City (which you can see at the Roman Square excavations), the Cardo would have been a wide colonnaded avenue flanked by roofed arcades. A section of it to the south has been restored to something like its original appearance, while the rest has been reconstructed as an arcade of expensive gift shops and galleries of Judaica. There are wells to allow visitors to see down to the levels beneath the street where there are strata of wall from the era of the First and Second temples.

Upstairs, above one of the Cardo galleries, is a permanent exhibition called **One Last Day**. This is a set of photographs taken by John Phillips, on assignment for *Life* magazine, on the day the Jewish Quarter fell to the Jordanians in 1948. The exhibition can be viewed from 9 am to 5 pm Sunday to Thursday, and from 9 am to 1 pm on Friday, closed Saturday. Admission is 4 NIS.

Broad Wall Just east of the Cardo and north of Hurva Square, looking like a derelict lot between blank-faced apartment blocks, is a stretch of crumbling masonry known as the Broad Wall. This is actually an exposed portion of the remains of a fortified stone wall dating from the time of King Hezekiah (c 701 BC).

Israelite Tower & Rachel Ben-Zvi Centre Buried beneath a modern apartment block on Shone HaLakhot St and reached by a short flight of steps, the **Israelite Tower** is a gate tower dating from the time of the Babylonian siege and the destruction of the First Temple. The site is open from 9 am, closing at 5 pm Sunday to Thursday, and 2 pm on Friday. Admission is 4 NIS, which also covers entry to the Burnt House and the Wohl Museum of Archaeology (see under Museums following).

Across from the Israelite Tower, the **Rachel Ben-Zvi Centre** (☎ 628 3448), also on Shone HaLakhot St, exhibits a scale model of Jerusalem in the First Temple period, which illustrates archaeological findings from the time of King David and his successors. Other exhibits include an audiovisual history of the city from 1000 to 586 BC. The centre is opens from 9 am to 4 pm Sunday to Thursday, and by appointment only on Friday. Admission is 8 NIS (students 6 NIS).

Hurva Square & Synagogues Hurva Square is the tree-shaded social centre of the Jewish Quarter. It's easily identifiable by a lone single-brick arch, almost all that remains of the **Hurva Synagogue**. The synagogue was originally dedicated by the

GREG ALFORD

The surviving arch of the Hurva Synagogue

Ashkenazi community in 1864 but was destroyed by the Jordanians in 1948. On regaining control of the Old City in 1967, the Jews decided to rebuild their place of worship but, despite a succession of plans being submitted by various renowned architects, no agreement on how to proceed could be reached. The re-creation of one of the arches that supported the synagogue dome was as far as the matter got.

Adjoining the Hurva Synagogue is the **Ramban Synagogue**, its name an acronym for Rabbi Moshe Ben Nahman. The synagogue was established in 1400 in a stable bought from an Arab landlord, but problems started when a mosque (the minaret of which still stands) was built nearby. The upshot was that in 1588 the Jews were banned from worshipping there and the synagogue was converted into a workshop. It was reconsecrated as a synagogue only in 1967, some 380 years later.

South of Hurva Square, on HaTupim St, are four **Sephardic Synagogues**, two of which date back at least as far as the 16th century. In accordance with a law of the time stating that synagogues could not be taller than neighbouring buildings, this grouping was sunk deep into the ground – a measure that certainly saved the buildings from destruction during the bombardment of the quarter in 1948. Instead, the synagogues were looted by the Jordanians and then used as sheep pens.

The synagogues have been restored using the remains of Italian synagogues damaged during WWII and are back in use for morning and evening services. They are open from 9.30 am, closing at 4 pm Sunday to Thursday, and 12.30 pm Friday. There is a small admission fee.

Batei Mahseh Square & Shelter Houses Batei Mahseh was at one time the quarter's largest square, presided over by the **Rothschild Building**, a grand old thing built in 1871 with funds provided by Baron Wilhelm von Rothschild of Frankfurt (his family emblem is visible, engraved on the upper part of the façade). The building now houses the offices of the Company for the Reconstruction and Development of the Jewish Quarter.

The **Shelter Houses** facing the Old City walls on Batei Mahseh St were built by Jews from Germany and Holland for the poor of the quarter. Little or no rent was charged and tenants were chosen by lottery. During the last fortnight of the battle for the quarter in May 1948, hundreds of resident Jews found shelter in their basements.

St Maria of the Germans Located on the northern side of the steps leading to the Western Wall, this was formerly a complex which comprised of a church, a hospital and a hospice, built by German Knights Hospitallers around 1128. When archaeologists first discovered and excavated these remains in the 1970s there were demands from the ultra-orthodox community to have them destroyed because the haredim objected to the existence of a church along a major route to the Western Wall.

Museums Perhaps the Jewish Quarter's most impressive complex is the **Wohl Museum of Archaeology** (☎ 628 3448), which details the lavish lifestyle enjoyed in Herod's city. Exhibits include frescoes, stucco reliefs, mosaic floors, ornaments, furniture and household objects. It's open from 9 am, closing 5 pm Sunday to Thursday, 1 pm Friday (closed Saturday). Admission is 10 NIS, which also covers entry to the Israelite Tower and the Burnt House.

The **Burnt House** (☎ 628 7211), next to the Quarter Cafe, is the reconstruction of a luxurious house in what was the Upper City of the Second Temple period. There's also an audiovisual show presented in a number of languages, including English. The Burnt House has the same opening hours as the Wohl Museum of Archaeology and one ticket is good for the two.

Following the same idea but jumping a long way forward in time, the **Old Yishuv Court Museum** (☎ 628 4636, 6 Or HaChaim St) west of the Cardo, is a reconstructed house in which each room illustrates an aspect of Jewish life in the quarter before the destruction of 1948. It's open from 9 am to 2 pm Sunday to Thursday. Admission is 12 NIS (students 10 NIS).

Of more limited interest is **Siebenberg House** (☎ 628 2341, 35 Misgav Ladakh St), on the corner of HaGittit St. It's a private residence with excavations in the basement. Finds include a Hasmonean cistern and parts of what may have been an aqueduct that carried water from Solomon's Pools to the Temple. It's open by appointment only.

Muslim Quarter (Map 7)

This is the most densely populated area of the Old City, with some 26,000 inhabitants – twice as many as the three other quarters combined. Depending on your tastes it's either claustrophobic and a hassle, or completely exhilarating. Enter the melee through the permanently congested Damascus Gate, squeezing by a tractor and dodging the young Arab boys riding their vendors carts down the slope. About 100m along, the street forks, and there is a busy felafel stall wedged between the two prongs.

Bearing to the left is Al-Wad Rd, lined with vast showrooms of brass items such as coffee pots and trays, in among sweet shops, vegetable stalls and an egg stall. This route leads directly to the Western Wall, crossing the Via Dolorosa along the way. The section of the Via Dolorosa heading uphill to the west (right) is crowded with Christian pilgrims, tour groups and shoppers battling for right of way. Souvenir shops line the route, with ceramics a speciality. Bearing to the right at the fork is Souq Khan as-Zeit St, which is even busier than Al-Wad Rd. It's lined with fruit, vegetable, sweet, hardware and oriental spice and nut shops.

St Anne's Church Constructed in a restrained and elegant Romanesque style, St Anne's is generally agreed to be the finest example of Crusader architecture in Jerusalem. Its popularity with pilgrims, however, has more to do with the traditional belief that the building's crypt is the site of the home of Joachim and Anne, the parents of the Virgin Mary. Next to the church are some impressive ruins surrounding the biblical Pool of Bethesda.

The Crusaders built the church in 1140, at the same time constructing a small adjacent chapel with a stairway leading down to the pool beside which Jesus is supposed to have healed a sick man (John 5:1-18). When Jerusalem fell to the armies of Saladin, St Anne's became a Muslim theological school; an inscription still to be seen above the church's entrance testifies to this. Successive rulers allowed the church to fall into decay, and by the 18th century it was roof-high in refuse. In 1856 the Ottoman Turks presented the church to France in gratitude for its support in the Crimean War against Russia, and it was reclaimed from the garbage heap.

Apart from its architectural beauty, the church is noted for its acoustics, and a prominent sign requests that only hymns be used for sound checks.

St Anne's is just off the Via Dolorosa, a short distance west of St Stephen's Gate. It is open from 8 am to noon and 2 to 6 pm (2 to 5 pm in winter) Monday to Saturday, closed Sunday. Admission is 3NIS. The entrance is marked 'St Anne – Peres Blanc'; do not use the other door marked 'Religious Birthplace of Mary'.

Ecce Homo Arch & the Convent of the Sisters of Zion East of Al-Wad Rd an arch punctured by two windows spans the Via

Dolorosa. This is the 19th century echo of an arch that was the eastern gate of the city during Roman times. The lower portion of the original Roman arch is preserved in the church belonging to the adjacent Convent of the Sisters of Zion. It's thought that the structure would have been a triumphal arch with a high portal in the middle flanked by two smaller gateways; the remains in the church are of one of the smaller arches (the bit spanning the street outside was designed to imitate the arc of the main central arch). The arch is traditionally, if improbably, the place where Pilate took Jesus out and proclaimed 'Ecce Homo' (Behold the Man) – improbably, because the arch wasn't constructed until the time of Hadrian, some 100 years afterwards.

The convent church is open from 8.30 am to 12.30 pm and 2 to 5 pm Monday to Saturday, closed Sunday. Admission is free.

Next door, is a basement chapel known as the **Prison of Christ**, which is supposedly the site of the rock-hewn cellars where Jesus and other criminals of his day were held. This is now the property of the Greek Orthodox Church.

Mamluk Buildings Overshadowed by the splendours of the Haram ash-Sharif/Temple Mount, and clustered outside its northern and western walls, are some excellent examples from the golden age of Islamic architecture. This area was developed during the era of the Mamluks (1250-1517), a dynasty of soldier-slaves ruling out of Egypt. They drove the Crusaders out of Palestine and Syria and followed this military success with an equally impressive campaign of construction, consolidating Islam's presence in the Levant with masses of mosques, *madrassas* (theological schools), hostels, monasteries and mausoleums. Their buildings are typically characterised by the banding of red and white stone (a technique known as *ablaq)* and by the elaborate carvings and patterning around windows and in the recessed portals.

All of these features are exhibited in the **Palace of the Lady Tunshuq**, built in 1388 and found halfway down Aqabat at-Takiya

(150m east of the Tabasco Hostel & Tearooms). The façade is badly eroded but the uppermost of the three large doorways still has some beautiful inlaid marble, while a recessed window is decorated with another Mamluk trademark, the stone 'stalactites' known as *muqarnas*. The palace complex now serves as workshops and an orphanage. The **Tomb of the Lady Tunshuq** (1398) is opposite.

Continue downhill to the junction with Al-Wad Rd, passing on your right, just before the corner, the last notable piece of Mamluk architecture built in Jerusalem, the **Ribat Bayram Jawish** (1540), a one-time pilgrims' hospice. Compare this with the buildings on Tariq Bab an-Nazir St, straight across Al-Wad Rd, which are Jerusalem's earliest Mamluk structures, built in the 1260s before the common use of ablaq. This street is named after the gate at the end which leads through into the Haram ash-Sharif/Temple Mount, but non-Muslims may not enter.

Some 100m south on Al-Wad Rd, opposite the Old City Restaurant, is **Tariq Bab al-Hadid St**; it looks uninviting but wander down, through the archway, and enter a street entirely composed of majestic Mamluk structures. Three of the four façades belong to madrassas dating from 1358 to 1440, while the single-storey building is a *ribat,* or hospice, from 1293. The last archway on the left gives access to the Small Wall (see that section following), while the green gate at the end of the street leads into the Haram; again, non-Muslims may not enter here.

Continuing south back on Al-Wad Rd, it passes the Souq al-Qattanin and then, on the left, Sabil Suleyman. It terminates in a police checkpoint at the mouth of the tunnel down to the Western Wall plaza; however, the stairs to the left lead up to the busy Bab as-Silsila St and the Bab as-Silsila Gate, one of the two ways into the Haram for non-Muslims. Just before the gate is the tiny kiosk-like **Tomb of Turkan Khatun** (1352), which features a façade adorned with uncommonly asymmetric carved geometric designs. In the early 20th century the tomb served as a stall for a lemonade seller.

Look out also for the restored **Khan as-Sultan**, a 14th century *caravanserai* (merchants' inn and stables) at the top end of Bab as-Silsila St. A discreet entrance just up from the large 'Gali' sign leads into a courtyard surrounded by workshops, and from a staircase tucked in the left-hand corner as you enter you can climb up to the Old City rooftops.

Souq al-Qattanin Founded on the remains of a Crusader market, the Mamluks built this tunnel-like arcade in the mid-14th century. Almost 100m long, it has 50 shops on the ground floor with residential quarters above. The name means 'market of the cotton merchants'. Sadly, little trade goes on here now and most of the former stores and workshops are just used for warehousing. The complex also included two *hammams* (public baths), one of which is undergoing restoration and may at some future point open to visitors.

Sabil Suleyman This is one of several *sabils* (drinking fountains) erected by the Ottoman Sultan Suleyman in 1536-37. As well as refreshing the populace, the fountains were used for the ritual ablutions that must be performed before a Muslim prays. Suleyman's other existing sabils are beside the Bab as-Silsila Gate, at the junction of Bab an-Nazir and Al-Wad Sts, on the Haram ash-Sharif/Temple Mount, and outside the city walls just south of Sultan's Pool.

Small Wall This site, also known as the Hidden Wall, is at the end of the last narrow passageway off Tariq Bab al-Hadid St. It is marked by a small sign, visible from Al-Wad Rd where Tariq Bab al-Hadid St begins. This section of wall, now part of a Muslim house, is the same Western Wall that thousands of Jews flock to a few hundred metres to the south. The Arabs living here don't seem to mind visitors' traffic and have provided an outside light on their 1st floor to enable Jews to read their prayers.

Zalatimo's A sweet shop famed for its pancakes and sticky confectionery, this place is also well known because its back room opens onto the remains of the original entrance to the Church of the Holy Sepulchre.

Christian Quarter (Map 6)

This quarter houses churches, monasteries and other religious institutions belonging to more than 20 different Christian sects, all subject to the pull of the Holy Sepulchre.

As you enter from Jaffa Gate, the first two streets to the left – Latin Patriarchate Rd and Greek Catholic Patriarchate Rd – indicate the tone of the neighbourhood, named as they are after the offices there. The roads lead to St Francis St, and in this quiet area around New Gate the local Christian hierarchy resides in comfort.

Elsewhere in the quarter, comfort and quiet give way to the chaos and crush of the tourist bazaars. Descending from Omar ibn al-Khattab Square into the heart of the Old City, **David St** is the main tourist trap, where visitors to the Holy City are victim to a barrage of persistent sales patter offering all manner of kitsch objects that no-one could conceivably ever have any use for. Branching north off David St, **Christian Quarter Rd** deals in a better class of souvenir with an emphasis on religious icons. South-east of the Church of the Holy Sepulchre, **Muristan Market** is usually less crowded than the other markets and specialises in leather goods, clothes and carpets.

As you approach the bottom end, David St switches from religious souvenirs over to food – a row of cavernous vaults on the left with fruit and vegetable stalls inside date from the time of the Crusades. The street ends by crashing into a trio of narrow alleyways which, if followed to the left, converge into Souq Khan as-Zeit St, one of the main thoroughfares of the Muslim Quarter. The squeamish should avoid the first of these narrow alleys, Souq al-Lahamin, (the **Butchers' Market**). Followed to the right, Souq Khan as-Zeit becomes the Cardo and leads into the Jewish Quarter.

Via Dolorosa

Winding up first through the Muslim Quarter and then the Christian Quarter, the Via Dolorosa, or Way of Sorrows, is the route that Jesus took as he carried his cross to Calvary. The sanctity of the modern-day route, however, is based purely on faith, not fact.

The history of the Via Dolorosa can be traced back to the days when Byzantine pilgrims, on the night of Holy Thursday, would go in procession from Gethsemane to Calvary along roughly the same route as today's Via Dolorosa, although there were no official devotional stops en route. By the 8th century, some stops had become customary but the route had changed considerably and now went from Gethsemane around the outside of the city walls to Caiaphas' house on Mt Zion, then to the Praetorium of Pilate at St Sophia near the Temple and eventually to the Holy Sepulchre.

In the Middle Ages, with Latin Christianity divided into two camps, the Via Dolorosa was twinned – each of the two claimed routes primarily visiting chapels belonging to either one or the other faction. In the 14th century, the Franciscans devised a walk of devotion that included some of the present-day stations but had as its starting point the Holy Sepulchre. This became the standard route for nearly two centuries but it was eventually modified by the desire of European pilgrims to follow the order of events of the gospels, finishing at the site of the Crucifixion rather than beginning there.

Historians, however, point to one devastating flaw in the routing of the Via Dolorosa, which is that it's more likely that Jesus was condemned to death by Pilate on the other side of the city at the Citadel, next to Jaffa Gate. This was Herod's palace and Pilate's official residence in Jerusalem. Various Bible references to the trial taking place on a platform and in the open support this theory, as the palace is known to have had such a structure. Hence, a more probable route for Jesus to have taken would be east along David St, north through the Butchers' Market of today, and then west to Golgotha.

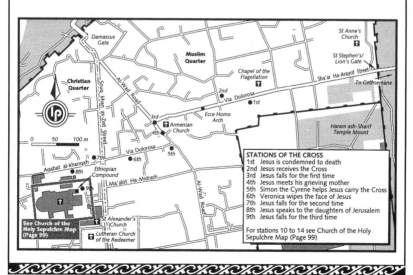

STATIONS OF THE CROSS
1st Jesus is condemned to death
2nd Jesus receives the Cross
3rd Jesus falls for the first time
4th Jesus meets his grieving mother
5th Simon the Cyrene helps Jesus carry the Cross
6th Veronica wipes the face of Jesus
7th Jesus falls for the second time
8th Jesus speaks to the daughters of Jerusalem
9th Jesus falls for the third time

For stations 10 to 14 see Church of the Holy Sepulchre Map (Page 99)

The Stations of the Cross

Every Friday at 3 pm, the Franciscan Fathers lead a cross-bearing procession along Stations of the Cross, which attracts many pilgrims, tourists and souvenir hawkers. See the Via Dolorosa map and the Church of the Holy Sepulchre map, on pages 95 and 99 respectively, for the locations of the 14 stations.

1st Station The place where Jesus was tried before Pilate, the 1st station is actually inside the working Islamic Al-Omariyeh College. The entrance is the door at the top of the ramp on the southern side of the Via Dolorosa, east of the Ecce Homo Arch. Entry is not always permitted so don't be surprised if you are asked to leave. There is nothing of official Christian value to see anyway, although there is a great view of the Haram ash-Sharif/Temple Mount through the barred windows on the upper level.

2nd Station The condemnation of Jesus and his receiving the cross, the 2nd station is in the Franciscan Church of the Condemnation. The Chapel of Flagellation to the right is where he was flogged. Built in 1929, the design on the domed ceiling incorporates the crown of thorns, and the windows of the chapel around the altar show the mob who witnessed the event. The church and chapel are open daily from 8 am to noon and 2 to 6 pm from April to September, and daily from 8 am to 5 pm during October-March. Admission is free.

3rd Station This is where Jesus fell for the first time while carrying the cross. It's the point at which the Via Dolorosa joins up with Al-Wad Rd. Adjacent to the entrance of the Armenian Catholic Patriarchate Hospice, the station is marked by a small Polish chapel.

4th Station This marks the spot where Jesus faced Mary, his mother, in the crowd, and is located beyond the hospice, next to the Armenian Church (the wonderfully named Our Lady of the Spasm), There is a mosaic of a pair of sandals inlaid in the church courtyard which supposedly marks the spot on which Mary stood as Jesus passed by.

5th Station Where the Romans co-opted Simon of Cyrene to help Jesus carry the cross. As Al-Wad Rd continues south towards the Western Wall, the Via Dolorosa breaks off to climb to the west, with the Station right on the corner. It is marked by signs around a door.

6th Station The place where St Veronica wiped Jesus' face. It is further along the street, on the left-hand side and easy to miss. The Greek Orthodox Patriarchate in the Christian Quarter displays what is claimed to be the cloth, which shows the imprint of a face.

7th Station This is where Jesus fell for the second time and it's marked by signs on the wall on the west of Souq Khan as-Zeit St, the main market street at the top of this section of the Via Dolorosa. In the 1st century, this was the edge of the city and a gate led out to the countryside, a fact which supports the claim that the Church of the Holy Sepulchre is the genuine location of the crucifixion, burial and resurrection.

8th Station Where Jesus told some women to mourn for themselves and their children and not for him; this is another station easy to miss. Cut straight across Souk Khan as-Zeit St from

The Stations of the Cross

the Via Dolorosa and ascend Aqabat al-Khanqah St. Just past the Greek Orthodox Convent on the left is the stone and Latin cross marking the spot.

9th Station Where Jesus fell for the third time. Come back down to where the Via Dolorosa and Aqabat al-Khanqah St meet and turn right (south, away from Damascus Gate) along Souq Khan as-Zeit St. Head up the stairway on your right and follow the path around to the Coptic Church. The remains of a column in its door mark the place.

LEE FOSTER

Jesus met his mother, Mary, at the 4th station of the cross.

Retrace your steps to the main street and head for the Church of the Holy Sepulchre; the remaining five stations are inside – see the Church of the Holy Sepulchre map on p 97.

10th Station This is where Jesus was stripped before crucifixion. As you enter the church, head up the steep stairway immediately to your right. The chapel at the top is divided into two naves. The right one belongs to the Franciscans, the left to the Greek Orthodox Church. At the entrance to the Franciscan Chapel is the Station.

11th Station Still in the chapel, this is where Jesus was nailed to the cross.

12th Station The Greek Orthodox Chapel is the site of the Crucifixion.

13th Station Between the 11th and 12th stations is the Deposition, where the body of Jesus was taken down and handed to Mary.

14th Station This is the Holy Sepulchre, the Tomb of Jesus. Walk down the narrow stairs beyond the Greek Orthodox Chapel to the ground floor and you will see that the Holy Sepulchre is to be found in the centre of the rotunda, which would be on your left if you were entering from outside.

The actual tomb is inside the Sepulchre. Candles lit by pilgrims who make a donation dominate the small tomb, with the raised marble slab covering the rock on which Jesus' body was laid. Around the back of the Holy Sepulchre is the tiny Coptic Chapel where pilgrims kiss the wall of the tomb, encouraged by a priest who expects a donation.

See the following page for more information about the Church of the Holy Sepulchre.

Church of the Holy Sepulchre Despite being the central shrine of Christianity, this church is much less distinctive than something like the Dome of the Rock or the Western Wall, and it happens that many people wander in and out without any idea of what they've just visited. Then again, many who do arrive in full knowledge of what the church represents often leave sorely disappointed. Hemmed in by a bunch of other buildings, from outside the church has no visual impact while inside it is dark, cramped and noisy. In his book *Winner Takes All*, travel writer Stephen Brook describes the interior as looking like 'a cross between a building site and a used furniture depot'.

If the church itself is lacking a little in the appearance of temporal splendour, at least

Rites & Wrongs

While the Greek Orthodox, the Armenians, the Copts and the Roman Catholics, along with the Christian Ethiopians and Syrians, are united in a shared set of central beliefs, the equitable shared possession of the Church of the Holy Sepulchre has proved completely beyond them all. Territorial claims are zealously guarded and something as seemingly insignificant as the moving of a rug by a few centimetres has in the past resulted in blood being spilt.

In the 19th century, clergymen at the church would display to visitors the scars and wounds sustained in the frequent sectarian punch-ups. When an earthquake in 1927 caused extensive damage and seriously weakened the already crumbling structure, the intense rivalry meant that it took over 30 years before the various factions could be brought to cooperate on an agreed program of repairs.

To circumvent at least one potential area of dispute, the keys to the church have been in the possession of a local Muslim family since the Ottoman period and it's their job to unlock the doors each morning and secure them again at night.

its claim to stand over Golgotha, the place of the crucifixion, burial and resurrection of Christ, is fairly well respected.

At the start of the 1st century this was a disused quarry outside the city walls. According to the Gospel of John (19:17, 41-2), Jesus' crucifixion occurred at a place outside the city walls with graves nearby. Archaeologists have discovered tombs dating from the correct period, so the site is at least compatible with the biblical account.

Until at least 66 AD Jerusalem's early Christian community held celebrations of public worship at the tomb. Hadrian filled in the area in 135 AD to build a temple dedicated to Venus/Aphrodite, but the Christian tradition persisted. Some 200 years later, Constantine and his mother, Helena, chose the site to construct a church to commemorate the Resurrection. To make room for the new development, substantial buildings had to be demolished; a move of a mere 100m either way would have saved a lot of time and expense but it was insisted that this had to be the church's location – a story which lends credence to the site's claims to authenticity. Work on Constantine's church commenced in 326 AD and it was dedicated nine years later.

When his armies took the city in 638 AD, Caliph Omar was invited to pray in the church but he refused, generously noting that if he did his fellow Muslims would have turned it into a mosque. In 1009, however, the church was destroyed by the mad Caliph Hakim. Unable to afford the necessary major repairs, Jerusalem's Christian community had to wait until 1042, when the Byzantine Imperial Treasury provided a subsidy.

This wasn't enough to pay for a complete reconstruction of the original church, so a large part of the building was abandoned, but an upper gallery was introduced into the rotunda and an apse was added to its eastern side as a sort of compensation. This was the building that the Crusaders entered in 1099 as the new rulers of Jerusalem. They made significant alterations and re-consecrated the building in 1149, on the 50th anniversary of their capture of the city.

CHURCH OF THE HOLY SEPULCHRE

1 Franciscan Convent
2 Church of the Apparition
3 Franciscan Sacristy
4 Mary Magdalene Chapel
5 Seven Arches of the Virgin
6 Byzantine Arcade
7 Crusader Arcade
8 Prison of Christ
9 St Longinus Chapel
10 Division of the Rainment Chapel
11 St Dimas Altar
12 Chapel of the Discovery of the Cross

13 Church of St Helena
14 Chapel of the Mocking
15 Greek Choir
16 St Nicodemus Chapel of the Syrians
17 Three Maries Altar
18 Tombs of Crusader Kings Baldwin I & Godfrey de Bouillon
19 Armenian Chapel
20 40 Martyrs' Chapel
21 St John's Chapel
22 St James' Chapel
23 Chapel of the Franks

24 Chapel of St Michael & All Saints
25 St John's Chapel (Armenian)
26 St Abraham's Monastery
27 Cisterns of St Helena
28 Golgotha
29 Greek Chapel
30 Chapel of Calvary
31 Medici Altar
32 Franciscan Chapel

STATIONS OF THE CROSS
10th Jesus is stripped of his garments
11th Jesus is nailed to the cross
12th Jesus dies on the cross
13th The body of Jesus is taken from the cross
14th Jesus is laid in the Holy Sepulchre

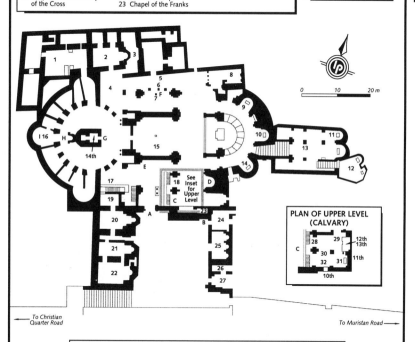

To Christian Quarter Road

To Muristan Road

A 12th century Crusader façade and entrance.
B Crusader entrance to Calvary, closed in 1187 to become the Chapel of the Franks.
C Calvary – reached by the steep stairs on the immediate right inside the entrance.
D The Chapel of Adam. The bodies of Baldwin I and Godfrey de Bouillon, the Crusader kings, lay on the two benches near the door until they were moved in 1810.
E The Stone of Unction commemorates Jesus' anointment before his burial. It is not the actual stone on which his body was laid out as it was only put in place in 1810.
F While all others have been restored, these two columns have been left in the same damaged condition as they were after the 1808 fire. Look carefully and you'll see that they are actually two halves of one column – it used to support the rum of the dome but was removed and sawn in two in the 11th century to carry the newly constructed upper gallery.
G The tomb monument, memorably described as a 'hideous kiosk'. The 1808 fire destroyed a previous 11th century structure which replaced the rock tomb that the mad Caliph Hakim had removed in 1009. There is usually a queue to get inside.
H Coptic Chapel at the rear of the Holy Sepulchre.
I This is part of the 4th century apse and wall, now part of the Syrian chapel.

The structure of the present church remains to a large extent a Crusader construction, although major repairs and additions were rendered necessary after a fire swept through the building in 1808. After much wrangling (and a sizeable bribe – see the 'Rites & Wrongs' boxed text earlier), the authorities gave the Greek Orthodox the job of carrying out the reconstruction, and they are still responsible for the much reviled structure over the tomb of Christ – described by a modern Franciscan author as looking 'like a gaudy newspaper kiosk in Salonika'.

In 1998 a British archaeological team was granted permission to excavate, on the proviso that worshippers are not disturbed.

The Church of the Holy Sepulchre is open daily from 4.30 am to 8 pm (closing at 7 pm in winter) to anyone suitably dressed – the guards are very strict and may refuse entry to anyone deemed not in compliance (see Society & Conduct in the Facts about Jerusalem chapter).

Christ Church Located just across from the Citadel in the Jaffa Gate area, this was the Holy Land's first Protestant church, consecrated in 1849. It was built by the London Society for Promoting Christianity Amongst the Jews (now CMJ – the Church's Ministry among the Jews). The society's founders were inspired by the belief that the Jews would be restored to what was then Turkish Palestine, and that many would then convert, acknowledging Jesus as the Messiah before he returned.

In order to present Christianity as something not totally alien to Judaism, Christ Church was built in the Protestant style with several similarities to a synagogue. Jewish symbols, such as Hebrew script and the Star of David, figure prominently at the altar and in the stained glass windows.

Greek Orthodox Patriarchate Museum On Greek Orthodox Patriarchate Rd this museum (☎ 628 4006) presents some of the treasures of the Patriarchate and goes a little way towards presenting the history of this locally dominant church.

It's open from 9 am to 1 pm and 3 to 5 pm Tuesday to Friday, and from 9 am to 1 pm Saturday, closed Sunday and Monday. Admission is 5 NIS. Follow Greek Catholic Patriarchate Rd north from Jaffa Gate, turn right into Greek Orthodox Patriarchate Rd and it's on the left.

St Alexander's Church On a corner just east of the Holy Sepulchre, this is the home of the Russian mission in exile. The attraction for visitors is a much-altered triumphal arch that once stood in Hadrian's forum, built here in 135 AD. Through the arch and to the left at the top of the steps you can see a section of the pavement that was once part of the platform of Hadrian's temple to Venus/Aphrodite.

St Alexander's Church is only open at 7 am on Thursday when prayers are said for Czar Alexander III. The excavations are open from 9 am to 1 pm and 3 to 5 pm Monday to Thursday; ring the bell for entry. There's a small admission fee.

Ethiopian Monastery Follow the route to the 9th Station of the Cross; up the steps off Souq Khan as-Zeit St, at the point at which the street to the Church of the Holy Sepulchre turns to the right, there is a small grey door directly ahead that opens onto a roof of that church. The cluster of huts here has been the Ethiopian Monastery (known as Deir as-Sultan) since the Copts forced them out of their former building in one of the many disputes between the various Christian groups.

The monks live among the ruins of a medieval cloister erected by the Crusaders on the site where Constantine's basilica had been previously. The cupola in the middle of this roof section admits light to St Helena's crypt below. Access to the Church of the Holy Sepulchre is possible via two nearby points. One is through the Ethiopian Chapel (most of these monks do not speak much English but are very friendly, so ask for directions); the other way is to go left out of the Ethiopian monastery and through the Copts' entrance.

Lutheran Church of the Redeemer

Dominating the Old City skyline with its tall white tower, the present structure was built in 1898 on the site of the 11th century church of St Mary la Latine. The closed northern entrance porch is a medieval remnant, and is decorated with the signs of the zodiac and the symbols of the months. The tower is popular for the excellent views to be had over the Old City. It's open from 9 am to 5 pm Monday to Saturday (closed between 1 and 1.30 pm and all day Sunday). Admission is 2 NIS.

Church of St John the Baptist Jerusalem's oldest church, St John the Baptist stands in a hidden section of the Muristan area and is usually overlooked by tourists, having been buried by the gradual rise in the level of the surrounding streets. However, the entrance from Christian Quarter Rd is clearly signposted. This leads you into the courtyard of a more recent Greek Orthodox monastery, where a monk will usually be present to open the church for you.

Originally built in the mid-5th century, the church was restored after the Persians destroyed it in 614 AD. In the 11th century Italian merchants of Amalfi built a new church using the walls of the earlier building, which became the cradle of the Knights Hospitallers. The present façade with the two small bell towers is a more recent addition, as are a few other alterations made to ensure the building's stability.

Armenian Quarter (Map 8)

Although they number only a few million worldwide, the Armenians have their own quarter within the Old City. Theirs was the first nation to officially embrace Christianity when the king converted in 303 AD, and they established themselves in Jerusalem sometime in the following century. The kingdom of Armenia disappeared at the end of the 4th century and Jerusalem was adopted as their spiritual capital. They've had an uninterrupted presence here ever since.

The core of the quarter is actually one large monastic compound, a reminder of the fact that until relatively recently the Armenian presence in Jerusalem was traditionally purely religious. This began to change earlier this century with the arrival of a large secular element fleeing Turkish persecution. That persecution escalated in 1915 to an attempted genocide in which over 1.5 million Armenians were killed.

The community today, which numbers about 1500, is still very insular, having its own schools, library, seminary and residential quarters discreetly tucked away behind high walls. The gates to this city within a city are closed early each evening.

There's little to see for the casual visitor, but if you can make it during the limited hours that its doors are open then it is well worth taking a look inside **St James' Cathedral**. Armenian ceramics are also justly famous and there are a couple of good showrooms off Armenian Orthodoxy Patriarchate Rd.

Armenian Compound About 1200 Armenians now live in what used to be a large pilgrims' hospice. It became a residential area after 1915, when refugees from the Turkish massacres settled here. The empty, wide courtyards are a rare sight in the Old City. The area is generally closed to visitors but you can telephone (☎ 628 2331) or ask at the entrance to St James' Cathedral to make an appointment for a visit.

St James' (Jacques') Cathedral Attending Mass here could seriously shake the nonfaith of an atheist. With its incense-loaded air, diffusely glowing golden lamps hung from the ceilings and floors covered in dark, richly patterned carpets, this place has a seductive aura of ritual and mystery lacking in every other Christian site in this most holy of cities.

It was the Georgians in the 11th century who first constructed a church here in honour of St James, on the site where he was beheaded and became the first martyred disciple. The Armenians, in favour with the ruling Crusaders, took possession of the church in the 12th century and the two parties shared restoration duties. The tiles date from much later (in the 18th century), and were imported from Turkey.

The Sunday service really is an impressive affair with no less than nine hooded Armenian priests taking part. There is quite a bit of to-ing and fro-ing around the altar area by the numerous helpers and there is impressive choral chanting from a 20-voice choir – all in Armenian. Most of the participants are foreign tourists.

The church is on Armenian Orthodoxy Patriarchate Rd and is only open for services, which are held from 6.30 to 7.15 am and 2.45 to 3.30 pm Monday to Friday, and from 2.30 to 3 pm Saturday and Sunday.

Armenian Museum Originally a theological seminary (1843), with an attractive courtyard enclosed by arched colonnades on two levels, the building that houses this museum (☎ 628 2331) is a lot more fascinating than most of the exhibits it presents. It's reasonably well-stocked and the displays are in English. There is a detailed display of the 1915 Armenian Genocide. Look out for the large Armenian globe dating from 1852 in the Paul Bedoukian Hall. It's open from 9 am to 4.30 pm Monday to Saturday, closed Sunday. Admission is 5 NIS (students 3 NIS).

St Mark's Chapel This is the home of the Syrian Orthodox community in Jerusalem, whose members here number about 200. (There are only about three million worldwide, of whom two million are in Malahar in central India.) The Syrian Orthodox believe the chapel, on Ararat St, occupies the site of the home of St Mark's mother, Mary, where Peter went after he was released from prison by an angel.

It is claimed that the Virgin Mary was baptised here, and according to Syrian Orthodox tradition this, not the Coenaculum on Mt Zion, is where the Last Supper took place. One thing to look out for is the painting on leather of the Virgin and Child attributed to St Luke and, according to the caretaker, painted from life.

The chapel is open from 7 am to noon and 2 to 5 pm Monday to Saturday, closed Sunday. Admission is free but donations are welcome.

Alex de Rothschild Craft Centre This is a small gallery (☎ 628 6076, 4 Or HaChaim St) displaying ceramics, glass, enamel and textiles by Jewish artists and craftspeople. It's open from 10 am to 4 pm Sunday to Thursday, and admission is free.

MT ZION (MAP 2)

Now denoting the steep slope south from the Old City walls beyond Zion Gate, 'Mt Zion' during the Old Testament period referred to a hill east of what is now known as the City of David. The name change came in the 4th century, based on new interpretations of religious texts. This compact area contains the possible site of the biblical Last Supper and, less probably the site of the Tomb of David.

Also located here is the **grave of Oskar Schindler**; from Zion Gate walk directly downhill, bearing left at the fork to go past the Chamber of the Holocaust. Go around the bend and cross the road to the entrance of the Christian cemetery. Ask the guard if you really get lost.

The hustlers who offer themselves as guides on Mt Zion are a particularly unpleasant lot, persistent and occasionally becoming quite nasty when their services are declined. They also have a scam going outside David's Tomb in which they ask for a donation in exchange for a cardboard *kippah*; men do need to cover their heads to visit but *kippot* are handed out gratis inside the tomb and no donations are requested. Studiously avoid these unwelcome hustlers and do not respond to them when approached.

King David's Tomb

A Crusader structure erected two millennia after his death, the Tomb of King David provides little spectacle. What's more, the authenticity of the site is highly dubious; the likelihood is that David is buried under the hill of the original Mt Zion, east of the

The Jerusalem Syndrome

It is a recognised medical fact that Jerusalem can send a person crazy. This happens to about 200 visitors a year. Overwhelmed by the impact of the Holy City, people suddenly believe themselves to be Biblical characters. Take, for instance, the story of the muscular Canadian Jew who, claiming to be Samson, proved his point by smashing his way through a hospital wall to escape. Or the elderly American Christian who believed she was the Virgin Mary and went to Bethlehem to look for the Baby Jesus, inviting anyone who would listen to his birthday party.

This sort of delusional behaviour has become a recognised phenomenon known as the Jerusalem Syndrome – the only documented psychiatric disorder to be named after a city.

Although many of these individuals arrived at Ben-Gurion airport with a recorded history of mental aberration, about a quarter of the cases on file had no previous psychiatric record. Although their ages and backgrounds vary, a significant proportion of those afflicted with the syndrome are unmarried 20 to 30-year-old Christians or Jews from North America and Western Europe who grew up in religious homes. Men seem to outnumber women two to one.

Most of the syndrome sufferers wind up at the state psychiatric hospital, Kfar Shaul, on the outskirts of West Jerusalem. Treatment tends to take the form of observation until the patient is deemed well enough to be flown home. Doctors have found it virtually pointless to try to persuade the deluded that they are not who they claim to be. Those with no pre-existing psychiatric condition tend to recover in a week or so, and are often extremely embarrassed by the whole incident.

Not surprisingly, all sufferers come from highly religious backgrounds. Dr Yair Barel, a past director of Kfar Shaul, suggests that the ultra-religious have such an idealised view of Jerusalem that they simply can't cope with the real city.

The Jerusalem Syndrome is nothing new. In 1033, the 1000th anniversary of the Crucifixion, crowds of pilgrims refused to leave Jerusalem. An Austrian in the 1870s went around introducing himself as Elijah, and in the 1930s, an English Christian woman was certain that Christ's Second Coming was imminent and would regularly climb Mt Scopus to welcome him back with a cup of tea.

Christians who develop the syndrome tend to break down at such traditional sites as the Mount of Olives, the Via Dolorosa or the Garden Tomb, and identify with such characters as Jesus or the Virgin Mary, although John the Baptist is apparently the most popular choice. In addition to Samson, 'incarnations' of Jewish sufferers have included Moses and King David.

While serious incidents in the past have included a deluded Australian Christian setting fire to the Al-Aqsa Mosque in 1969 and an American Christian smashing up the interior of the Church of the Holy Sepulchre in 1992, Israeli authorities have gone on high alert in the run-up to the year 2000. Shin Bet and Mossad agents have been seconded to a special unit created to deal with 'millennial madness'.

The authorities' worst nightmare is a mass influx of assorted Jewish and Christian 'end-timers' who believe that attacking the Haram ash-Sharif/Temple Mount will hasten Armageddon and the arrival/return of the Messiah. There is also the fear of mass hysteria and possibly suicide if the Messiah does not appear 'on time'. To make matters worse, Muslims, who aren't usually affected, may become paranoid that apocalyptic Christians and messianic Jews may join together to blow up the Haram ash-Sharif/Temple Mount.

The Israeli authorities signalled their intentions in 1998 and 1999 with the pre-emptive arrest and deportation of various Christian groups and individuals suspected of being a danger to Jerusalem's holy places.

City of David. However, this is one of the most revered of the Jewish holy places, and from 1948 to 1967, when the Western Wall was part of the territory held by the Jordanians and off-limits to Jews, the tomb was the stand-in main centre of pilgrimage. It still serves as a popular prayer hall.

To get to the tomb head south from Zion Gate, bear right at the fork and then left. It's open daily from 8 am, closing at 6 pm Saturday to Thursday and 2.20 pm Friday. Admission is free.

The Coenaculum

Popularly thought to be the site of the Last Supper (*coenaculum* is Latin for 'dining hall'), this is the only Christian site in Israel which is administered by the local government. Part of the King David's Tomb complex, the Coenaculum (also known as the Cenacle) was a site of Christian veneration during the Byzantine period. The Franciscans acquired it in the Middle Ages, but they were later expelled by the Turks. Under Ottoman rule the Coenaculum became a mosque and Christians were barred from entering, just as Jews were kept from King David's Tomb.

Like the Tomb, the Coenaculum dates from the time of the Crusaders, and to the right of the entrance there is a pair of faded Crusader coats of arms. The southern wall still bears the *mihrab*, the prayer niche hollowed by the Muslims when they converted the chapel into a mosque.

The Coenaculum is above King David's Tomb, reached via a discreet stairway (behind a door to the left) that leads up from the courtyard. Many visitors mistake the first large room for the real thing, but you need to walk across the hall to enter the much smaller chamber beyond, which is where Jesus is believed to have shared the Last Supper with his disciples.

The Coenaculum Chapel is open daily from 8 am to noon and 3 to 6 pm, but the Last Supper room closes at 4 pm. Admission to both is free. Special services are occasionally held; contact the Christian Information Centre for details.

Museum of King David

This museum next to King David's Tomb is associated with the Diaspora Yeshiva, the adjacent Jewish school for religious study. The main exhibit is some rather bizarre modern art. The only reason for the museum's existence appears to be to raise money for the *yeshiva* – donations of at least 5 NIS are strongly encouraged. It's open from 10 am, closing at 5 pm Sunday to Thursday, and 2 pm Friday (closed Saturday).

Church & Monastery of the Dormition

This beautiful neo-Romanesque church is the site believed to be where the Virgin Mary fell into 'eternal sleep'; its Latin name is *Dormitio Sanctae Mariae* (Sleep of Holy Mary). The current sturctures, owned by the German Benedictine order, were designed by a German architect, Heinrich Renard, and consecrated in 1906. The church was damaged during the battles for the city in 1948 and 1967 when its tower, which overlooked Jordanian army positions on the Old City ramparts below, was used by Israeli soldiers.

The church's interior is a bright contrast to many of its older and duller peers nearby. A golden mosaic of Mary with the Baby Jesus is set in the upper part of the apse; below it the Prophets of Israel are portrayed. The chapels around the hall are dedicated to saints: St Willibald, an English Benedictine who visited the Holy Land in 724; the Three Wise Men; St Joseph, whose chapel is covered with medallions featuring kings of Judah as Jesus' forefathers; and St John the Baptist. The floor is decorated with names of saints and prophets and zodiac symbols.

The crypt has a stone effigy of Mary asleep on her deathbed with Jesus calling his mother to heaven. The surrounding chapels were donated by various countries. In the apse is the Chapel of the Holy Spirit, who is shown coming down to the Apostles.

The church is open daily from 8 am to noon and 2 to 6 pm. Admission is free. The complex also has a pleasant café where cakes and drinks (including beer) are served.

THINGS TO SEE & DO

Church of St Peter in Gallicantu

Almost hidden by the trees and the slope of the hill, the Church of St Peter 'at the Crowing of the Cock' is the traditional site of the denial of Jesus by his disciple Peter 'before the cock crowed three times' (Mark 14:66-72). Built on the foundations of previous Byzantine and Crusader churches, the modern structure is also believed to stand on the site of the house of the High Priest Caiaphas, where Jesus was taken after his arrest. A cave beneath the church is said to be where Christ was incarcerated.

Whatever your beliefs, the view from the balcony of the church across to the City of David, the Arab village of Silwan and the three valleys that shape Jerusalem is reason enough to justify a visit.

The church is open from 8 to 11.45 am and 2 to 5 pm Monday to Saturday (from 2 to 5.30 pm during May-September), closed Sunday. Admission is free. The church is reached by turning east (left) as you descend the road leading from Mt Zion down and around to Sultan's Pool. Roman steps lead down from the church garden to the Gihon Spring in the Kidron Valley.

KIDRON VALLEY

Apart from the wonderful views, the points of interest here are the tombs. These can be reached by following the road north from the entrance to Hezekiah's Tunnel or by taking the downhill path off Jericho Rd about 150m south of the Church of All Nations. The Arab village that clings to the eastern slope of the valley is Silwan.

Valley of Jehoshaphat (Map 2)

The northernmost part of the Kidron Valley, this is the area between the Haram ash-Sharif/Temple Mount and the Mount of Olives. Jehoshaphat in Hebrew means 'God Shall Judge', and this narrow furrow of land is where the Bible says that the events of the Day of Judgement are to take place. All of humanity will be assembled together on the Mount of Olives, with the Judgement Seat on the Haram opposite. Two bridges will appear, spanning the valley, one made of iron and the other made of paper. According to God's judgement each person will be directed to cross one or the other. We know the ending of course, for the Bible gives it away: the iron bridge will collapse and those sent across it will die, while the paper bridge will hold up and offers the promise of eternal life.

At the southern end of the Valley of Jehoshaphat are four Jewish tombs (known collectively as the Kidron Valley tombs), some of the most complete monuments from the time of the Second Temple.

Absalom's Pillar Dating from the 1st century BC, this monument is easily identified by its inverted funnel-shaped roof. The anachronistic Absalom after whom it was named was one of the sons of King David. The roof aside, the monument is wholly carved in one piece from out of the hillside.

Tomb of Jehoshaphat Located behind Absalom's Pillar, this 1st century burial cave is notable for the impressive frieze above its entrance.

Tomb of B'nei Hezir Just to the south of Absalom's Tomb, this is a burial cave hewn out of the rock face. The gaping entrance is framed by a Greek-style pediment supported by two columns. An inscription on the frieze between the columns indicates that this is the tomb of the B'nei Hezirs (sons of the Hezirs), a family of Jewish priests. St James is popularly believed to have hidden here when Jesus was arrested nearby in the Garden of Gethsemane.

Tomb of Zechariah Like the neighbouring Tomb of B'nei Hezir, that of Zechariah, which features a cube with a pyramid on top, betrays a Hellenistic influence – in this case, in the form of Ionic pilasters decorating the façades. According to Jewish tradition, this is the place where the prophet Zechariah is buried, but, as usual, the archaeological evidence suggests otherwise; Zechariah died in the 6th century BC while the tomb dates from the 1st century BC.

City of David (Map 2)

The oldest part of Jerusalem, dating from before the 20th century BC, this is the confirmed site of the city captured and developed by King David. The excavations are the result of work – still in progress – that started in 1850.

Of interest to archaeologists is a signposted path that leads around the excavations. These include the Canaanite citadel of the Jebusite town that David conquered, a fortress built by David, and Jerusalem's Upper City where the wealthy resided and where buildings destroyed in the Babylonian conquest of 586 BC once stood.

The site is open daily from 9 am to 4 pm and admission is free. From the Dung Gate, head east (downhill), take the road to the right (just past the car park), then take a left along the path with the sign (just past the grocery shop) and follow it down to the bottom of the hill, where you turn right. If you don't see a sign ask for directions, as the slopes are too steep to want to get lost on. Continue downhill to reach Warren's Shaft.

Warren's Shaft (Map 2)

This was built by the Jebusites to ensure their water supply during a siege. It is just inside their city's defence wall and this is possibly where Joab entered the City of David. About 100m down from the entrance to the City of David excavations, a small museum features photos of the excavation work with explanations of the water supply situation as it used to be. A spiral staircase leads to a tunnel extending into the shaft, so bring a torch.

The shaft (☎ 628 8141) is open from 9 am to 5 pm Sunday to Thursday, 1 pm Friday (closed Saturday). Admission is 5 NIS (students 3 NIS).

From Warren's Shaft, you can proceed down to Hezekiah's Tunnel at the bottom of the hill.

Gihon Spring, Pool of Shiloah & Hezekiah's Tunnel (Map 2)

The Gihon Spring was the main reason why the Jebusites settled on the low Ophel Ridge rather than choosing the adjacent higher ground. Gihon means 'gushing', which is quite suitable as the spring acts like a siphon, pouring out a large quantity of water for some 30 minutes before almost drying up for between four and 10 hours. There is believed to be enough water to support a population of about 2500. The tunnel was built in about 700 BC by King Hezekiah to bring the water of the Gihon into the city and store it in the pool of Shiloah, or Siloam. Its purpose was to prevent invaders, in particular the Assyrians, from locating the city's water supply and cutting it off. The tunnel's length is 533m (335m as the crow flies).

Although narrow and low in parts, you can wade through the tunnel; the water is normally about half a metre to a metre deep. Due to the siphon effect it does occasionally rise, but only by about 15 to 20 cm.

The entrance steps leading down to the water are medieval. After about 20m the tunnel turns sharply to the left, where a chest-high wall blocks another channel leading to Warren's Shaft (near the City of David excavations, see the City of David section). Towards the tunnel's end the roof rises. This is because the tunnellers worked from either end and one team slightly misjudged the other's level, requiring them to lower the floor so that the water would flow. A Hebrew inscription was found in the tunnel, and a copy can be seen in the Israel Museum in West Jerusalem. Carved by Hezekiah's engineers, it tells of the tunnel's construction.

Enter the tunnel at its source at the Gihon Spring on HaShiloah Rd down in the Kidron Valley and just south of the resthouse. Turn left as you get to the foot of the hill from Warren's Shaft.

The tunnel is open from 9 am, closing at 5 pm Sunday to Thursday, and at 3 pm pn Friday (it's closed Saturday). Admission is 7 NIS. The wade takes about 30 minutes; wear shorts and suitable footwear. A torch is also required because the candles sold at the entrance won't stay alight in the draughty tunnel.

MOUNT OF OLIVES (MAP 2)

Rising above the city on the east, the Mount of Olives is dominated by the world's oldest and largest **Jewish cemetery**, as well as the many churches commemorating the events of the Passion and the Resurrection.

The cemetery dates from biblical times. Its importance is based on the belief that this will be the site of the resurrection of the dead when the Messiah comes on the Day of Judgement. One of those waiting here is former media baron Robert Maxwell, interred in one of the hillside tombs.

Most of the mount's churches and gardens are open in the morning, closing for at least two hours towards noon and reopening again in the mid-afternoon. However, the real draw – and what makes a visit to the Mount of Olives a 'must' – is the panoramic view it affords of the Old City. Up at the top, in front of the **Seven Arches Hotel** (cause of much controversy as it was built by the Jordanians over part of the ancient Jewish cemetery) is a promenade which triggers compulsive camera clicking in all who visit. Sunset isn't necessarily the best time to visit, as at this time of day the Old City is usually thrown into silhouette; instead come first thing in the morning, when the light is best.

You can walk from East Jerusalem or from St Stephen's Gate in the Old City, or take the bus to avoid what most find to be a strenuous walk. Arab bus No 75 runs from the station on Sultan Suleyman St.

Augusta Victoria

The Augusta Victoria complex was constructed in the late 19th century, a German entry in the 'bigger, bolder, more imposing' competition to achieve pre-eminence in the Holy City through overbearing architecture. Though nominally a church and attached hospice, this grouping of buildings has been called a vast monument to German imperialism. Fittingly, it became the headquarters of the German-Turkish military command during WWI. After their defeat, the compound was taken over by the British and put into use as the residence of their high commissioner. These days Augusta Victoria

Warning

The *Jerusalem Post* has reported that a priest who brings visitors to the Mount of Olives noted that during one week alone several people had had their pockets picked, a guide had been beaten up and a woman had been sexually assaulted.

Lonely Planet has also received letters from women readers who suffered unpleasant experiences while walking around here. In light of this, our advice is that women definitely should not visit the Mount of Olives alone or even in pairs – go with a male companion or as part of a group.

serves as an UNRWA-run hospital for Palestinians.

The Augusta Victoria **Church of the Ascension** has some noteworthy mosaics, paintings and masonry work, while the 65m-high tower has great views across to the Old City and the Judean Desert. The church is open from 8 am to 5.30 pm Monday to Saturday. Admission is free, but it costs 2 NIS to climb up the tower (6 NIS for the elevator). Arab bus No 75 stops outside.

Russian Chapel of the Ascension

Marked by a needle-point steeple – the tallest structure on the Mount of Olives – this church and monastery is built over the spot from which the Christian Orthodox church claims Jesus made his ascent to heaven. It is a bit hard to find, so look for a narrow alleyway leading off the main street, in among the shops and cafes. It is open from 9 am to 12 pm Tuesday and Thursday. Admission is free.

Mosque of the Ascension

Confusingly also sometimes referred to as the Church or Chapel of the Ascension, this is an alternative site for Jesus' journey skyward. The spot is marked by an odd little octagonal Crusader structure which stands on the site of an earlier Byzantine church. Saladin authorised two of his followers to acquire the site in 1198 and it has remained in Muslim possession ever since, functioning as a mosque. Christians are permitted to celebrate here each year on Ascension Day, 40 days after Easter.

The stone floor bears an imprint said to be the footstep of Jesus. Perhaps the reason for its unconvincing appearance today is that pilgrims in the Byzantine period were permitted to take bits of it away.

Opening hours vary but the cost of admission is 2 NIS.

Church of the Pater Noster

Helena, the mother of the emperor Constantine, had this church built beside the cave in which is it believed Jesus spoke to his disciples. (It is also known as the Church of the Eleona – derived from the Greek word *elaionas*, meaning 'olive grove'.) Destroyed by the Persians in 614, the site later became known as the place where Jesus taught the Lord's Prayer, a belief which inspired the Crusaders to construct an oratory among the ruins in 1106.

The most interesting things here are the attractive tiled panels on which the Lord's Prayer is inscribed in over 60 languages. In Latin, it begins 'Pater noster', hence the name of the church.

As you enter the gate, turn left and then right. The tomb is that of Princess de la Tour d'Auvergne, who purchased the property in 1886 and built the neighbouring Carmelite convent. The actual cave can be reached by going around the cloister to the left, down some stairs and through the first door on the right.

The site is open from 8.30 to 11.45 am and 3 to 4.45 pm Monday to Saturday, closed Sunday. Admission is free.

Tombs of the Prophets

Slightly to the north and below the viewing promenade are some ancient tombs, reputedly those of the prophets Haggai and Malachi, who lived in the 5th century BC.

The site is open from 9 am to 3 pm, Sunday to Friday, closed Saturday. Admission is free.

Church of Dominus Flevit

The original church on this site was built by Medieval pilgrims who claimed to have found the rock on the Mount of Olives where Jesus had wept for Jerusalem, hence the name Dominus Flevit ('the Lord wept').

When the modern, tear-shaped church was being built between 1954 and 1955 (designed by the Italian architect Antonio Barluzzi), excavations unearthed a 5th century monastery, the mosaic floor of which is on display, and a large cemetery dating back to about 1500 BC. The view of the Dome of the Rock from the window of the altar is particularly attractive.

The church is open daily from 8 to 11.45 am and 2.30 to 5 pm. Admission is free.

Russian Church of Mary Magdalene

Although badly tarnished by the weather, the seven gilded 'onion' domes of this White Russian church still form one of Jerusalem's most attractive and surprising landmarks. Built by Alexander III in 1886 in memory of his mother, Maria Alexandrovna, it is styled in the manner of of the 16th and 17th century Muscovite churches.

Russian Church of Mary Magdalene

The church is now a convent and has one of the city's best choirs. It's only open from 10 to 11.30 am on Tuesday and Thursday. Admission is free.

Church of All Nations & Garden of Gethsemane

Designed by the same architect responsible for Dominus Flevit up the hill, the classically styled Church of All Nations is notable for the glistening golden mosaic that adorns its facade (the mosaic depicts Jesus carrying the suffering of the world, hence the church's alternative name, the Basilica of the Agony). Built in 1924, it was financed by a consortium drawn from 12 nations. It's the successor to two earlier churches, the first erected in the 4th century but destroyed by an earthquake in the 740s, the second an oratory built over the ruins by the Crusaders but abandoned in 1345 for reasons unknown.

Around the church is the popularly accepted site of Gethsemane, the garden where Jesus was betrayed and arrested. The garden has some of the world's oldest olive trees (in Hebrew *gat shmanim* means 'oil press'), three of which have been dated as over 2000 years old, making them witnesses to whatever biblical events may have occurred here.

The garden is open daily from 8 am to noon and 2.30 to 4 pm. Admission is free. Entrance is not from the main road but from the narrow, steeply inclined alleyway running up behind the church.

Church of All Nations

Tomb of the Virgin Mary

On her death in the middle of the 1st century, Mary is believed to have been interred here by the disciples. A monument was first constructed in the 5th century but was repeatedly destroyed. Almost hidden in the valley, the present monument is a 12th century Crusader edifice, built on Byzantine foundations. It is owned by the Greek Orthodox Church, while the Armenians, Syrians and Copts have shares in the altar.

The tomb is open from 6 to 11.45 am and 2.30 to 5 pm Monday to Saturday, closed Sunday. Admission is free.

On the main road beside the stairs down to the tomb, the small cupola supported by columns is a memorial to Mujir ad-Din, a 15th century Muslim judge and historian.

St Stephen's Church

This Greek Orthodox church is on the southern side of the main Jericho road as it curves away from the Old City walls towards the Mount of Olives. Largely ignored by guides and visitors alike, it was completed in 1968 as a 'modern Byzantine' church. It is near the site where Stephen, the first Christian martyr, was stoned to death. The two pleasant ladies who look after the church are happy to guide visitors around. Ring the bell to see if anyone is in – there are no set hours. Admission is free.

MT SCOPUS

Scopus (from the Greek *skopeo*, 'to look over') lies on the same ridge to the north of the Mount of Olives. It overlooks one of the most vulnerable approaches to Jerusalem and its strategic location has played a decisive role in the many battles for the city over the centuries. In 70 AD the Roman legions of Titus camped here, as did the Crusaders in 1099 and the British in 1917. During the 1948 War, Arab forces attacked from here. One of the anomalies of the 1949 cease-fire was that Mt Scopus became an Israeli enclave in Jordanian territory. Every fortnight a convoy under UN protection was allowed to cross from Jewish West Jerusalem with supplies and relieve the Israeli garrison.

In addition to the Hebrew University campus and the military cemetery, other places of note here include **Hadassah Hospital** (Map 1), designed in the 1930s by German architect Erich Mendelsohn and renowned as one of the world's top medical centres, and the Mormon University. Take Arab bus No 75 to the Augusta Victoria Hospital and walk 20 minutes, or take Egged bus Nos 4, 4A, 9, 23 or 28 from Jaffa Rd in the New City to the university.

Hebrew University (Map 2)

Founded in 1925 and featuring some distinctive modern architecture, the Hebrew University was the world's first secular Hebrew institute of higher learning. Between 1948 and 1967, when Mt Scopus was a Jewish enclave isolated in Jordanian-held territory, the university was relocated to Givat Ram, and it is now divided between the two campuses. There are free guided tours in English from Sunday to Thursday at 11 am lasting from 1-1½ hours. These leave from the Bronfman Visitors Centre in the Sherman administration building.

The modern **Hecht Synagogue** stands out as the major attraction for visitors, although the best views are from the **amphitheatre**. Call ☎ 588 2819 for full details.

Mormon University (Map 2)

Brigham Young University was opened in 1987 amid much protestation, particularly by Orthodox Jews who feared the Mormons were intent on missionary activity. Largely due to the support of then mayor Teddy Kollek, a firm advocate of religious and cultural tolerance, the Mormons were finally permitted to establish their university. The resulting building is quite beautiful – a stepped structure that ripples down the slope of Mt Scopus in a series of landscaped terraces.

Guided tours of the campus are available at 10.30 and 11.30 am and 2.30 and 3.30 pm from Tuesday to Friday. Public concerts are also regularly held in the university's glass-enclosed auditorium, which has stunning views over the Old City.

WWI Cemetery (Map 2)

This is the burial site for those soldiers from the British Commonwealth forces who died in the Palestinian campaign of 1917. Various remembrance services, including ANZAC Day (for Australians and New Zealanders), are held here and are attended by the mayor, local dignitaries and military personnel.

EAST JERUSALEM

East Jerusalem is the Palestinian Arab sector of the city. It stretches north from the Old City walls up to Sheikh Jarrah, and to the east encompasses the swell of the Mount of Olives and the cluster of villages on its slopes, including Silwan, Abu Dis and Bethany. The heart of the district is centred on converging Salah ad-Din St and Nablus Rd, which is where you'll find most of the shops, eating places and accommodation.

Recognisable tourist sites are few, although the Garden Tomb is pleasant and the Rockefeller Museum contains some impressive exhibits (see that section following). Lively and chaotic during the day, East Jerusalem completely closes down at dusk.

Solomon's Quarries (Map 5)

Midway between Damascus and Herod's gates is this vast cave beneath the north wall of the Old City. Part of a quarry, stone chiselled from here was, in all likelihood, used by Herod the Great for his many construction projects, and maybe even by Solomon in the construction of the First Temple. Far more recently (1933), the builders of the YMCA in the New City received special dispensation to use stone from the quarry in the construction of the communion room in that building's tower.

In Jewish tradition the cave is known as Me'arat Zidkiyahu (Zedekiah's Cave), because legend has it that the last king of Judah, Zedekiah, used it as an escape route to flee the armies of Nebuchadnezzar. The cave extends for over 200m beneath the Old City, and while there's little to see it does offer cool refuge on a hot day. It's also actually great fun exploring all the little pathways and nooks and crannies.

The Freemasons' Society, intriguingly enough, holds annual ceremonies in the main hall of the cave since they believe that King Solomon was the first Freemason and come here to pay homage to his memory.

The cave is open from 9 am, closing 2 pm Sunday to Thursday, 5 pm Friday, and 4 pm Saturday. Admission is 7 NIS (students 3.50 NIS).

Rockefeller Museum (Map 2)

Set up with a gift of US$2 million donated by the Rockefeller family in 1927 and opened 11 years later, the Palestine Archaeological Museum, as it was then known, was at one time the leading museum of antiquities in the region.

The museum has, however, received little attention in recent times; while some of the exhibits are impressive – particularly the carved beams from the Al-Aqsa Mosque and the stone ornamentation recovered from Hisham's Palace in Jericho – the presentation is off-puttingly dour and musty compared to other more modern Israeli museums. The central courtyard with its tiled fountain – loosely inspired by the Alhambra in Spain – is still a pleasant place to sit and escape the city's noise and fumes. The pockmarks on the walls are bullet holes from the fighting in the Six Day War of 1967.

The Rockefeller museum (☎ 628 2251, fax 620 4624) is open from 10 am, closing at 5 pm Sunday to Thursday, and 2 pm Friday and Saturday. Admission is 22 NIS (students 14 NIS).

Armenian Mosaic

Unfortunately, at the time of our last visit there was no admission to this site, but anyone interested in seeing what is possibly the most attractive mosaic floor in all the Middle East should enquire at the Mardigian Museum in the Armenian Quarter of the Old City.

Laid in the late 5th or early 6th century, the mosaic depicts a vast grapevine within which are perched some 45 colourful birds and baskets of fruit. The detail is superb and the colours are still incredibly brilliant. The floor belongs to what was the Mortuary Chapel of St Polyeuctus, an Armenian officer in the Roman army who was martyred for being Christian. An inscription in Armenian where the apse should begin reads 'For the memory and salvation of the souls of all Armenians whose names are known to God alone'.

The building housing the mosaic is just around the corner from, and behind, the Ramses Youth Hostel on HaNevi'im St.

Garden Tomb (Map 5)

This is believed by some to be an alternative site for the Crucifixion and Resurrection of Christ and, although enjoying little support for its biblical claims, it is appreciated by many for its tranquillity and charm. As one Catholic priest is reported to have said: 'If the Garden Tomb is not the true site of the Lord's death and resurrection, it should have been'.

Biblical significance was first attached to this location by General Charles Gordon (of Khartoum fame) in 1883. Gordon refused to believe that the Church of the Holy Sepulchre could occupy the site of Golgotha, and on identifying a skull-shaped hill just north of Damascus Gate, he began excavations. The suitably ancient tombs he discovered under the mound confirmed his conviction that this was the true site of the crucifixion and burial of Jesus.

More objective archaeologists have subsequently scotched this theory by dating the tomb to the 5th century BC. Cynics suggest that the continued championing of the Garden Tomb as an authentic site has more to do with the fact that it's the only significant holy site in Jerusalem that the Protestants have any stake in.

The Garden Tomb is open from 8.30 am to noon and from 2 to 5.30 pm Monday to Saturday, closed Sunday. Admission is free. On Sunday at 9 am an ecumenical service with singing is held, it lasts about 50 minutes. To get to the tomb from Sultan Suleyman St, head north along Nablus Rd and turn right onto Schick St.

St George's Cathedral (Map 5)

Named after the patron saint of England, traditionally believed to have been martyred in Palestine early in the 4th century (see the boxed text 'St George of Lod and England' below), this is the cathedral church of the Anglican Episcopal Diocese of Jerusalem and the Middle East. It was consecrated in 1912, but very soon after the Turks closed the church; the bishop's house was used as their army headquarters during WWI.

When the British took Jerusalem in 1917, the truce was signed here in the bishop's study. The cathedral has two congregations, Arabic and English-speaking, and the complex includes a popular guesthouse (see the Places to Stay chapter) and school.

The church compound is a piece of the British Mandate frozen in time. The church features many symbols of the British presence: a font donated by Queen Victoria, memorials to British servicemen, a royal coat of arms, an English oak screen and the tower built in memory of Edward VII. The cathedral is just south of the junction of Salah ad-Din St and Nablus Rd. It has no set opening hours and no admission fee.

Tombs of the Kings (Map 5)

The first archaeologist to excavate here decided that this complex must be the tombs of the Kings of Judah because of the majesty of its façade. While the name has stuck, it has since been proved that this is the 1st century tomb of Queen Helena of Adiabene in Mesopotamia, who converted to Judaism in 45 AD and travelled to Jerusalem with her children. It has been described as one of the country's 'most interesting ancient burial places', but only serious archaeology buffs are likely to agree.

The tomb is to the north of St George's Cathedral, and it's open to visitors from 8 am to 12.30 pm and 2 to 5 pm Monday to Saturday, closed Sunday. Admission is 5 NIS (students 3 NIS).

Tourjeman Post Museum (Map 5)

Overlooking the former Mandelbaum Gate area (which was the UN-supervised access point between the Israeli New City and Jordanian-occupied Jerusalem between 1948 and 1967, and not a gate at all) this museum is in an old Turkish house used by the Israelis as a frontier position. With the touchy theme of 'a divided city reunited', it presents a distinctly Zionist picture of the period when the city was physically divided by concrete barriers and barbed wire.

A little tricky to find, the museum (☎ 628 1278) is on HaShalom Rd. If approaching

---

St George of Lod (& England)

Several flights a day connect London with Ben-Gurion airport, located on the outskirts of the small town of Lod, but few of those travelling this route would be aware of the little quirk of history that links these two places. Lod is the burial site of St George, the dragon-slayer and patron saint of England.

Tradition has it that George was a conscript in the Roman army who was executed in 303 AD for tearing up a copy of Diocletian's decree that reinforced the illegal status of Christianity. He was buried in Lod (then Lydda) and a Byzantine church was built over his tomb. This church was subsequently dismantled by the Mamluk Sultan Baybars (the stones were used to build a nearby bridge) and replaced with a mosque dedicated to Al-Khadr, the 'Green One', a saintly Islamic figure who roughly equates to George.

How this character came to be patron saint of England and the Italian port city of Genoa is unknown, although the fantastical legends of George that were doing the rounds in the Levant would have been carried back to Europe by the Crusaders.

View of the Old City from the Dominus Flevit church

Church of the Holy Sepulchure: jewelled statue of the Virgin Mary and exterior view of the apse

JOHN BORTHWICK

PAUL HELLANDER

CHRISTINE OSBORNE

CHRISTINE OSBORNE

Clockwise from Top: Dachau Memorial at Yad Vashem; Armenian tile design; Palestinian embroidery; Hasmonean relief from the Damascus Gate area, walk north up HaNevi'im St, turn right after the Ramsis Hostel onto HaShalom Rd, and it's on your left after a few minutes' walk.

The museum was closed for repairs at the time of research, check with the tourist offices for opening times.

Ammunition Hill (Map 1)

Although not strictly in East Jerusalem, Ammunition Hill is just north of the Palestinian neighbourhood of Sheikh Jarrah. Another partition-era site, this was Jordan's main fortified outpost on the Jerusalem front and during the Six Day War it was taken by the Israelis in the first major battle for the Old City. Now a public park, the bunker complex has been converted into a Six Day War museum and memorial to the many Israeli lives lost in the fighting.

The museum (☎ 582 9132) is open from 9 am, closing at 5 pm Sunday to Thursday, 1 pm Friday (closed Saturday). Admission is 3NIS. To get to the park walk north along Nablus Rd, straight on through Sheikh Jarrah, and turn left at the sports ground. Alternatively, take Egged bus Nos 9, 25 or 28 from the New City and ask for 'Givat HaTahmoshet' (Ammunition Hill).

THE NEW CITY CENTRE (MAP 3)

The central district of the New City largely took shape during the time of the British Mandate. Although now primarily a place to shop, dine and drink, the sense of history – albeit recent – is no less acute here than in the Old City.

Notre Dame

Whether it's the predominant use of stone or the result of a paranoid defensiveness that comes from having so many various creeds and sects vying for influence in one place, much of the city's religious architecture has a distinct bastion-like appearance. This reaches its pinnacle in the Notre Dame de France Hospice (begun in 1884, completed in 1904), a hostel for French pilgrims that takes the form of a vast, imposing fortress that even manages to dominate

Suleyman's Old City walls. Reinforcing the muscular imagery, up on the roofline a 5m-high statue of Mary stands flanked by two crenellated turrets.

It's fitting that between 1948 and 1967, when Jerusalem was divided, the south wing of the Notre Dame was used as an IDF bunker and frontier post. The heavy battle damage the building suffered was patched up in the 1970s, and now Notre Dame operates as a busy international pilgrims' centre with a highly rated guesthouse and restaurant (see the Places to Stay chapter and under Other International in the Places to Eat chapter). It also includes an arts centre promoting traditional local Christian art.

Immediately to the west of the Notre Dame, on the corner site, is the St Louis Hospital built by the French between 1879 and 1896, which is still in use as a hospice for terminally ill patients.

Old & New City Hall

Just west of Notre Dame, on Zahal Square, the building with the rounded façade is Jerusalem's former City Hall. It was built during the Mandate and was originally the headquarters of Barclays Bank – you can still see 'BB' wrought into the iron grills on the ground floor windows. Between 1948 and 1967 it served as a frontline bunker on the border between Jewish West Jerusalem and the Arab-held areas, a period recorded in the bullet-pocked stonework. At the time of writing the building was no longer in use, having been replaced by the adjacent new City Hall complex.

Completed in summer 1993, the City Hall complex is a mix of new and renovated old buildings around a newly created public plaza, Safra Square. Picking up on elements of traditional Jerusalem architecture, such as the ablaq stonework, the complex is quite attractive, especially the date palm court at the Jaffa Rd edge of the plaza. The municipality's Department of Information (☎ 624 1379) is based here and gives guided tours of the new City Hall complex every Monday at 9.30 am; meet in Safra Square near the palms, opposite the main post office.

Russian Compound

During the 19th century the masses of Russian pilgrims visiting Jerusalem far outnumbered pilgrims from any other country. Thus in 1860 the Russian Church acquired this site outside the city walls and within just a few years developed it into a virtually self-contained compound that included a cathedral-church, residences, a hospital, several hospices and quarters for the Russian consulate.

Although the Soviet government sold most of the buildings to the Israeli government in 1964 for oranges, the compound today is still dominated by the Kremlin-inspired green cupolas of the **Church of the Holy Trinity**, consecrated in 1872. The church (closed to the public) occupies the site where the Assyrians camped in about 700 BC, and where, in 70 AD, Roman legions assembled to crush the Great Revolt. In front of the building, under a grille, is the 12m-high **Herod's Pillar**, believed to have been intended for the Second Temple. It cracked and was abandoned here.

Most of the Russian pilgrims were poor peasants who paid for their journey with their life savings, but the nobility also visited, and for them a large hostel was built with deluxe facilities and furnishings. Known as the **Sergei Building**, after its patron Prince Sergei Romanoff, son of Czar Alexander II, the hostel (on present-day Heleni HaMalka St) is easily distinguishable by its two round crenellated towers. After the 1917 Revolution halted the flow of pilgrims from Russia, the empty hostel was taken over by the British mandatory government. It now houses Israel's Agriculture Ministry and is home to the Jerusalem offices of the Society for the Protection of Nature in Israel (see the Tourist Offices section in the Facts for the Visitor chapter).

During the Mandate period, certain other compound buildings were requisitioned by the British, earning the area the nickname of 'Bevingrad' after the British Foreign Secretary Ernest Bevin, a man much reviled by the Jews of Palestine. The building behind the church to the right was the British head-

quarters, while the adjacent former Russian women's hostel was used as a prison. As such, these were targets for attacks by the Jewish paramilitary underground. The hostel/prison is now the **Underground Prisoners' Museum 1918-1948** (☎ 623 3166), devoted to those same resistance organisations that once attacked it. It is open from 8 am to 4 pm Sunday to Thursday, closed on Friday and Saturday. Admission is 6 NIS (students 3 NIS).

Nahalat Shiv'a

Situated at the heart of the New City centre, Nahalat Shiv'a is the bar and cafe-filled equivalent of London's Covent Garden. One of the first residential areas to be created outside the walls of the Old City, it was founded in 1869 by a consortium of seven families – hence the name, 'Quarter of the Seven'. However, by the time of the British Mandate its narrow alleys and tight courtyards had become almost deserted and the area was slated for clearance.

It survived, but was threatened with destruction once again in the 1950s by a city administration intent on modernisation. Somewhere along the line someone saw the light, and instead of being flattened the neighbourhood received a facelift. Commercial revitalisation followed and the small cluster of picturesque lanes is now the flourishing focus of the New City's nightlife, home to a cache of trendy eateries and open-all-hours cafes bars. See under New City in the Places to Eat chapter for details.

Museum of Italian Jewish Art & Synagogue

In 1952, with no Jews left in Conegliano Veneto near Venice, the interior of that town's 18th century synagogue was dismantled and reassembled here. It now serves the needs of Italian Jews in Jerusalem and is the only synagogue outside Italy where the ancient Italian liturgy is performed.

The architecture and art displayed in the adjacent museum is there for public appreciation. The museum/synagogue (☎ 624 1610) is on the south-west fringe of Nahalat Shiv'a at 27 Hillel St. It's open Sunday, Monday, Tuesday and Thursday from 10 am to 1 pm, and Wednesday from 4 to 7 pm (closed Friday and Saturday). Admission is 10 NIS.

Zion Square & Ben Yehuda St

Pedestrianised Ben Yehuda St (known in Hebrew as the *midrahov*, combining the words for street and pavement) is the secular heart of Jerusalem. Much of the city's best shopping is on or around here. With the absence of traffic, the broad sloping street is instead congested with the street furniture of countless cafes, making it a favourite place for quick lunches or languorous coffees.

Entertainment, of sorts, is provided by buskers who are typically Russian immigrants with accordion-accompanied songs of melancholy or, in summer, young Americans with acoustic guitars and an excruciating preference for Don McLean.

At its lower end, Ben Yehuda is linked to Jaffa Rd by Zion Square. This is a cramped and shabby plaza that nonetheless continues to serve as the focal point of the New City. It is a popular rallying point for demonstrations, a venue for agitated orators to get up on their soapboxes, and a place to meet and hang out for the city's youth. The square is also home to one of the city's biggest planning foul-ups: a hideous multistorey tower block that is totally out of keeping with the surrounding architecture.

The Time Elevator

If you like virtual 'rides' you might enjoy this whiz-bang potted presentation of the history of the city. Opened in September 1998, the Time Elevator (☎ 625 2227, fax 625 2228) is a high-tech experience combining gut-wrenching virtual roller coaster effects through time and space with light-hearted historical documentary.

It starts with the establishment of the City of David and ends with a spectacular aerial panorama of present-day Jerusalem, all projected onto a large split screen. The only unlikely element is an obviously computer-contrived El Al 747 plane flying low over the skyline at dusk. It is actually a very enjoyable experience though a little pricey at 37 NIS for the half-hour show.

Pregnant women and sufferers of motion sickness can take a static version for the ride, but that's like eating a cheeseburger without the cheese! It is in the Beit Agron building at 37 Hillel St. Rides are every half-hour and it is open daily from 10 am to 9 pm, closed Saturday.

Ticho House (Beit Ticho)

The former home of Dr Abraham Ticho and his artist wife, Anna, this combination of museum, art gallery, shop, library and café is now administered by the Israel Museum.

Dr Ticho was a leader in the field of ophthalmology and during the time of the British Mandate was responsible for saving hundreds of Palestinian Arabs from blindness. Included in the exhibits is Dr Ticho's study and documents and letters of interest, in particular those dealing with his work for the Arabs, as well as his collection of Hanukkah lamps and some examples of Anna Ticho's art.

However, the appeal of the museum is secondary to the popularity of its charming ground floor café, which also spills out onto a terrace overlooking a large, tranquil garden.

Ticho House (☎ 624 5068) is just off Harav Kook St. It's open from 10 am, closing 5 pm Sunday, Monday, Wednesday and Thursday, 10 pm Tuesday, and 2 pm Friday (closed Saturday). Admission is free.

The café is open 10 am to midnight Sunday to Thursday, 10 am to 3 pm Friday, and from sunset to midnight on Saturday.

The neighbouring building, along the north side of Ticho St – the little alley leading to Ticho House – is also of some historical significance. Known as **Beit David** (David's House), this large block was another of the earliest settlements outside the city walls and would have originally housed a number of Jewish families. The upper storey, which is a later addition, was home to the first Ashkenazi Chief Rabbi of Palestine and is open to the public as the **Rabbi Kook Museum**.

Gan Ha'Atzmaut

Created by the British during the Mandate, Gan Ha'Atzmaut (Independence Park) is Jerusalem's largest public park. That said, it has little to recommend it – it is unkempt, surrounded by traffic and offers none of the wonderful views that other grassy areas such as the Bloomfield Gardens do. The eastern part of the park is actually a Muslim cemetery, within which is the **Mamilla Pool**, a large and ancient rainwater cistern.

Bezalel School of Art

Near the junction of King George V and Ben Yehuda Sts, at 10 Shmuel HaNagid St, is Israel's premier art school, founded in 1906. It is named after the Old Testament artist Bezalel Ben-Ouri (Exodus 31:2-11).

Next door to the main school building, at 12 Shmuel HaNagid St, the **Artists' House** (☎ 223 653) features an art gallery, shop and a bar/restaurant. The gallery is open daily from 9 am to 1 pm and 4 to 7 pm (open 10 am Saturday and Sunday). Admission is free. The bar/restaurant is open daily, usually until after midnight.

Heichal Shlomo & the Great Synagogue

At the southern end of King George V St, facing the Sheraton Plaza Hotel, this 1960s complex is supposedly styled along the lines of Solomon's Temple – Heichal Shlomo literally means 'Solomon's Mansion' – and is the seat of the Chief Rabbinate of Israel and the Supreme Religious Centre. The emblem of the scales of justice is featured on both sides of the entrance.

The **Wolfson Museum** (☎ 624 7112) housed inside this massive building features presentations of religious and traditional Jewish life. Built with funds donated by Sir Isaac Wolfson, the English philanthopist, it's open from 9 am to 1 pm Sunday to Thursday, (closed Friday and Saturday). Admission is 5 NIS.

Next door to Heichal Shlomo, and part of the same complex, is the Great Synagogue. This building has been condemned by many as an extravagant waste of money.

MEA SHE'ARIM & THE BUKHARAN QUARTER (MAP 2)

Mea She'arim and the Bukharan Quarter, along with neighbouring Ge'ula and other small adjacent neighbourhoods, are the heartland of Jerusalem's haredi communities. The residents mostly dress in 18th century Eastern European styles, with the slight differences in their heavy garb denoting the different groups. They are mainly devoted to Torah study and are frequently financed by haredi communities of the Diaspora.

Mea She'arim

Possibly the world's most reluctant tourist attraction, this haredi district is the only remaining example of the *shtetl* (ghettos) which existed before the Holocaust in Eastern European Jewish communities.

A result of the uncompromising interpretation of Judaic law here is the attitude of residents towards strangers. Signs proclaim 'Daughters of Israel! The Torah requires you to dress modestly'. The edict applies equally to non-Jewish daughters too, as other notices make plain. Women visitors to the area must not wear shorts or off-the-shoulder tops – loose fitting skirts (trousers are frowned upon for showing off the figure too much) and long-sleeved shirts are recommended. Male visitors should also refrain from walking through Mea She'arim in shorts. Do not walk arm in arm or even hand in hand with anyone, and kissing in public is most definitely out of the question. Most haredim dislike being photographed – some even see it as a contravention of the law against making 'graven images'.

The more extreme characters have been known to stone those, Jewish and gentile alike, who break these codes of conduct, however unwittingly. Signalled or verbal objections are more common, though.

The district's main artery is **Mea She'arim St**. Note all the graffiti and posters – the many different haredi communities inhabiting the area don't necessarily see eye to eye, and the walls of the neighbourhood are busy with propaganda, denunciations and ripostes. At the top of Harav Shmuel

Salant St (the first left coming from Shivtei Y'Israel St) is the site of the former **Jerusalem Gate**, one of the six gates of the original settlement. At night these gates were locked to keep out bandits. Today only an iron bar remains and potential intruders are instead warded off with a barrage of warnings about immodest dress, mixing of the sexes and the unwelcome nature of gawping tourists.

The undeterred who press on will enter a warren of narrow alleys. Mea She'arim is a tight collection of small communities, each of which was designed to be a self-contained unit. The blocks of housing all face inwards, focused on one large building that serves as the religious teaching centre, synagogue and communal hall. One such building, **Beit Avraham** (Abraham's House), lies about 100m north-west beyond the Jerusalem Gate (walk along the narrow alleyway and take the second left).

If you cut north, back onto Mea She'arim St, walk west for 50m then head down the short flight of stairs on your right, you'll enter **Batei Ungarin** (Hungarian Houses), one of the best preserved of the area's *kolel* (neighbourhoods comprising residents from one particular country or city in Europe that are administered by a committee).

Jewish holidays are always the best time to visit Mea She'arim, as the entire area throws itself into the celebrations with an enthusiasm not to be witnessed anywhere else in the city. See the Jewish Festivals special section.

HaNevi'im St

HaNevi'im, or Street of the Prophets, divides the worldly central New City (Map 3) from the isolationist haredi neighbourhoods that lie just to the north (Map 2). During the 19th century it was one of the city's main thoroughfares and the address of choice for many European (and other) consulates, missions and agencies. The street remains the most convenient route for anyone staying in East Jerusalem or around Damascus Gate to reach the Russian Compound or Zion Square in the New City.

One of the most prominent and striking structures on the street is the **Italian Hospital**, built in the early 20th century, but with decoration, red roof tiles and square tower borrowed from the building style of 16th century Florence. The architect was Antonio Barluzzi, who also designed two of the churches on the Mount of Olives. It wasn't a hospital for long, as during the Mandate it was taken over by the British air force. It's now home to the Israeli Ministry of Education & Culture.

Just to the east of the Italian Hospital is the **Ethiopian Consulate**, a memorial to the times when Israel enjoyed a close relationship with the government of Haile Selassie. It has an attractive blue and gold lion mosaic above the door (see Ethiopia St following).

At No 58 HaNevi'im is **Thabor House**, which was built and occupied by a Swiss Protestant missionary turned architect and amateur archaeologist, Conrad Schick. A self-taught draughtsman, Schick is most famous for designing the original settlement of Mea She'arim, the Leper Hospital in Talbiyeh, and this, his eccentric house. It's fashioned like a mini German castle, and various ancient artefacts that Schick discovered are embedded in the façade. The house is now owned by the Swedish Theological Institute – curious visitors are usually allowed into the courtyard.

A few doors down from Thabor House at No 64 is the one-time Jerusalem home of the English pre-Raphaelite painter **William Holman Hunt** (1827-1910), who arrived in the city in 1854. During his time here, the evangelical Holman Hunt painted several of his best known biblically-inspired works using local residents as his models. The house is now a private residence and is closed to the public.

Further west on HaNevi'im St is the **Anglican School**, built in 1901 as the English Mission Hospital. It takes the form of seven pavilions built in a semicircle around a front lawn. HaNevi'im St was a prime site for missionary activities because of the proximity of the new Jewish neighbourhoods.

These activities infuriated the local haredi communities and they boycotted the hospital facilities. It might be sweet revenge then that the school, which is attended by the children of diplomats and UN personnel, is soon to close – the building has been bought by an ultra-orthodox organisation.

HaNevi'im St ends – or starts, depending on where you set out from – with the **Davidka Monument**, at Davidka Square, where an example of the primitive and unreliable mortar of the same name is displayed. This weapon was used by the Jews to great effect in 1948; it did little physical damage but the story goes that it made such a loud noise that it scared the living daylights out of the enemy.

Ethiopia St

Tucked away on narrow, leafy Ethiopia St, the impressive, domed **Ethiopian Church** would be a major feature in most cities, but in Jerusalem it is often overlooked. Built between 1896 and 1904, the church's entrance gate features the carved Lion of Judah, an emblem believed to have been presented to the Queen of Sheba (Ethiopia) by Solomon when she visited Jerusalem.

This church is open daily from 7 am to 6 pm between March and September (slightly shorter hours in winter). Admission is free.

Opposite the church is **Ben Yehuda House**, where the great linguist lived and did much of his work on the revival of the Hebrew language (see the Literature section in the Facts about Jerusalem chapter). A plaque marking the house was stolen by ultra-orthodox Jews who strongly disapprove of the language's everyday use, feeling that the language of the Torah should be reserved for religious use only.

Mahane Yehuda Market

About a kilometre west of Zion Square between Jaffa Rd and Agrippas St, this fabulous market is a spectacle in its own right even if you don't want to do any shopping. You'll never see bigger, redder strawberries than here, and you'll need an unflinching nature to buy the fish, which have to be

brained into submission before they can be wrapped. Other stalls laden with all manner of fruit, vegetables, pickles, olives and cheeses stand among cheap butchers, bakeries and wholesale *mahkolets* (grocers).

This is the best place to stock up on produce if you are using self-catering accommodation. To shop effectively, just grab what you want, hand it to the stallholder after estimating the approximate price (prices are shown) and hand over the approximate amount. You won't be ripped off and prices really are very low here. The only hassle is hauling it all back to your room, but there is a major bus stop just outside the market on Jaffa Rd. The market is at its gloriously bustling best on Thursday and Friday during the pre-Shabbat scramble. Be alert for pickpockets though, as this is a great arena for the deft-of-hand and thefts have been reported.

On Agrippas and Jaffa Sts there are several great places for spicy Yemenite *meorav Yerushalmi* (barbecued meats), and these are open from the early evening until early morning. See the Oriental (Sephardic) section in the Places to Eat chapter.

Bukharan Quarter

Established towards the end of the 19th century by Jews from the Central Asian *khanates* (now cities) of Bukhara and Samarkand, this was one of Jerusalem's most wealthy and exclusive districts. Unlike neighbouring Mea She'arim, an area dedicated to cramped communal dwelling and humility, the Bukharan Quarter was laid out on a spacious grid of wide tree-lined streets, and featured a collection of regal and elegant one-family mansions. Many of these houses were used purely as summer residences – more often than not used only every second summer because the trip to Jerusalem and back was too long to make annually.

In the aftermath of the Russian Revolution, Central Asia's Jews were stripped of their wealth and prevented from travelling. The sumptuous homes in Jerusalem were either lost or had to be rented out and the quarter began a slide into decline. The change in character was further hastened when the haredim of Mea She'arim moved in to fill the vacuum.

Though now neglected and decaying, the Bukharan Quarter is still worth a visit. Most impressive of all is **Beit Yehudayoff** at 19 Ezra St, a great birthday cake of a building designed by an Italian architect for a particularly well-off Bukharan family. Known locally as 'the Palace', it has more than 30 rooms and once served as the headquarters of the Ottoman administration in Jerusalem. A reception for General Allenby and his victorious officers was also held in this mansion when the British took Jerusalem in 1917. It now houses two girls' schools. Also of note are the pagoda-roofed **Davidoff House** and the **Mosheioff House**, built by one of the quarter's founding families.

REHAVIA & TALBIYEH (MAP 4)

Built in the earlier part of this century by Jewish intellectuals (Rehavia) and wealthy Christian Arabs (Talbiyeh), these districts are among the city's more fashionable neighbourhoods, although the steadily increasing number of haredi residents is said to be changing that.

Rehavia stands in strict opposition to the conservative religious Jewish enclaves such as Mea She'arim and Batei Ungarin. It has traditionally been home to intellectuals, Zionists and politicians and is still home to the residences of both the prime minister and president. Much of the local architecture reflects the neighbourhood's progressive origins; at No 6 Balfour St, for example, is the **Schocken Library**, designed by the modernist German architect Erich Mendelsohn (who fled to Jerusalem to escape the Nazis).

The houses of Talbiyeh (also known as Komemiyut) are more traditional in nature, but in many cases are also wonderfully self-indulgent. Take a look at No 17 Alkalay St, a house called **Beit Jalad**, built by an Arab contractor with a fondness for the imagery of *The Thousand and One Nights*.

Place de France & Ramban St

Place de France (also known as Zarfat Square) marks the junction of the city centre with Rehavia. It's dominated by the bulk of the **Terra Sancta** building, an underused college built by the Catholic Church in 1927. Just 100m west along Ramban St is the **Rehavia windmill** (Map 3) one of two in Jerusalem (the other is in Mamilla). This was a functioning mill last century and it stood in an area of wheat fields. In the 1930s it became the home and offices of the architect Erich Mendelsohn while he designed the Hebrew University and Hadassah Hospital buildings on Mt Scopus. It is now part of a shopping complex.

Jason's Tomb

It's not worth the long walk to get here because the only thing to see is a cave barred by a rusting iron gate in a leafy suburban street. For archaeologists, however, this was one of the city's most interesting tombs because it provided a wealth of historical information. Built in the early 1st century BC by someone called Jason, it contains two or three generations of his family. The tomb revealed a good deal about 1st century concepts of the afterlife – lighting and cooking pots, complete with food, were provided in the individual graves, and dice were also found (gambling in heaven?!) The porch's charcoal drawings of a warship in pursuit of two other vessels suggest that either Jason or his son was a naval officer.

If you're in the neighbourhood you may want to visit the tomb, which is on Alfasi St; look through the iron grille to see the burial chamber. Eight shaft graves can be seen through the small opening on the left.

MAMILLA

Bordering the Old City walls from Jaffa Gate up to Zahal Square and rolling across the valley to busy HaMelekh David St, Mamilla links old and new Jerusalem. At the beginning of this century it was a busy commercial district shared between Arabs and Jews, but the fighting in 1948 resulted in the border being drawn through Mamilla, and for 19 years the place existed as a sniper-infested no-man's-land.

Such prime real estate wasn't going to lie fallow for too long, however, and since reunification numerous new developments have either been completed or are well under way. The most high profile of these is **David's Village** (Map 3), a cluster of prestige residential blocks across the valley from Jaffa Gate. The sales pitch for these apartments – 'for those who can afford to live like a king' – seems appropriate; however the village is not named, as you might assume, after the biblical King David but after the developer behind the project, David Taic. Adjacent to the village is a new luxury **Hilton Hotel**, and there's also a shopping centre, parks and new highways to come.

HaMelekh David St, which runs south from the New City centre down to the railway station, escaped the fighting relatively unscathed and is home to several important landmarks, including the architecturally noteworthy **Hebrew Union College** building, the King David Hotel and the YMCA. The road leads to Herod's Family Tomb, the Yemin Moshe neighbourhood and Liberty Bell Gardens.

St Vincent de Paul Hospice (Map 3)

On HaEmek St (also known as Mamilla Rd) down from Jaffa Gate, this large convent is another of those wonderful Jerusalem buildings that gets lost in the crowd. It's an orphanage built in the late 19th century by the Sisters of Charity, a Paris-based order of nuns.

Note also the house at No 33 HaEmek St that bears a plaque recording the fact that **Dr Theodor Herzl**, the founder of political Zionism, stayed here during his visit to Palestine in 1898. However, in 1998 the whole area was under renovation and the house was inaccessible. What they will do with the house or even where they will put it, is anyone's guess, since there was talk of relocating the whole building.

The YMCA & King David Hotel (Map 3)

Designed by the architect of New York's Empire State Building and completed in 1933, Jerusalem's YMCA building on HaMelekh David St is an appealing mix of Romanesque and Oriental architecture. The vaulted lobby is especially attractive and it's worthwhile poking your nose inside. Although for a time closed to the public after being used for an attempted suicide, the building's distinctive tower is open again, from 9 am to 2 pm Monday to Saturday, closed Sunday. Admission is 3 NIS. At the YMCA is the well-appointed Three Arches Hotel (see the Places to Stay – Top End section of the Places to Stay chapter for details).

The stadium behind the main building used to be home to Jerusalem's football team but it's now moved to a new, modern ground (the Teddy Stadium) beside the Kanyon shopping centre in the west of the city.

Opposite the YMCA, and obscuring its view of the Old City, is the ungainly bulk of the King David Hotel (see the Places to Stay chapter). What the Savoy is to London and Raffles to Singapore, so is the King David to Jerusalem. Designed in 1930 by a Swiss architect, Emil Vogt, for an Egyptian Jewish family, the hotel has been host to the likes of Winston Churchill, Anwar Sadat, the last five US presidents, Elizabeth Taylor and Kirk Douglas, to name but a few. Home to the British military high command during the Mandate, in 1946 the hotel's southern wing was blown up by the Irgun, the underground terrorist organisation led by the future prime minister Menachem Begin.

Herod's Family Tomb (Map 4)

Discovered in 1892, archaeologists believe that this may be the tomb of the family of King Herod because of its size and grandeur. Unfortunately, little was found inside to back up this theory, as tomb robbers had been there first. Herod himself is not buried here but at Herodian, near Bethlehem. The tomb is at the northern edge of Bloomfield Gardens on Aba Sikra St, just south of King David Hotel.

Yemin Moshe & the Windmill (Map 4)

The small Yemin Moshe neighbourhood can be identified immediately by its windmill, one of the very first structures to be built outside the secure confines of the Old City.

The windmill was part of a scheme developed by Sir Moses Montefiore, a Jewish English philanthropist who wanted to ease the overcrowding within the city walls. He built a single block of 24 small apartments, buttressed either side by a synagogue, called **Mishkenot Sha'ananim** or 'Dwellings of Tranquillity'. The windmill was to have provided the basis for a flour industry. This aspect of the scheme failed (not enough wind) and the windmill is now an eccentric landmark serving as a museum dedicated to the life and work of Montefiore. It's open from 9 am, closing 4 pm Sunday to Thursday, 1 pm Friday (closed Saturday).

Even if the windmill proved inappropriate, the idea of living outside the city walls was a success, and Yemin Moshe came into being in the 1890s. Despite being in the firing line, many of its residents clung on through the partition years of 1948 to 1967, only ironically to be turfed out after reunification as part of the Jerusalem municipality's gentrification plan for the area. Yemin Moshe is now one of the city's most desirable addresses.

The Mishkenot Sha'ananim complex is now a guesthouse for 'creative' visitors to Jerusalem, and past tenants have included Simone de Beauvoir, Isaiah Berlin, Marc Chagall, Milan Kundera and VS Naipaul.

Arts & Crafts Lane (Khutsot HaYotser)

Originally a small settlement of Sephardic Jews, Khutsot HaYotser was rebuilt in the 1920s as an Arab market and workshop complex. From 1948 onwards it sat abandoned in the middle of no-man's-land, and it was only when the barbed wire was removed in 1967 that reconstruction could begin. Today, it's a curious arcade (which oddly leads from nowhere to nowhere) of art galleries, craft workshops and a couple of cafes (see the Shopping chapter). It's not really worth a special trip but you might conceivably pass this way walking from the Old City to the Cinematheque or the neighbourhood of Talbiyeh.

Liberty Bell Gardens (Map 4)

Just west of the Montefiore windmill, across traffic-logged David Remez St, are these gardens, which cover three hectares and have as their central point an exact replica of the Liberty Bell in Philadelphia. The gardens are often a venue for public events and are popular with picnickers. Avoid them at night though, since suspicious characters are reputed to haunt its shadowy ways.

St Andrew's Church (Map 4)

Also known as the Scottish Church, St Andrew's was built in 1927 in memory of the Scottish soldiers lost in the campaign to capture Palestine in WWI. It's owned by the Church of Scotland and the floor features an inscription to the memory of Robert the Bruce, who requested that his heart be buried in Jerusalem when he died. Sir James Douglas made an attempt at fulfilling Bruce's wish but he was killed en route in Spain, fighting the Moors. The heart was recovered and returned to Scotland; it's now buried at Melrose.

Jerusalem Film Centre & Cinematheque (Map 4)

Perched on the hillside below Hebron Rd, with great views across to Mt Zion and the Old City, this complex (☎ 671 5398) houses several cinema screens, a small museum, a library and archives relating to the film industry. It's open from 10 am, closing at 3 pm Sunday and Monday, 7 pm Tuesday and Thursday, and 1 pm Friday. Also part of the complex is the Cinematheque (see the Entertainment chapter) and a popular vegetarian restaurant (see under New City in the Cafés section of the Places to Eat chapter).

Sultan's Pool (Map 4)

Now a unique open-air amphitheatre used for a variety of concerts, this was originally a city reservoir created by the Mamluk Sultan Barquq in the 14th century and later renovated by Sultan Suleyman the Magnificent. Its location, nestled below the walls of the Old City, makes it a spectacularly atmospheric venue. Check the listings in the *Jerusalem Post* or ask at the tourist information office on Jaffa Rd in the New City, and if anybody is performing here (some well-known international rock acts have played here in the past including Neil Young and Stevie Wonder), get a ticket.

Sultan's Pool lies between Yemin Moshe and Hativat Yerushalayim, and beside the road above it is a beautiful 16th century *sabil* (drinking fountain), erected during the reign of Suleyman.

THE GERMAN COLONY (MAP 4)

South of Talbiyeh, the German Colony (HaMoshava HaGermanit) was founded in 1873 by a group of Templers, a Protestant sect, from rural southern Germany. The community arrived with the idea of founding in Jerusalem 'a small kingdom of heaven upon earth', which they modelled along the lines of a typical German village. The Germans were initially admired by the Jews for their work ethic and efficiency, but relations soured when the existence of a branch of the Nazi Party was uncovered in the colony during the mid-1930s.

In 1939 the Templers were deported by the British, who then appropriated their property. With the end of the Mandate the abandoned homes were filled by Jewish immigrants. The area has subsequently undergone a process of gentrification similar to that in Khutsot HaYotser is now one of the city's classier neighbourhoods.

The main drag through the colony, Emek Refa'im, is now home to a thriving restaurant and cafe scene and the area in general now offers some good bed & breakfast accommodation (see under New City in the Places to Stay – Mid-Range section of the Places to Stay chapter).

TALPIOT (MAP 1)

Talpiot (divided geographically into Talpiot, East Talpiot and North Talpiot) is one of Jerusalem's new suburbs. Lying astride the Bethlehem and Hebron Rds, and incorporating a large industrial estate, other than the few highlights described below it has nothing to offer apart from a multiplex cinema.

Haas Promenade

This terraced promenade was created to take advantage of some of the most spectacular views of the Old City and surroundings. A little difficult to get to without a car, it is nonetheless always busy, especially at night when Jerusalemites flock here to sit at the outdoor cafes or dine in the picture-windowed restaurants. In Hebrew it's sometimes referred to as the Tayelet. Adjoining it is the similar Sherover Promenade. To get here take bus No 8 from Jaffa Rd and get off at the Kiryat Moriah stop.

Hill of Evil Counsel

A little to the east and below the Haas Promenade is the so-called Hill of Evil Counsel. This is a possible alternative location for the house of Caiaphas, the High Priest who had paid Judas to betray Jesus. Since 1933 it has also been the site of **Government House**, built as the residency of the British High Commissioner for Palestine during the Mandate, and now the headquarters of the United Nations in Israel, unfortunately this beautiful building is sadly closed to the public. In Hebrew the place is known as Armon HaNatziv (the Palace of the Commissioner).

Agnon House (Beit Agnon)

The former residence of Nobel laureate and author SY Agnon, the house contains his library plus sundry exhibits and a video screening on the man and his work. There are guided tours in English, call for details (☎ 671 6498, 16 Joseph Klausner St). The house is open 9 am to 1 pm Sunday to Thursday, and 10 am to 1 pm Saturday. Take bus No 7 from the city centre.

GIVAT RAM & MUSEUM ROW

West of central Jerusalem and due south of the central bus station is the green swathe of Givat Ram, which over the last 30 years or so has developed as the institutional heart of the city. As well as being home to the Knesset (the seat of the Israeli parliament) and the several museums mentioned next, it is also the site of the **prime minister's office** (usually easily identified by the placard-wielding protesters outside), the headquarters of the **Bank of Israel** and the Supreme Court building. You can get here from Jaffa Rd on bus Nos 9, 24 or 28 (to the university).

Bible Lands Museum (Map 2)

One of the latest additions to the New City's cultural scene, this museum is billed as 'a non-denominational centre for the appreciation of the history of the Bible'. Covering 6000 BC to 600 AD and presented chronologically, the exhibits include some 2000 artefacts. These range from mosaics and other art pieces, seals, ivories and bronzes to simple household items from all over Asia, Europe and Africa.

Bible Lands Museum (☎ 561 1066) is on Granot St, adjacent to the Israel Museum. It's open from 9.30 am, closing at 5.30 pm Sunday, Monday, Tuesday and Thursday, 9.30 pm Wednesday, and 2 pm Friday (open from 11 am to 3 pm Saturday). Admission is 20 NIS.

The Knesset (Map 2)

A few minutes walk from the Israel Museum is HaKirya (The City), the government centre, dominated by the Knesset, Israel's parliament building. Belonging to the multistorey car park school of architecture, the building was inaugurated in 1966 – previously the parliament had met in what is now the Ministry of Tourism on King George V St. At least the modern Knesset is a lot more attractive inside than out, and it has a foyer decorated with three tapestries and a mosaic by Marc Chagall.

The building is open to the public on Sunday and Thursday from 8.30 am to 2.30 pm,

when free guided tours are given. Bring your passport. You can also see the Knesset in session from 4 to 7 pm Monday and Tuesday, and from 11 am to 7 pm Sunday and Thursday. The proceedings are conducted mainly in Hebrew and occasionally in Arabic. For further information call ☎ 675 3333.

Next to the bus stops opposite the Knesset is a bronze **menorah**, a gift from British supporters of the State of Israel. It's decorated with panels representing important figures and events in Jewish history. Just north of the menorah is the **Wohl Rose Park**, with over 10,000 bushes representing some 650 varieties of roses.

Supreme Court Building (Map 2)

Not an obvious tourist attraction, the court (dedicated in 1993) nevertheless attracts many visitors who come to admire what is considered to be one of the most important and impressive architectural creations in Israel. It's open to the public from 8.30 am to 2.30 pm Sunday to Thursday, with free guided tours in English given at 11 am Sunday and Wednesday. For further information and to confirm tour times, call ☎ 675 9612.

Bloomfield Science Museum (Map 1)

Part of Hebrew University (see the following section), this museum is devoted to aiding the understanding of the natural and technological worlds through a series of hands-on exhibits. It's designed primarily with the young in mind and is a great place to take kids. The museum (☎ 561 8128) is open daily from 10 am, closing 6 pm Monday, Wednesday and Thursday, 8 pm Tuesday, 1 pm Friday, and 3 pm Saturday. Admission is 12 NIS.

Hebrew University & Botanical Garden (Map 1)

The Givat Ram campus was created after 1948 when the original Hebrew University on Mt Scopus was cut off from Israeli-held Jerusalem by the Jordanian frontline. The **University Library** here is the largest in the

(continued on page 131)

THE ISRAEL MUSEUM

No visit to Jerusalem or Israel could be considered complete without a visit to the country's leading showcase of its cultural and historical heritage – the Israel Museum. The coach loads of daily visitors are testament to its endurance as a major cultural attraction, and like many major museums in the world, a single day can hardly do justice to the treasures on display.

The Israel Museum is a purpose-built grouping of several buildings on a specially created, landscaped site. It includes the excellent **Arts Wing**, which brings together works that range from Islamic calligraphy to Francis Bacon and is, as would be expected, strong on Jewish artists, including Chagall and Soutine. The **Archaeological Wing** houses finds made in the Holy Land from prehistoric artefacts through to Roman and Byzantine remains. There's also a wing devoted to **Judaica & Jewish Ethnography**.

Indisputably the museum's biggest drawcard is the **Shrine of the Book**, the distinctive pot lid-shaped building at the northern end of the site. Displayed in a dimly lit subterranean chamber are five of the 2000-year-old Dead Sea Scrolls found in caves at Qumran, near the Dead Sea.

There's also an **Art Garden** with work by Henry Moore, Picasso and Rodin, among others, as well as a **Youth Wing** for children where there are always several exhibitions at any one time, as well as programs of concerts, lectures and films.

Beginnings

The founding of the museum had its roots in a speech given by then prime minister David Ben-Gurion in the Knesset, Israel's parliament.

Below: The Shrine of the Book

© THE ISRAEL MUSEUM JERUSALEM/ANN LEVIN

The speech was delivered on 30 May 1960 during a debate on the up-coming budget allocation for the establishment of the National Museum of Israel. Ben-Gurion announced that Israel should have an 'impressive cultural centre' to reflect the revival of the country's 'inde-pendence in its ancient land' and the enduring spirit of the people.

The main initiator behind this move to establish a home for Israel's cultural treasures was Teddy Kollek, then director of the prime minis-ter's office (later to serve as the mayor of Jerusalem for 28 years). It was he and a group of like-minded pioneers who had the dream to create a national museum in the new homeland of Israel, and Ben-Gurion's support was crucial in securing the funds for the building of the nascent museum.

After funding was finally secured, a grand debate ensued over the placement of the new museum. The present site Neveh Sha'anan (Hill of Tranquillity), west of the Old City, was decided upon mainly because it would be accessible to visitors. It was not until 11 May 1965 that the dream was finally realised and the museum opened its doors to the public.

Now over 30 years old, the museum has grown in stature and size and serves as a focus and repository for the nation's cultural and ar-chaeological wealth. It attracts over 700,000 visitors each year and hosts many fascinating exhibitions. The museum itself consists of a series of low, interconnected buildings blending almost imperceptibly into Jerusalem's landscape. If you are planning to explore archaeolog-ical sites around Israel, you should make sure you begin or end your visit in the Israel Museum.

Practicalities

Get to the museum by 10 am if at all possible to avoid the long queues that form when the tour buses start arriving. The main entrance build-ing contains the ticket office, information stand and the well-stocked museum shop. Maps showing the layout of the museum are on promi-nent display.

It is a good 30 to 40 minute hike to the museum from the Old or New City. If you're on foot the best route is to follow Agron St west from where it begins near the Jerusalem Hilton, until you come out by the big intersection with Ben Tsvi Boulevard. Cross the intersection (via the underpass) and follow Rupin St to the museum entrance which is prominently signposted.

The museum is open Sunday, Monday, Wednesday and Thursday from 10 am to 5 pm, Tuesday from 4 to 10 pm, Friday from 10 am to 2 pm, and Saturday from 10 am to 4 pm. Admission is 20NIS (students 15NIS). For recorded information, call ☎ 02-670 8811 or check the tourist information office and the *Jerusalem Post* for details of special exhibitions and events.

Guided tours in English are included in the admission price. They start from the main entrance and deal with specific areas rather than the whole complex. There's a good museum highlights tour daily (except Saturday and Tuesday) at 11 am and also at 3 pm on Sunday, Monday, Wednesday and Thursday.

If you can't get to the Israel Museum in Jerusalem, check out their Web site at www.imj.org.il.

Highlights

If you have time on your hands, you can conveniently get around most of the major exhibits in one (albeit exhausting) day. Allow two days if time and funds allow. The following section deals with the highlights of the museum.

Shrine of the Book This discrete building houses the remarkable Dead Sea Scrolls which were found by a shepherd boy at Qumran near the Dead Sea in 1947. The scrolls, totalling 800 in all, were found in clay pots and date back to the time of the Bar Kochba Revolt (132-35 AD). Made mainly of leather, they deal with both secular and religious issues and were thought to have been written by an ascetic group of Jews called the Essenes who inhabited the area for about 300 years.

An enormous amount of often controversial and contradictory material has been written about the Dead Sea Scrolls; the bottom line is that no one really knows what they signified, or who the Essenes really were, despite several biblical references to their existence.

The most important scroll is the **Great Isaiah Scroll**, the largest and best preserved. It is the only biblical scroll that has survived in its entirety, and takes centre place in the room. The 54 columns of the scroll contain all 66 chapters of Isaiah without an apparent division between what modern scholars regard as First and Second Isaiah. It dates from about 100 BC and predates the previously oldest biblical document ever found by about 1000 years.

The **Temple Scroll** is a halachic composition dealing with laws as interpreted by the Essenes. It deals with five major subjects: the temple, the king's statutes, the feast and their sacrifices, the Temple City, and the laws of purity. Dating from the 2nd century BC, this is the longest of the Dead Sea Scrolls.

Left: Torah finials (© The Israel Museum Jerusalem)

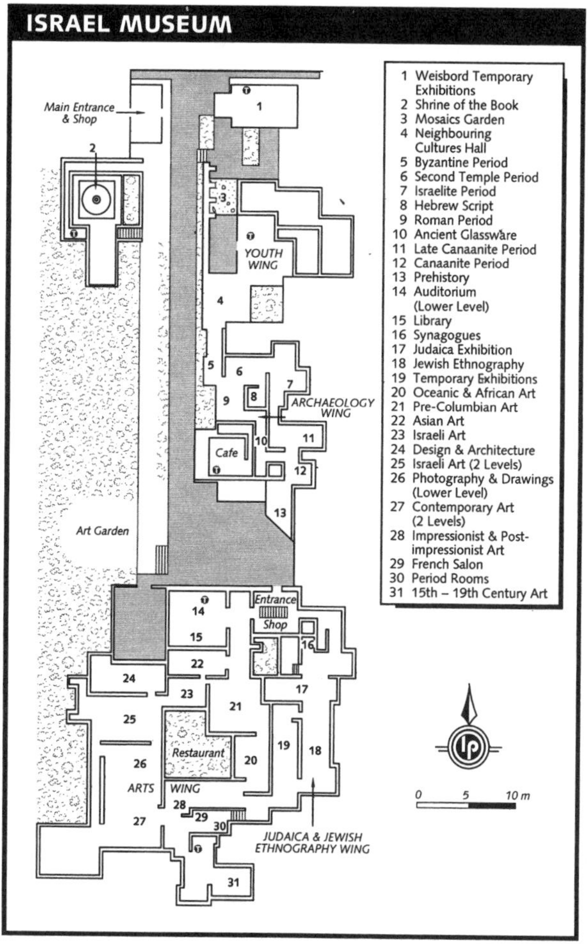

ISRAEL MUSEUM

Main Entrance & Shop

Art Garden

YOUTH WING

ARCHAEOLOGY WING

Cafe

Entrance
Shop

Restaurant

ARTS WING

JUDAICA & JEWISH ETHNOGRAPHY WING

0   5   10 m

1 Weisbord Temporary Exhibitions
2 Shrine of the Book
3 Mosaics Garden
4 Neighbouring Cultures Hall
5 Byzantine Period
6 Second Temple Period
7 Israelite Period
8 Hebrew Script
9 Roman Period
10 Ancient Glassware
11 Late Canaanite Period
12 Canaanite Period
13 Prehistory
14 Auditorium (Lower Level)
15 Library
16 Synagogues
17 Judaica Exhibition
18 Jewish Ethnography
19 Temporary Exhibitions
20 Oceanic & African Art
21 Pre-Columbian Art
22 Asian Art
23 Israeli Art
24 Design & Architecture
25 Israeli Art (2 Levels)
26 Photography & Drawings (Lower Level)
27 Contemporary Art (2 Levels)
28 Impressionist & Post-impressionist Art
29 French Salon
30 Period Rooms
31 15th – 19th Century Art

The **Manual of Discipline** is the book of social regulations of the ancient Jewish community that lived in Qumran. The scroll deals with issues such as the acceptance of new members, conduct at meals and assemblies, punishment for infringements of rules and so on.

The **Habbakuk Commentary Scroll** deals with the life and times of the Qumran community and gives a revealing sociological commentary on the activities of the people who lived in this ancient town.

The **War Scroll** is a war manual, but it also alludes to a so-called battle between the 'Children of Light' and the 'Children of Darkness'.

The lower section of the hall contains artefacts from the Bar Kochba Revolt found in a cave in Nahal Hever not far from Qumran. The corridor to the main hall contains letters found in the same cave along with fragments of other writings.

Judaica & Jewish Ethnography Wing This is one of the richest and most colourful of the museum's exhibitions comprising of a huge range of artefacts both large and small detailing all facets of Jewish life. Probably due to the long centuries of the Diaspora, the Jewish world has had a long-held interest in its own people and religion – the oldest religion still practised today. This exhibition is a repository for the spiritual and cultural wealth of the Israeli nation

The exhibition is in two parts; the Judaica section is comprised of objects made of metal – primarily silver – and centres around five major themes: the Shabbat, the synagogue, the Torah, illuminated manuscripts, and Jewish holidays. The most outstanding features are the three complete synagogues brought from various locations and reconstructed. Of the three, the **Vittorio Veneto Synagogue** is the most impressive. It dates from 1700 and was transported from Vittorio Veneto in Italy in 1965. It was used by the Ashkenazi (European Jewish) community in Italy for more than 200 years, but fell into disuse after WWI.

Look out for the excellent examples of lavishly designed *parochets* (Torah Ark curtains), Torah mantles and scroll cases. There are also spice boxes, alms boxes, Torah ornaments, *haggadot* (illuminated manuscripts) and superb manuscripts of marriage contracts.

The second part of this exhibition focuses on Jewish ethnography; the variety of folk costumes on display is most impressive. Foremost among the exhibits are a Jewish bride's outfit from San'a in Yemen dating from the turn of the 19th and 20th centuries, a Druze woman's apparel from Galilee dating back to the late 19th century, and richly embroidered Palestinian costumes from Bethlehem of the 1930s. Look out for costumes from Jewish communities in Ethiopia and Kurdistan.

The **Ortenau Room** is a replica of a middle-class Jewish home featuring domestic trappings from the early 19th century to around 1938. The room belonged to the Ortenau family of Bad Reichenhall near Munich in Germany and was preserved in its entirety through the duration of WWII before being donated to the Israel Museum. As such it is testimony not only to Jewish life in Europe before WWII, but also stands as a memorial to the victims of that same war.

Archaeology Wing If it's pots, shards, coins and bones that you like, the **Archaeology Wing** will keep you engrossed for hours. Constituting a long serpentine segment of the museum complex, the exhibition starts chronologically from the ground floor level of the main entrance building and should ideally be tackled from this starting point. It is the most comprehensive archaeological collection in the whole country and features finds made in Israel since 1948.

Top: Restoration work on a Hellenistic relief in the Archaeology Garden
Bottom: 'Beit Shean' bust of the Roman emperor Hadrian

Top: Archaeology Gallery
(Second Temple Period)
Middle: The
Design Pavillion
Bottom: Japanese
Netsuke (left); the
Rothschild Room, a re-
creation of 18th century
Paris (right)

There is a varied display of prehistory material in the first gallery including hand axes, picks, chopper tools and spheroids. All of these items have been found at sites in Israel and paint a rich tableau of the country's first inhabitants. An impressive collection of Judean Treasure artefacts from the Chalcolithic period are worth looking out for. The collection of heads, maces, standards and sceptres are made of arsenic and antimony copper and were moulded using the *cire perdue* (lost wax) process; they were found in a Judean desert cave in 1961.

Right: Ivory pomegranate from the First Temple Period (© The Israel Museum Jerusalem/ Nachum Slapak)

The Canaanite period gallerys feature anthropoid sarcophagi, gold jewellery and various clay figurines and jugs. The Israelite period gallery houses the '*House of David' Victory Stele* – a fragmentary monumental inscription from the First Temple period and the only extra-biblical reference to the Davidic dynasty to have come to light so far. Other notable artefacts from this period include a curious ivory pomegranate and an unusual pottery stand decorated with clay musicians, from the late 11th to early 10th century BC.

The **Roman period** is well represented by Jewish sarcophagi, ossuaries and some impressive statues including a bronze bust of Hadrian from the 2nd century AD. Found at Beit She'an, it is considered to be one of the finest portraits of Hadrian ever discovered.

The exhibits in the neighbouring cultures hall include rock reliefs from Simurrum in north-eastern Iraq, stelae from the Zagros Mountains in western Iran, an Egyptian board game called senet and an ingenuously entitled *Votive Statue of the Singer Imeni* from Cusae in Middle Egypt.

Arts Wing The **Arts Wing** takes up a considerable portion of the museum complex, occupying two floors of the southern wing as well as an annexe at Beit Ticho in the New City. There is a lot to see – art for every taste, from curious plastic nude statues to traditional European impressionist paintings. There are galleries for prints, drawings, paintings, sculpture and photography as well as Israeli art since 1906. There are also sections on the arts of Oceania, Asia, Africa and the Americas.

The **modern art and sculpture** collections, including the Art Garden outside the museum's main building (see later in this section for more details) are prominent features of the museum complex. Inside the museum proper are galleries of **impressionist** and **postimpressionist art** – admire works by Renoir, Pissaro, Gauguin, Matisse and Van Gogh. One of the most arresting displays is a complete **French Salon** from the 18th century (viewed from two entrances leading off from the postimpressionist art gallery).

Israeli art is well represented in the **Israeli Art** pavilion with striking paintings by Reuven Rubin and Yosef Zaritsky, and less conventional work by Igael Tumarkin (see his odd exhibit made of wood, textiles, iron, a stretcher and paint entitled *Mita Meshunah* – Unnatural Death). The upper floor of this pavilion has a series of changing exhibitions while the lower floor houses the permanent exhibit of modern Israeli art.

There is an extensive photography collection showing impressive works by Man Ray and Manuel Alvarez Bravo as well as Israeli photographers Mendel Diness and Yaakov Ben Dov. One of the most curious exhibits is an erotic-inspired photo-painting by Salvador Dali and Horst P. Horst – *Costume Design for the Dream of Venus* – in which Dali has painted over a photograph of a naked woman.

Left: Seated Male figure Mexico. Late Classic Period, 600-900 AD (© The Israel Museum Jerusalem)

Art Garden The art theme extends to the **Art Garden** on the eastern side of the complex and is reached by a paved pathway from the Shrine of the Book. The hard-to-miss, black bronze sculpture called *Vertebrae* by British artist Henry Moore is a semiabstract creation reminding one of both the shape of a woman through its suggestive curvature, and the internal structure of the human body with pieces resembling the vertebrae of the spine. Also look out for the striking sculpture *Mother and Child* by Jacques Lipchitz.

The Art Garden provides visitors with a welcome respite from the heady collections of the Israel Museum. Before wandering inside, enjoy the splendid views over the western side of Jerusalem's New City.

Youth Wing The **Youth Wing** serves as the education department of the museum. Children can enjoy hands-on educational activities including playing with model houses conveniently positioned at children's eyelevel. Groups of school children are given guided tours and art classes are offered to interested parties.

(continued from page 123)

Middle East. Other features of interest include the **Academy of the Hebrew Language**, which displays the library and furniture of Eliezer Ben Yehuda, who was responsible for the revival of the Hebrew language (see the boxed text 'Ben Yehuda & the Revival of Hebrew' in the Facts about Jerusalem chapter), and the **Rubin Academy of Music & Dance**, which has a collection of old and ancient musical instruments. It's open from 10 am to 8 pm Sunday to Thursday during the academic year only. The campus also features a strikingly designed puffball-shaped synagogue. Free daily guided tours of the campus start at 9 and 11 am at the old Sherman building.

On the eastern slopes of Givat Ram and part of the university, the **Botanical Garden** is one of the city's best hidden beauty spots, a 12 hectare haven featuring flowers, pools and trees. Admission is free and it is open from early morning to sunset every day of the week. For further details call ☎ 663 6342.

Monastery of the Cross (Map 2)

This great walled compound looks like a desert monastery and appears completely out of place in the middle of the large urban sprawl of the New City (up until the 20th century the city lay a mile or more from this then isolated valley). Founded by King Bagrat of Georgia, the monastery was built to commemorate the traditional belief that Jesus' cross was made from a tree that grew here. The monastery is basically 11th century, although various additions have been made since then. The Greek Orthodox Church purchased the complex in 1685.

It's worth a visit just to appreciate the incongruity of the monastery's location, which is even greater once inside, but there are also some interesting 17th century frescoes, a bit of 5th century mosaic floor in the chapel and a small museum. The monastery is open from 9 am to 4 pm Monday to Friday, closed Saturday and Sunday. Admission is 5 NIS. It can be reached by walking through Rehavia along Ramban St, cross-ing Khay'in Hazaz Ave (Hanasi Ben Zvi) and following the path down the hillside. From the city centre take bus Nos 31 or 32; from Jaffa Gate, bus No 19. Get off at the first stop on Harav Herzog St and follow the path down.

WEST OF THE NEW CITY (MAP 1)
Model of Ancient Jerusalem

About 2.5km south-west of Givat Ram in the grounds of the Holyland Hotel (☎ 643 7777) is a huge 1:50 scale model of Jerusalem as it was in 66 AD, at the end of the Second Temple period. While the model is fantastic and the attention to detail is incredible, it's a long way out of town and only those with a keen interest in Jewish history or archaeology are going to find the trip worthwhile.

The model is open for viewing from 8 am, closing 8 pm Sunday to Thursday, and 5 pm Friday and Saturday (closing daily at 4 pm during winter). Admission is 10 NIS (students 6 NIS). Take bus Nos 21 or 21A.

New Biblical Zoo

Also known as the Tisch Family Zoological Gardens, since 1993 this has replaced the much reviled old Biblical Zoo that once existed in the north of the city. While fairly small, the new zoo (☎ 643 0111) is attractively landscaped with lakes, streams and grassy picnic areas. The animals seem to be well looked after with few cramped cages in evidence. One major aim of the zoo is to breed and reintroduce into Israel various species that through references in the Bible are known to have once inhabited this region. Biblical quotes accompany the scientific names and descriptions (in English as well as Hebrew and Arabic) tagged to the pens.

The zoo is open 9 am to 7.30 pm Sunday to Thursday, 9 am to 4.30 pm Friday, and 10 am to 6 pm Saturday. Admission is 20 NIS (children 15 NIS). The zoo is out in the Manahat (or Malkha) district; take bus Nos 26, 33 or 99 travelling westbound from the central bus station.

Mt Herzl

In November 1995 world leaders from over 86 nations assembled here to pay their last respects to the assassinated Israeli prime minister, Yitzhak Rabin. He was laid to rest beside the graves of other former holders of the office, including Levi Eshkol, Golda Meir and Menachem Begin. Also buried here is the founder of political Zionism, Theodor Herzl, the man after whom this pleasant parkland area is named.

Herzl Museum (☎ 6511 108) includes a replica of Herzl's Vienna study, library and furniture. It's open from 9 am, closing 5 pm Sunday to Thursday, and 1 pm Friday, closed Saturday. Admission is free. Take bus Nos 13, 18, 20, 23 or 27.

Yad Vashem

Anyone who spends much time in the country will soon become aware of just how much the spectre of the Holocaust continues to haunt Israeli society. The modern Jewish state was born out of the tragic experiences of persecution, flight and the death camps, and from the desire to make sure that such horrors would never be repeated. As a columnist in the *Jerusalem Report* put it, the Holocaust is, in effect, the civil religion of Israel. If that is so, then Yad Vashem ('A Memorial and a Name', from 1 Isaiah 56:5) is its greatest shrine. It's telling that while the Western Wall doesn't necessarily make it on to the program, nearly all visiting heads of state are taken on an official visit to Yad Vashem.

While it's not going to make for the cheeriest day of your holiday, there are good reasons to come here. The history and tragedy documented at the site speaks of far more than the Nazis and the nation of Israel.

Yad Vashem (☎ 675 1611, www.yad-vashem.org.il) is open from 9 am, closing at 4.45 pm Sunday to Thursday, and 1 pm Friday (closed Saturday). Admission is free. There are free guided tours on Sunday and Wednesday at 10 am. Take bus Nos 13, 18, 20, 23 or 27.

The 45 acres of the Yad Vashem complex, established in 1953 by an act of the Knesset, are divided into these main areas: the historical and art museums, the Hall of Rememberance, the Valley of the Communities, the Children's Memorial, and the Righteous Among the Nations. Vad Yashem also houses an extensive Shoah library and archive, including the Hall of Names, which is an ongoing project to record the name of every person who died in the Holocaust.

Historical & Art Museums The format of the Historical Museum was established in 1973 and is currently being restructured. The five halls reflect the five stages of the Shoah (Holocaust), from 1933 to the aftermath of 1945.

The Art Museum originally housed art works 'predominantly created by Jewish artists living under German occupation, in cities, ghettos and concentration camps during WWII', but has recently been expanded to include contemporary art by second and third generation survivors, and also by artists with no direct connection to the Holocaust.

Hall of Rememberance This is the most immediately dramatic of the components of Vad Yashem. The names of concentration-camp sites are engraved on the floor, surrounding an eternal flame, in front of which is a crypt containing the ashes of victims. The tradition is for IDF recruits to pay a visit on the eve of battle.

Valley of the Communities & Children's Memorial Inspired by the biblical Valley of the Dry Bones, the Valley of the Communities was excavated by Lippa Yahalom and Dan Zur in the grounds of Vad Yashem. It records the names of some 5000 Jewish communities destroyed in the Shoah; these names are now symbolically engraved into the bedrock of Israel.

Set in a cavern, the Children's Memorial is dedicated to the 1.5 million children who died in the camps. It is lit with memorial candles, and the names of the children can be heard in the background, recorded on a looped tape.

YAD VASHEM

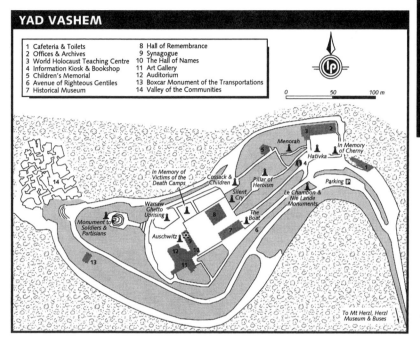

1 Cafeteria & Toilets
2 Offices & Archives
3 World Holocaust Teaching Centre
4 Information Kiosk & Bookshop
5 Children's Memorial
6 Avenue of Righteous Gentiles
7 Historical Museum
8 Hall of Remembrance
9 Synagogue
10 The Hall of Names
11 Art Gallery
12 Auditorium
13 Boxcar Monument of the Transportations
14 Valley of the Communities

Righteous Among the Nations This memorial was dedicated in 1963 by an additional act of the Knesset to commemorate the Gentiles who risked their lives to save Jews. Some 16,000 people have been recognised, some posthumously. Notable figures include the industrialist Oskar Schindler, and diplomats Raoul Wallenberg and Sempo Sugihara. Entire communities are also honoured, including the French village of Le Chambon-sur-Lignon and the Dutch village of Nieuwlande. The small rowboat commemorates the collective Danish effort to smuggle 7200 of their 8000 Jews to neutral Sweden.

A recent posthumous addition is Frank Foley. An MI6 agent stationed as the head of the passport and visa section of the British embassy in Berlin, Foley is said to have saved 10,000 German Jews, hiding some of them in his own apartment.

Ein Kerem

Now enveloped by the expanding New City, the ugly apartment blocks of which threaten to blight the terraced valley slopes, this picturesque village contains several attractive churches commemorating the traditional birthplace of John the Baptist.

It's a very pleasant walking area, and although bus No 17 from Jaffa Rd comes directly to the village, you might instead take bus Nos 5, 6, 18 or 21 to reach Ein Kerem via the Jerusalem Forest. Get off at the Sonol petrol station on Herzl Blvd, continue walking in the same direction and take the first right onto Ye'fe Nof and then the second left, Pirhe Chen, to enter the forest. Head for the Youth Centre in the middle of the forest; the village is visible most of the way.

Church of St John This church is owned by the Franciscans and built over the grotto

THINGS TO SEE & DO

where St John is believed to have been born. Steps lead down to the grotto, with its remains of ancient structures and a Byzantine mosaic.

The church is open from 9 am to noon and 2.30 to 5 pm Sunday to Friday (closing 4 pm in winter), closed Saturday. Admission is free. It's on the street to the right of the main road.

Church of the Visitation This church is also Franciscan and was built on the traditional site of the summer residence of Zecharias and Elizabeth, the parents of St John. The church commemorates the visit to their home by the Virgin Mary, who was at that time pregnant with Jesus. Note also the ancient cistern and, in an alcove, the stone behind which John supposedly hid from Roman soldiers. Upstairs is the apse of a Crusader church. It's open daily from 8 to 11.45 am and 2.30 to 6 pm. Admission is free.

You'll find it on the street to the left of the main road, opposite that leading to the Church of St John. The spring which gives the village its name is nearby. The wall bears the words of the prophet Isaiah, 'Everyone who thirsts, come to the waters' (Isaiah 55:1).

Russian Church & Monastery Higher up the steep slope, this monastery (☎ 622 2565, 565 4128) can only be visited by appointment.

Hadassah Medical Centre & the Chagall Windows

Often confused with its namesake on Mt Scopus, the Hadassah Medical Centre is the Middle East's largest hospital. However, it's far more famous internationally for the synagogue, which features a set of stained-glass windows by French Jewish artist Marc Chagall (see the Chagall boxed text). Each of his 12 colourful, abstract panels depicts one of the tribes of Israel. Created in 1960-61 and installed soon after, four of the windows were shattered during the 1967 war and had to be repaired

Chagall

Marc Chagall was never a resident of Jerusalem (or even Israel), but he is possibly the artist closest to the heart of the city. Born in a small city in what is now Belarus in 1887, Chagall had a religious Jewish upbringing. This intrinsic Jewishness permeates many of his paintings, which are dreamy semi-folkloric scenes incorporating fiddlers on rooftops and heavily bearded rabbis.

His greatest artistic legacies to Jerusalem are the tapestries he designed for the foyer of the Knesset building and the 12 stained glass windows he created for the synagogue of the Hadassah Medical Centre. Works by Chagall also hang in the Israel Museum in Givat Ram.

by the artist who, as a testimony to the event, allowd a single symbolic bullet hole to remain unrepaired in the lower part of the green window.

The synagogue and tourist centre (☎ 641 6333, 644 6271) are open to visitors from 8 am to 3.45 pm Sunday to Thursday, and from 8.30 am to 12.30 pm on Friday, closed Saturday. Admission is 12 NIS (students 7 NIS), which includes a guided tour (held every hour on the half-hour until 12.30 pm). Take bus Nos 19 or 27 and get off at the last stop. The Hadassah Medical Centre is als within walking distance from Ein Kerem.

ACTIVITIES

Jerusalem generally panders to one's the spiritual and cerebral sides; for the more physical forms of recreation it's usually necessary to look elsewhere. Hiking and climbing are possible in the nearby Jericho and Dead Sea regions and beach culture and water sports thrive in Tel Aviv, only a 45 minute bus ride away (see the Excursions chapter), with buses departing from Jerusalem's central bus station every 15 minutes throughout the day.

Aerial Tours

Jerusalem Wings (☎ 583 1444, fax 583 1880, email lljrwing@inter.net.il) is an aerial tour company offering 30 minutes in a small plane over Jerusalem and its environs for US$50 per person, or a 60 minute whirl down to Masada and back for US$90 per person. Reservations must be made a few days in advance.

Archaeological Digs

Definitely not for gold-diggers, most archaeological digs require that you pay to work. In January of each year the Israeli Antiquities Authority (IAA), which is part of the Ministry of Education & Culture, publishes a list of the archaeological excavations open to volunteers for the coming year. To get a copy, contact the IAA at the Rockefeller Museum (☎ 629 2627, fax 629 2628, PO Box 586, Jerusalem 91004). To volunteer you must be over 18 years old, fit and fully insured.

The digging season is May to September, when universities are in recess and the weather is hot and dry. No previous excavating experience is usually necessary, but volunteers should be prepared to participate for a minimum of one or two weeks, depending on the individual dig. A fee for food and accommodation (varying from sleeping bags to three star hotels) is required. Some expeditions do provide volunteers with an allowance for food, accommodation and/or travel expenses within Israel.

The Institute of Archaeology at the Hebrew University of Jerusalem (☎ 588 2403, fax 582 5548, Mt Scopus, Jerusalem 91905), takes volunteers for week-long digs at a cost of US$180, including room and meals, lectures and field trips.

For those interested in trying archaeology one day at a time, there's a tourist-oriented 'Dig for a Day' program operating during July and August and involving a three hour excavation, seminars and a tour. It costs about US$55. Contact Archaeological Seminars (☎ 627 3515, fax 627 2660, email office@archesem.com, PO Box 14002, 34 Habad St, Jerusalem 91140).

Cycling

The Jerusalem Cycle Club (☎ 561 9416, 16 Rachael Imenu St) in the German Colony, organises Saturday morning rides around the environs of Jerusalem. The excursions start at 7 am and usually last about four hours; the club can rent out bicycles.

For do-it-yourself pedal power check out Walk Ways (☎ 533 6294, fax 533 2402, email rockman@netvision.net.il). Owner Chaim Rockman rents out bicycles at a reasonable rate and although this outfit is located out in Mevesseret Zion on the Tel Aviv road, he will drop off and pick up bicycles at your hotel or hostel. Walk Ways also organises adventurous cycling and camping tours throughout Israel, Jordan and Egypt's Sinai region. See the Bicycle section of the Getting Around chapter.

COURSES
Bible Studies

St George's College (☎ 628 4372, 31 Salah a-Din St, Jerusalem 95908) describes itself as a centre for fieldwork, study and reflection in the Holy Land, allowing you to study the Bible in its appropriate geographical setting. The college offers courses that include Bible study and field trips throughout the Holy Land and to Sinai, lasting from 16 days (US$1500) to three (US$1720), four (US$2250) and 10 weeks (US$5100).

Course subject headings include 'The Bible and the Holy Land Today', 'The Palestine of Jesus', and 'The Bible and its Setting'. Food and board are included.

Language

The *ulpanim* (language schools) network caters for new Jewish immigrants and generally doesn't welcome Gentiles. Contact the Ulpan Office, Division of Adult Education (☎ 625 4156, 11 Beit Ha'am, Bezalel St, Jerusalem 94591).

Birzeit University in the West Bank offers course in Arabic language and literature to beginners and more experienced students. For details check out the Birzeit University Web site (see the boxed text 'Online Services' in the Facts for the Visitor chapter).

Places to Stay

Jerusalem has a wide range of accommodation with plenty of scope for both the budget and the business traveller. Before you convert all your currency into shekels, remember that by paying in US dollars (where the option exists) you avoid the 17% VAT; in such cases the rates are given in dollars rather than shekels.

The best location to stay really depends on your requirements. The Old City and East Jerusalem tend to have the cheapest places and the best atmosphere, and of course they're the most convenient for the major sites nearby. However, some hostels and hospices have strict curfews, and being at least a good 20 minute walk from the nightlife of the New City centre, they aren't so great for those who want to stay out late (the Old City and East Jerusalem completely close down at dusk).

Newcomers to the Jerusalem accommodation scene are a growing string of nifty bed & breakfast establishments that are conveniently filling the gap between the backpacker hostels and the generally expensive hotels. They are certainly worth looking at if you are a traveller with a mid-range budget.

The Israel Hotel Association (see under Hotels opposite) lists many hotels in Jerusalem – but not all of them. Only member hotels that have paid their subscription dues are listed, so hotels that are not listed are not necessarily substandard. However, there is no longer a star rating system for hotels in Jerusalem or Israel, so price is the only real guide here to quality. All hotels are signposted around town with standardised orange and black signs showing the hotel name in Roman, Hebrew and Arabic script as well as a picture of a bed.

HOSTELS
Jerusalem has dozens of privately run hostels, mainly clustered in the Old City and just outside Damascus Gate, in addition to

Christian Hospices

Various Christian denominations have accommodation in the vicinity of their religious sites. They are often the best value in the low-to-moderate price range, with cleanliness apparently the top priority.

You do not need to be a Christian to stay in most of these hospices, but you must be prepared to abide by the rules, which usually involve a strict curfew, an early check-out time and no double rooms for unmarried couples.

Some hospices are extremely informal and are more like regular guesthouses or hotels.

---

five (at last count) large establishments administered by Hostelling International (HI). Nonmembers can stay at HI hostels for usually only a handful more shekels than card holders, so it isn't especially worth buying a card. For a list of HI hostels countrywide or for any further information, contact the Israel Youth Hostels Association (☎ 655 8400, fax 655 8432, email iyha@netvision .net.il, International Convention Centre, PO Box 6001, Jerusalem 91060). The International Convention Centre is west of the city centre and about 500m south of the new bus station. The office is open from 8.30 am to 3 pm Sunday to Thursday and from 9 am to noon on Friday and you can also check out its Web site at www.youth-hostels.org.il.

BED & BREAKFAST
The Home Accommodation Association of Jerusalem (HAAJ) maintains a growing list of over 30 establishments that offer informal B&B arrangements. These range from self-contained apartment studios to simple rooms with private facilities. In many cases breakfast is offered as part of the deal. The

atmosphere at B&Bs is usually informal and friendly and gives a chance for travellers to meet not only the owners, but fellow-travellers and locals as well.

These establishments are often located only 10 to 20 minutes from the New and Old cities, and are ideal for both short and longer-term visitors who prefer a more homely atmosphere to an often sterile hotel environment. In any case, the availability of buses to and from these places are fairly painless to get to. Prices range from US$25 to US$70 and in at least 13 cases, bookings can be made effortlessly via email.

Check the HAAJ's Web site (www.bnb .co.il) for further details.

HOTELS

In comparison with the number of budget and mid-price beds available, Jerusalem has a disproportionately high percentage of luxury accommodation; in fact, the Israeli State goes as far as sponsoring and subsidising the construction of new upmarket hotels. Except during the high season (see When to Go in the Facts for the Visitor chapter), prices at these hotels compare favourably with those in other parts of the world and, attuned as they are to a predominantly North American clientele, the facilities and level of service are top class.

Prices have in fact shot up enormously since this book was last published – by as much as 50% in some cases – and finding reasonably cheap hotel accommodation may mean a sacrifice in quality. Prices are also determined by high, low and regular seasons and even these seasons change according to region. The price difference between low and high seasons can be as little as US$20 or as much as US$100. However, these seasonal price hikes tend to apply mainly to mid-range and top-end hotels only.

The Israel Hotel Association (☎ 03-517 0131, fax 510 0197, email infotels@ israelhotels.org.il, Web site www.israelhotels .org.il) maintains a Web site with an up-to-date list of hotels and prices. It is suggested you look at the site and contact hotels individually to make bookings; you may be able to secure a better deal this way. Wherever possible, hotels' email addresses have been listed throughout this chapter.

LONG-TERM RENTALS

Anyone intending to spend two months or more in Jerusalem may want to consider renting a room or an apartment. If you look around you should be able to pay less rent than you would in a hostel (the going rate for a room in a shared flat is around 750 NIS or US$250 per calendar month), and you may have more privacy and independence.

To find a cheap room or studio, or someone who needs an extra person to share an apartment, scan the 'In Jerusalem' section of Friday's *The Jerusalem Post* or, better still, get someone who reads Hebrew to take you through the classifieds in *Kol Ha'Ir*, a local weekly. The notice boards at the two campuses of Hebrew University are at the Israel Centre on the corner of Strauss and HaNevi'im Sts, and at the Sefer VeSefel and Tmol Shilshom bookshops, both in the New City centre; these can also be good places to look.

She'al (Map 3, ☎ 622 6991, 21 King George V St) is a property agency that keeps lists in English, although it charges a small fortune to let you look at them. It is open from 8.30 am to 1 pm and 4 to 7 pm Sunday to Thursday, and from 8.30 am to 1 pm Friday (closed Saturday).

PLACES TO STAY – BUDGET
Old City

Most of the Old City's budget accommodation is found near Jaffa and Damascus gates, which is convenient because they are the main access points to the Old City and are well served by buses. From outside the central bus station, across the other side of Jaffa Rd, take bus Nos 13 or 20 for Jaffa Gate and bus Nos 23 or 27 for Damascus Gate.

The main contender in the popularity stakes is *Tabasco Hostel (Map 6, ☎/fax 628 3461)* on Aqabat at-Takiya St (you can see the sign from Souq Khan as-Zeit St). This place is very lively, animated and clean, though it is sometimes crowded. It has a busy notice board and no curfew, though you will have to identify yourself to get in after 1 am. Downstairs is the Old City's most partyin' venue (see the Entertainment chapter), though the veneer was dented in August 1998 when hooded thugs entered and smashed up the bar. Presumably they were objecting to the open sale of alcohol in a Muslim-dominated quarter. Nevertheless, Tabasco Hostel is cheap: dorm beds are 18 NIS and a mattress on the roof is 15 NIS. A rather small private room, however, is a hefty 75 NIS.

In the vicinity of Damascus Gate *Al-Arab Hostel (Map 6, ☎ 628 3537, Souq Khan as-Zeit St)* is another backpackers' hang-out. Its reputation has waxed and waned over the years, as has the sometimes gruff attitude of staff. Avoid talking politics here, if at all possible. As well as large airy, cat-prowled dorms (15 NIS), there are beds on the roof (12 NIS) and a couple of private double rooms at 50 NIS. Showers and toilets are communal and are perhaps too few, but it has a tiny kitchen with free tea and a table tennis room, and each night videos are shown in the cushion-strewn common room. Curfew is 1.30 am. Take note, though: at the Al-Arab beds are usually paid for when checking-out. Keep a record of any transactions.

Far cleaner, far quieter and a much better option altogether is the fairly austere *New Hashimi Hostel (Map 6, ☎ 628 4410, fax 628 4667, Souq Khan as-Zeit St)*. The dorms have only eight beds (20 NIS), and each room has its own shower and toilet, as do the very attractive private doubles at 90 NIS. There's a large common area with plenty of tables and chairs and a well-equipped kitchen. Reception is open 24 hours a day. Note that this is primarily a Muslim hostel and that means no alcohol and no open association between the sexes. The New Hashimi is just two doors along from the Al-Arab hostel.

Right next to the mosque on Al-Wad Rd is *Al-Ahram Youth Hostel (Map 6, ☎ 628 0926, fax 992 1027)*, another fairly quiet and reasonably clean place that seems to at-

tract an older crowd. Dorm beds are 20 NIS, a comfortable mattress up on the roof terrace goes for between 24 NIS and 30 NIS. There is an enforced midnight curfew. Across from the Al-Ahram, on the corner of the Via Dolorosa, is *Austrian Hospice (Map 7, ☎ 627 1466)*. Secluded behind high walls, this place is almost monastic in its asceticism and sobriety. You may find, however, it redeemed by the wonderful garden terraces that overlook the streets below. Dorm beds are US$26 for the first night and US$13 for each subsequent night. Double rooms (married couples only) cost US$72 including breakfast. There's a midnight curfew but a US$20 deposit gets you a night key. The hospice is open to arriving guests from 7 am to 10 pm.

In the Jaffa Gate area is *Petra Hostel (Map 6, ☎ 628 6618, 626 2434)*. It's set in a superb location on Omar ibn al-Khattab Square, so see if you can get into a dorm with a balcony overlooking the action. It's an airy, breezy place, with lots of room to move and breathe. Located in what was once a grand hotel in the Old City, it is now a popular backpackers' home, however the attitude of one or two of the staff here is somewhat diffident. Dorm beds are 23 NIS and a spot on the roof with a great view of the Dome of the Rock – if you ignore the abandoned wasteland of Hezekiah's pool below – is 15 NIS.

Not far away is *New Swedish Hostel (Map 6 ☎ 626 4124, fax 628 7884, 29 David St)* some 100m into the bazaar. While it's clean and generally quite acceptable overall and draws a regular backpacker crowd (many of whom come from Sweden) it is somewhat cramped and pokey. Dorm beds cost 15 NIS and tiny private rooms are between 50 NIS and 75 NIS. There is a 3 am curfew.

Jaffa Gate Youth Hostel (Map 6, ☎ 627 6402), behind the Christian Information Centre, is a popular, occasionally crowded place that has a kitchen and cosy TV lounge. Dorm beds (women only) are 25 NIS and a double room is 90 NIS. There's a midnight curfew.

For a couple of better hostels, head into the bazaar along David St from Omar ibn al-Khattab Square, take the first right and then turn left immediately onto St Mark's Rd. *Citadel Youth Hostel (Map 6, ☎ 627 4375, email citadelhostel@netscape.net)* is 50m along on the right. The reception and the small double rooms (60 to 100 NIS) on the ground floor look like they've been burrowed into the stone. A tight, narrow stairway leads up to some clean and comfortable dorms (20 NIS), a small lounge and kitchen, and access to the roof with views over the Old City.

Just beyond the Citadel Youth Hostel, on the opposite side of the street, is the *Lutheran Hospice (Map 6, ☎ 628 2120, fax 628 5107, email luthhosp@netvision.net.il)*, the closest thing to a 'five star' hostel in Jerusalem. It is beautiful. There are shady cloisters, a huge spotless kitchen and a palm garden with a fountain and views of the Dome of the Rock. The dorms are single sex and beds are 25 NIS. Private single rooms are priced in Deutschmarks and go for between DM66 and DM78, doubles are from DM59 to DM65. The hospice is closed from 9 am to noon and has a strict 10.30 pm curfew, though you may stay out later if you tell the front desk when you'll be back.

Finally, tucked away on quiet El-Malak St is the only private accommodation option in the Jewish Quarter. This is *El-Malak Youth Hostel (Map 9, ☎ 628 5362)*, a cool, cosy oasis in the basement of an old house not far from the Western Wall. Dorm beds go for 20 NIS and small private rooms, some of which are in a separate part of the house, go for between 75/100 NIS. Ask for Isaac, the custodian of the hostel.

East Jerusalem

'Hostel Row' is the stretch of HaNevi'im St across from Damascus Gate, beside the service taxi rank. There are four possibilities here, the best of which are the two nearest the Old City walls. *Faisal Hostel (Map 5, ☎ 627 2492, 4 HaNevi'im St)* is the closest, and it has a good terrace on which guests can laze around and watch the activity around the gate. There's a kitchen with free tea and coffee, and a common room. It's worth noting that the hostel's occupants seem to be a semipermanent migrant crowd rather than backpackers. Dorm beds (a bit cramped) are 20 NIS and there are a few doubles at 50 NIS. There's a flexible 1 am curfew.

Palm Hostel (Map 5, ☎ 627 3189, 6 Ha Nevi'im St), next door to the Faisal, has a great common room with plants and a glass roof. There's also a kitchen with a fridge, and videos are shown most nights. There is no curfew. Beds in large, spacious dorms are 20 NIS, and there are a few private rooms at 80 and 100 NIS.

Much harder to recommend are *New Raghadan Hostel (Map 5, ☎ 628 3348)* and *Ramsis Hostel (Map 5, ☎ 627 1651)*, a few doors up at 10 and 20 HaNevi'im St respectively. These places seem to cater primarily to transient migrants.

Around the corner from the Ramsis and just north of the Nablus Rd Arab bus station is *Cairo Hostel (Map 6, ☎ 627 7216, 21 Nablus Rd)*. It's a bit soulless and not particularly friendly, but there's a large lounge with satellite TV, and free tea and coffee in the kitchen. Dorm beds are 15 NIS, and there are private rooms for 60 NIS that take three or maybe four people.

New City

Although it is way more expensive than the Old City and East Jerusalem hostels, *Jerusalem Inn Hostel (☎ 625 1294, 6 HaHistradrut St)* just off pedestrianised Ben Yehuda St, right in the centre of the New City, is recommended. It's a converted apartment building with dorms on three floors, all kept immaculately clean. It further endears itself to some by having a strictly enforced no smoking policy (and you don't want to mess with Olga, the manager on this or any other issues). There's no kitchen, but at the reception/bar area you can get breakfast, snacks, tea, coffee and beer. The place has a midnight curfew but a deposit will get you a front door key. Dorm beds are 42 NIS and singles are 96 NIS, while doubles start at 120 NIS.

A relative newcomer to the hostel scene here is *My Home (Map 3, ☎ 623 2235, fax 623 2236, email myhome@netvision.net.il, 15 King George St)*, close to Ben Yehuda Street. It's clean enough, though the floors are a bit grungy and could do with a scrub, and dorm beds (US$14/17) are certainly not as cheap as in the Old City or even nearby. Double rooms are a better buy at US$20/24 and breakfast is included. Nonetheless, it is handy for city nightlife and most amenities.

Another option is *Jasmine Ben Yehuda Hostel (Map 3, ☎ 624 8021, fax 625 3032, 1 Solomon St)* more or less above the Underground disco. This place is reasonably clean and well run but the management are a bit diffident and timeworn, as is the feel of the hostel generally. There is a small kitchen area and tea, coffee and breakfast if you want them. There's no curfew. Dorm beds are 30 NIS.

Hotel Noga (Map 3, ☎ 625 4590 before noon, or 566 1888 after, 4 Bezalel St) is something different altogether: a clean family-owned apartment in a quiet part of town alongside the Bezalel School of Art. The comfortably furnished rooms share a well-equipped kitchen and bathroom. Singles/doubles are 75/90 NIS, and there's also a triple for 120 NIS and a quad for 144 NIS. There's no curfew, as guests get their own front door key. Reservations must be made; ask for Mr or Mrs Kristal.

There are six HI-affiliated hostels in Jerusalem and surrounds, two of which are central. The best is *Beit Shmuel Hostel (Map 3, ☎ 620 3491, fax 620 3467, 6 Shama St)* next to the Hebrew Union College near the junction of HaMelekh David and Agron Sts. This place is highly recommended. It's a beautiful building, more like a hotel than a hostel, and it's only a few minutes walk from both the Old City and the New City centre.

HaDavidka Youth Hostel (Map 2, ☎ 538 4555, fax 538 8790, 67 HaNevi'im St) is at the junction of HaNevi'im St and Jaffa Rd. It's just a few minutes' walk from the city centre and a bus ride (Nos 23 and 27 stop outside on their way to Damascus Gate)

from the Old City. The HaDavidka has good facilities and is well maintained, but is not particularly friendly and is often busy with Israeli school groups. In these HI hostels, dorm beds are between US$13/19 and there are usually also private singles for around US$42, breakfast included in all cases.

Louise Waterman-Wise Hostel (Map 1, ☎ 642 3366, 8 Hapisga St) is out in the Beit Vegan area, about 30 minutes by bus from the New City centre (take bus Nos 18 or 20 to Mt Herzl). *Ein Kerem Youth Hostel (Map 1, ☎ 641 6282)* is off Ma'ayan St in the village of the same name (take bus No 17 to Ein Kerem and get off at the second last stop – ask the driver). Meals are served at both. Last buses from town out in this direction are at 11.15 pm, except on Friday when they stop mid-afternoon. Prices are comparable to those at the city centre HI hostels.

PLACES TO STAY – MID-RANGE
Old City

Most of the Old City's mid-range accommodation is offered by the Christian hospices in the Jaffa Gate area. These tend to be quiet, sober places from which unmarried couples are likely to be turned away. They all have curfews.

Christ Church Hospice (Map 6, ☎ 627 7727, fax 627 7730, email christch@netvision .net.il) at Omar ibn al-Khattab Square, opposite the Citadel entrance, has pleasant staff and is very clean, quiet and comfortable, with a pretty courtyard and comfortable public rooms (see Christ Church in the Things to See & Do chapter for more information). Singles cost from US$41/50, and doubles from US$72/90. As well as its cheap dorm beds, the very popular *Lutheran Hospice* (see under Old City in the Places to Stay – Budget section earlier in this chapter) has an attached guesthouse in which singles go for between DM66/78 and doubles range from DM59/65, with breakfast provided.

Casa Nova Pilgrims' Hospice (Map 6, ☎ 628 2791, fax 626 4370, 10 Casa Nova St), run by the Franciscans with the help of some officious Arab staff, is clean and has vaulted ceilings and massive marble pillars in the dining room. The food is great and the rooms, mainly twins with bathrooms and central heating, are pleasant. The hospice is often full with European pilgrims. Singles/doubles are US$32/42. Approaching from Jaffa Gate, take the second left onto Greek Catholic Patriarchate Rd, and follow it until it becomes Casa Nova St. The hospice is on your left after you enter a narrow alley and climb a set of stairs.

The *Greek Catholic Patriarchate Hospice* (Map 6, ☎ 628 2023, fax 628 6652) is a bit unfriendly, but the basic singles/doubles (US$36/52) are comfortable and breakfast is included. From Jaffa Gate take the second left onto Greek Catholic Patriarchate Rd, which becomes St Dimitri's Rd; the hospice is on the right on the bend.

Although the building is owned by the Greek Orthodox Church, *New Imperial Hotel* (Map 6, ☎ 628 2261), on your left as you enter Jaffa Gate, has few religious trappings. It was built in the late 19th century, and Wilhelm II stayed here when he visited in 1898. The hotel retains an air of dusty, faded grandeur, although the rooms have all been cleaned up and are reasonably comfortable. Heating might be a problem in winter, though renovation of the heating system is planned. Singles/doubles are a bit of a bargain, starting at US$30/33.

Up behind the New Imperial on Latin Patriarchate Rd, *Gloria Hotel* (Map 6, ☎ 628 2431, fax 628 2401) is very modern inside and has large, quiet rooms, with pleasant views from the dining room, across the Citadel. Singles/doubles cost from US$50/75 with breakfast, and there's no curfew.

Deep in the Muslim Quarter on the Via Dolorosa, 50m west of the junction with Al-Wad Rd, is perhaps the most comfortable of the Christian-run establishments. The *Armenian Hospice* (Map 7, ☎ 626 0880, fax 626 1208) has recently been renovated and now offers immaculate doubles with en suite bathroom and TV for $US60.

Around 100m further east along the Via Dolorosa, on the left, is the *Convent of the Sisters of Zion* (Map 7, ☎ 627 7292, fax 628 2224, email eccehomo@inter.net.il), run by the Sisters of Zion. It's very clean, with a study area and kitchen. Singles/doubles are US$40/66 with breakfast. The hospice reception is open from 7 am to 12.30 pm and from 5.30 to 8 pm. There's an 11 pm curfew.

East Jerusalem

This was where all the pilgrims to the Old City would stay when Jerusalem was a divided city, so most of these hotels are found mainly on or around Salah ad-Din St and date from the 1950s and 1960s – and the majority are still firmly stuck in that era. The facilities are generally not as good as those in the New City hotels with comparable prices, but the East Jerusalem places tend to be more friendly.

One of the best accommodation deals in Jerusalem, *St George's Cathedral Guesthouse* (☎ 628 3302, fax 628 2253, email sghotel@netvision.net.il, 20 Nablus Rd) is part of the St George's Cathedral compound, just 10 minutes walk from the Old City. It's a delightful cloistered building with an attractive garden. The atmosphere is very relaxed and friendly, with no curfew. The comfortable rooms, most with private bathroom, cost in the high season US$50/78 for singles/doubles with breakfast.

On the same street but a little closer to Damascus Gate is *Capitolina Hotel* (☎ 628 6888, fax 627 6301, 29 Nablus Rd) next door to the US Consulate and once Jerusalem's YMCA. The decor is dowdy but there are good facilities, including a swimming pool and squash and tennis courts; rooms are US$55/75.

The *Jerusalem Golden Walls Hotel* (☎ 627 2135, fax 589 4658, email admin@pilgrimpal .com) on Sultan Suleyman St facing the Old City walls definitely has the prime location of the more conventional hotels. Unfortunately, it's also next to the bus station, so rooms on that side suffer from chronic noise pollution. It is, though, one of East Jerusalem's best-appointed hotels; rooms cost US$105/140.

Not much further from the Old City (just a few minutes walk from Damascus Gate),

Jerusalem Hotel (☎/fax 628 3282), just off Nablus Rd facing the Nablus Rd Arab bus station, is not a bad option. It's a beautiful building with an attractive courtyard and has a cool, welcoming stone-clad interior; rooms are US$59/85.

Many of the other hotels in East Jerusalem suffered badly from a lack of trade in the *intifada* years and are now seriously in need of some money being spent on them. A case in point is **Rivoli Hotel** (☎ 628 4871, fax 627 4879, 3 Salah ad-Din St) on the corner of Sultan Suleyman St. It has rooms that are adequate, if a little dingy, and what was once quite a decent lounge. Rooms are US$50/70.

Over the road and 50m along is **Metropole** (☎ 628 2507, fax 628 5134, 6 Salah ad-Din St) another downmarket down-at-heel place where rooms cost US$40/60. Do not confuse it with the adjacent **New Metropole Hotel** (☎ 628 3846, fax 627 7485, 8 Salah ad-Din St) which is a much better place. It has a roof garden with views of Mt Scopus, the Mount of Olives and the Rockefeller Museum. Comfortable, with air-conditioned rooms with good facilities cost US$45/70.

Continuing north up the same street is the aged **Lawrence Hotel** (☎ 626 4208, fax 627 1285, email karine@actom.co.il, 18 Salah ad-Din St), which has basic rooms from US$40/60, while over the road is the more modern **Capitol Hotel** (☎ 628 2501, fax 626 4352, email hotcap@p-ol.com), with a bar and well-equipped air-conditioned rooms with balconies facing the Mount of Olives. The hotel is popular with European package tour groups. Rooms start from US$65/85.

From the Capitol Hotel, continue north up Salah ad-Din St and turn right onto As-Zahra St, where you'll find **National Palace Hotel** (☎ 627 3273, fax 628 2139, email ranzi@trendline.co.il), which is rather characterless but does well from the pilgrim trade, packing them into rooms at US$70/96.

Equally unexceptional, though smaller and more private, are **Victoria Hotel** (☎ 627 3858, fax 627 4171, 8 Al-Masoudi St) round the corner to the right of the National Palace, which has rooms at US$45/65, and

Christmas Hotel (☎ 628 2588, fax 626 4417, email garo@netvision.net.il), off Salah ad-Din St opposite St George's Cathedral, which has clean and comfortable rooms from US$75/95.

New City

Bed & Breakfast The majority of bed and breakfast places are in the New City (see the Bed and Breakfast section earlier in this chapter). An excellent and very convenient option for arrivals by bus is **Allenby #2** (Map 2, ☎ 052-578 493, fax 534 4113, email nmr@netvision.net.il), an old, homey Jerusalem house on Allenby Square that is a five minute walk east of the central bus station. Here you will find several single/double rooms and a couple of roomy self-contained apartments that can accommodate up to five people. Danny Flax, the irrepressible owner, is a fount of knowledge on Jerusalem and a most delightful host. Prices range from US$45 to US$70.

Over in the Givat Hamivtar neighbourhood, 3km north of the Old City, are a couple of places that merit serious consideration. **House 57** (Map 1, ☎ 581 9944, fax 532 2929, email house57@netvision.net.il, 57 Midbar Sinai) was the first opened of the now popular B&B option. Built on the side of a hill it offers comfortable rooms with a view and easy bus access to the Old and New cities. Singles/doubles go for US$45/65.

Further along the same street is **Le Sixteen** (Map 1, ☎ 532 8008, fax 581 9159, email le16@virtual.co.il, 16 Midbar Sinai) run by French and English-speaking Ari. This beautifully-designed house has five small studio apartments, all opening out onto a green lawn – a rarity in Jerusalem – and views over the valley to the north. Rooms have air-con and cable TV and range in price from US$35/70.

Down in the German Colony, 3km south of the New City, are three places worth looking at. Just off the main drag, Emek Refa'im, **B-Green Guest House** (Map 1, ☎ 566 4220, fax 563 8505, email b-green@virtual .co.il, 4 Rachel Imenu) is a friendly place with a relaxing garden. Owner Boaz Green has well-appointed rooms for around US$50.

Not far away next to Smadar Cinema is *A Little House In The Colony (Map 1, ☎ 563 7641, fax 563 7645, email melonit@netvision .net.il, 4/a Lloyd George St)* an obvious play on the TV series of a similar name. Rooms are somewhat small, but the location is good. Singles are from US$49/59 and doubles are from US$59/71. Breakfast is included.

In a little side street off Emek Refa'im is a single cosy studio offered by *Tami's Bed & Breakfast (Map 1, ☎ 563 4657, fax 563 5348, 7 Hannya St)*. This is perfect if you want to be on your own for a while, yet not far from the action of the café and restaurant strip of Emek Refa'im. The studio is US$65.

Further west along Emek Refa'im is another single studio, *Beit Oren (Map 1, ☎/fax 671 7102, email orenjer@hotmail .com, Peretz 3)* a neat self-contained apartment in the cool basement of a private home. There is a little garden for guests and easy bus access to the Old and New cities. Rates range from US$50 to US$70, depending on season.

Finally, in sight of the Knesset in the Nahalat Ahim district just west of the New City is *Noah's House (Map 2, ☎ 625 0842, fax 625 0849, email katsir@hum.huji.ac.il, 33 Narkiss St)*, so named in reference to its passing similarity to the Ark of the same name. These are more like apartments than B&B rooms and are great for longer-term stays or for families with children. Rates range from US$40 to US$90 for singles in low season to US$55 to US$110 for doubles in high season. Lower rates apply for long-term stays.

Hotels A wonderful location outside one of the Old City gates (and just 10 minutes walk from the city centre) help make the guesthouse at *Notre Dame of Jerusalem Centre (Map 3, ☎ 627 9111, fax 627 1995, 1-3 HaTzanhanim Rd)* one of the city's better mid-range accommodation options. The rooms have three star-style facilities, and the surroundings and views are just excellent. Singles/doubles cost US$79/98, breakfast included.

YMCA Three Arches Hotel (Map 3, ☎ 569 2692, fax 623 5192, email y3arches@netvi sion.net.il, 26 HaMelekh David St) is probably the best-looking YMCA in the world. Guests have free use of the pool, gym and squash and tennis courts. Rooms are US$104/127. The YMCA can be reached on bus Nos 7, 8, 21 or 30 from Jaffa Rd. On foot it will take you 10 minutes to reach Jaffa Gate, while the city centre area is some 15 minutes away.

Another place of great character is *St Andrew's Hospice (Map 4, ☎ 673 2401, fax 673 1711)* which, belonging to the church of the same name, has a friendly Scottish country house atmosphere – very comfortable and peaceful. Singles/doubles are US$50/75 with breakfast included. However, despite its appealing location near Bloomfield Gardens, overlooking Mt Zion and the Old City, the hospice is a little far away from the action. It's a 15 to 20 minute steep walk to Jaffa Gate and more than that to the New City centre. During the day take bus Nos 4, 7, 14, 15, 21 or 30 to get here; later at night you may find yourself having to resort to taxis.

If you value being in the middle of the action then there are several extremely central options, the best of which is possibly *Jerusalem Inn Hotel (Map 3, ☎ 625 2757, fax 625 1297, 7 Horkenos St)*, which has an almost Scandinavian-looking interior with masses of open space and a large lounge and bar/restaurant. Singles cost from US$52/72 and doubles from US$58/78. It's not far from Zion Square; head north up Eliyshar St (look for MacDonald's on the corner), up the steps at the end and it's on the left.

Right across from Zion Square is *Hotel Ron (Map 3, ☎ 622 3122, fax 625 0707, email ronhotel@inter.net.il, 44 Jaffa Rd)*. It's from one of this building's balconies that Menachem Begin, former underground guerilla leader and future prime minister of Israel, made his first major public speech. The rooms at Hotel Ron are large and reasonably pleasant, although those facing the front may be a little noisy; singles/doubles are US$89/94. Around the corner from the Ron is the less appealing **Hotel Kaplan** *(Map 3, ☎ 625 4591, fax 623 6245, 4 HaHavazelet St)*, which offers rooms without bathroom for US$28/38 or with facilities for US$40/60.

Eyal Hotel *(Map 3, ☎ 623 4161, fax 623 4167, 21 Shamai St)*, one block south of Zion Square, has a good central location but prices have crept up to US$86 per person. The Eyal also has a sister establishment in the **Hotel Zion** *(Map 3, ☎ 623 2367, fax 625 7585)*, which is as central as it gets, lying between Jaffa Rd and Ben Yehuda St on Luntz St, one of the small café-filled pedestrian alleys. It's reasonably attractive inside, but the staff's attitude is a bit gruff. It is surrounded on all sides by some of Jerusalem's liveliest all-night streets, and some people might have problems with the noise. Singles are from US$53 to US$72 while doubles are US$76 to US$80.

PLACES TO STAY – TOP END

Jerusalem is top-heavy with luxury hotels. Most are in the New City, with just one or two in East Jerusalem and none in the Old City. During 1997 the Hilton chain opened what is now the city's brashest and most glitzy hotel the **Jerusalem Hilton** *(Map 3, ☎ 621 1111, fax 621 1000, email jrshiew@ netvision.net.il, 7 HaMelekh David St)* located in Mamilla, a champagne cork's arc away from the Old City walls. Singles cost from US$236/333 and doubles cost from US$282/380.

The country's top hotel is probably still **King David** *(Map 4, ☎ 620 8888, fax 620 8882, email danhtls@danhotels.co.il, 23 HaMelekh St)*, which has been given the seal of approval by a stream of visiting heads of state. While the place does have the benefits of a distinguished history, a superb high-class restaurant and excellent, uninterrupted views of the Old City from its eastern side, it's difficult not to suspect that the major attraction of the King David is its pure, traditional snob appeal. Singles cost from US$283 to US$506, while doubles go from US$306 to US$529.

Not far behind the King David in the luxury stakes is **Laromme Jerusalem Hotel** *(Map 4, ☎ 675 6666, fax 675 6777, email managment@laromme-hotel.co.il, 3 Ze'ev Jabotinsky St)* beside the Liberty Bell Gardens and overlooking the Old City. Owned by El Al airlines, this place has excellent standards of service and is again an occasional host to heads of state. Singles cost from US$151 to US$348 and doubles from US$170 to US$368.

Next in ranking is **Sheraton Plaza Hotel** *(Map 3, ☎ 629 8666, fax 623 1667, 47 King George V St)* overlooking Ha'Atzmaut Park, although the upper floors of this 18-storey monolith enjoy views across the whole city. The Plaza is very convenient for the New City and about 15 minutes walk from the Old City. Singles cost from US$173 to US$303 and doubles from US$193 to US$322.

The other five star-style hotels that are within an easy walk of the Old City are **King Solomon** *(Map 4, ☎ 569 5555, fax 624 1774, email solhotel@netvision.net.il, 32 HaMelekh David St)* just south of King David Hotel, and **Radisson-Moriah Plaza** *(Map 4, ☎ 569 5695, fax 623 2411, 39 Keren HaYesod St)*, one block west. The Solomon was originally built for the Sheraton chain and it maintains their high standards. Singles cost from US$136/230 and doubles cost from US$135/245. The prices at the Radisson-Moriah Plaza are US$170/ 242 and US$212/327.

Jerusalem's other top hotels suffer badly from unfavourable locations. The village-size **Hyatt Regency** *(Map 1, ☎ 533 1234, fax 581 5947, email hyattjrs@trendline .co.il, 32 Lehi St)* has excellent facilities and the Hyatt reputation ensures the hotel's popularity with US visitors; however, the hotel is stuck out over towards Mt Scopus, miles from anywhere of interest and impossible to get to by public transport. Singles cost from US$154/236 and doubles from US$169/251.

Similarly isolated, **Seven Arches** *(Map 2, ☎ 627 7555, fax 627 1319, email svnarch@ trendline.co.il)* is up on the Mount of Olives. It has a classic view over the Old City but once that's savoured and the nearby churches

The Colony

The *American Colony Hotel (☎ 627 9777, fax 628 3357, email reserv@amcol.co.il, 1 Louis Vincent St)* off Nablus Rd is the East Jerusalem counterpart to the King David Hotel. Both places have served as unofficial no-man's-lands where in recent Middle Eastern history the key players and observers have gathered. But while the King David has been host to statesmen and women, the Colony has been the favoured haunt of journalists, writers, diplomats and spies. Past guests have included TE Lawrence, John Le Carre, Graham Greene, Lord Allenby and Lauren Bacall.

Once the home of a Turkish pasha, the Colony is the city's only top-notch Arab hotel (albeit English-owned and Swiss-managed), although the Israelis used to disparagingly refer to it as the 'PLO hotel' because of alleged links between staff and the Palestinian movement. It has beautiful oriental architecture, a lovely swimming pool and a popular garden terrace. It also serves non-kosher food, including a renowned lunch buffet on Saturday.

Singles cost from US$207 to US$219 while doubles range from US$253 to US$276.

have been explored there's a long way to go to get anywhere else. Business has not been great here and singles/ doubles are a low US$100/130.

For good value and a central location we recommend *Kings Hotel (Map 3, ☎ 620 1201, fax 620 1211, 60 King George V St)*, close to the Sheraton Plaza – it's just over the road from a late night Supersol supermarket. Rooms are from US$105/130. Even more central but with inferior facilities, *Jerusalem Tower (Map 3, ☎ 620 9209, fax 625 2167, 23 Hillel St)* is a three or four star hotel that is very popular with package tour operators. Singles cost from US$121/138 and doubles cost from US$145/182.

Another good place is the modest *Mount Zion (Map 4, ☎ 568 9555, fax 673 1425, 17 Hebron Rd)* just south of the Cinematheque. It has an unusual design in that it's built into the side of the valley and the street level reception area is actually on the top floor. Most rooms have good views of the Old City; singles range from US$132 to 184, doubles from US$145 to 196.

There are also several hotels west of the New City centre in the Givat Ram area, which is quite a bus or taxi ride from the Old City. *Crown Plaza (Map 2, ☎ 658 8888, fax 651 4555)* was originally a Hilton and has five star facilities, but because of the awful location (behind the conference centre – the great glass block facing the new bus station) prices are as for a four star-style establishment; rooms are from US$198 to 218.

Even further afield are *Park Plaza (Map 1, ☎ 658 2222, fax 658 2211, 2 Vilnai St)*, *Four Points Sheraton (Map 1, ☎ 655 8888, fax 623 1667, 4 Vilnai St)* and *Renaissance Jerusalem Hotel (Map 1, ☎ 659 9999, fax 651 1824, email renjhot@netvision.net.il, Ruppin Bridge at Herzl Blvd)*. All are top-end hotels with excellent facilities. They are hindered by being west of Givat Ram, virtually on the outskirts of the city, but they seem to do well serving a steady flow of foreign tour groups. As a result, rates are reasonable for the quality: in the region of US$100 to US$175 for singles and US$110 to US$198 for doubles.

Places to Eat

With all the exotic and varied international ingredients that go into making up Jerusalem's society, much of the food on offer in the city's restaurants and cafes is, not surprisingly, diverse and representative of the city's ethnic mix. You can find anything from home-style Jewish cooking to Argentinian steaks, from Chinese banquets to Persian grills. Finding a good restaurant at a reasonable price can take some searching, however.

The city's oriental cuisine – ie Sephardic cooking originating in Maghreb and Spain, Iraq, Yemen and other Arab countries – is well represented and presents probably the best range of choices at realistic prices. These dishes rely heavily on salads dressed with olive oil, accompanied by dips of *humous* (cooked chickpeas ground into a paste and mixed with garlic and lemon) and *tahina* (a thinner paste made from sesame seeds). Pickled vegetables are also prevalent, as is the use of eggplant. The accompanying meat is almost always grilled on skewers or the spit and is typically lamb or turkey – both Islam and Judaism forbid the consumption of pork, while eating beef is uncommon.

The other pleasure is fruit, and Israel, with its varied climate, produces a wide range, including oranges, apples, mangos, guavas, melons, persimmons, pomegranates, figs, dates and avocados. Mahane Yehuda Market, in the New City, is the most plentiful and cheapest source of fruit and other foodstuffs. The best bargains are to be had towards the end of the day (packing up time is about 8 pm Sunday to Thursday), particularly on a Friday (go between 3 and 4 pm).

Look out for the *sabra* (prickly pear), a cactus fruit that looks like a hand-grenade, which was imported to Palestine from Mexico a few centuries ago. Native-born Israelis are nicknamed 'sabra' after the fruit: tough and prickly on the outside, soft and sweet on

the inside. Sabra is sold on the streets everywhere when in season, but it's an acquired taste. The seeds give the locals another chance to demonstrate their unsurpassed spitting skills.

Most places to eat are in the central area of the New City, especially on or around Ben Yehuda St and in the Nahalat Shiv'a Quarter. There is also a swathe of cheaper but excellent eating places along Agrippas St, just west of Mahane Yehuda Market. These places are mainly frequented by locals, but offer an alternative to the trendy central area.

Eating out in Jerusalem can be expensive, especially in comparison with other cities of the Middle East. Prices at midrange to top-end establishments can be on a par with Western Europe, though if you are prepared to walk away from the tourist traps you can find good food at reasonable prices. One good policy is to take advantage of the 'lunch time specials' offered between noon and 5 pm by many restaurants. These are generous set meals for between 25 and 35 NIS – 30 to 40% less than you would pay in the evening.

VEGETARIAN & HEALTH FOOD

The dietary laws of *kashrut* ensure that Israel is a dream for vegetarians, with numerous dairy-only restaurants.

Established for over 30 years, the *Village Green* restaurants *(Map 3, ☎ 625 2007, 10 Ben Yehuda St & 1 Bezalel St)* both in the New City centre, are reliable places for good-value vegetarian food and refreshments. Also worth a visit is the attractive stone and foliage-filled *Alumah Natural Food Restaurant (Map 3, ☎ 625 5014, 8 Yaabez St)* close to the first Village Green restaurant. Service is pretty laid-back and slow and main dishes are 30 to 40 NIS, but they do cheaper takeaways. It's open from 10 am, closing 11 pm Sunday to Thursday, and 2 pm Friday (closed Saturday).

At the other end of Salomon St, next to Underground disco is *Potato Guy (Map 3)*, with simple, unassuming, but tasty and quick food. Choose your own fillings and get your serving of protein and carbohydrates in an easy-to-eat package. A basic bare spud costs 10 NIS and fillings are 2.9 NIS each.

The 7th Place (Map 3, ☎ 625 4495, 37 Hillel St) is a southern Indian-style establishment which offers a dairy and vegetarian menu. Prices are very reasonable, with most of the menu going for between 2 and 35 NIS. Try the popular *thali* dish at 34 NIS. The restaurant's in the Beit Agron building just east of the junction with Yoel Salomon St. It's open from 8 am to 1 am Sunday to Thursday, 8 am to 3 pm Friday, and from sunset Saturday until 1 am Sunday morning.

Te'Enim (Map 4, ☎ 563 0048, 21 Emek Refaim St), not far from the now disused railway station, is a vegetarian's delight. The menu is varied and imaginative and there is absolutely no meat in sight. However, this place will even appeal to hardcore carnivores. Mouth-watering dishes such as skewered mushrooms with tofu and vegetables in red wine with olives and herbs go for 32 NIS, imaginative salads for around 30 NIS and their sandwiches for 25 to 30 NIS,

For dairy-based food in a neat courtyard topped by a once-working windmill, drop by *Off The Square (Map 3, ☎ 566 5956)* just off Zarfat Square. This long-established and popular establishment serves fish dishes for around 45 NIS and inventive pasta dishes for around 35 NIS. They also do tasty hot pies, crepes and stuffed potatoes for between 26 and 35 NIS. It is open from 9 am to 11 pm Sunday to Thursday, 9am to 2 pm Friday, and from sunset until midnight Saturday.

Other places offering similar fare are *Ticho House Cafe* and *Cacao* at the Cinematheque – see the Cafés section later in this chapter for the details of both places. For Italian vegetarian food see *Angelo* in the Italian section later in this chapter.

FELAFEL, SHWARMA & HUMOUS

Felafel, shwarma and humous are the three staples of Jerusalem 'fast food'. Felafel is ground chickpeas blended with herbs and spices, shaped into balls and then deep-fried. They tend to be a bit on the bland side, but covered in tahina and served with an assortment of salads in a pitta bread (a type of flat pocket bread), it's palatable, fairly substantial and cheap. The most popular way to eat meat is as shwarma, also known elsewhere as *doner kebab*. This is lamb, or sometimes turkey or chicken, sliced from a revolving vertical spit and stuffed, along with salad, into a pitta or rolled in a plate-sized piece of *laffa* bread.

Old City & East Jerusalem

Considering that felafel originates in the Arab world, there is surprisingly little of it to be found in the (predominantly Arab) Old City – and what you do find isn't particularly good. The most popular place to get felafel is at a stall just down from Damascus Gate, at the point at which the road forks. For good humous head down Al-Wad Rd and, by the 5th Station of the Cross, where the Via Dolorosa turns west (right), is *Abu Shukri, (Map 7)* on the left-hand side. A good humous platter is 8 NIS, but stay off the *fuul* (fava bean paste) and felafel, both of which are terrible here.

Most shwarma and grilled meat shops are found along Souq Khan as-Zeit St, but sadly most of them are not very good and they also overcharge, possibly as a result of the large numbers of tourists around. However, *El-A'elat Restaurant (Map 7, ☎ 628 3435, 77 Khan as-Zeit St)* open since 1950, is worth visiting for its good shwarma. This place also hosted the late King Hussein of Jordan's wedding party when he married his first wife, Dina.

For better food overall, head out of Damascus Gate and try the places on Sultan Suleyman St. Down towards the junction with Salah ad-Din St, *Al-Quds Arabic Restaurant (Map 7)* and neighbouring *Candy's* both do superb shwarma and *shashlik* (grilled kebabs). For those with skip-sized appetites, they sell roast chicken, a whole or half bird, hot off the skewer.

Something of a cult establishment among humous freaks is **Abu Ali Restaurant** *(Map 5)* although it may be greeted with something less than bounding enthusiasm by the hygiene conscious. It's hidden away off Salah ad-Din St; head north from Herod's Gate and turn right along an alley at the sign for 'Geneve Exhibition'; it's downstairs on your left. Abu Ali is open daily from 6 am to about 2 pm.

Be very wary of eating at new-looking restaurants offering shwarma or felafel, which don't display obvious menu details with prices – you will be unceremoniously ripped off. **Morocco** and **Friends Restaurant** along Chain St (Bab as-Sisila), not far from the Bab as-Sisila Gate to the Temple Mount in the Old City, are two such places. Avoid them.

New City

Most New City felafel is sold on King George V St between Jaffa Rd and Ben Yehuda St – just follow the trail of tahina and squashed felafel balls on the pavement. Many of the places selling felafel also have shwarma. None of them stands above the others in price or quality, but one of the most popular with locals is **King of Felafel & Shwarma** *(Map 3)* on the corner of King George V and Agrippas Sts. If you want to sit while eating go to the curiously named **Thailand Food Sandwich Bar** *(Map 3, 6 Ben Hillel St)* on the pedestrianised street running between Ben Yehuda and King George V Sts, and get some felafel (7 NIS) or shwarma (12 NIS).

Humous is available in most Sephardic restaurants and is reputably very good at **Ta'ami** *(Map 3, 3 Shamai St)*, which is parallel with and to the south of Ben Yehuda St (no English sign). It's also said to be good at the long-established **Rahmo** *(Map 2)* just off Mahane Yehuda Market, on the corner of Ha'Armonium and HaEshkol Sts. See the oriental (Sephardic) section later in this chapter.

CAFÉS
Old City & East Jerusalem

For breakfast, **Cafeteria St Michel** *(Map 6)* on Omar ibn al-Khattab Square at Jaffa Gate does a decent omelette, bread and jam, and tea or coffee spread. Two doors away, **City Restaurant** *(Map 6)* also serves breakfast and has various Middle Eastern snacks such as grilled cheese and felafel or humous platters. It's open from 8 am to 8 pm daily except Sunday. Across the square, the **Coffee Shop** *(Map 6)*, next to the Christian Information Centre, is a lovely place – clean, and decorated with Christian-theme Jerusalem tiles. It features a modestly priced all-you-can-eat salad bar with soup and bread. It's open daily from 10 am to 6 pm, except Sunday.

A popular meeting spot for travellers (and proud of it!) **Backpacker Tearooms** *(Map 8, 100 Aftimus St)*, in the Christian Quarter's Muristan area, offers cheap food and beer all day, as well as nightly videos. Another favourite backpacker hang-out is **Tabasco Tearoom** *(Map 6)*, downstairs from Tabasco Hostel. Food is mainly western, though they throw in the odd curry or two. Travellers come mainly for the cheap beer and the company.

In the sanitised New York-accented Jewish Quarter, **Tzaddik's Old City Deli** *(Map 9)* fuels the hungry with heavily loaded submarine rolls, plus things like chilli dogs and draught beer. It's open Sunday to Thursday until 8 pm, and Friday until mid-afternoon.

Decorated with pink lacy curtains and embroidered 'God Bless Our Home' pennants, and with a waiter who switches effortlessly between Arabic and half a dozen different European languages, **Cafe Europe** *(Map 5, 9 As-Zahra St)* seems way out of place in the heart of blaring, wailing Arab East Jerusalem. The menu is as quirky but the food is superb and offers some of the best-value quality eating in the whole of the city. The platters are particularly recommended, and the ice cream cocktails are excellent too, although a little pricey. Try their famous chicken sandwiches or hamburgers. It's east of Salah ad-Din St and open daily from 10 am to 10.30 pm, closed Sunday.

The Coffeehouse

The Arab version of the café is the *qahwa* – a coffeehouse (the word also means coffee). These places are generally much plainer than their European-originated counterparts, often no more than a collection of battered chairs and tables in a sawdust-strewn room open to the street.

The drink served is, (surprise, surprise) coffee – of the strong Turkish-style variety, often flavoured with *hehl* (cardamom). *Shai* (tea) is also popular, served in a glass, black, very sweet (if you don't want sugar say so when you order – minREEYA sukar) and often with *na'ana* (mint), which is extremely refreshing even on a hot day.

The hubbub of conversation is sometimes accompanied by the incessant clacking of slammed domino and backgammon pieces and, inevitably, by the bubbling sound of smokers drawing hard on their *nargilas* (the cumbersome waterpipe, also known as a *sheesha*). Palestinian women rarely enter a qahwa but there's no reason why female tourists shouldn't.

Most of Jerusalem's qahwas can be found in the Old City; there's a particularly popular and long-established place at the top of Al-Wad Rd, just on the left when entering from Damascus Gate, and a couple on Bab as-Silsila St.

New City

The Nahalat Shiv'a Quarter and the pedestrianised areas around Ben Yehuda St are crowded with cafés. Take your pick, there's little to distinguish between most of them.

The majority offer basic hot dishes and salads as well as cakes, ice cream and beverages. Coffee here comes black and strong, and if what you want is something like a Nescafe then ask for 'milk coffee' or 'nes'. Beware the cappuccino, which usually resembles something like a warmed up ice cream sundae.

Bonkers Bagels is a 24 hour place on the east side of Zion Square that offers the full gamut of bagels as well as coffee, beverages and other goodies baked on the premises. Try the peanut butter brownies.

Tmol Shilshom (☎ 623 2758, 5 Yoel Salomon St) is a crowded little coffee shop cum restaurant that is also a bookshop and meeting place for frequent literary readings in Hebrew (and sometimes English). Its walls are lined with shelves of mostly second-hand books. You can also check your email here (see the Facts for the Visitor chapter). The place gets packed at lunch times but it's quieter early on and there's a good breakfast spread, including waffles with homemade jam. Try also their delicious salmon steak, cooked in a fig and wine sauce with secret spices. Tmol Shilshom is sandwiched between Salomon and Shiv'a Sts.

Another good place to sit and read (bring your own book) is the tranquil ***Ticho House Cafe*** (☎ 624 4186, 9 Harav Kook St). The house provides cool and pleasant surroundings, or you can sit out in the tree-shaded garden. It's open from 10 am to midnight Sunday to Thursday, from 10 am to 3 pm on Friday, and from sunset to midnight on Saturday. On Thursday from 8.30 pm onwards they have live jazz plus wine and cheese evenings. Phone for bookings.

Despite the name, ***Strudel*** (☎ 623 2102, 11 Monbaz St) in the Russian Compound area, is a pastry-free zone; the name comes from the Hebrew term for the '@' common to all email addresses. It's an Internet cafe-cum-wine bar, with tables for dining, a sofa area and four computer stations in alcoves. It has a menu of homemade soups, salads and sandwiches and an impressive array of beers and wines, including a mean draught Guinness. It is open from noon until late, and from 3 pm onwards on Saturday.

Bagels & Bread

Jerusalem offers a delicious selection of breads, both Jewish and Arabic. Not surprisingly, bagels are very popular. Perhaps closer to their Central European origins, Jerusalem bagels are different to the more famous New York version, being crisper and drier. A traditional way to end a night out is to visit the bagel factory and pick up a hot bagel or two – *Bonkers* on Zion Square is open 24 hours.

Hallah, a brioche-style soft bread made with dough enriched with eggs, is baked for Shabbat. Jewish bakeries produce sweet breads too. Glazed with sugar syrup, filled with currants or chocolate, they vary in quality but can be great. *Matza* is the unleavened, unsalted flat bread eaten during Pesah, when ordinary bread products are forbidden to the observant (see the Jewish Festivals section).

Arab and Sephardic bakers mainly make pitta bread or a kind of bagel thickly covered with sesame seeds or sprinkled with *za'atar*, a heady mixture of herbs (mainly oregano) and spices.

Back down in the centre of the New City is a popular café/restaurant called **Trio** *(5 Luntz St)*. It is open 24 hours, offers a dance party every Friday at noon and live jazz music on Tuesday and Saturday from 7 pm onwards. They serve a hearty Israeli breakfast for between 22 and 26 NIS and pasta dishes in the 30 to 38 NIS range.

Rif-Raf *(Hillel St)*, on the corner of Rabbi Akiva St and opposite American Express, is a 24 hour café that is very popular with the student community. It's a great place to get a snack or just to hang out and watch or be watched.

Away from the city centre, **Cacao** *(Map 4, ☎ 671 0632, 1 Hebron Rd)* the vegetarian café at the Cinematheque, has great views of the Old City, Mt Zion and the Judean Desert from its terrace. It's open daily from 10 am until after midnight.

BURGERS & PIZZA

Jerusalem has an enormous *McDonald's (Map 3, 4 Shamai St)* one block south of Ben Yehuda St, with all the usual McFavourites. Even decidedly non-kosher cheeseburgers are aravilable here.

About the best place to eat in the Old City is **Abu Shanab** *(Map 6, 35 Latin Patriarchate Rd)* near Jaffa Gate. It specialises in excellent pizza, made on the premises, which comes in three sizes: filling (10 NIS), very filling (20 NIS) and 'do you want half of this?' (35 NIS). Abu Shanab also does hot sandwiches, salads, lasagne and spaghetti, all for about 15 NIS. It's open daily from 9 am until midnight.

For a very different pizza-eating experience visit the *Green Door Bakery*, *(Map 6)* a large, empty cave of a room in which Mohammed Ali tends a furnace-like oven and bakes for the whole neighbourhood. For travellers, he rustles up rough cheese, egg and tomato pizzas – although the pleasure is more in watching them being prepared than it is in the eating. The pizzas cost just a few shekels and he will happily use any ingredients that you care to bring along. The bakery is open daily from early morning to late at night. It's on Aqabat ash-Sheikh Rihan just left off Al-Wad Rd at the bottom of the slope from Damascus Gate.

ORIENTAL (SEPHARDIC)

Best exemplified by Jerusalem's many Yemeni restaurants, oriental (Sephardic) cooking, originating in Jewish communities in the Middle East, is especially renowned for offal dishes. Turkey testicles, cow's udder, spleen and heart all taste a lot better than they sound. Nonvegetarians should not miss trying the city's speciality, *meorav Yerushalmi* (literally 'Jerusalem meats'). This is a mix of chopped livers, kidneys, hearts and beef with onions and spices sizzled on a great hot plate and scooped into pockets of bread. The best place to try it is on Agrippas St, in the vicinity of Mahane Yehuda *(Map 2)*, where there are any number of restaurants frying from early evening through until early morning.

One of the tastiest aspects of Sephardic cooking is the art of stuffing vegetables and meat with rice, nuts, meat and spices. Most Yemeni restaurants have a varied selection of stuffed vegetables as starters, but one or two on their own make for an ample meal.

For basic favourites like salads, soups and stuffed vegetables, try *Chen*, *(Map 3, 30 Jaffa Rd)* a busy lunch time spot in the New City where you can eat well for under 25 NIS. Former president Chaim Herzog is said to favour this place. It's across from the main post office (no English sign), sandwiched between a pastry shop and a gift shop. It's open from 8 am, closing 6 pm Sunday to Thursday, and 3 pm Friday (closed Saturday). *Ma'adan (Map 3, 35 Jaffa Rd)* is a similar sort of place, where a full meal including soup or salad starts at around 20 NIS. The menu is wider than that at Chen and Ma'adan is open until late.

Upmarket Orientalism is best represented by *The Yemenite Step (Map 3, ☎ 624 0477, 10 Yoel Salomon St)*, open daily from 10 am to midnight. The mainstay of the menu is *malawach*, which is a thin, flaky-pastry bread stuffed with meat, mushrooms or other savoury fillings (15 NIS). It's extremely filling, though a little monotonous eaten on its own.

ASHKENAZI

What most people think of as typically 'Jewish food' is Eastern European, typified by such dishes as goulash, schnitzel, *klops* (chopped meat) and *gefilte* (fish balls). Most Israelis will completely deny enjoying the last of these, which basically consists of sweet-and-sour fish balls served chilled. Much more appetising are *blintzes*, a type of heavy pancake typically filled with something savoury such as mushrooms or cheese – though never meat because of the rules of kashrut. On Shabbat, most secular Jews join the religious and follow the traditional rule of no cooking. For many, this will mean eating *cholent*, a heavy, cassoulet-like stew prepared before sunset on Friday and kept simmering until Saturday.

One restaurant that advertises itself as specialising in Jewish Eastern European cuisine is *Heimishe Essen (Map 3, ☎ 563 9845, 19 Keren Kayemet St)* in the classy Rehavia district. Here you can sample a gefilte fish appetiser for 14 NIS or a cholent and meat main course for 36 NIS. It is open from 11.30 am to 10 pm Sunday to Thursday, and 8 am to 3.30 pm Friday (closed Saturday).

Romanian restaurants are particularly good for steaks and liver, and one of the best is *Gilly's (Map 3, ☎ 625 5955, 33 Hillel St)* on the corner of Yoel Salomon St. It is quite pricey though, with main dishes in the 60 to 110 NIS range.

In the Jewish Quarter of the Old City, just up from the Western Wall is the upstairs and self-service *The Quarter Cafe (Map 9, ☎ 628 7770, 11 Tiferet Y'Israel St)*. It has decent, reasonably priced kosher food served in pleasant surroundings, including a great view across to the Dome of the Rock and the Mount of Olives from the top level. It's open daily from 8.30 am, closing 6.30 pm Sunday to Thursday, and 4 pm Friday, closed on Saturday.

ARABIC

Felafel originated in the Arab world, as did its close cousin, humous, not to mention tahina. These three basics, accompanied with vinegar-laced salads and and a wide selection of breads, form the mainstay of most menus at the cheap sit-down Arab restaurants, along with *fuul* (pronounced 'fool') – mashed fava beans. More upmarket places will also serve grilled chicken, shwarma and shashlik and, if you're lucky, *mansaf*, a Palestinian dish of rice cooked with small pieces of lamb, seasoned with nuts, lemon juice and herbs. Other Palestinian dishes include *melok*, a soup made from greens, and *kubbe*, minced spiced lamb or beef mixed with *burghul* (cracked wheat) and deep fried. If you are offered *mezze*, this is a selection of starters which typically includes humous, brain salad, eggplant puree, stuffed vine leaves, olives and pickles.

At the cheaper end of the price range are places like *Al-Quds Arabic Restaurant* (see the Felafel, Shwarma & Humous section earlier in this chapter) and, in the Old City on Al-Wad St close to Damascus Gate, *Jerusalem Star (Map 6)*, which produces basic grilled meat dishes. Half a grilled chicken served with potatoes and salad costs 15 NIS. There are often special offers – check at the door. Jerusalem Star is open daily until 9.30 pm.

Philadelphia Restaurant (Map 5, ☎ 628 9770, 1800 255 155, 9 As-Zahra St) off Salah ad-Din St in East Jerusalem, is known to be one of the city's best Arab restaurants. This establishment specialises in mezzes as well as grilled lamb dishes and seafood. It's open daily from noon to 10 pm. Prices here range from 40 NIS for the grilled chicken to 65 NIS for grouper. They even offer a free shuttle service to/from your hotel.

Arab Sweets & Pastries

Usually soaked in honey and full of sugar, these highlights of Arab cuisine can't be good for you, but who cares? *Baklava* is toasted layers of wheat, stuffed with pistachios or hazelnuts and drowned in honey, while *katayeef* and *kunafeh* are concoctions of vanilla, vermiccelli pastry, sugar and honey.

Souk Khan as-Zeit St is the honey-soaked sweet street in the Old City and of all its syrupy confections the best are made at *Zalatimo's*, just back from the stairs leading up to the 9th Station of the Cross. The speciality of this unremarkable looking little bakery is *moutabak*, made to order by Abu Ali Hawash, the baker here for over 20 years. Super-light pastry is kneaded and rolled over and over with a fresh cheese filling and served straight from the traditional oven with hot sugar syrup. If you fancy some get there early, because by about 11 am the pastry is gone and Abu Ali has locked up and gone home.

ARMENIAN

Near Jaffa Gate in the Old City is the *Armenian Tavern (Map 8, ☎ 627 3854, 79 Armenian Patriarchate Rd)*, which has a beautiful tiled interior with a fountain gently splashing in one corner. The strongly flavoured meat dishes (30 to 40 NIS) are without exception excellent and it is recommended you try the *khaghoghi derev*, a spiced minced meat mixture bundled in vine leaves and served in a light, yogurt-based sauce. There is a cheaper, but not as good Armenian restaurant, *Yerevan (Map 6)* close to the New Gate in the Christian Quarter. This places dishes up 'Armenian Pizzas' among a few other Armenian staples.

GREEK

For a city with a surprisingly large Greek Orthodox presence, there are few places that can call themselves Greek restaurants. One little place worth seeking out is *Kostas' Restaurant (Map 6, Ha-Koptim St)* tucked away in a corner of the Christian Quarter of the Old City. The menu is limited but the food is tasty and reasonably cheap and is popular with local Arabs. Chicken fillet goes for 33 NIS and a Macabbee beer is 7 NIS. Open only from lunch time to early evening. Don't be surprised at the passing gaggles of tourists – especially Greeks – who tend to gawk at the diners.

ITALIAN

There are several Italian-oriented restaurants in Nahalat Shiv'a, but despite their popularity many of these establishments are unapologetically mediocre. Instead, try *Spaghettim (Map 3, ☎ 623 5547, 8 Rabbi Akiva St)*, off Hillel St. Occupying the ground floor of a villa, it has a spacious, cool, bare stone interior that is refreshingly uncluttered when compared with most restaurants in Jerusalem. The menu features spaghetti only, but it's served in over 50 different ways, from the predictable bolognaise through to the decidedly exotic spaghetti with ostrich in hunter sauce. Prices are 20 to 40 NIS and it's open daily from noon to midnight.

Mamma Mia (Map 3, ☎ 624 8080, 38 King George V St) is also extremely good. The pasta dishes here, all homemade, cost between 36 and 40 NIS. It's at the back of the car park, 100m south of the junction with Hillel St, and is open from noon to midnight Sunday to Thursday, noon to 4 pm Friday, and from sunset to midnight Saturday.

The newer *Angelo (Map 3, ☎ 623 6095, 9 Horkanos St)* near the Russian Colony, is a dairy (and therefore meat-free) kosher establishment which will will have an obvious appeal for vegetarians. It offers cosy streetside dining in a quiet corner of the New City. Main pasta dishes range in price from 33 to 35 NIS. It is open from noon to 11 pm Sunday to Thursday, and from half an hour after sunset on Saturday.

KURDISH & PERSIAN

Kurdish and Persian restaurants have recently made an appearance on the culinary scene in Jerusalem and there is a good one on the Agrippas St restaurant strip, west of the New City. *Gidi's (Map 2, ☎ 624 3454, 121 Agrippas St)* is a Persian and Middle Eastern restaurant with main stewed courses for about 22 NIS. Grilled meat dishes are in the 40 NIS bracket. You can browse amongst the pots and pans in the kitchen if you are not sure what you want to eat, and make your choice visually. It is open most days until midnight but closed Friday.

Halfway along the same street is *Mordoch (Map 2, ☎ 624 5169, 70 Agrippas St)*, a popular lunch time stop for students and local workers alike, with not a tourist in sight. It's only a small joint but very popular so get here before 1 pm. Kubbe soup, a tangy soup with semolina dumplings filled with nuts or meat, is their speciality, although their *musaka* and stuffed courgettes are pretty tasty too. Prices are between 14 and 20 NIS.

Nearer the centre and just off the Solomon St restaurant stretch is *Misadonet (Map 3, ☎ 624 8396, 12 Solomon Nahalat Shiva)* with outdoor tables in an open square with a fountain. Mains range from 30 to 50 NIS. Their kubbe soup is reputedly the best in Jerusalem.

SOUTH AMERICAN

El Gaucho (Map 3, ☎ 624 2227, 22 Rivlin St) is Israel's first South American restaurant. It's a pleasant, if somewhat brash eatery with al fresco dining and a predominantly meat menu. It is open from noon to midnight Sunday to Thursday and from sunset to midnight Saturday. Prices range from 49 NIS for an *asado* veal dish to 82 NIS for a 500g *chorizo* steak.

Blues Brothers (Map 3, ☎ 625 8621, 3 Luntz St) is an Argentinian steak house slap-bang in the middle of the New City. If you like your meat in large quantities this is where to come. It's all fully kosher and grilled in front of you at the table. Main meat dishes are in the 60 to 70 NIS range. It's open daily from 10 am to 1 am.

ASIAN

Jerusalem has seen substantial growth in the Asian restaurant scene with half a dozen or more places offering far-eastern and southeast Asian cuisine. One of the cheapest and easiest to stumble upon is *Papi Tai (Map 3, 35 Jaffa Rd)*. It's nothing flash, but it's cheap (around 17 NIS for stir-fry), convenient and they do takeaway.

Chinese food is probably best represented by Israel's first such establishment, *Mandarin (Map 3, ☎ 625 2890, 2 Shlomzion HaMalka St)* just east of Zion Square. Szechuan and Cantonese dishes feature too. Meat dishes are around 40 NIS but there are cheaper lunch time special set menus.

Korea House (Map 3, ☎ 625 4756, 7 Ma'alot Nahalat Shiva St) just off Salomon St in the New City centre, has a very atmospheric and tranquil setting and prices are surprisingly reasonable. A lunch time (noon to 3 pm) *pulgogi* (grilled meat and vegetables) set menu will cost you 30 NIS, jumping to 50 NIS in the evening.

For another taste of the Orient, *Rungsit (Map 45, ☎ 561 1757, 2 Jabotinsky St)* diagonally opposite the Laromme Hotel in Talbiyeh, offers superior Thai/Japanese food in opulent Oriental (Far Eastern as opposed to Middle Eastern) surroundings. It's a sister restaurant to the Rungsits in New

The Wee Small Hours

Trio is an American-style diner open 24 hours, seven days a week. It serves burgers, hot dogs, chicken, pancakes and an all-day (and all-night) breakfast special of grilled sausage and eggs. It's on Luntz St just off Ben Yehuda mall. On Zion Square, *Bonkers* keeps the same hours as Trio, but serves only bagels and coffee. The stretch of street running east from Bonkers also features a clutch of popular bagelries open all hours of the night.

For general provisions, the large *Supersol* supermarket on Agron St, near the junction with King George V St, is open until late during the week, and is open 24 hours over the weekend.

On Jaffa Rd, near the corner with HaMalka St, is a small delicatessen that is open on Shabbat. Here you can buy soft and alcoholic drinks and tobacco products as well as smaller grocery items when all the other shops in the New City are closed.

York and Bangkok. It is open from noon to midnight Sunday to Thursday, from noon to 1 hour before sunset Friday, and from one hour after sunset to midnight Saturday.

Japanese food can also be found at *Sakura (Map 3, ☎ 623 5464, 31 Jaffa Rd)* in the Feingold Building of the Jerusalem Courtyard, enter from Rivlin Mall. Sushi is the speciality here and it's of good quality but comes at a typically inflated Japanese price: 56 NIS per person for 12 pieces of sushi. The 36 to 60 NIS business lunch of soup, sushi, salad and tea is a marginally better option.

OTHER RESTAURANTS

The Wild Bull (Shor HaBar) (Map 3, ☎ 624 4395, 3 Yaabez St) is a good South African-run steak restaurant that could be described as 'excellent' at lunch time because of its cheap and filling business lunches (burgers and steak sandwiches with heaps of potato wedges and salad) starting from 25 NIS.

Stanleys (Map 4, ☎ 625 9459, 3 Horkanos St) gets raves reviews from the local press. The emphasis is on South African meat dishes, from sirloin to *boerwoers*, a kind of farmer's sausage, and if you are lucky, some of Stanley's homemade *biltong*, which is dried beef (similar to jerky) served sliced with salad. The lunch specials are a good deal at 24 to 35 NIS. It is open daily from noon to midnight.

Similarly substantial is the fare at *Norman's Bar & Grill (Map 4, ☎ 566 6603, 27 Emek Refa'im St)*, an American-style place specialising in burgers, steaks and chicken. It also offers good value lunch specials – best eaten out on the lovely tree-shaded patio. The only drawback is the location, way down in the German Colony. It's open from noon to 11.30 pm Sunday to Thursday and from sunset Saturday to 1 am Sunday morning.

One of the city's great kitchens can be found at *Notre Dame of Jerusalem Centre (Map 3)* opposite New Gate. This Catholic-run complex features a terrace coffee shop, and a restaurant with excellent food served in grand surroundings. It's open daily for lunch and dinner; expect to pay about 40 NIS.

PLACES TO EAT – TOP END

As well as a vast array of fine wines and spirits, the semi-legendary *Fink's Restaurant (Map 3, ☎ 623 4523, 2 HaHistadrut St)* on the corner with King George V St and 50m north of the junction with Ben Yehuda St, serves a menu of consistently excellent Austro-Bavarian food. A house speciality is the goulash soup, described as a 'Jewish ploughman's lunch'. With less than a dozen stools at the bar and only six tables, reservations are advisable. It's open from 6 pm until midnight Saturday to Thursday, (closed Friday).

Mishkenot Sha'ananim (Map 4, ☎ 625 1042) below the Montefiore Windmill, serves award-winning French cuisine combined with a few Moroccan appetisers. It also claims to possess one of the largest and best restaurant wine cellars in the world. Whether or not its cellar is that good (this writer is sadly unqualified to comment), the views of the floodlit Old City walls are undeniably terrific. Some of their more imaginative advertised dishes include Mixed Kissinger Hors d'oeuvres, terrine de foie gras, and goose liver with strawberry. Business lunches are US$28. It's open daily from 11 am to 1 am.

For superior seafood, head for the *Ocean (Map 3, ☎ 624 7501, 7 Rivlin St)*, a restaurant once described by the Jerusalem correspondent of the *London Times* as 'unhappily pretentious' but also as having fresh fish on a par with anything served in any European capital. Ocean is open daily from 1 to 4 pm and 7 to 11 pm. It is probably the most expensive restaurant in Jerusalem.

PLACES TO EAT

Entertainment

Despite the best attempts of the religious
element, things have picked up a little since
then. Those in search of 'amusement' in present-day Jerusalem can enjoy classical concerts or jazz jamming sessions, catch the
latest Hollywood blockbuster or some obscure Swedish brain squeeze at the cinema,
watch 22 men sweat it out on a football field
or do plenty of perspiring themselves ham-
mering the dance floor at an all-night rave.

Pick up *The Jerusalem Post,* in particular
the Friday edition, for an up-to-date and
comprehensive list of events, and also stop
by the Jaffa Rd tourist information office for
a free copy of the current *Your Jerusalem*
brochure. Unfortunately, *Traveller* newspaper, which was available free in bars and
hostels and which had a good bar and
nightlife guide, seems to have disappeared.

Hebrew speakers can call the ☎ 106 hotline for details on what is currently happening on the Jerusalem cultural scene.
For those callers outside of Jerusalem the
number is ☎ 02-531 4601.

BARS & CLUBS

While East Jerusalem and the Old City seem
to close up completely at sunset, with just
Abu Shanab, *Tabasco Tearooms* and *Backpacker Tearooms* providing any alternative
to beer and a book back at the hostel, the
New City buzzes till sunrise. Yoel Salomon
and Rivlin, the two parallel main streets in
Nahalat Shiv'a (Map 3), are lined with
enough late night bars and cafés to defeat
the most alcohol-absorbent of pub-crawlers.

Down at the bottom of Rivlin St, *The Tavern Pub* was the original pub in Jerusalem
and it attracts a mainly expatriate, bar-prop-
ping, beer-drinking crowd. It's nothing particularly special, but it's at the centre of

action and the tables outside make a good
vantage point for people watching. *The Blue
Hole*, down a little side alley about midway
along Yoel Salomon St, is a similar sort of
place,but considerably more dingy and it's
also away from the real action. Like most of
the bars it has a popular happy hour, only in
this case it's a whole 3½ hours long.

Near Zion Square, *Underground*, *(Map 3,
1 Yoel Salomon St)* is possibly Jerusalem's
most popular nightspot. It's a crowded pub
on the ground floor with a disco downstairs
– not recommended for those who enjoy
breathing. This place doesn't get going until
around 10 or 11 pm and is open until everyone's way past caring what time it is. It's had
some negative reports from travellers about
its rowdiness and it really is for the under-
25s – you have been warned.

Stardust (Map 3, 6 Rivlin St) is a small,
cosy bar with different musical offerings.
Monday is club night, considered by the
local beat press to be a true standout on the
sometimes stagnant music scene.

The other main concentration of bars is
crowded around the upper part of Heleni
HaMalka St in the Russian Compound area
(Map 3). These places are less congested
with travellers and visitors and tend to be
where locals hang out. Best of the lot are the
suitably laid-back *Kanabis* on Monbaz St,
and the ever-popular *Glasnost*, which features live music three nights a week (see
Live Music opposite). Also worth dropping
by at is *Strudel*, the Internet café/wine bar
(see Email & Internet Access in the Facts
for the Visitor chapter).

Decent Guinness (18 NIS; 9 NIS during
happy hour) is served at *Champs (Map 3, 19
Jaffa Rd)* a lone English-style pub midway
between the New City centre and the Old
City walls, opposite the new City Hall complex. It's open from 1 pm to 5 am. Happy
'hour' is from 4 to 7 pm and again from 10
to 11 pm, at these times drinks listed in red
on the menu are all half price.

Israeli Beer

Israelis are not a nation of big drinkers, and this is reflected in their relative disinterest in the brewing business. One company, National Brewery Ltd, controls 98% of the beer market – a position of dominance attained not through aggressive marketing or competitive prices, but simply through lack of any competition.

At the bottom of the range is the rarely spotted Nesher (3.8% alcohol), which isn't served by most bars or cafes but, when found, is the cheapest beer on the market. Goldstar (4.7%) is the most popular beer with travellers, both bottled and draught, while Maccabee (4.9%) is the Israeli favourite, considered upmarket as it's the only Israeli beer exported to the world.

A relative newcomer is Taybeh, the product of a small, private Palestinian-run brewery in the West Bank town of the same name. While not yet widely available around the city, you can get it in draught form at *Strudel* Internet cafe/wine bar where it is worth a taste.

Live Music

Musicians have been having a hard time of it in Jerusalem of late; at the time of research the city's municipality was putting a dampener on the live music scene. Check the local beat press for up-to-date information as venues may change.

The best place for live music is at *Mike's Place* (Map 3, Horkonos St), a tiny bar which, aside from the guy with the guitar and the bartender, has room for only about a dozen customers. It has live folk, rock and blues nightly between 10 pm and midnight; it's off Heleni HaMalka St in the Russian Compound area.

Up the hill, *Glasnost* (Map 3, ☎ 625 6954, 15 Heleni HaMalka St) has live music, varying from rock to reggae to jazz funk and samba, depending on what night of the week it is. At the time of research, Monday, Tuesday and Friday were live music nights. There's a cover charge of 15 NIS.

A newcomer on the scene is *NetCafe*, near the Russian Compound area, which usually has live music – everything from acoustic folk to 'HippieJamRock' – a couple of nights a week from 9.30 pm. This place also doubles as an Internet cafe (for details see Email & Internet Access in the Facts for the Visitor chapter).

In the centre of the New City, the popular 24 hour café/restaurant *Trio* (5 Luntz St) offers live jazz on Tuesday and Saturday from 7 pm onwards and a dance party every Friday at noon.

For jazz, folk and Arabic music, as well as the odd buzzsaw guitar band, check the schedule at *Pargod Theatre* (Map 2, ☎ 625 8819, 94 Bezalel St). Friday afternoons feature free jazz jamming sessions from 1.30 to 4.30 pm. *The Yellow Submarine* (Map 1, ☎ 678 1387, HaRakavim St) way down in Talpiot, usually has live Israeli rock and alternative music.

GAY & LESBIAN VENUES

At the time of research, only *Orion* (Map 3, 4 Shammai St) in the centre of town, above McDonald's in Ben Yehuda St, offered anything like a gay scene, though in practice it is a mixed straight-gay club. It has had mixed reviews in the local press since opening, but is considered a better option for city clubbers who don't care to drag themselves out to Talpiot, a suburb south of the Old City that's host to a sometimes club scene.

The Yellow Submarine is considered to be 'gay-friendly', but it too is essentially a mixed venue (see the Live Music section). *Tmol Shilshom* is a laid-back, gay-run establishment that doesn't discriminate against nongays. It's a fine place to stop by for a coffee or a meal irrespective of your sexual orientation (see also Literary Readings later in this chapter and under New City in the Cafés section of the Places to Eat chapter).

LITERARY READINGS

If head-banging to loud music is not your cup of tea, you may prefer the more gentle cerebral form of entertainment offered by literary readings. Poetry and prose is regularly read out by its exponents at *Tmol Shilshom (Map 3 ☎ 623 2758, 5 Yoel Salomon St)* coffee shop and restaurant (see also under New City in the Cafés section of the Places to Eat chapter). Readings are usually of Hebrew prose and poetry so you won't get much out of it if you don't speak Hebrew, but you can always dine, have a bottle of wine and watch the Jerusalem intelligentsia at work.

FOLK/TRADITIONAL MUSIC

At the *International Cultural Centre for Youth (ICCY) (Map 4, ☎ 566 4144, 12A Emek Refa'im St)* in the German Colony, south of Talbiyeh, the Pa'amez Teyman Folklore Ensemble regularly performs from a repertoire that includes Israeli folk dances, traditional Yemente, Haredi and Arabic dances, Israeli folk songs and Khalifa Arabic drumming. Tickets are sold at the door and at many hotels. You could also try *Pargod Theatre* (see the Live Music section earlier in this chapter).

CLASSICAL MUSIC

Classical music lovers are well catered for in Jerusalem. *Henry Crown Concert Hall (Map 4)* at Jerusalem Sherover Theatre (see the Theatre section) is the home base of the Jerusalem Symphony Orchestra. If one orchestra isn't enough, *Binyanei Ha'Umah Conference Centre (Map 2, ☎ 622 2481)*, opposite the new (under construction) central bus station and adjacent to the Holiday Inn Crown Plaza, is the national residence of the Israel Philharmonic Orchestra.

Free classical performances are held occasionally at a number of venues including the *YMCA Auditorium (Map 4)* on Ha Melekh David St; *Mishkenot Sha'ananim (Map 4)*, held on alternate Fridays, *Beit Shmuel (Map 3)*, part of the Hebrew Union College on HaMelekh David St, held on Saturday mornings; and at the *Church of the Dormition (Map 2)* on Mt Zion. Immigrant musicians also give performances at *Ticho House* every Friday morning (see the New City Centre section of the Things to See & Do chapter).

CINEMAS

Central Jerusalem is very poorly served when it comes to cinemas. Unfortunately, the two or three that existed, around the Shamai and Hillel St area, have closed down. Movie-goers now have to travel some distance out to the suburbs to one of the big new multiplexes where standard Hollywood fare prevails. Films are nearly always left in their original language and subtitled into Hebrew. Tickets cost about 22 NIS.

Cinematheque *(Map 4, ☎ 672 4131)* shows a variety of classic, avant-garde, new wave and off-beat films, and presents a festival each July. The majority of tickets go to members but usually a number of tickets are available just before the performance. It's part of the Jerusalem Film Centre complex, which includes a café, archives and museum, tucked below Hebron Rd, down from St Andrew's Church. For more details see the Mamilla section in the Things to See & Do chapter.

Gil 1-10 *(Map 1, ☎ 678 8448)* is out at the Malkha shopping mall, take bus Nos 19 or 24 from Jaffa Rd.

Lev *(Map 3, ☎ 624 7507, 37 Hillel St)*, just two blocks south of Ben Yehuda St.

Orion *(Map 3, ☎ 625 2914)* on Shamai St, just one block south of Ben Yehuda St.

Rav-Chen 1-7 *(Map 1, ☎ 679 2799, 19 Ha'Oman St)* in the Rav Mecher building, way down in Talpiot near the Haas Promenade.

Ron *(Map 3, ☎ 623 4176, 18 Hillel St)* near the Jerusalem Tower.

Semadar *(Map 4, ☎ 561 8168, 4 Lloyd George St)* in the German Colony, south of Liberty Bell Gardens.

Films are also shown at the Jerusalem Sherover Theatre in Talbiyeh (see the Theatre section opposite) and at the Israel Museum in Givat Ram. French-language films are screened regularly at the Alliance Française *(Map 3, ☎ 625 1204, 625 7167)* on Agron St.

What to do on Shabbat

'Shabbat Shalom' for the secular and the Gentile in Jerusalem need not be a password for boredom. For Jerusalem's large Arab population, Shabbat is just another day and nothing is closed in most of the Old City, Mt Zion, the Mount of Olives and East Jerusalem. The exception in the Old City is, of course, the Jewish Quarter, which completely shuts down for the day – wander over to the Western Wall to see the crowds and the singing and dancing that welcomes 'Queen Shabbat' on Friday at sunset.

While the Egged buses are off the road, the Arab bus network and service taxis still operate from the Damascus Gate area, and Shabbat is as good a time as any to head for Bethlehem, Jericho, Hebron, Ramallah or Nablus.

You might also try beating Shabbat by taking a bus down to the Dead Sea on Friday before the shutdown and staying somewhere overnight like Ein Gedi or Masada – the parks and reserves are all open seven days a week. You can return after sunset on Saturday when the buses start running again. Even better, sign up for the all-inclusive Masada-Ein Gedi-Qumran-Jericho trip offered by many of the Old City hostels. This departs every morning, Shabbat included, at 3 am, and gets you back into Jerusalem at about 3 pm – in time for a quick snooze before sunset, when the city comes back to life for its busiest night of the week.

If you do elect to stay in town on Friday night then you'll find that, much to the annoyance of observant Jews, most of the bars on and around Yoel Salomon and Rivlin Sts and the Russian Compound defy Shabbat and open as usual.

During the day on Saturday, with only slightly reduced hours, distraction is also offered by, among others, the Israel Museum and neighbouring Bible Lands Museum, the Bloomfield Science Museum and the Citadel (Tower of David Museum).

THEATRE

Israel has a pretty active theatre and dance scene, but as in many places today it faces an increasing struggle for funds and audiences. Most performances are in Hebrew, although there are occasional foreign language productions.

Al-Masrah Centre for Palestinian Culture & Art and Al-Kasaba Theatre *(Map 5, ☎ 628 0957)* are on Abu Obeida St off Salah ad-Din St, behind the Tombs of the Kings in East Jerusalem. Plays, musicals, operettas and folk dancing are performed here in Arabic, often with an English synopsis.

Jerusalem Sherover Theatre *(Map 4, ☎ 561 7167, 20 David Marcus St, Talbiyeh).* This is a modern theatre complex featuring the classics and modern works. Simultaneous English-language translation headsets are available for certain performances.

Khan Theatre *(Map 4, ☎ 671 8281, fax 673 3095)* is on David Remez St across from the railway station entrance. A converted and refurbished Ottoman-era caravanserai, this complex features mainly Hebrew plays in its theatre. It also has a nightclub. Take bus Nos 6, 7, 8 or 30.

Train Theatre *(Map 4, ☎ 561 8514)* is in the Liberty Bell Gardens. This is a converted railway carriage that now serves as a puppet theatre.

Pargod Theatre *(Map 2, ☎ 623 1765, 94 Bezalel St)* is just west of the New City centre. It mainly serves as a music venue, but occasionally it hosts small-scale theatre productions.

SPECTATOR SPORTS

The two big sports in Jerusalem are basketball and football. The city's main sporting venue is the Teddy Stadium *(Map 1)*, named after former mayor Teddy Kollek, which is out in Malkha district, west of the city centre and adjacent to the Kanyon shopping mall; take bus Nos 6, 24 or 31. For dates and further details of what's on, check with the Jaffa Rd tourist office.

ENTERTAINMENT

Shopping

The prime city centre shopping street is King George V St (Map 3), which has a couple of multistorey shopping malls and also the large Hamashbir department store. Jerusalem has also succumbed to the out-of-town-mall malaise, and the Kanyon mall (Map 1), out in the Malkha district, is the largest shopping centre in Israel. Take bus Nos 6, 24 or 31 from Jaffa Rd.

For more interesting buys take a look around Nahalat Shiv'a (Map 3), which is full of arts and crafts boutiques or, for those with Rockefeller-like financial reserves, browse HaMelekh David St (Maps 3 & 4), the Jerusalem equivalent of Knightsbridge.

The bazaars of the Old City (Maps 6, 7, 8 & 9) are prime souvenir territory. Their tightly compacted stalls are completely devoted to filling the mantelpieces and wall units of the world with multidenominational kitsch, from glitter-dusted prints of the Dome of the Rock and glow-in-the-dark crucifixes, to 'Shalom Y'All' plaques.

Standard Israeli shopping hours are from 8 am to 1 pm and 4 to 7 pm or later Monday to Thursday, and from 8 am to 2 pm on Friday, with some places re-opening after sunset on Saturday. Even taking into account the 15% tax refund available to visitors (see the Money section in the Facts for the Visitor chapter), Jerusalem's prices (with the exception of camping gear) are not particularly competitive compared with prices in the USA or most of Western Europe.

WHAT TO BUY
Prints & Paintings
Most of the commercial galleries are on HaMelekh David St, in the area of King David Hotel and adjacent luxury places to stay – which is indicative of their prices. And not only is the work ridiculously pricey, it's also very disappointing, much of it falling into the sub-Chagall genre or simply recycling old Judaic cliches. Slightly more variety is to be found at the

25 galleries and studios that make up the Arts & Crafts Lane (Khutsot HaYotser) in Mamilla. Opening hours are generally 10 am to 5.30 pm.

Far more interesting are some of the portfolios at **Artists' House** (Map 3, ☎ 223 653, 12 Shmuel HaNagid St). There are always two or three exhibitions hanging in the galleries, plus a lot of other artists' work in storage (available for viewing and for sale). The gallery is open daily from 9 am to 1 pm and 4 to 7 pm, opening an hour later Saturday and Sunday.

Jeru Art Israeli poster centre (Map 3, 29 King George V St) has a vast selection of prints and limited edition posters by local artists.

Hiking & Camping Gear
Israel is a surprisingly good place to stock up on hiking, camping and outdoor adventure gear. Prices are more often than not considerably lower for the same items in western European countries. Hiking boots in particular are a good buy. **Lametayel** (Map 3, ☎ 528 6894, Yoel Salomon St) is by far the best shop in Jerusalem for your travel gear. You can buy a wide range of Lonely Planet books here as well (see Books following). Lametayel also have stores in Tel Aviv and Haifa.

Books
For English-language reading matter try any of the bookshops belonging to the **Steimatzky** chain, three of which are in the New City; all are within a couple of hundred metres of each other. You'll find them at 39 Jaffa Rd, just east of Zion Square; at 7 Ben Yehuda St; and at 9 King George V St (Map 3). The *Jerusalem Post* also has a bookshop at 12 Harav Kook St, near Zion Square (Map 3), which specialises in Israel-oriented and Judaic publications. The **Academon Academic Bookstore** at the Mt Scopus campus of the Hebrew University

Textiles in the Old City

Vegetables at Mahane Yehuda market

GREG ELMS

CHRISTINE OSBORNE

Roast on the hoof – Friday's Arab animal market in Jerusalem

CHRISTINE OSBORNE

LEE FOSTER

PAUL HELLANDER

ISRAELI MINISTRY OF TOURISM

EDDIE GERALD

PAUL HELLANDER

The selection of bread, sweets, olives, nuts and pastries makes Mahane Yehuda a dieter's nightmare

(Map 2) is also very well stocked and, among everything else, carries lots of Lonely Planet titles.

Lametayel has quite a wide range of travel guides, including some that you may not find at Steimatzky. They also have a reading section with lots of cushions and beanbags on the floor where you can read your books before buying them (or putting them back on the shelves); see Hiking & Camping Gear earlier this chapter for contact details.

Probably Jerusalem's most interesting bookshop is **Sefer VeSefel** (Map 3, upstairs at 2 Yaabez St), in a little alley off Jaffa Rd, one block east of King George V St. It's a creaky little place packed from floor to ceiling with new and second-hand titles, both fiction and nonfiction. It also has a small balcony cafe. It's open from 8 am to 8 pm Sunday to Thursday, from 8 am to 2.30 pm on Friday, and from sunset to 11.30 pm Saturday.

In the Old City, **The Bookshelf** (Map 9) at the southern end of Jewish Quarter Rd, has piles of dog-eared thrillers, while **Moriah Bookstore** on nearby Misgav Ladakh is the place for English-language material on Judaism. In East Jerusalem, **Educational Bookshop** (Map 5, 22 Salah ad-Din St) carries an assortment of Palestinian-oriented publications.

French-readers will find a limited selection of books in Steimatzky bookshops but are much better catered for at Librarie Française (Map 3) on Jaffa Rd, across from the main post office.

For information about books written about Jerusalem, see under Books in the Facts for the Visitor chapter.

Newspapers & Magazines

Steimatzky is also the place to pick up your copy of the *Economist*, *Time*, *Paris-Match* or *Wired*. For a more varied and eclectic selection try **Tower Records** (Map 3) on Hillel St behind McDonald's, which has a wide range of UK and US-style music and arts publications. See also this section in the Facts for the Visitor chapter.

Antiquities

Israel is alone among the Mediterranean seaboard nations in allowing the free sale and export of its antiquities. What could earn you a stiff jail sentence in Greece or Egypt can provide you with an unusual and often inexpensive memento from biblical times for your mantelpiece or your collection of travel artefacts.

The best place to look for antiquities is in the Old City. Probably the most famous, though unlikely looking shop is **Baidun** (Map 7, ☎ 628 2937) on the Via Dolorosa. Owner Khader Baidun lists among his clients such luminaries as Moshe Dyan, Bill Clinton and Pope John Paul II. His relic-scattered studio is a curator's dream, while his shop next door showcases both antiquities and newer ceramics and pottery for sale.

Further west along the same street is **Aweidah Gallery** (☎ 628 4417, 4 Via Dolorosa), a rather snobbier and more pretentious place, but with a wide selection of good quality antiquities at proportional prices.

Ethics & Antiquities

Anyone thinking about buying antiquities in Israel should bear in mind that looting archaeological sites is at epidemic proportions, and that anything you buy may well have been stolen. The sites, predominantly tombs, are also severely damaged by looters interested in stealing anything saleable. The counterfeiting of antiquities, especially 'Roman' silver coins and glass, is also rife.

By law, the buyer must apply for a (free) permit from the Israel Antiquities Authority (IAA) before any artefact over 200 years old leaves the country; and the IAA has a right to prevent the export of any piece with national or historical value. With the antiquities dealers gearing up for the millennium pilgrim trade, the IAA plans to open a desk at Ben-Gurion airport to allow people to register their purchases.

Ceramics

The tiling on the Dome of the Rock was made in Armenian craftshops, as are the ceramic street name plaques that adorn the walls of the Old City. Tiles and plates fashioned in the same manner are one of the most attractive buys in Jerusalem. Probably the best sales studio to visit is **Jerusalem Pottery** on the Via Dolorosa next to the 6th Station of the Cross. Commissions are accepted here. Also recommended are the two ceramic shops on Armenian Patriarchate Rd (Map 9); and **Palestinian Pottery** (Map 5, 14 Nablus Rd) across from the US consulate in East Jerusalem.

Handicrafts & Souvenirs

The sale of Oriental coffee pots, inlaid lapis boxes, *nargilas* (water pipes) and a bewildering array of other ornaments sometimes seems to be the *raison d'être* of the Old City. 'Jerusalem candles', prettily patterned spherical things that become translucent when the wick is lit, are the mainstay of the handicrafts industry. They are genuinely attractive and sell for between 15 and 30 NIS, depending on the size.

Olive wood items are similarly ubiquitous, most commonly fashioned into crucifixes, camels, worry beads and carvings of biblical scenes and characters.

Dead Sea Products

An unusual line of products are those manufactured from the minerals of the Dead Sea. These include soaps made from mineral mud, bath salts and a line of body products that would make original gifts for friends as well as for your own personal use (see the 'Dead Healthy?' boxed text in the Excursions chapter). **Ahava** (Map 3, ☎ 628 3998) is a minuscule, but easily found shop on the corner of Zahal Square near the New Gate of the Old City. You may also find Ahava's products in pharmacies and other shops selling cosmetics. You can usually buy a wide range of Dead Sea products at Ben-Gurion airport's duty free shops at cheaper prices.

Excursions

AROUND JERUSALEM
Kibbutz Ramat Rachel

Its location between Jerusalem and Bethlehem meant that this kibbutz was the unwitting scene of bloody fighting during the 1948 War. Today, though, that same location has helped the kibbutz develop itself as a full-scale tourist attraction.

Its name means 'the Heights of Rachel', referring to the Matriach Rachel, Jacob's wife, whose tomb is in Bethlehem. Tours of the kibbutz offer visitors a glimpse of life on a collective farm, and there's a museum with exhibits on the 1948 War, open daily from 8 am to noon.

It's also possible to stay at the *Kibbutz Guesthouse* (☎ *670 2555, fax 673 3155, email resv@ramatrachel.co.il*), where the rates are US$117 to US$156 for a single, and US$130 to $178 for a double.

Take bus No 7 from Jaffa Rd or Keren HaYesod St in Talbiyeh.

Kennedy Memorial (Map 1)

South of the Hadassah Medical Centre and about 11km from the city centre, this fine memorial to John F Kennedy sits atop Mt Orah. Unfortunately, you may need a car to get here as the nearest bus stop (bus Nos 20 and 50) is a good 30 minute walk away.

Sorek/Avshalom Stalagmite & Stalactite Cave

The stunning Sorek, or Avshalom (Absalom's), cave is some 20km west of Jerusalem along the road from Ein Kerem. The predominance of limestone in the region has caused these geological formations, which are floodlit for effect. Opening hours are from 8.30 am to 3.45 pm Sunday to Thursday and 8.30 am to 12.45 pm on Friday. Admission is 18 NIS (children 10 NIS). For more information call ☎ 691 1117.

The pleasant scenery en route from Jerusalem is almost worth an excursion itself. No

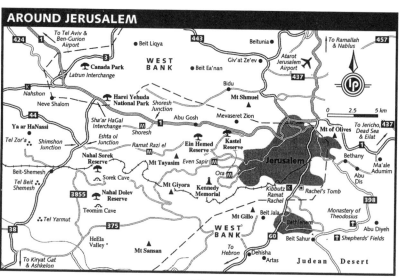

163

regular bus goes directly to the cave, but Egged Tours offers two half-day guided tours, each for around US$20. If you are driving there from Jerusalem, take the Beit Shmesh road via Ein Kerem. The cave is well signposted.

Beit Guvrin-Maresha National Park

This splendid set of underground caves together with the ruins of both the biblical and Hellenistic city of Maresha and the Roman-Byzantine city of Beit Guvrin (ancient Eleutheroupolis) is worth a day trip. The site extends over 500 hectares and consists of some 4000 hollows and chambers that create a Swiss cheese landscape. Some of the caves are natural, the result of water eroding the soft limestone surface. Others, however, are thought to be the result of quarrying by the Phoenicians. Among the more interesting attractions are the Sidonian Burial caves, an olive oil processing plant and a partly restored dwelling.

Getting to the site can be difficult without a car, as public transport is limited. Bus No 11 runs twice a day from Kiryat Gat to the kibbutz nearby, at 8 am and 5 pm, with return journeys at 8.25 am and 12.30 pm. Alternatively, SPNI Tours do a one-day tour of Beit Guvrin from Jerusalem for US$59; if there are at least three of you a special taxi should work out cheaper.

Shoresh Junction

West of this junction on the Jerusalem-Tel Aviv highway, the road descends into a gorge. On both sides you can see the rusted remains of vehicles that were part of the Jewish supply convoys attacked by the Arabs during the 1948 siege of Jerusalem. Some have been daubed with red paint and inscriptions, and they now form a memorial to the Jews who were killed here.

Abu Gosh

This peaceful and picturesque Arab village (13km from Jerusalem and off the main highway to Tel Aviv) is significant because it is the site of the biblical Kiriath-Jearim

(Town of Forests) where the Ark of the Covenant stayed for 20 years until David moved it to Jerusalem (I Chronicles 13:5-8). Before the new highway bypassed the village it was a popular beauty spot for Israelis, but now it sees fewer visitors.

There are two interesting churches here. **Notre Dame de l'Arche** (Our Lady of the Ark) was built in 1924 and is a local landmark, with its statue of Mary carrying the Baby Jesus. It belongs to the French Sisters of St Joseph of the Apparition, and they believe that it stands on the site of Abinadab's house, where the Ark of the Covenent was kept (I Samuel 7:1). Ring the bell at the door of the adjacent building if no one is about and the church is closed. The church is built on the same site as a larger Byzantine church, and you can see its mosaic floor inside and out. It can be reached from the top of the hill overlooking the village and facing Jerusalem. Turn right coming out of Caravan Restaurant and head up the hill. It's open daily from 8 to 11.30 am and 3.30 to 6 pm. Admission is free.

Crusader Church & Monastery is one of the country's best-preserved and most attractive Crusader remains. It was built about 1142 and destroyed in 1187. It is believed that the monastery stands on the remains of a Roman fort. A stone from the castle is displayed in the church and bears an inscription of the 10th Legion, a renowned Roman unit stationed in Jerusalem in the 1st century AD.

Used for many centuries as an animal shelter, the church was acquired in 1859 by the French government, who placed it under the guardianship of the French Benedictines. Since 1956 it has belonged to the Lazarist Fathers. There is a small spring in the subterranean section of the building.

The complex is next door to the mosque, so look for the minaret in the valley. The sign outside reads 'Eglise de Croisse' (Crusaders' Church). Ring the bell to enter. The monastery is open Monday to Wednesday, Friday and Saturday from 8.30 to 11 am and 2.30 to 5.30 pm, closed Thursday and Sunday. Admission is free, but donations are requested.

Getting There & Away Abu Gosh is conveniently reached from Jerusalem on bus Nos 185 or 186, both of which depart frequently between 6 am and 11 pm from the central bus station.

Bethany

On the western slopes of the Mount of Olives, Bethany is renowned as the site of the resurrection of Lazarus (John 11:1-44). A Franciscan church commemorates the site where this miracle is traditionally believed to have been performed by Jesus. The church features some impressive mosaics, one of which illustrates Lazarus' resurrection. Built in 1954, this is the fourth church to occupy the area. The first was constructed in the mid-1st century, the second in the Byzantine period and the third by the Crusaders.

A Greek Orthodox church stands by the Tomb of Lazarus. In the 16th century, Muslims built a mosque here and Christians later dug their own entrance to enable them to worship. Local guides are often on hand and do a decent job of telling their interesting version of local history. If you listen, you should tip a couple of shekels. The tomb is open daily from 8 am to noon and 2 to 6 pm. Admission is 2 NIS.

The church itself is only open on the Feast of Lazarus, in early April. The Greek Orthodox convent preserves the rock upon which Jesus sat while waiting for Martha to arrive from Jericho. Ring the bell to enter.

Getting There & Away To reach Bethany you can take either of two Arab buses – the No 36 service (there are two No 36 services, so ask for 'El-Azariya' [Lazarus] before boarding) or No 28 to Jericho – and get off on the way through. Another option is to walk. If it's not too hot (or wet), you can walk up and over the Mount of Olives and around the side to Bethany. You can't really get lost, as you'll never be far from a busy road on which to hitch or hail a service taxi.

Latrun

About halfway between Jerusalem and Tel Aviv lies Latrun. Latrun means 'Home of the Good Thief'; it is believed to have been the home of one of the thieves crucified with Jesus. In the 1948 War, the Arabs closed the road here, thus cutting off supplies to Jerusalem. It was not until the Six Day War in June 1967 that the Israelis took Latrun. Further back in time, this area saw its fair share of conflict. Greeks, Romans, Arabs, Crusaders, British and the Ottoman Turks have all passed through en route to Jerusalem.

A modern highway now cuts through the area, and to the west (ie the left-hand side heading towards Tel Aviv) is the attractive Latrun Monastery, while to the east is Canada Park and the ruins of Emmaus Church.

The popular **wine-producing monastery** at Latrun enjoys views of many biblical

EXCURSIONS

Latrun Monastery

Founded in 1890 by French Trappists as a contemplative monastery, Latrun Monastery is now widely renowned for its wine, as well as its lovely location, architecture and gardens.

The wine-making began in 1899. The monks reclaimed and cultivated the land, planting olive groves, grain fields and vegetable gardens, as well as vineyards. In the rocky areas pine trees and cypresses were planted. In WWI the monks were expelled by the Turks, but they were able to return, and in 1926 the present monastery was constructed.

Visitors are welcome to enjoy the gardens and the architecture and to buy the wine, spirits, vermouth and olive oil. The shop by the gate is open from 8.30 to 11.30 am and 2.30 to 4.30 pm Monday to Saturday, closed Sunday.

sites: Emmaus, Ayalon, Bethoron, Gezer, Modin, Lydda and Sorec (see the boxed text 'Latrun Monastery' earlier).

Also near Latrun is **Canada Park**, the result of a tree-planting program initiated by the Jewish National Fund. This park is one of the country's many beautifully forested areas, and you can wander around and picnic here. There is a well-preserved Roman bath near the church, dating from around 640 AD. Various water holes, conduits and the remains of an amphitheatre can also be found in the park.

Above the ruins of **Emmaus Church** rises a monastery that formerly belonged to the Beit-Haram brothers, but now functions as the French Prehistorical Research Centre. This site is believed to be where Jesus appeared to two of His disciples after the Resurrection.

Latrun can be easily reached by bus, with a service departing Jerusalem every 30 minutes.

BETHLEHEM

Modern-day Bethlehem may be a cynic's delight, with Manger Square, Manger St, Star St, Shepherds' St, two Shepherds' Fields and an unheavenly host of 'Christmases', but for most travellers with even the faintest Christian background, a trip to Jerusalem without visiting the nearby site of the Nativity is unthinkable, even if only to please a pious relative back home.

Orientation & Information

Manger Square is at the centre of town and the Church of the Nativity is on its southern side. At the time of research, renovations to the square (a joint Palestinian-Swedish project) were incomplete but should be finished by the time you read this. Around the square are the tourist information office, police station, post office and various shops, hotels and eating places. Milk Grotto St heads off to the south-east, down past the Milk Grotto Chapel, while Paul VI St, which heads uphill to the north-west, has the museum, outdoor market and more shops and hotels.

Manger St, off the north side of the square, is the main winding route through the new town. It eventually intersects with the Jerusalem-Hebron highway opposite the shrine of Rachel's Tomb.

Accommodation in Bethlehem has improved immeasurably in recent times but it can still get crowded, especially at Easter and Christmas (some things never change!) so try and make sure you have a booking before attempting to stay overnight.

Things to See

The **Church of the Nativity**, one of the world's oldest operational churches, is built like a citadel over the cave where it is believed that Jesus was born. Happily, it's a suitably august and venerable building, which unlike Jerusalem's Holy Sepulchre or Nazareth's Basilica, manages to avoid the 'holy site as sideshow' feel. One such sideshow is found down Milk Grotto St at the **Milk Grotto Chapel**, a kitsch little shrine that owes its existence to the Virgin Mary's clumsy lactations (at least that's the legend).

North-west of the square, on Paul VI St, **Bethlehem Museum** exhibits traditional Palestinian crafts and costumes; it's open from 10 am to noon and 2.30 to 5.30 pm Monday to Saturday, closed Sunday.

One of Judaism's most sacred shrines, also revered by Muslims and Christians, **Rachel's Tomb** is housed in a small white domed building on the edge of town at the intersection of Hebron Rd and Manger St.

Getting There & Away

Arab bus No 22 runs frequently from East Jerusalem to Bethleham (40 minutes), stopping outside Jaffa Gate en route. Service taxis (3 NIS) from outside Damascus Gate are more convenient, they tend to depart more frequently and make the journey in half the time.

Walking from Jerusalem to Bethlehem is another option. At Christmas there's an official procession, but the two to 2½ hour, up hill and down dale hike will be shared with often heavy traffic. Follow Hebron Rd out past Jerusalem's railway station and eventually you will emerge into the countryside. Once past the Greek Orthodox Elias Monastery, you'll see Bethlehem ahead of you.

JERICHO
Jericho is best known for the biblical account of Joshua and the tumbling walls. There are some ancient, well-visited ruins on the outskirts of town but these are surpassed by the shabby beauty of the surrounding landscape.

Orientation & Information
Service taxis from Jerusalem drop their passengers off in the main square with its shops, eating places, police station, taxi ranks and foreign exchange facilities.

To reach the sights, follow the 6km loop formed by Qasr Hisham and Ein as-Sultan Sts. Moving anti-clockwise is the popular choice: head north up Qasr Hisham St to Hisham's Palace, a walk (or cycle) of about 2.5km, then west to the old synagogue and ancient Jericho.

With the distances involved between the town and the sights, cycling is a popular mode of transport. The roads are relatively flat and free from traffic, so decide for yourself whether the heat is easier to bear on foot or in the saddle of a rented boneshaker. Zaki's bicycle shop is on the town square, bicycle hire costs 5 NIS per hour. You may be asked to leave a passport or something similar as security.

Ancient Sites
Hisham's Palace is the impressive ruins of a 7th century hunting lodge. It includes a beautiful Byzantine mosaic floor depicting a lion pouncing on one of a group of gazelle grazing beneath a great leafy tree.

There's another **mosaic floor** – part of the ruins of a 5th or 6th century **synagogue**. This is passed on the way to the site of **ancient Jericho**, otherwise known as the Tel as-Sultan excavations. Only true archaeology buffs are likely to be impressed here, and even visitors blessed with the most

visionary imaginations are going to struggle to make anything of the signposted trenches and mounds of dirt.

The **Mount & Monastery of Temptation**, on the other hand, is well worth the steep climb. This 12th century Greek Orthodox monastery clings to the cliffside on the site where the Devil is believed to have tempted Jesus. It's closed Sunday.

Wadi Qelt
Wadi Qelt is a nature reserve with a natural spring where you can swim in a pool under a waterfall and hike along an aqueduct to **St George's Monastery**, built into the cliff face of a canyon. The hike takes about four hours. The starting point is the Wadi Qelt turn-off on the Jerusalem to Jericho road (ask the bus driver to drop you off here) and the finishing point is Jericho, from where you can continue sightseeing in the town or easily find transport back to Jerusalem.

Places to Stay
Hisham's Palace Hotel (☎ 992 2156) on Ein as-Sultan St, is the oldest place to stay in Jericho. Large and shabby, the place is so neglected that the carpets have started to sprout grass. Prices are negotiable, but count on paying around 135 NIS, which is more than the room is worth.

New Jericho Pension (☎ 992 2215, Sharia al-Quds) is slightly better but it's not all that flash. Singles/doubles are negotiable but should be around the 130/160 NIS mark.

Jerusalem Hotel (☎ 992 1329, fax 992 3109), 2.5km east of the main square, is the most upmarket hotel in town. Smart, bright new rooms go for US$65 to US$90.

Getting There & Away
There are, at present, no bus services to Jericho; instead, you could use the sheruts (special taxis). Operating from the rank opposite Jerusalem's Damascus Gate, the stretch-Mercedes or Peugeots depart whenever they're full, and that's rarely more than a 10 minute wait. The fare is 5 NIS for the pleasant 30 minute drive. In Jericho, service taxis depart from the town square, usually

until about 7 pm. You can find them after this time but with a shortage of passengers you may have to fork out a higher fare.

It is possible to get a service taxi from Jericho to other West Bank towns such as Bethlehem, Nablus and Ramallah; ask at the rank on the southern side of the square.

THE DEAD SEA

It's the ultimate Israel cliche, the image of a swimsuited bather lying in – almost on – the water, feet up and newspaper open, like a Sunday morning in bed. But unlike a camel ride at the Pyramids or wrapping a kufeyya around your neck, this is one Middle Eastern cliche well worth indulging in. With a shoreline of some 90km there is no one bathing spot, but you are advised to take your dip somewhere with shower facilities (the Dead Sea 'water' has a slightly slimy quality); the beach at Ein Gedi is one of the most popular spots.

Masada

After the obligatory float in the Dead Sea, the next popular thing to do is to visit Masada, a place that readers consistently rate as Israel's number one attraction. On a free-standing, sheer-sided plateau high above the Dead Sea, the seriously paranoid Herod the Great built a fortified palace complex, including a synagogue and even a *mikveh* (ritual bath).

In 66 AD, as part of the Great Revolt, a group of Jewish *sicarii* (dagger-men) captured the lightly guarded Masada. After the fall of Jerusalem in 70 AD, the Romans began to mop up the remnants of the rebellion, including the rebels at Masada. During the ensuing two-year siege, the Romans built a massive ramp from the valley floor up to the walls of the fortress. The tale of the mass suicide of the defenders figures large in the Israeli national psyche. See the boxed text 'The (very complex) Masada Complex'. The site and views are superb, and you can reach the top by cable car or on foot.

Ein Gedi

Not as well known or as well frequented by travellers, **Ein Gedi Nature Reserve** also deserves some exploration. One of the country's most attractive oases, Ein Gedi is a lush area of freshwater springs, waterfalls, pools and tropical vegetation nestled in the arid desert landscape of the lowest place on earth.

Dead Healthy?

Compared with regular sea water, the water of the Dead Sea contains 20 times as much bromine, 15 times as much magnesium and 10 times as much iodine – it is, in effect, 33% solid substance. Bromine, a component of many sedatives, relaxes the nerves, magnesium counteracts skin allergies and clears the bronchial passages, while iodine has a beneficial effect on certain glandular functions – or so it's claimed, especially by local health spa owners and the various Dead Sea cosmetic companies.

Due to the low altitude (400m below sea level), there is 10% more oxygen in Dead Sea air than at sea level, and the lack of urban development has kept it free of pollution. All of this purportedly increases the body's metabolic rate and has a bracing effect.

Healthy or not, soaking in the Dead Sea can also be extremely painful. Wade in with any exposed cuts or grazes and you will gain instant enlightenment as to the meaning of the phrase to 'rub salt in your wounds'. We guarantee that you are going to discover scratches and sores that you never knew you had! The magnesium chloride in the water gives it a revolting bitter taste and if you swallow any, it's stomach pump time. Don't get the water in your eyes either as it will sting and inflame. If this happens, rinse your eyes immediately with fresh water.

Carpets for sale in a Tel Aviv flea market

The unmistakably modern skyline of Tel Aviv's Esplanade

View of Jaffa from the harbour

CHRISTINE OSBORNE

PAUL HELLANDER

CHRISTINE OSBORNE

LEE FOSTER

Top: Lent candles and a fresco in the Church of the Nativity in Bethlehem
Middle: Ancient Jericho being uncovered at the Tel as-Sultan excavations.
Bottom: The Dead Sea, the world's largest flotation tank

The (very complex) Masada Complex

Masada is one of the few symbols powerful enough to unite most Jews – the religious, the secular Zionists, and those of the Diaspora communities. IDF recruits are sworn in here, and 'Masada shall not fall again!' is a perennially popular slogan. A Masada opera was premiered in 1998, timed to coincide with the 'Israel at 50' celebrations. There's even a psychological condition called the Masada Complex.

It's at Masada that the occupying Jewish forces made a last stand against the Romans in the seige of 70 AD, one of the final acts of the the Great Revolt, which ended when the 960 defenders – men, women and children – chose mass suicide rather than surrender. Masada is one of the great defining stories of the Jewish people that is also demonstrated historical fact. Or is it?

The site was excavated in 1963-65 by the late Yigael Yadin, then Professor of Archaeology at the Hebrew University (who had also excavated the Dead Sea caves at Qumran). What Yadin found seemed to corroborate the details of the account written by Flavius Josephus, a 1st century AD Jewish historian, in his work *The Jewish War*. Yadin even found a piece of broken pottery with the name of Eleazar, the commander at Masada, scratched into it. Since pottery shards were commonly used as 'straws' with which to draw lots, this find seems to tally with Josephus' claims that the mass suicide was done by means of a lottery (in which one man out of each group of ten was chosen to kill the others) until the last survivor was left to kill himself.

But archaeological finds must be interpreted after they are recovered, and this process is heavily influenced by the archaeologists' own theories. Yadin had been the Chief of Staff of the IDF from 1949-52, and may have approached the dig expecting to find evidence to back Josephus' record of events.

Yadin's interpretations of the finds at Masada have since been questioned. For example, Yadin had assumed that the 25 skeletons discovered in a nearby cave had belonged to Jews and were tossed there by Romans; it has been pointed out that the legionaries would most likely have thrown bodies over the fortress walls, not dragged them halfway up a dangerously steep cliff. Also, since lotteries were often used for everyday things, the pottery shard with Eleazar's name on it could just as easily be connected to the guard duty roster.

Josephus' historical account of the Great Revolt, which Yadin's conclusions so neatly corroborated, is also less than concrete. Josephus was certainly alive at the time, but he was hardly an impartial observer. Captured very early on in the rebellion, he spent most of the war as a prisoner of the Romans, sometimes acting as an interpreter for them. By the time Masada fell, Josephus is likely to have already left Judaea for Rome, where he was to spend the rest of his life as an imperial courtier.

The details of Josephus' account of the fall of Masada also have a suspicious similarity to the fall of Jotapata, the Galilean fort which he had commanded at the beginning of the Great Revolt. Like Masada, the situation was hopeless, and also like Masada, the defenders resolved to commit an honourable mass suicide. But unlike Masada, the lots were rigged, and when Josephus was one of the last two left alive, he persuaded his companion to join him in surrendering to the Romans. Did Josephus romanticise the Masada story into an ideal version of what should have happened at Jotapata? Perhaps. Without conclusive archaeological evidence (such as a large pile of skeletons and some Jewish swords!) we cannot tell, but Masada legend has certainly taken on a life and significance of its own.

It's a haven for desert wildlife, which hangs in there despite the terrifyingly raucous coach loads of kids that rampage through the reserves on an almost daily basis.

Ein Gedi sprawls over an area of 4 sq km. The nature reserves, field school and youth hostel are in the north; 1km south are the bathing beach, restaurant and camp site. Another 2.5km south is the turn-off for Kibbutz Ein Gedi, with the Hamme Mazor sulphur baths a further 2.5km south. Avoid visiting on weekends and holidays when Ein Gedi is noisy and crowded.

North of Ein Gedi is **Qumran**, where the Dead Sea Scrolls were discovered. The site includes the settlement and caves of the Essenes, the Jewish sect who wrote the scrolls between 150 BC and 68 AD. The bus stops on the main road; follow the turn-off up the hill. There is a self-service cafeteria at the site. It's a hot climb up to the caves, so bring plenty of drinking water.

Tours

By far the cheapest way of sampling the Dead Sea region is to sign up for the 12 hour tour you'll see advertised in almost all the hostels in Jerusalem. It departs the Old City at 3 am each morning, getting you down to Masada in time to watch the sun rise over the desert. The tour includes a visit to Ein Gedi Nature Reserve and a float in the Dead Sea before making photo stops at Qumran and Jericho's Mount of Temptation. Despite the stopwatch-timed schedule, most travellers find that they get to see all they want. SPNI Tours operate a very similar program but it's about three times more expensive.

Metzoke Dragot (☎ 994 4222, fax 994 4333, email metzoke@netvision.net.il) offers various tours and activities in the Judean Desert, either with or without accommodation. They are highly recommended by those who have experienced them.

Places to Stay

The Ein Gedi *HI – Beit Sara Hostel (☎ 07-658 4165, fax 658 4445)* charges US$16.50 to stay in an air-con eight bed dorm. Double rooms are US$40 (nonmembers pay a few

dollars more). Breakfast is included and dinner is available. Check-in is between 3 to 7 pm and check-out is at 9 am. The hostel is about 250m north-west of the Ein Gedi Nature Reserve bus stop.

The Masada, *HI – Isaac H Taylor Hostel (☎ 07-658 4349, fax 658 4650)* has air-con dorm beds for US$16.50, with breakfast included. Sleeping out on top of Masada is no longer permitted, but the hostel does have tent-pitching space.

Back at Ein Gedi and moving up in price is the guesthouse at *Kibbutz Ein Gedi (☎ 07-659 4222, fax 658 4328, email eb@kibbutz .co.il)* which, while expensive, is one of the most popular in the country. Surrounded by tree-filled gardens beside the Dead Sea, it has a swimming pool and a hot spa – the use of which are included in the price (half board only). Singles range from US$122 to 143 and doubles from US$174 to 204. Booking is recommended.

Getting There & Away

The entire 90km-long west coast of the Dead Sea is served by a single main road (Route No 90) which is part of the Tiberias-Eilat highway running from the Sea of Galilee to the Red Sea. The road follows the shoreline south to Sodom and continues to Eilat. There is a comprehensive bus service from Jerusalem's central bus station. Buses to Eilat and Beersheba run via Qumran (20 NIS, 1 hour), Ein Gedi (25 NIS, 1½ hours) and Masada; there should be a bus departing at least every hour or so.

TEL AVIV

Tel Aviv is a greatly underrated Mediterranean city. Barely a century old, it thumbs its nose at the 3000-year-history of Jerusalem. Forsaking synagogues for stock exchanges and tradition for the latest fads and fashions, the concerns of secular Tel Aviv are finance, business and fun. The city has an absorbing array of distinctive neighbourhoods, the result of the diverse backgrounds of its inhabitants, all of whom arrived in the last few generations with piles of cultural baggage intact. A short walk can encompass the spicy orientalism of the Yemenite Quarter, the seedy vodka cafés of Russian-influenced lower Allenby St and the Miami chic of pastel pink and blue glass beachfront condominiums.

Possibly the major attraction is the lengthy stretch of fine white sand fringing the city centre area. When the sun is out (and it usually is) the beaches are a strutting ground for local poseurs and a vast sandy court for pairs playing *matkot*, Israeli beach tennis. On summer nights the beaches remain crowded as they become impromptu sites for concerts and discos.

Visitors should make a point of visiting both the **Diaspora Museum** up in the northern suburb of Ramat Aviv, and the former Arab port of **Jaffa**, now an unashamed till-ringing tourist attraction and popular Israeli venue for candle-lit, waterfront seafood dinners.

Fast food is big business in Tel Aviv, with sandwich bars, felafel joints, pizza parlours and all the big-name hamburger retailers saturating the food scene. With increasing Israeli travel experience in Far East destinations, Asian street food is becoming popular. Around central Tel Aviv you will soon come across little hole-in-the-wall places offering stir-fried whatever you fancy. Look out for the flaming woks in the windows and pop your head in to see what is on offer.

For fresh fruit, head for Carmel Market. For one-stop shopping there's a convenient Supersol supermarket at 79 Ben Yehuda St, between Gordon and Mapu Sts. It's open from 7 am to midnight Sunday to Tuesday, all night Wednesday and Thursday, and from 7 am to 3 pm Friday (closed Saturday).

For information on getting to Tel Aviv, see the Getting There & Away chapter.

Language

Thanks to the efforts of Eliezer ben Yehuda in reviving a language which to all intents and purposes was as 'dead' as Latin, (see the Language section of the Facts about Jerusalem chapter), Hebrew is the national language of Israel, and also the most widely spoken.

Next in popularity is Arabic, and you should have little trouble finding someone who understands English. Most of the major road and street signs are in all three languages.

Because of the long and continuing history of Jewish immigration to Israel from Diaspora communities spread across the world, other languages are common in Israel – French, German and Yiddish are the main ones, but also Spanish and Russian.

HEBREW
Basics

Hello.	sha-LOM
Goodbye.	sha-LOM
Good morning.	BO-ker tov
Good evening.	erev tov
Goodnight.	lie-la tov
See you later.	le-HIT-rah-OTT
Thank you.	to-DAH
Please.	be-va-ka-SHA
You're welcome.	al low da-VAAR
Yes.	ken
No.	loh
Excuse me.	slee-KHA
Wait.	REG-gah
What?	mah?
When?	mah-tye?
Where is ...?	AYE-fo ...?
right (correct)	na-CHON
money	KES-sef
bank	bank
I don't speak Hebrew.	AH-NEElo m'dah-BEHR ee-VREET
Do you speak English?	ah-TAH m'dah-BEHR ang-LEET?

Time & Days

What is the time?	MA ha-sha-AH?
seven o'clock	ha-sha-AHSHEV-vah
minute	da-KAH
hour	sha-AH
day	yom
week	sha-voo-ah
month	KHO-desh
year	sha-NAH
Monday	shey-NEE
Tuesday	shlee-SHEE
Wednesday	reh-vee-EE
Thursday	cha-mee SHEE
Friday	shee-SHEE
Saturday	sha-BAT
Sunday	ree-SHON

Getting Around

Which bus goes to ...?	AYE-zeh auto-boos no-SE-ah le ...?
Stop here.	ah-TSOR kahn
airport	sde t'oo-FAH
bus	auto-boos
near	ka-ROV
railway	rah-KEH-vet
station	ta-cha-na

Food & Accommodation

food	OKHEL
water	my-im
restaurant	MISS-ah-DAH
breakfast	ah-roo-CHAT BO-ker
lunch	ah-roo-KHAT-tsa-ha-RYE-im
dinner	ah-roo-KHAT erev
menu	taf-REET
egg	bay-TSA
vegetables	YEH-rah-KOHT
bread	LEKH-hem
butter	khem-AH
cheese	g'VEE-nah
milk	kha-LAV
ice cream	glee-DAH

fruit	*pay-ROT*
wine	*yain*
bill	*KHESH-bon*
hotel	*ma-LON*
room	*khe-der*
toilet	*she-ru-TEEM*

Around Town

How much is it?	*KA-mah zeh ule?*
post office	*dough-ar*
letter	*mich-tav*
stamps	*boolim*
envelopes	*ma-ata-FOT*
postcard	*gloo-yah*
telegram	*miv-rack*
airmail	*dough-ar ah-veer*
pharmacy	*bait mer-kah-KHAT*
shop	*kha-NOOT*
expensive	*ya-KAR*
cheap	*zol*

Numbers

1	*eh-HAD*
2	*SHTA-yim*
3	*sha-LOSH*
4	*AR-bah*
5	*cha-MAYSH*
6	*shaysh*
7	*SHEV-vah*
8	*sh-MO-neh*
9	*TAY-shah*
10	*ESS-er*
11	*eh-HAD-ess-RAY*
12	*shtaym-ess-RAY*
20	*ess-REEM*
21	*ess-REEM v'ah-KHAD*
30	*shlo-SHEEM*
31	*shlo-SHEEM v'ah-KHAD*
50	*cha-MEESHLEEM*
100	*MAY-ah*
200	*mah-tah-YEEM*
300	*shlosh may-OAT*
500	*cha-MAYSH may-OAT*
1000	*alef*
3000	*shlosh-ET alef-EEM*
5000	*cha-maysh-ET alef-EEM*

ARABIC

Any attempts, however unsuccessful, to speak Arabic will endear you to the Arabs of the region. Learning the characters for the Arab numerals is useful, as much of your shopping will be done in Arab markets.

Useful Words

Hello.	*a-halan/mahr-haba*
Goodbye.	*salaam aleicham/ ma-ah-salameh*
Good morning.	*sabah-al-kheir*
Good evening.	*masa'al-kheir*
Please.	*min fadlach*
Thank you.	*shoo-khran*
You're welcome.	*afwan*
I don't understand.	*mish faahim*
Do you speak English?	*tech-kee Ingleesi?*
How much is this?	*ah-desh hadah?*
Yes.	*ay-wah*
No.	*la*
Pardon?	*sa-mech-nee?*
Where?	*feen?*
right	*yemine*
left	*she-mal*
straight	*doo-ree*

Time & Days

Sunday	*el-ahad*
Monday	*itnein*
Tuesday	*talaata*
Wednesday	*el-arbi'a*
Thursday	*khamis*
Friday	*jumu'a*
Saturday	*sabit*
What is the time?	*gaddesh saa'ah?*
minute	*da'iah*
hour	*saa'ah*
day	*yawm*
week	*jum'a/usbuu'*
month	*shahr*
year	*saneh*

Getting Around

Which bus goes to ...?	*ayya baas yaruh 'ala ...?*

Is it far?	*ba'id?*	tea	*schai*
Stop here.	*wa'if huna*	coffee	*kah-wah*
train station	*mahattat train*	hotel	*oteyl*
airport	*mataar*	room	*odah*
bus stop	*mawif al-baas*	toilet	*beyt al-may*

Around Town

post office	*al-bostah*
letter	*maktuub*
stamps	*tabi'*
envelope	*mughallaf*
airmail	*al-barid al-hawwi*
pharmacy	*farmashiyyeh*
shop	*dukkaan*
expensive	*ghaali*
cheap	*rakhis*

Food & Accommodation

food	*akil*
water	*may*
restaurant	*mat'am*
breakfast	*futuur*
lunch	*ghada*
dinner	*'asha*
menu	*menu*

Numbers

Arabic numerals are read from left to right, unlike the language, which is read from right to left.

0	.	*sifr*
1	١	*wa-hid*
2	٢	*tinen*
3	٣	*talatay*
4	٤	*arbaha*
5	٥	*khamseh*
6	٦	*sitteh*
7	٧	*sabah*
8	٨	*tamanyeh*
9	٩	*taisah*
10	١٠	*ahsharah*
100	١٠٠	*miyyah*
500	٥٠٠	*khamsmiyyah*
1000	١٠٠٠	*alf*
5000	٥٠٠٠	*khamasta alaf*

Glossary

HEBREW, YIDDISH & ARAMAIC

agam – lake

agora (pl **agorot**) – smallest unit of the *shekel*, 1 shekel = 100 agorot

aliyah – (literally 'stepping up') Jewish immigration to Israel; also, a specific wave of immigration (eg the First Aliyah, 1882-1903; the Second Aliyah 1904-14; the Third Aliyah 1919-23); also refers to being called up to read from the *Torah* in the synagogue

Arkia – a domestic Israeli airline

Aron Hakodesh – originally the Ark in the Temple that contained the Tablets of the Law given at Mount Sinai; today, the ark in which the Torah scrolls are kept

Ashkenazi (pl **Ashkenazim**) – Yiddish-speaking Jews of Central and East European descent

atar – site

bar mitzvah – (Aramaic, literally 'son of the commandments') the ceremony which marks a boy's coming of age at 13 years

bat mitzvah – the equivalent to a bar mitzvah for girls, only in Reform and Conservative Judaism

be'er – a well

Begin, Menachem – prime minister of Israel from 1977 to 1983

beit or **beth** – house ('bayit' when used before another noun)

beit knesset – synagogue

Ben-Gurion, David – head of the Jewish Agency in 1935-48 and twice prime minister of Israel in 1948-53 and 1955-63

beth midrash – house of study

bimah – central platform in a synagogue

Cardo (pl **Cardines**) – the main street of Roman and Byzantine Jerusalem

chutzpah (Yiddish-Hebrew) – brazenness, cheekiness or downright rudeness; CHU-tzpah is Yiddish whereas chuts-PAH is Hebrew)

Dan – bus cooperative with a near monopoly in greater Tel Aviv

derekh – street or road

Diaspora (Greek) – Jewish dispersion or exile from the Land of Israel; also the world-wide Jewish community

Egged – bus company with a near monopoly in all parts of Israel except greater Tel Aviv

ein – a spring

El Al – Israel's national airline

Eretz Yisra'el – the Land of Israel

Falashas (Amharic, literally 'strangers') – the Jews of Ethiopia; this term is considered derogatory and has been superseded by the term 'Ethiopian Jews'

gan – a garden or park

Golah – Diaspora

goy (pl **goyim**) – gentile

gush (literally 'bloc') – used in such names as Gush Emunim (Bloc of Believers), the West Bank settler movement, and Gush Etzion (Etzion Bloc), a group of Jewish settlements south of Bethlehem; also Gush Dan (the Greater Tel Aviv area)

ha – 'the'; always connected to the following word as in 'HaRehov' (the street)

HaAvoda – Israel's Labor Party

halacha (adj **halachic**) – Judaic law

har – mountain

hasid (adj **hasidic**) – member of an ultra-orthodox Lubavitcher movement with mystical tendencies that was founded in Poland in the 18th century

haredi (pl **haredim**) – an ultra-Orthodox Jew, either *Ashkenazi* or *Sephardic*

hefetz hashud (literally, 'suspicious object') – an object, eg a bag or backpack, whose owner is nowhere to be found, that may be a bomb; passers-by are kept at a distance until the police sappers finish their work.

hof – beach

hursha – grove

hurva – ruin

IDF – Israeli Defence Forces, the Israeli army

Irgun – Jewish underground terrorist group active during the British Mandate, led by *Menachem Begin*; also known as the Etzel

iriya – city hall or municipality

Judaea – (in Hebrew, Yehuda) in ancient Jewish history and in the modern-day right wing terminology, the southern lobe of the West Bank

kanyon – shopping mall

kashrut (adj **kosher**) – Judaic dietary laws

Keren Keyemet l'Yisra'el – the Jewish National Fund, founded in 1902 to purchase land in Palestine for Jewish settlement; since 1948, it is best known for its massive afforestation programs

kfar – village

kibbutz (pl **kibbutzim**) – communal settlement run cooperatively by its members; kibbutzim, once based solely on farming, are now involved in a range of industries

kibbutznik – member of a *kibbutz*

kikar – city, town or village square

kippah – skullcap worn by observant Jewish men (sometimes by Reform or Conservative women)

klezmer – traditional music of Eastern European Jews

knesiya – church

Knesset – Israeli national parliament

kosher – see *kashrut*

Likud – the major Israeli right-wing political party

ma'agar – reservoir

ma'ayan – a spring

Magen David Adom – (literally, 'Red Star of David') the Israeli first-aid organisation that provides emergency ambulance and paramedic services, equivalent to the Red Cross

malon – hotel

mapal – waterfall

masu'a – beacon

matzeva – pillar, monument, gravestone

me'ara – cave

Meir, Golda – Israel's first and so far only female prime minister (from 1969 to 74)

menorah – a seven-branched candelabrum that adorned the ancient Temple in Jerusalem and has been a Jewish symbol ever since; it is now the official symbol of the State of Israel

metzuda – fortress, castle

mezuzah (pl **mezuzoth**) – a small receptacle fixed to doorways, these contain passages from Deuteronomy; see also *tefillin*

migdal – tower

midrahov – pedestrian mall

mikveh – ritual bath

Mishnah – the first codification of Jewish oral law, assembled in Palestine by Yehuda HaNasi (Judah the Prince) around 200 AD

mitnachel – Israeli settlers who have created new communities on territory captured from Jordan, Egypt and Syria during the 1967 war

mitzvah (pl **mitzvot**) – a commandment; colloquially, a good deed

Mizrahi (pl **Mizrahim**) – a Jew from one of the Oriental Jewish communities, eg from Morocco, Yemen or Iraq; this term is often used interchangeably with 'Sephardi'; see *Sephardim*

MK – member of the Knesset

moshav – cooperative settlement, with a mix of private and collective housing and economic activity

moshavnik – a member of a *moshav*

Mossad – Israel's intelligence agency, equivalent to the CIA

nahal – river

NIS – New Israel Shekel, Israel's currency

oleh (pl **olim**) – new immigrant, someone who has made *aliyah*

Palmach – the Haganah's elite strike force that played a decisive role in the 1948 War of Independence

parochet – the curtain that covers the Torah Ark in synagogues (except in certain Sephardic communities)

Passover – see *Pesach*

Pesach – Passover

Rabin, Yitzak – IDF chief-of-staff 1964-67, twice prime minister in 1974-77 and 1992-5, shared 1994 Nobel peace prize with Yasser Arafat; assassinated in 1995 in Tel Aviv by a right-wing Jewish extremist opposed to the Oslo Accords
rehov – street
Rosh HaShanah – (literally, 'the head of the year') Jewish New Year

sabra – the fruit of a prickly pear cactus; also a native-born Israeli
Sephardim (adj **Sephardic**) – technically, the descendants of the Jews of expelled from Spain in the Middle Ages, but often used to denote all non-Eastern European Jews; see *Mizrahi*
settler – see *mitnachel*
sha'ar – gate
Shabbat – the Sabbath, observed from sundown on Friday evening to an hour after sundown on Saturday
shderot – boulevard
shekel – Israel monetary unit
sherut – (short for 'monit sherut') shared taxi for a fixed route
Shin Bet or **Shabak** – Israel's internal security service, equivalent to MI5 or the FBI
shmura or **shmurat teva** – nature reserve
Shoah – the Holocaust
shofar – ram's horn trumpet, sounded particularly on *Rosh HaShanah* and Yom Kippur
shtetl – small, traditional Eastern European Jewish village
shuq – market
shvil – trail
speshel – (from the English 'special') a regular taxi (as opposed to a service taxi)

tallit – prayer shawl
Talmud – compilation of *Mishnah* plus commentary; exists in Palestinian and Babylonian versions
tayelet – promenade
tefillin – phylacteries, ie the two cube-shaped leather boxes containing passages from the *Torah* that are worn on the forehead and left arm by observant Jewish men during weekday morning prayers
tel – a hill; also an archaeological mound

Torah – the Books of Moses, ie the first five books of the Old Testament; also used to denote *halacha* in general
Tu B'Shevat – the New Year for Trees
tzitzit – ritual tassels worn by *haredi* men

ulpan – an intensive Hebrew language school for new immigrants
UNRWA – United Nations Relief & Works Agency in Palestine
UNSCOP – United Nations Special Committee on Palestine

WZO – World Zionist Organisation

ya'ar – forest
yad – memorial
yarmulke – (Yiddish) see *kippah*
yeshiva – Jewish seminary

zimmer – (German, 'room') a bed and breakfast
Zionism – the movement to establish a Jewish State in the Land of Israel

ARABIC
abu – father (of), often used as part of name
ain/ein – water spring or source
al – the definite article, ie 'the'
al-Naqba – (literally, 'the Catastrophe') Palestinian name for the 1948 war

bab – door, gate
bir – well
burj – fortress or tower

caliph – (literally, a successor of Mohammed) Islamic rulers, precursors of the Turkish sultans

Druze – member of a religious-political community that evolved out of Islam in 10th century Egypt
dunam – (from Turkish) 1000 sq metres

Eid al-Adha – feast comemmorating the near-sacrifice of Ishmael by his father, Abraham
Eid al-Fitr – feast which marks the end of *Ramadan*

Fatah – Arafat's political party

Haj – annual Muslim pilgrimage to Mecca
Hamas – (abbreviation of Harakat al-Muqaama al-Islamiya) militant Islamic organisation which aims to create an Islamic state in the pre-1948 territory of Palestine
hamma – hot spring
hammam – public baths
haram – (literally 'forbidden') holy sanctuary
Haram ash-Sharif – Islamic complex in the Temple Mount area
hejab – headscarf worn by Muslim women
Hezbollah – (literally, Party of God) Iranian-backed Shi'ia guerrilla group active in southern Lebanon
Hijra – Mohammed's flight from Mecca to Medina in 622 CE

Intifada – (literally 'shaking off') the Palestinian uprising against Israeli authorities in the West Bank, Gaza and East Jerusalem that began at the end of 1987

jebal – hill, mountain

khan – also called a caravanserai; a travellers' inn usually constructed along main trade routes, which consisted of accommodation on the 1st floor and stables around a central courtyard and storage on the ground floor
khatib – low, railed wooden platform where the reader sits to recite from the Quran
khirbet – ruins (of)
kuffiyya – the chequered headscarf worn by Palestinian men
kufr – village

Lailatul Miraj – the night on which the Prophet Mohammed ascended into heaven from Mt Moriah (the *Haram ash-Sharif/* Temple Mount) in Jerusalem
madrasa – school, especially one associated with a mosque
majdal – tower

masjid – mosque
mihrab – prayer niche in a mosque, indicating the direction of Mecca
minaret – the tower of a mosque from which the call to prayer is sung
minbar – pulpit used by the immam for mosque sermons
muezzin – the man who sings the call to prayer, traditionally from atop a minaret
mufti – a jurist who interprets Islamic law

nargila – a water pipe

PA – Palestinian Authority
PLO – Palestine Liberation Organisation
PNC – Palestinian National Council, ruling body of PLO

qibla – the direction of Mecca, towards which Muslims pray; within a mosque the qibla is indicated the *mihrab*
Quran – the Islamic holy text revealed to Mohammed by the archangel Gabriel
qubba – dome, cupola

Ramadan – the holiest Islamic month of dawn-to-dusk fasting and self-control
ribat – pilgrim hostel

sabil – public drinking fountain
saray – palace
servis – shared taxi (like Hebrew sherut)
Sharia'a – Islamic law
sheikh – learned or old man
souq – market
sufi – Islamic mystic

tariq – road
turba – tomb or graveyard

UNRWA – United Nations Reliefs & Works Agency for Palestine Refugees

wadi – dried up river bed, arroyo
wali – Muslim saint or holy man

zawiya – Muslim religious dwelling
zuqaq – alleyway

FOOD GLOSSARY

baklava – a sweet made with filo pastry, honey and almonds

beygaleh – a bread ring covered with sesame seeds

blintzes – (from Russian via Yiddish) pancakes stuffed with a variety of sweet and savoury fillings

burghul – cracked wheat

cholent – (Yiddish) a heavy stew prepared before sunset on Friday and kept simmering until Saturday

dogga – a mixture of herbs (mainly oregano) and spices; see *za'atar*

felafel – ground chickpeas blended with herbs and spices, shaped into a ball and then deep-fried; usually served in pitta bread with *tahina*, *homous* and salad

gefilte fish – (Yiddish) sweet and sour fishballs served either chilled or warm, often with horseradish

glatt kosher – ultra-orthodox kosher meat

fuul – paste made of fava (broad) beans, similar to *humous*

halal – (literally, 'allowed') meat from an animal slaughtered in accordance with Islamic practice

hallah – soft, braided bread made with eggs eaten on *Shabbat*

humous – thick paste made from chickpeas, seasoned with *tahina*, lemon juice and olive oil

ka'ak – cakes; also a ring of bread covered with sesame seeds

kanafeh – a sweet pastry made with cheese and honey

katayeef – dessert made of shredded filo pastry, honey and almonds

kubbeh – traditional Kurdish vegetable soup with dumplings

maklubi – an upside-down dish of rice, lamb, eggplant and other vegetables

mansaf – Palestinian dish of rice with lamb, nuts, lemon juice and herbs.

matza (pl **matzot**) – flat, unsalted and unleavened bread eaten during *Pesach*

meorav yerushalmi – (literally 'Jerusalem-style meats') a fried concoction of liver, kidney, heart and beef eaten in pitta bread

parve – food that is in *halacha* neither milk nor meat (eg fruit, vegetables, bread, eggs and fish)

shwarma – lamb, turkey or chicken sliced from a revolving vertical spit

tahina – a thin paste made from ground sesame seeds

za'atar – a Sephardic mixture of herbs and spices

Phrasebooks

Lonely Planet phrasebooks are packed with essential words and phrases to help travellers communicate with the locals. With colour tabs for quick reference, an extensive vocabulary and use of script, these handy pocket-sized language guides cover day-to-day travel situations.

- handy pocket-sized books
- easy to understand Pronunciation chapter
- clear & comprehensive Grammar chapter
- romanisation alongside script to allow ease of pronunciation
- script throughout so users can point to phrases for every situation
- full of cultural information and tips for the traveller

'...vital for a real DIY spirit and attitude in language learning'
　　　　　　　　　　　　　　　　　　　　　　　　　　 – Backpacker

'the phrasebooks have good cultural backgrounders and offer solid advice for challenging situations in remote locations'
　　　　　　　　　　　　　　　　　　　　　　 – San Francisco Examiner

Arabic (Egyptian) ● Arabic (Moroccan) ● Australian *(Australian English, Aboriginal and Torres Strait languages)* ● Baltic States *(Estonian, Latvian, Lithuanian)* ● Bengali ● Brazilian ● British ● Burmese ● Cantonese ● Central Asia ● Central Europe *(Czech, French, German, Hungarian, Italian, Slovak)* ● Eastern Europe *(Bulgarian, Czech, Hungarian, Polish, Romanian, Slovak)* ● Ethiopian (Amharic) ● Fijian ● French ● German ● Greek ● Hill Tribes ● Hindi/Urdu ● Indonesian ● Italian ● Japanese ● Korean ● Lao ● Latin American Spanish ● Malay ● Mandarin ● Mediterranean Europe *(Albanian, Croatian, Greek, Italian, Macedonian, Maltese, Serbian, Slovene)* ● Mongolian ● Nepali ● Papua New Guinea ● Pilipino (Tagalog) ● Quechua ● Russian ● Scandinavian Europe *(Danish, Finnish, Icelandic, Norwegian, Swedish)* ● South-East Asia *(Burmese, Indonesian, Khmer, Lao, Malay, Tagalog Pilipino, Thai, Vietnamese)* ● Spanish (Castilian) *(also includes Catalan, Galician and Basque)* ● Sri Lanka ● Swahili ● Thai ● Tibetan ● Turkish ● Ukrainian ● USA *(US English, Vernacular, Native American languages, Hawaiian)* ● Vietnamese ● Western Europe *(Basque, Catalan, Dutch, French, German, Greek, Irish)*

LONELY PLANET

Lonely Planet Journeys

Journeys is a unique collection of travel writing – published by the company that understands travel better than anyone else. It is a series for anyone who has ever experienced – or dreamed of – the magical moment when they encountered a strange culture or saw a place for the first time. They are tales to read while you're planning a trip, while you're on the road or while you're in an armchair in front of a fire.

These outstanding titles explore our planet through the eyes of a diverse group of international writers. JOURNEYS books catch the spirit of a place, illuminate a culture, recount a crazy adventure or introduce a fascinating way of life. They always entertain, and always enrich the experience of travel.

MALI BLUES
Traveling to an African Beat
Lieve Joris (translated by Sam Garrett)

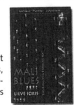

Drought, rebel uprisings, ethnic conflict: these are the predominant images of West Africa. But as Lieve Joris travels in Senegal, Mauritania and Mali, she meets survivors, fascinating individuals charting new ways of living between tradition and modernity. With her remarkable gift for drawing out people's stories, Joris brilliantly captures the rhythms of a world that refuses to give in.

THE GATES OF DAMASCUS
Lieve Joris (translated by Sam Garrett)

This best-selling book is a beautifully drawn portrait of day-to-day life in modern Syria. Through her intimate contact with local people, Lieve Joris draws us into the fascinating world that lies behind the gates of Damascus. Hala's husband is a political prisoner, jailed for his opposition to the Assad regime; through the author's friendship with Hala we see how Syrian politics impacts on the lives of ordinary people.

THE OLIVE GROVE
Travels in Greece
Katherine Kizilos

Katherine Kizilos travels to fabled islands, troubled border zones and her family's village deep in the mountains. She vividly evokes breathtaking landscapes, generous people and passionate politics, capturing the complexities of a country she loves.

'beautifully captures the real tensions of Greece' – *Sunday Times*

KINGDOM OF THE FILM STARS
Journey into Jordan
Annie Caulfield

Kingdom of the Film Stars is a travel book and a love story. With honesty and humour, Annie Caulfield writes of travelling in Jordan and falling in love with a Bedouin with film-star looks.

She offers fascinating insights into the country – from the tent life of traditional women to the hustle of downtown Amman – and unpicks tight-woven western myths about the Arab world.

Lonely Planet Travel Atlases

L onely Planet has long been famous for the number and quality of its guidebook maps. Now we've gone one step further and produced a handy companion series: Lonely Planet travel atlases – maps of a country produced in book form.

Unlike other maps, which look good but lead travellers astray, our travel atlases have been researched on the road by Lonely Planet's experienced team of writers. All details are carefully checked to ensure the atlas corresponds with the equivalent Lonely Planet guidebook.

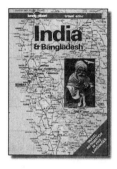

- full-colour throughout
- maps researched and checked by Lonely Planet authors
- place names correspond with Lonely Planet guidebooks
- no confusing spelling differences
- legend and travelling information in English, French, German, Japanese and Spanish
- size: 230 x 160 mm

Available now: Chile & Easter Island ● Egypt ● India & Bangladesh ● Israel & the Palestinian Territories ● Jordan, Syria & Lebanon ● Kenya ● Laos ● Portugal ● South Africa, Lesotho & Swaziland ● Thailand ● Turkey ● Vietnam ● Zimbabwe, Botswana & Namibia

---

Lonely Planet TV Series & Videos

L onely Planet travel guides have been brought to life on television screens around the world. Like our guides, the programs are based on the joy of independent travel, and look honestly at some of the most exciting, picturesque and frustrating places in the world. Each show is presented by one of three travellers from Australia, England or the USA and combines an innovative mixture of video, Super-8 film, atmospheric soundscapes and original music.

Videos of each episode – containing additional footage not shown on television – are available from good book and video shops, but the availability of individual videos varies with regional screening schedules.

Video destinations include: Alaska ● American Rockies ● Australia – The South-East ● Baja California & the Copper Canyon ● Brazil ● Central Asia ● Chile & Easter Island ● Corsica, Sicily & Sardinia – The Mediterranean Islands ● East Africa (Tanzania & Zanzibar) ● Ecuador & the Galapagos Islands ● Greenland & Iceland ● Indonesia ● Israel & the Sinai Desert ● Jamaica ● Japan ● La Ruta Maya ● Morocco ● New York ● North India ● Pacific Islands (Fiji, Solomon Islands & Vanuatu) ● South India ● South West China ● Turkey ● Vietnam ● West Africa ● Zimbabwe, Botswana & Namibia

The Lonely Planet TV series is produced by: Pilot Productions
The Old Studio
18 Middle Row
London W10 5AT, UK

Lonely Planet On-line

Whether you've just begun planning your next trip, or you're chasing down specific info on currency regulations or visa requirements, check out Lonely Planet On-line for up-to-the minute travel information.

As well as mini guides to more than 250 destinations, you'll find maps, photos, travel news, health and visa updates, travel advisories, and discussion of the eco-logical and political issues you need to be aware of as you travel. You'll also find timely upgrades to popular guidebooks which you can print out and stick in the back of your book.

There's also an on-line travellers' forum where you can share your experience of life on the road, meet travel companions and ask other travellers for their recommendations and advice.

And of course we have a complete and up-to-date list of all Lonely Planet travel products including travel guides, diving and snorkeling guides, phrasebooks, atlases, travel literature and videos, and a simple on-line ordering facility if you can't find the book you want elsewhere.

Lonely Planet Diving & Snorkeling Guides

Known for indispensible guidebooks to destinations all over the world, Lonely Planet's Pisces Books are the most popular series of diving and snorkeling titles available.

There are three series: **Diving & Snorkeling Guides**, **Shipwreck Diving** series and **Dive Into History**. Full colour throughout, the **Diving & Snorkeling Guides** combine quality photographs with detailed descriptions of the best dive sites for each location, giving divers a glimpse of what they can expect both on land and in water. The **Dive Into History** series is perfect for the adventure diver or armchair traveller. The **Shipwreck Diving** series provides all the details for exploring the most interesting wrecks in the Atlantic and Pacific oceans. The list also includes underwater nature and technical guides.

FREE Lonely Planet Newsletters

We love hearing from you and think you'd like to hear from us.

Planet Talk

Our FREE quarterly printed newsletter is full of tips from travellers and anecdotes from Lonely Planet guidebook authors. Every issue is packed with up-to-date travel news and advice, and includes:

- a postcard from Lonely Planet co-founder Tony Wheeler
- a swag of mail from travellers
- a look at life on the road through the eyes of a Lonely Planet author
- topical health advice
- prizes for the best travel yarn
- news about forthcoming Lonely Planet events
- a complete list of Lonely Planet books and other titles

To join our mailing list, residents of the UK, Europe and Africa can email us at go@lonelyplanet.co.uk; residents of North and South America can email us at info@lonelyplanet.com; the rest of the world can email us at talk2us@lonelyplanet.com.au, or contact any Lonely Planet office.

Comet

Our FREE monthly email newsletter brings you all the latest travel news, features, interviews, competitions, destination ideas, travellers' tips & tales, Q&As, raging debates and related links. Find out what's new on the Lonely Planet Web site and which books are about to hit the shelves.

Subscribe from your desktop: www.lonelyplanet.com/comet

Guides by Region

Lonely Planet is known worldwide for publishing practical, reliable and no-nonsense travel information in our guides and on our Web site. The Lonely Planet list covers just about every accessible part of the world. Currently there are nine series: travel guides, shoe-string guides, walking guides, city guides, phrasebooks, audio packs, travel atlases, diving and snorkeling guides and travel literature.

AFRICA Africa – the South • Africa on a shoestring • Arabic (Egyptian) phrasebook • Arabic (Moroccan) phrasebook • Cairo • Cape Town • Central Africa • East Africa • Egypt • Egypt travel atlas • Ethiopian (Amharic) phrasebook • The Gambia & Senegal • Kenya • Kenya travel atlas • Malawi, Mozambique & Zambia • Morocco • North Africa • South Africa, Lesotho & Swaziland • South Africa, Lesotho & Swazi-land travel atlas • Swahili phrasebook • Tanzania, Zanzibar & Pemba • Trekking in East Africa • Tunisia • West Africa • Zimbabwe, Botswana & Namibia • Zimbabwe, Botswana & Namibia travel atlas
Travel Literature: The Rainbird: A Central African Journey • Songs to an African Sunset: A Zimbabwean Story • Mali Blues: Traveling to an African Beat

AUSTRALIA & THE PACIFIC Australia • Australian phrasebook • Bushwalking in Australia • Bush-walking in Papua New Guinea • Fiji • Fijian phrasebook • Islands of Australia's Great Barrier Reef • Melbourne • Micronesia • New Caledonia • New South Wales & the ACT • New Zealand • Northern Ter-ritory • Outback Australia • Papua New Guinea • Papua New Guinea (Pidgin) phrasebook • Queensland • Rarotonga & the Cook Islands • Samoa • Solomon Islands • South Australia • Sydney • Tahiti & French Polynesia • Tasmania • Tonga • Tramping in New Zealand • Vanuatu • Victoria • Western Australia
Travel Literature: Islands in the Clouds • Sean & David's Long Drive

CENTRAL AMERICA & THE CARIBBEAN Bahamas and Turks & Caicos • Barcelona • Bermuda • Central America on a shoestring • Costa Rica • Cuba • Dominican Republic & Haiti • Eastern Caribbean • Guatemala, Belize & Yucatán: La Ruta Maya • Jamaica • Mexico • Mexico City • Panama
Travel Literature: Green Dreams: Travels in Central America

EUROPE Amsterdam • Andalucía • Austria • Baltic States phrasebook • Barcelona • Berlin • Britain • British phrasebook • Canary Islands • Central Europe • Central Europe phrasebook • Corsica • Croatia • Czech & Slovak Republics • Denmark • Dublin • Eastern Europe • Eastern Europe phrase-book • Edinburgh • Estonia, Latvia & Lithuania • Europe • Finland • France • French phrasebook • Germany • German phrasebook • Greece • Greek phrasebook • Hungary • Iceland, Greenland & the Faroe Islands • Ireland • Italian phrasebook • Italy • Lisbon • London • Mediterranean Europe • Mediterranean Europe phrasebook • Norway • Paris • Poland • Portugal • Portugal travel atlas • Prague • Provence & the Côte d'Azur • Romania & Moldova • Rome • Russia, Ukraine & Belarus • Russian phrasebook • Scandinavian & Baltic Europe • Scandinavian Europe phrasebook • Scotland • Slovenia • Spain • Spanish phrasebook • St Petersburg • Switzerland • Trekking in Spain • Ukrainian phrasebook • Vienna • Walking in Britain • Walking in Italy • Walking in Ireland • Walking in Switzer-land • Western Europe • Western Europe phrasebook
Travel Literature: The Olive Grove: Travels in Greece

INDIAN SUBCONTINENT Bangladesh • Bengali phrasebook • Bhutan • Delhi • Goa • Hindi/Urdu phrasebook • India • India & Bangladesh travel atlas • Indian Himalaya • Karakoram Highway • Nepal • Nepali phrasebook • Pakistan • Rajasthan • South India • Sri Lanka • Sri Lanka phrasebook • Trekking in the Indian Himalaya • Trekking in the Karakoram & Hindukush • Trekking in the Nepal Himalaya
Travel Literature: In Rajasthan • Shopping for Buddhas

LONELY PLANET

Mail Order

Lonely Planet products are distributed worldwide.They are also available by mail order from Lonely Planet, so if you have difficulty finding a title please write to us. North and South American residents should write to 150 Linden St, Oakland, CA 94607, USA; European and African residents should write to 10a Spring Place, London NW5 3BH, UK; and residents of other countries to PO Box 617, Hawthorn, Victoria 3122, Australia.

ISLANDS OF THE INDIAN OCEAN Madagascar & Comoros ● Maldives ● Mauritius, Réunion & Seychelles

MIDDLE EAST & CENTRAL ASIA Arab Gulf States ● Central Asia ● Central Asia phrasebook ● Iran ● Israel & the Palestinian Territories ● Israel & the Palestinian Territories travel atlas ● Istanbul ● Jerusalem ● Jordan & Syria ● Jordan, Syria & Lebanon travel atlas ● Lebanon ● Middle East on a shoestring ● Turkey ● Turkish phrasebook ● Turkey travel atlas ● Yemen
Travel Literature: The Gates of Damascus ● Kingdom of the Film Stars: Journey into Jordan

NORTH AMERICA Alaska ● Backpacking in Alaska ● Baja California ● California & Nevada ● Canada ● Chicago ● Florida ● Hawaii ● Honolulu ● Los Angeles ● Louisiana ● Miami ● New England USA ● New Orleans ● New York City ● New York, New Jersey & Pennsylvania ● Pacific Northwest USA ● Rocky Mountain States ● San Francisco ● Seattle ● Southwest USA ● USA ● USA phrasebook ● Vancouver ● Washington, DC & the Capital Region
Travel Literature: Drive Thru America

NORTH-EAST ASIA Beijing ● Cantonese phrasebook ● China ● Hong Kong ● Hong Kong, Macau & Guangzhou ● Japan ● Japanese phrasebook ● Japanese audio pack ● Korea ● Korean phrasebook ● Kyoto ● Mandarin phrasebook ● Mongolia ● Mongolian phrasebook ● North-East Asia on a shoestring ● Seoul ● South-West China ● Taiwan ● Tibet ● Tibetan phrasebook ● Tokyo
Travel Literature: Lost Japan

SOUTH AMERICA Argentina, Uruguay & Paraguay ● Bolivia ● Brazil ● Brazilian phrasebook ● Buenos Aires ● Chile & Easter Island ● Chile & Easter Island travel atlas ● Colombia ● Ecuador & the Galapagos Islands ● Latin American Spanish phrasebook ● Peru ● Quechua phrasebook ● Rio de Janeiro ● South America on a shoestring ● Trekking in the Patagonian Andes ● Venezuela
Travel Literature: Full Circle: A South American Journey

SOUTH-EAST ASIA Bali & Lombok ● Bangkok ● Burmese phrasebook ● Cambodia ● Hill Tribes phrasebook ● Ho Chi Minh City ● Indonesia ● Indonesia's Eastern Islands ● Indonesian phrasebook ● Indonesian audio pack ● Jakarta ● Java ● Laos ● Lao phrasebook ● Laos travel atlas ● Malay phrasebook ● Malaysia, Singapore & Brunei ● Myanmar (Burma) ● Philippines ● Pilipino (Tagalog) phrasebook ● Singapore ● South-East Asia on a shoestring ● South-East Asia phrasebook ● Thailand ● Thailand's Islands & Beaches ● Thailand travel atlas ● Thai phrasebook ● Thai audio pack ● Vietnam ● Vietnamese phrasebook ● Vietnam travel atlas

ALSO AVAILABLE: Antarctica ● Brief Encounters: Stories of Love, Sex & Travel ● Chasing Rickshaws ● Not the Only Planet: Travel Stories from Science Fiction ● Travel with Children ● Traveller's Tales

Index

Text

A

Abraham 84
Abu Gosh 164-5
accommodation 136-46
    bed & breakfast 136-7, 142-3
    Dead Sea 170
    hostels 136-40
    Jericho 167
    Kibbutz Ramat Rachel 163
    mid-range 140-4
    rental 137
    top end 144-6
activities 134-5
Aelia Capitolina 13
Agnon, SY 122
air travel 63-7
    departure tax 67
    to/from Asia 66
    to/from Australia &
        New Zealand 66
    to/from Egypt 67
    to/from Europe 66
    to/from North America 63-6
    to/from the UK 66
    within Israel 63
airport 63-7, 73
Al-Aqsa Mosque 86-7, **85**
Alex de Rothschild Craft
    Centre 102, **Map 8**
aliyah 20
al-Malik, Abd 87
Alternative Information Centre 53
Amichai, Yehuda 22
Ammunition Hill 113, **Map 1**
ancient Jerusalem, model of
    131, **Map 1**
ANZAC 110
Arabic 174-5, 177-8
    courses 135
archaeological excavations 135
    Broad Wall 90
    City of David 106
    Israelite Tower 90
    Jericho 167
    Masada 168
    Roman Square excavations 79
    Siebenberg House 92

Warren's Shaft 106
Western Wall Tunnel 89
architecture 23-4
    Crusader 92, 164
    Mamluk 88, 93-4
Ark of the Covenant 10, 87, 164
Armenian Compound 101,
    Map 8
Armenian Mosaic 111,
    Map 8
Armenian Quarter 101-2
art galleries, *see* museums &
    art galleries
arts 21-25, **Map 8**
Arts & Crafts Lane, *see* Khutsot
    HaYotser
Augusta Victoria 107, **Map 2**

B

Balfour Declaration 16
bargaining, *see* money
bar Kochba, Simon 13
Barluzzi, Antonio 108, 117
Batei Ungarin 117, **Map 2**
Beit David 115
Beit Guvrin-Maresha National
    Park 164, **Map 1**
Beit Ticho, *see* Ticho House
Beit Yehudayoff 119, **Map 2**
Ben-Gurion, David 16
Ben Yehuda, Eliezer 22, 35, 188
Ben Yehuda House 118, **Map 2**
Ben Yehuda St 115, **Map 2**
Bethany 165
Bethlehem 166-7, **Map 1**
Bethlehem Museum 166
Bezalel School of Art 116,
    Map 3
Bible Lands Museum 123, **Map 2**
Bible studies 135
Biblical Zoo 131, **Map 1**
Bloomfield Science Museum
    123, **Map 1**
boat travel 67-8
books 48-9
Botanical Garden 131, **Map 1**
British Mandate 16
Broad Wall 90, **Map 9**
Bukharan Quarter 118-19, **Map 2**
Burnt House 92, **Map 9**

bus travel 68-4
    Arab 74
    Egged 73-4
    to/from Egypt 68-9
    to/from Jordan 69-70
    within Israel 70-1
business 57
business hours 54

C

car travel 71, 74-5
    rental 74-5
    road rules 74
Cardo 13, 90, **Map 9**
CD ROMs 49
Chagall, Marc 88, 123, 134
Chagall Windows 134, **Map 1**
children
    travel with 52-3
Christ Church 100, **Map 6**
Christian Quarter 94-101,
    Map 6
Christianity 33-4
Church & Monastery of the
    Dormition 104, **Map 2**
Church of the Holy Sepulchre
    98, **99**
Church of the Nativity 166
churches
    Christ Church 100, **Map 6**
    Church & Monastery of the
        Dormition 104, **Map 2**
    Church of All Nations 109
    Church of Dominus Flevit 108
    Church of St John 133-4
    Church of St Peter in
        Gallicantu 105
    Church of the Ascension 107
    Church of the Holy Sepulchre
        98, **99**, **Map 6**
    Church of the Holy Trinity 114
    Church of the Nativity 166
    Church of the Pater Noster
        108
    Church of the Visitation 134
    Coenaculum 104, **Map 2**
    Convent of the Sisters of
        Zion 92-3, **Map 7**
    Crusader church &
        monastery 164

Bold indicates maps.

Emmaus Church 166
Ethiopian Church 118, **Map 2**
Ethiopian Monastery 100, **Map 6**
Lutheran Church of the Redeemer 101, **Map 6**
Milk Grotto Chapel 166
Monastery of the Cross 131, **Map 2**
Mt & Monastery of Temptation 167
Notre Dame 113, **Map 3**
Notre Dame l'Arche 164
Russian Chapel of the Ascension 107
Russian Church & Monastery 134
Russian Church of Mary Magdalene 108-9
St Alexander's Church 100, **Map 6**
St Andrew's Church 24, 121, **Map 4**
St Anne's Church 92
St George's Cathedral 112, **Map 5**
St George's Monastery 167
St James' Cathedral 101-2, **Map 8**
St John the Baptist 101
St Maria of the Germans 91
St Mark's Chapel 102
St Stephen's Church 109, **Map 2**
Tomb of the Virgin Mary 109
Cinematheque 121, **Map 4**
Citadel 81-4, **Map 6**
City Hall 113, **Map 3**
City of David 106, **Map 2**
climate 18
Coenaculum 104, **Map 2**
Constantine 13
consulates, see embassies
Convent of the Sisters of Zion 92-3, **Map 7**
costs, see money
Crusades 15, 33
cultural centres 53
cultural events 56-7
currency, see money
cycling 76
  rental 135, 167

Bold indicates maps.

D
Damascus Gate 78-9, **Maps 6 & 7**
Dana International 21-2
David 10
Davidka Monument 118, **Map 2**
Dead Sea 18, 168-70
departure taxes, see air travel
Deri, Aryeh 26
Diaspora Museum 171
disabled travellers 52
Dome of the Rock 15, 87, **85**
Dung Gate 80, **Map 9**

E
East Jerusalem 36-7, 110-13, **Map 5**
Ecce Homo Arch 92-3, **Map 7**
economy 19
Ein Gedi 168-70
Ein Kerem 133-4, **Map 1**
electricity 50
email 46-8
embassies 40-2
Emmaus Church 166
entertainment 156-9
  bars 156-8
  cinemas 158
  clubs 156-8
  theatre 159
environment 18-19
Eshkol, Levi 132
Ethiopian Church 118, **Map 2**
Ethiopian Monastery 100, **Map 6**
Ethiopian consulate 117, **Map 2**
excavations, see archaeological excavations

F
fax 46
ferry companies 68
festivals, see holidays
First Revolt 13
First Temple 10, 84
Flavius Josephus 12
Foley, Frank 133
food 146-55
  Arabic 151-2
  Ashkenazi 151
  cafés 148-50
  fast food 147-8, 150
  health food 146-7
  international 152-5
  Sephardic 150-1
  vegetarian 146-7

G
Gan Ha'Atmaut 116, **Map 3**
Garden of Gethsemane 109, **Map 2**
Garden Tomb 111, **Map 5**
gardens, see parks & gardens
gates
  Damascus Gate 78, **Maps 6 & 7**
  Dung Gate 80, **Map 9**
  Golden Gate 80, **Map 7**
  Herod's Gate 79-80, **Map 7**
  Jaffa Gate 80-1, **Map 6**
  New Gate 81, **Map 6**
  St Stephen's Gate 80, **Map 7**
  Zion Gate 80, **Maps 8 & 9**
gay travellers 52
  entertainment 157-8
German Colony 122, **Map 4**
Gihon Spring 106, **Map 2**
Givat Ram 123-31, **Map 1**
glossary 179
Golden Gate 80, **Map 7**
government 19

H
Haas Promenade 122, **Map 1**
Hadassah Hospital 24, **Map 1**
Hadassah Medical Centre 134, **Map 1**
Hadrian 13, 78-9
halal 32
HaNevim St 117-18, **Map 2**
Haram ash-Sharif/Temple Mount 84-8, **85**
Hasmonean Revolt, see Maccabean Revolt
health 50-1
Hebrew 22, 34-5, 173-7
  courses 135
Hebrew University 110, 123-31, **Maps 1 & 2**
Heichal Schlomo 116, **Map 3**
Helena 13
Herod the Great 12, 81
Herod's Gate 79-80, **Map 7**
Herod's Pillar 114, **Map 3**
Herzl Museum 132, **Map 1**
Herzl, Theodor 132
Hezekiah's Tunnel 106
Hill of Evil Counsel 122
history 10-18
hitching 71-2
holidays 54-6, 58-62
Holman Hunt, William 117
hostel cards 40
Hurva Synagogue 90-1, **Map 9**

I

Independence Park, see Gan Ha'Atmaut
insurance 40
Internet 46-8
Islam 31-2
Israel Antiquities Authority 161
Israel Defence Force (IDF) 20
Israel Museum 24, 124-30, **127, Map 2**
Israelite Tower 90, **Map 9**

J

Jaffa 171
Jaffa Gate 80-1, **Map 6**
Jericho 167-8
Jerusalem Film Centre 121, **Map 4**
Jerusalem Gate 117, **Map 2**
Jesus 13, 165
  betrayal 109
  birth 166
  crucifixion 111
  Last Supper 102, 104
  Lord's Prayer 108
  resurrection 166
  Stations of the Cross 96-7
  temptation 167
  tomb 98-100, 111
Jewish Quarter 90-2, **Map 9**
Jewish society 26
Judaism 27-31

K

kashrut 28
Kennedy Memorial 163, **Map 1**
Kfar Shaul psychiatric hospital 103, **Map 1**
Khan as-Sultan 94, **Map 7**
Khutsot HaYotser 121, **Map 4**
Kibbutz Ramat Rachel 163, **Map 1**
Kidron Valley 105-6, **Map 2**
King David's Tomb 102-4, **Map 2**
Knesset 123, **Map 2**
Kollek, Teddy 19

L

Latrun 165-6, **Map 1**
Latrun Monastery 165-6, **Map 1**
laundry 50
Law of Return 31
lesbian travellers 52
  entertainment 157-8
libraries 53

literature 22-3, see also books
Lutheran Church of the Redeemer 101, **Map 6**

M

Maccabean Revolt 12
Madaba map 80, 90
magazines 49
Mahane Yehuda Market 118, **Map 2**
Mamilla 119-22, **Map 3**
Mamilla Pool 116, **Map 3**
Mamluks 15
maps 37
Masada 168, 169
Maxwell, Robert 107
Mea She'arim 116-19, **Map 2**
Meir, Golda 132
Milk Grotto Chapel 166
Mohammed 13, 31, 87
Monastery of the Cross 131, **Map 2**
money 42-5
  ATMS 43
  bargaining 44
  costs 44
  credit cards 43
  exchange rates 42
  tipping 44
  transfers 43
  travellers cheques 43
Mormon University 110, **Map 2**
motorcycle travel 74-5
  road rules 74
mosques 32
  Al-Aqsa Mosque 86-7
  Dome of the Rock 87
  Mosque of the Ascension 107-8
motorcycle travel 71
Mount of Olives 107-9, **Map 2**
Mt & Monastery of Temptation 167
Mt Herzl 132, **Map 1**
Mt Moriah 10, 84
Mt Scopus 109-10, **Map 2**
Museum of Italian Jewish Art 114-15, **Map 3**
Museum Row 123-31, **Map 2**
museums & art galleries
  Academy of the Hebrew Language 131
  Alex de Rothschild Craft Centre 102, **Map 8**
  Armenian Museum 102
  Artists' House 116

Beit Agnon 122
Bethlehem Museum 166
Bible Lands Museum 123, **Map 2**
Bloomfield Science Museum 123, **Map 1**
Burnt House 92, **Map 9**
Diaspora Museum 171
Greek Orthodox Patriciate Museum 100
Herzl Museum 132, **Map 1**
Islamic Museum 86
Israel Museum 24, 124-30, **127, Map 2**
Mt Zion 102-5
Museum of Italian Jewish Art 114-15
Museum of King David 104
Old Yishuv Court Museum 92, **Map 9**
Rabbi Kook Museum 115
Rachel Ben-Zvi Centre 90, **Map 9**
Rockefeller Museum 111, **Map 2**
Rubin Academy of Music & Dance 131
Siebenberg House 92
Ticho House 25, 115
Tourjeman Post Museum 112-13, **Map 5**
Tower of David Museum of the History of Jerusalem 83-4, **Map 6**
Underground Prisoners' Museum 114
Wohl Museum of Archaeology 91, **Map 9**
Wolfson Museum 116
Yad Vashem 132-3, **133, Map 1**
music 21-2
  classical 21, 158
  folk 158
  klezmer 21
  live 157-8
  popular 21-2
Muslim Quarter 92-4, **Map 7**

N

Nahalat Shiv'a 114, **Map 3**
Nebuchadnezzar 12, 84
New City 16, 36, 113-16, **Map 3**
New Gate 81, **Map 6**
newspapers 49
Notre Dame 113, **Map 3**
Notre Dame de l'Arche 164

O

Old City 36, 78-102, **Maps 6-9**
Old Yishuv Court Museum 92,
    Map 9
Olmert, Ehud 19
organised tours 76-7
Orient House 17
Oz, Amos 22

P

painting 24-6
Palace of the Lady Tunshuq 93,
    Map 7
Palestinian Archaeological
    Museum, see Rockefeller
    Museum
Palestinian society 27
parks & gardens
    Ammunition Hill 113
    Beit Guvrin-Maresha National
        Park 164, **Map 1**
    Botanical Garden 131, **Map 1**
    Canada Park 166
    Ein Gedi Nature Reserve
        168-70
    Gan Ha'Atmaut 116, **Map 3**
    Garden of Gethsemane 109,
        Map 2
    Liberty Bell Gardens 121
    Mt Herzl 132, **Map 1**
    Wolh Rose Park 123
photography 50
Pontius Pilate 13
Pool of Bethesda 92, **Map 7**
Pool of Shiloah 106, **Map 2**
post 45
Prison of Christ 93, **Map 7**

Q

Qumran 170
Quran 31

R

Rabin, Yitzhak 26, 132
Rachel Ben-Zvi Centre 90, **Map 9**
Rachel's Tomb 166, **Map 1**
radio 49
Ramban Synagogue 91, **Map 9**
Rehavia 119, **Map 4**
responsible tourism 37

Bold indicates maps.

Ribat Bayram Jawish 93, **Map 7**
Rockefeller Museum 111, **Map 2**
Roman Square excavations 79,
    Maps 6 & 7
rooftop promenade 81
Rothschild Building 91, **Map 9**
Russian Compound 114, **Map 3**

S

Sabil Suleyman 94, **Map 7**
safety 43, 53-4, 107
Saladin 15
Schindler, Oskar 102, 133
sea travel 67
    disembarkation fee 67
    fares 67
    tickets 67-8
Second Temple 12, 84, 88
Shabbat 28, 159
Sharon, Ariel 89
Shelter Houses 91, **Map 9**
sheruts 71, 75
shopping 160-2
Shoresh Junction 164, **Map 1**
Six Day War (1967) 17, 88
Small Wall 94, **Map 7**
Society for the Preservation of
    Nature in Israel (SPNI) 18-19,
    38, 77
Solomon 10
Solomon's Quarries 110-11,
    Map 5
Sorek/Avshalom Stalagmite &
    Stalactite Cave 163-4,
    Map 1
Souq al-Qattanin 94, **Map 7**
souvenirs, see shopping
St Alexander's Church 100,
    Map 6
St Andrew's Church 121, **Map 4**
St Anne's Church 92
St George's Cathedral 112,
    Map 5
St George's Monastery 167
St James' Cathedral 101-2,
    Map 8
St Maria of the Germans 91,
    Map 9
St Mark's Chapel 102, **Map 8**
St Peter in Gallicantu 105,
    Map 2
St Stephen's Church 109, **Map 2**
St Stephen's Gate 80, **Map 7**
St Vincent de Paul Hospice 120,
    Map 3

Stations of the Cross 96-7
student cards 40
Sugihara, Sempo 133
Suleyman the Magnificent 15,
    78-9, 83, 122
Sultan's Pool 122, **Map 4**
Supreme Court Building 123,
    Map 2
synagogues 30
    Beit Avraham 117
    Great Synagogue 116
    Hecht Synagogue 110
    Hurva Synagogue 90-1
    Italian Synagogue 114-15
    Ramban Synagogue 91
    Sephardic Synagogues 91

T

Talbiyeh 119, **Map 4**
Talmud 28
Talpiot 122, **Map 1**
taxes 44-4
taxis 76, see also sheruts
Tel Aviv 170-1
telephone 45-6
television 49
telex 46
Temple Mount, see Haram
    ash-Sharif/Temple Mount
Terra Sancta 119, **Map 4**
Thabor House 117, **Map 2**
Ticho House 25, 115, **Map 3**
Ticho, Abraham 115
Ticho, Anna 115
time 50
Time Elevator 115, **Map 3**
tipping, see money
tombs
    Absolom's Tomb 105
    Garden Tomb 111
    Herod's Family Tomb 120
    Jason's Tomb 119
    Jesus, see Church of the
        Holy Sepulchre
    Rachel's Tomb 166, **Map 1**
    Tomb of B'nei Hezir 105
    Tomb of Jehoshaphat 105
    Tomb of Lazarus 165
    Tomb of the Lady Tunshuq 93
    Tomb of the Virgin Mary 109
    Tomb of Turjan Khatun 93
    Tomb of Zechariah 105
    Tombs of the Kings 112
    Tombs of the Prophets 108
Torah 28

tourist offices 37-8
Tourjeman Post Museum 112-13,
    Map 5
tours
    aerial tours 135
    cycling tours 135
    Dead Sea 170
    West Bank 77
    walking tours 81, 82-3
Tower of David, see Citadel
Tower of David Museum of the
    History of Jerusalem 83-4,
    Map 6
travel agents 67

V
Valley of Jehoshaphat 105-6,
    Map 2
Via Dolorosa 95, **95**

video 50
visas 38
Volunteer Tourist Service 53

W
Wadi Qelt 167
Wailing Wall, see Western Wall
walking tours 76-77, 81
Wallenberg, Raoul 133
War of Independence (1948) 17
Warren's Shaft 106, **Map 2**
Western Wall 88-9, **Map 9**
Western Wall Tunnel 89, **Map 9**
Wilson's Arch 89, **Map 9**
Wohl Museum of Archaeology
    91, **Map 9**
women travellers 51-2
work 57
WWI cemetery 110, **Map 2**

Y
Yad Vashem 132-3, **133**
    Map 1
    Children's Memorial 132
    Hall of Rememberance 132
    Historical & Art Museums
        132
    Righteous Among the
        Nations 133
    Valley of the Communities 132
Yadin, Yigael 169
Yemin Moshe 121, **Map 4**
Yiddish 14

Z
Zion Gate 80, **Maps 8 & 9**
Zion Square 115, **Map 3**
zoo, see Biblical Zoo

Boxed Text

Air Travel Glossary 64-5
Arab Sweets & Pastries 152
Bagels & Bread 150
Ben Yehuda & the Revival of
    Hebrew 35
Boys, Girls & Guns 20
Chagall 134
Christian Hospices 136
Coffeehouse, The 149
Colony, The 145
Dana International – Israel's
    Pride or Shame? 22
Dead Healthy? 168
Ethics & Antiquities 161
Everyday Health 50
God's Fax Line 88
Holy Fire 56

Internet Resources 47
Introducing the eKno 46
Israeli Beer 157
Israeli Stamp Stigma, The 39
Jerusalem in Print 23
Jerusalem Syndrome, The 103
Jerusalem Time Line 11
Kippot 29
Latrun Monastery 167
Medical Kit Check List 51
Orthodox & Gay – Oxymoron
    or Personal Paradox? 27
Psalm 137 12
Public Holidays in 2000 55
Rites & Wrongs 98
Road Orthodoxy 75
Sorry for What? 25

St George of Lod (& England)
    112
Stations of the Cross, The 96-7
There Goes the Neighbour-
    hood 89
(Very Complex) Masada
    Complex, The 169
Via Dolorosa 95
Views of the City 79
Walking Tours of the Old City
    82-3
Warning 107
Wee Small Hours, The 154
What to do on Shabbat 159
Yiddish 14

St James' Cathedral door, Armenian Quarter

The Church of the Holy Sepulchre, Old City

An Ethiopian priest contemplates his Bible at an entrance of the Church of the Holy Sepulchre.

MAP 1 – Greater Jerusalem

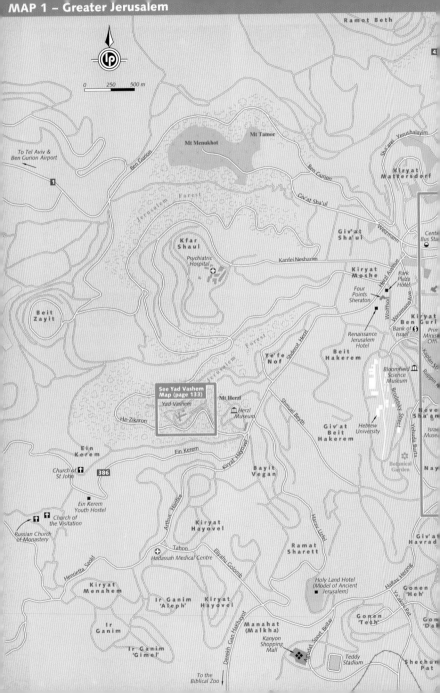

0   250   500 m

To Tel Aviv &
Ben Gurion Airport

1

Ramot Beth

Shalem Yerushalayim

Miryat
Mattersdorf

Ben Gurion

Mt Tamor

Mt Menukhot

Ben Gurion

Jerusalem   Forest

Giv'at Sha'ul

Giv'at
Sha'ul

Weizmann

Central
Bus Sta

Kfar
Shaul

Kanfei Nesharim

Kiryat
Moshe

Park
Plaza
Hotel

Psychiatric
Hospital

Four
Points
Sheraton

Herzl Avenue

Wolfson

Weizmann Ave

Kiryat
Ben Guri

Bank of
Israel

Prim
Minist
Offi

Renaissance
Jerusalem
Hotel

Beit
Zayit

Beit
Hakerem

Yefe
Nof

Kaplan St

Bloomfield
Science
Museum

Jerusalem   Forest

Shderot Herzl

Brodetsky Street

Neve
Sha'ani

Ruppin St

Israe
Muse

See Yad Vashem
Map (page 133)

Mt Herzl

Herzl
Museum

Yad Vashem

Ha-Zikaron

Samuel Beyth

Giv'at
Beit
Hakerem

Hebrew
University

Yehuda Burla

Botanical
Garden

Nay

Ein
Kerem

Ein Kerem

Kiryat Hayovel

Bayit
Vegan

Church of
St John

386

Ein Kerem
Youth Hostel

Arthur Hantke

Eliyahu Golomb

Kiryat
Hayovel

Ramat
Sharett

Harav Uziel

Giv'at
Havrad

Church of
the Visitation

Russian Church
of Monastery

Tahon

Hadassah Medical Centre

Henrietta Szold

Kiryat
Menahem

Ir Ganim
'Aleph'

Kiryat
Hayovel

Holy Land Hotel
(Model of Ancient
Jerusalem)

Gonen
'Heh'

HaRav Herzog

Yaakov Pat

Ir
Ganim

Ir Ganim
'Gimel'

Derekh Gan HaKhayot

Manahat
(Malkha)

Kanyon
Shopping
Mall

Agudat Sport Betar

Gonen
'Teth'

Gon
'Da

Shechun
Pat

Teddy
Stadium

To the
Biblical Zoo

Ramot Forest

Yigael Yadin

60

Sha'afat Road

Giv'at Shapira

Ma'aleh Adumim Road

1

Le Sixteen Bed & Breakfast

Giv'at Ramivtar House 57 Bed & Breakfast

Ramot Eshkol

Sderot Levi Eshkol

Sderot Golda Meir

Hativat Harel

Sanhedria

Ammunition Hill

Hyatt Regency

Hadassah Hospital

Ezrat Torah

Kiryat Belz

Mahanaym

Bar Ilan Street

Shmuel HaNavi Street

UNRWA Headquarters

French Consulate

Kiryat Hamemshala

Shderot sayeret Har HaTzdim

Isawiya

Ma'alot Dafna

Kiryat Aryeh

Sheikh Jarrah

Shikun Habad

Bukharan Quarter

Yirmiyahu

Kerem Avraham

Malchei Yisra'el

Yaltezkei Street

UK Consulate

Nahalat Shim'on

HaShalom Road

American Colony

Hebrew University (Mt Scopus)

mema

Mekor Baruch

Ge'ula

Mea She'arim

Beit Yisra'el

Nablus Street

Salah ad Din Street

Mt Scopus

Wad El-Joz

Augusta Victoria Hospital

Zichron Moshe

Jaffa Road

Mea She'arim

Heil HaHandasa Road

Mormon Brigham Young University

Agrippas Street

HaNevi'im Street

East Jerusalem

Bab Ez'Zahra

Shmuel Ben Adaya

Es-Suwaneh

Mahane Yehuda

Bezalel Street

Nahla'ot

Ben Yehuda St

Yisrael Street

Garden Tomb

Suleyman Street

Rab'a El Adawiyeh

Nahal HaEgoz

Jericho Road

'vat am

Ben Zvi Avenue

me Court

Nahalat Ahim

King George V Street

Nahalat Shiv'a

SPNI Jaffa Road

Morasha

Sultan

Muslim Quarter

Mount of Olives

Et Tur

esset

Sha'arei Hessed

New City

Christian Quarter

Old City

Dome of the Rock

Kiryat Wolfson

Agron Street

Mamilla

HaEmek Refa'im

Jaffa Gate

Jewish Quarter

Jewish Cemetery

Ramban Street

Keren Ha-Yesod St

Yemin Moshe

Armenian Quarter

Kidron Valley

Jericho Road

417

astery the oss

Rehavia

Ze'ev Jabotinsky Street

Mt Zion

Ras El-Amud

veh anot

Kiryat Shmuel

Gaza (Aza) Road

Talbiyeh

Silwan

lerzog

HaPalmach Street

Elazar HaModa'i

Hinnon Valley

ikun ssco

Gonen

(The German Colony) HaMoshava HaGermanit

Train Station

Giv'at Hananya

To Abu Dis & Jericho

MAP 2 – Inner Jerusalem

Abu Tor

Emek Refa'im

Hamoshava Hayvanit

Emek Refa'im

St Claire's Convent

Peace Forest (Ya'ar HaShalom)

Khirbet Beit Sakhur

Gonen 'Vav'

Baka

Hebron Road

Yehuda

North Talpiot

Haas Promenade

Government House

Gonen 'Aleph'

Mekor Nayim

60

Daniel

Yanovsky

en 'h'

Bethlehem Road

Talpiot

Ma'alot Moriah

To Bethlehem

Agnon House

MAP 2 – Inner Jerusalem

Shikun Habad

Bukharan Quarter

Yirmiyahu

Bar-Ilan Street

Schmuel HaNavi Street

Kerem Avraham

Zephaniah

Yehezkel Street

Malchei Yisra'el

Romema

Allenby #2

Central Bus Station

Jaffa Road

Sarei Yisra'el

Nordau

Mekor Baruch

Rashi Street

Mea She'arim Street

Ge'ula

Bet Yisra'el

Zalman

Zichron Moshe

Mea She'arim

Binyanei Ha'Umah Conference Centre & Israel Youth Hostels Association

Strauss Street

Foreign Ministry

Davidka Memorial

HI – HaDavidka Youth Hostel

HaNevi'im

Ethiopian Church

Crown Plaza Hotel

Agrippas Street

Gidi's

Mordo B.

Mahane Yehuda

Mahane Yehuda Market

HaNevi'im Street

Ben Yehuda House

Bnei Brith St.

Ethiopia St.

Jaffa Road

Klal Building/Arkia

MAP 3 – New City Central

Mahane Yehuda

Pargod Theatre

Betzalel Street

Ben Zvi Avenue

Nahla'ot

Ben Yehuda Street

Nahalat Shiv'a

Jaffa Road

Supreme Court

Noah's House

Nahalat Ahim

Givat Ram

Wohl Rose Park

Sha'arei Hessed

King George V Street

Gan Ha'Atzmaut (Independence Park)

Mamilla

HaEmek

Keren Street

Ministry of the Interior

Ruppin Road

Kiryat Wolfson

Ussishkin Street

Diskin Street

Agron Street

Ha-Melekh David Street

Knesset

Ramban Street

Ben Maimon

MAP 4 – New City South

Bible Lands Museum

Khav'in Ha'az Avenue

Afesi Street

Gaza (Azza) Road

Rehavia

Balfour Street

Ze'ev Jabotinsky Street

Keren HaYesod Street

HaMelekh David

Neveh Sha'anan

Israel Museum

Clore Gardens

Kaf Nisar Road

Talbiyeh

Billy Rose Sculpture Garden

Monastery of the Cross

Baruch Marcus Rd.

Liberty Bell Gardens

Neveh Granot

Kiryat Shmuel

Chopin Street

Nayot

Kiryat Shmuel

HaMovilim Street

HaLamech David

Habaimach Street

Harav Herzog

Tchernichowsky

Baruch Hermdar

(The German Colony) HaMoshava HaGermanit

Emek Refaim

Shikun Rassco

Gonen

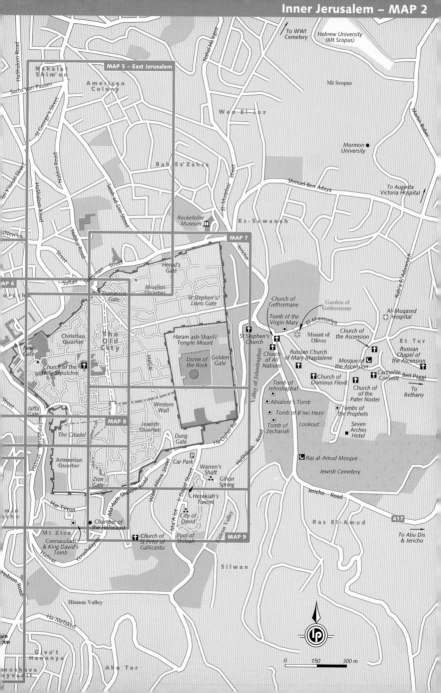

To WWI Cemetery

Hebrew University (Mt Scopus)

Mt Scopus

Nablus Road

HaShalom Road

HaShalom Road

Sachs Van Paasen

St George's Street

Ben-Hillel Street

Nahalat Shim'on

American Colony

Was El-Joz

Martin Buber

Mormon University

Ashtara Road

HaNeviim Street

al-Neviim

Bab Ez Zahra

Shmuel Ben Adaya

To Augusta Victoria Hospital

El-Mordhai Street

Saladin Street

South al-Din Street

Rockefeller Museum

Es-Suwaneh

Jericho Street

MAP 5 – East Jerusalem

MAP 7

Herod's Gate

Rabi'a El Adawiyeh

Suleyman Street

MAP 6

Sultan

Damascus Gate

Muslim Quarter

St Stephen's/ Lions Gate

Church of Gethsemane

Garden of Gethsemane

Al-Muqased Hospital

Tomb of the Virgin Mary

El-Mansuriya

Et Tur

Christian Quarter

The Old City

HaNevi'im

Haram ash-Sharif/ Temple Mount

St Stephen's Church

Mount of Olives

Church of the Ascension

Russian Chapel of the Ascension

New Gate

Dome of the Rock

Golden Gate

Church of All Nations

Russian Church of Mary-Magdalene

Mosque of the Ascension

Church of the Holy Sepulchre

Jaffa Gate

Church of Dominus Flevit

Carmelite Convent

Beit Pagei

To Bethany

Valley of Jehoshaphat

Western Wall

Jewish Quarter

Tomb of Jehoshaphat

Church of the Pater Noster

The Citadel

MAP 8

Absalom's Tomb

Tombs of the Prophets

Ha Ophel Rd

Dung Gate

Tomb of B'nei Hezir

Hativat Yerushalayim

Armenian Quarter

Ma'aleh Shalom Road

Car Park

Warren's Shaft

Tomb of Zechariah

Lookout

Seven Arches Hotel

HaShiloah Road

Zion Gate

Wadi Hilwe Street

Gihon Spring

Ras al-Amud Mosque

Har Tsiyon

Ir-David Street

Hezekiah's Tunnel

Jewish Cemetery

Chamber of the Holocaust

Ma'alot

City of David

Jericho Road

417

Mt Zion

Coenaculum & King David's Tomb

Church of St Peter of Gallicantu

Pool of Shiloah

Kidron Valley

MAP 9

Ras El-Amud

Hativat

Yerushalayim

Silwan

To Abu Dis & Jericho

Hebron Road

Hinnon Valley

Ha-Mefaked

Giv'at Hananya

Abu Tor

0   150   300 m

MAP 3 – New City Central

Mahane Yehuda

Nahla'ot

Nahalat Shiv'a

Sha'arei Hessed

Me'ir Sherman Garden

To Pargod Theatre

To Mahane Yehuda Market

Iftis Road

Rishonim

To Rehavia & Talbiyeh

MAP 4

PLACES TO STAY
2 Hotel Noga
10 Jerusalem Tower
15 My Home
16 Jerusalem Inn Hotel
26 Hotel Zion
31 Eyal Hotel
54 Jasmine Ben Yehuda Hostel
58 Hotel Ron
61 Hotel Kaplan
63 Jerusalem Inn Hotel
85 Jerusalem Hilton
86 HI-Beit Shmuel Hostel
88 King David Hotel
89 YMCA Three Arches Hotel
92 Sheraton Plaza Hotel
95 Kings Hotel

PLACES TO EAT
4 Mamma Mia
8 Spaghettim
9 Rif-Raf
12 McDonald's
17 Fink's
19 Thailand Food Sandwich Bar
20 King of Felafel & Shwarma
21 Alumah Natural Food Restaurant
22 Wild Bull
23 Blues Brothers
28 The Village Green
30 Trio
35 Gilly's
37 The 7th Place
38 Mandarin
40 Ocean
42 Korea House
43 El Gaucho
44 The Yemenite Step
45 Misadonet
47 Sakura
51 Papi Tai; Ma'adan
55 Potato Guy
56 Bonkers Bagels
60 Ticho House Cafe
62 Angelo
64 Stanleys
78 Eten
97 Off the Square
99 Helmeshe Essen

OTHER
1 Post Office
3 Bezalel Art School
5 Ministry of Tourism
6 Mona Tours
7 Schwartz
11 Tower Records
13 Orion
14 Nesher Taxis (for the airport)
18 Steimatzky Bookshop
23 Sefer VeSefel Bookshop
24 Change Point
25 Solan Telecom
29 Steimatzky Bookshop
32 Laundry Place
33 The Blue Hole
34 Museum of Italian Jewish Art & Synagogue
36 The Time Elevator
39 Tzipor Hanefesh
41 The Tavern Pub
46 Stardust
48 Tmol Shilshom
49 Underground
50 Change Point
52 Kodak Express
53 Lametayel
57 Video City
59 Ticho House
65 Mike's Place
66 Netcafe
67 SPNI Office & Bookshop
68 ISSTA Student Travel
69 Strudel
70 Kanabis
71 Glasnost
72 Vibe Dance Bar
73 Underground Prisoners' Museum 1918-1948
74 Church of the Holy Trinity
75 Central Police Station
76 Libraire Française
77 Main Post Office
79 New City Hall Complex; Jerusalem Information & Tourism Centre
80 Champs
81 Mazada Tours
82 Old City Hall
83 Ahava
84 St Vincent de Paul Hospice
87 Hebrew Union College
90 US Consulate
91 Mamilla Pool
93 Alliance Française
94 Supersol Supermarket
96 Heichal Shlomo & The Great Synagogue
98 Rehavia Windmill

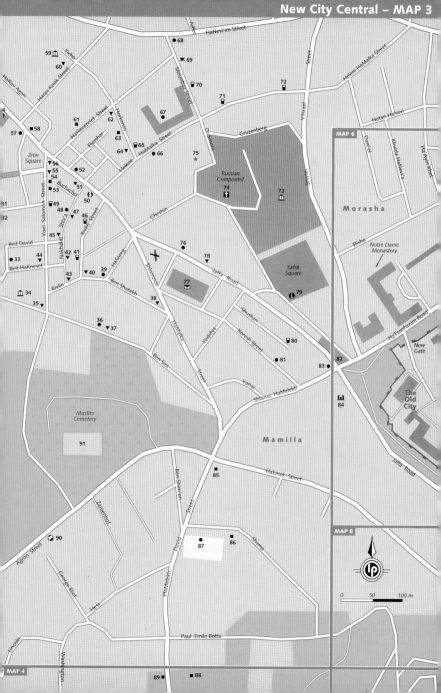

MAP 6

MAP 8

MAP 4

Morasha

Notre Dame
Monastery

Elisha

New
Gate

The
Old
City

Safra
Square

Russian
Compound

Zion
Square

Beit David

Beit HaKneset

Muslim
Cemetery

Mamilla

HaNevi'im Street

Heleni HaMalka Street

Notan HaNevi

Daniel

Khulda HaNevi'a

Ha'Ayin Khet

Y-Israel

Shivtei

Gruzenberg

Cheshin

Jaffa   Road

Shushan

Koresh Street

Shlomo   HaMelekh

Yanai

HaTzanhanim Road

Jaffa Road

HaEmek Street

Shama

Ben-Shimon

David

Hatzvi

HaTzfira

Zamenhof

Agron Street

George Eliot

Hess

Lincoln

Washington

Paul Emile Botta

Ben Sira

Parnaka

Yeddye

Silomron

Ben Shatakh

HaSoreg

Shiv'a

Rivlin

Nakhalat

Rivlin

Buchacha

Yoel–Salomon Street

HaRav Agan

Harav Kook Street

Ticho

Helene

HaMalkha Street

HaHistov

HaTevezelet Street

Eyeshar

Monbaz Street

D-Sisneta

HaRav Agan

59 60 61 62 63 64 65 66 67 68 69 70 71 72 73 74 75 76 77 78 79 80 81 82 83 84 85 86 87 88 89 90 91 57 58 96 55 54 53 52 51 50 49 48 47 46 45 44 43 42 41 40 39 38 37 36 35 34 33

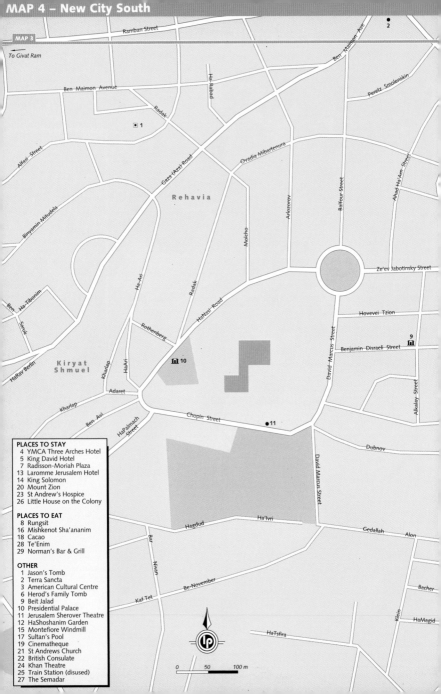

MAP 4 – New City South

MAP 3

To Givat Ram

Rehavia

Kiryat Shmuel

Ramban Street

Ben Maimon Ave

Peretz Smolenskin

Ben Maimon Avenue

Ha-Rabad

Radak

Gaza (Aza) Road

Ovadia Mibertenura

Balfour Street

Ahad Ha'Am Street

Alfasi Street

Binyamin Mitudela

Arlozorov

Molcho

Ha-Ari

Radak

HaNasi Road

Ze'ev Jabotinsky Street

Ben Sarulk

Ha-Tibonim

Rothenberg

Hovevei Tzion

David Marcus Street

Benjamin Disraeli Street

HaRav Berlin

Kharlap

Ha-Ari

Adaret

9

10

Alkalay Street

Kharlap

Ben Avi

HaPalmach Street

Chopin Street

11

Dubnov

Bar

Nissan

David Marcus Street

Hagdud

Ha'Ivri

Gedallah

Alon

Be-November

Kaf Tet

Bacher

HaTsfira

Klein

HaMagid

PLACES TO STAY
4 YMCA Three Arches Hotel
5 King David Hotel
7 Radisson-Moriah Plaza
13 Laromme Jerusalem Hotel
14 King Solomon
20 Mount Zion
23 St Andrew's Hospice
26 Little House on the Colony

PLACES TO EAT
8 Rungsit
16 Mishkenot Sha'ananim
18 Cacao
28 Te'Enim
29 Norman's Bar & Grill

OTHER
1 Jason's Tomb
2 Terra Sancta
3 American Cultural Centre
6 Herod's Family Tomb
9 Beit Jalad
10 Presidential Palace
11 Jerusalem Sherover Theatre
12 HaShoshanim Garden
15 Montefiore Windmill
17 Sultan's Pool
19 Cinematheque
21 St Andrews Church
22 British Consulate
24 Khan Theatre
25 Train Station (disused)
27 The Semadar

0   50   100 m

MAP 3

MAP 8

Yemin Moshe

Talbiyeh

Bloomfield Gardens

Liberty Bell Gardens

Pinsker Street

(The German Colony)
HaMoshava HaGermanit

To Bethlehem

Keren HaYesod Street
George Washington
Sokolov
Sokolov
Mocher
Sfarim
Mendele
Shalom
Yitzkhak Elhanin
Mane
Aba
Sikra
Mapu
Alrichem
HaMigdal
HaBrekha
Yemin
Moshe
Arts & Crafts Lane
Ha'Mevasser
Bloomfield Avenue
HaTsayar
HaMelekh David Street
Mishkenot
Sha'ananin
Nahon
Hebron Road
David Remez Street
Bethlehem Road
Emek Refa'im Street
Peterson
Hebron Road
Cremieux
Dor Vedorshav
Zvi Graetz
osanis
Immanu'el No'akh
Lloyd George Street
Wedgewood
Smuts

3
4
5
6
7
8
13
14
15
16
17
18
19
20
21
22
23
24
25
26
27
28
29
12

MAP 5 – East Jerusalem

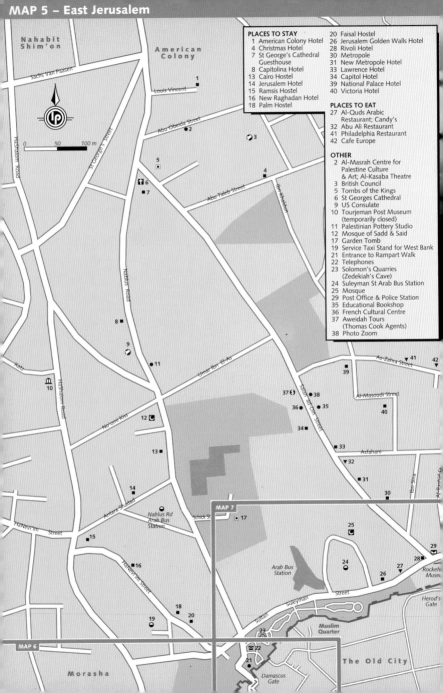

PLACES TO STAY
1 American Colony Hotel
7 St George's Cathedral
  Guesthouse
8 Capitolina Hotel
13 Cairo Hostel
14 Jerusalem Hotel
15 Ramsis Hostel
16 New Raghadan Hotel
18 Palm Hostel
20 Faisal Hostel
26 Jerusalem Golden Walls Hotel
28 Rivoli Hotel
30 Metropole
31 New Metropole Hotel
33 Lawrence Hotel
34 Capitol Hotel
39 National Palace Hotel
40 Victoria Hotel

PLACES TO EAT
27 Al-Quds Arabic
  Restaurant; Candy's
32 Abu Ali Restaurant
41 Philadelphia Restaurant
42 Cafe Europe

OTHER
2 Al-Masrah Centre for
  Palestine Culture
  & Art; Al-Kasaba Theatre
3 British Council
5 Tombs of the Kings
6 St Georges Cathedral
9 US Consulate
10 Tourjeman Post Museum
  (temporarily closed)
11 Palestinian Pottery Studio
12 Mosque of Sadd & Said
17 Garden Tomb
19 Service Taxi Stand for West Bank
21 Entrance to Rampart Walk
22 Telephones
23 Solomon's Quarries
  (Zedekiah's Cave)
24 Suleyman St Arab Bus Station
25 Mosque
29 Post Office & Police Station
35 Educational Bookshop
36 French Cultural Centre
37 Aweidah Tours
  (Thomas Cook Agents)
38 Photo Zoom

PLACES TO STAY
7 Al Ahram Youth Hostel
8 Al-Arab Hostel
10 New Hashimi Hostel
11 Tabasco Hostel & Tearooms
21 Casa Nova Pilgrims' Hospice
23 Greek Catholic
   Patriarchate Hospice
24 Gloria Hotel
30 New Imperial Hotel
32 Petra Hostel
34 Jaffa Gate Youth Hostel
39 Christ Church Hospice
45 Citadel Youth Hostel
48 New Swedish Hostel
49 Lutheran Hospice

PLACES TO EAT
4 Green Door Bakery
6 Jerusalem Star
12 El-A'Elat Restaurant
17 Zalatino's
19 Kostas' Restaurant
22 Yerevan
25 Abu Shanab
29 City Restaurant
31 Cafeteria St Michel
36 Coffee Shop
44 Armenian Tavern
47 Backpacker Tearooms

OTHER
1 Telephones
2 Entrance to Ramparts Walk
3 Money Changer
5 Ariel Sharon's House
12 Lutheran Church
   of the Redeemer
13 St Alexander's Church
14 Ethiopian Monastery
15 Khanqah Salahiyya
16 Church of the Holy Sepulchre
18 Omar Mosque
20 Greek Orthodox
   Patriarchate Museum
26 Tourist Information Office
27 Entrance & Tickets for
   Ramparts Walk
28 Telephones
33 Pool of Hezekiah
35 Christian Information Centre
37 Branch Post Office
38 Christ Church
40 Bank Leumi
41 Zion Walking Tours
42 Armenian Ceramic Shop
43 Police
46 Church of St John the Baptist
50 Butchers' Market
51 Stairs to Rooftop Promenade
52 Stairs to Rooftop Promenade
53 Branch Post Office
54 Hurva Synagogue
55 Ramban Synagogue
56 Jewish Student Information
   Centre
57 Archaeological Seminars
58 St Mark's Church
59 Old Yishuv Court Museum

Backpackers taking a break at the Damascus Gate.

errusal

MAP 7 – The Old City, Muslim Quarter

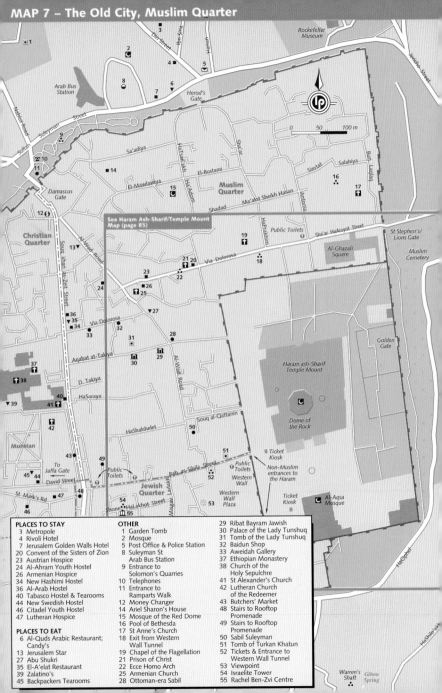

Rockefeller Museum

Arab Bus Station

Damascus Gate

Christian Quarter

Sa'adiya

El-Mawlawiya

El-Bustami

Muslim Quarter

Shadad

Ma'alot Sheikh Hasan

Herod's Gate

Simtat Salahiya

Burj Laqlaq

See Haram Ash-Sharif/Temple Mount Map (page 85)

Public Toilets

Sha'ar HaArayot Street

Al-Ghazali Square

St Stephen's/Lions Gate

Muslim Cemetery

Via Dolorosa

Al-Wad Road

Souq Khan as-Zeit Street

Aqabat at-Takiya

D. Takiya

HaSaraya

HaShalshelet

Souq al-Qattanin

Haram ash-Sharif Temple Mount

Golden Gate

Dome of the Rock

Muristan

To Jaffa Gate

David Street

St Mark's Rd

Jewish Quarter

Bab as-Silsila Street

Misgav Ladakh

HaLakhot Street

Stone

Public Toilets

Western Wall Plaza

Western Wall

Non-Muslim entrances to the Haram

Ticket Kiosk

Ticket Kiosk

Al-Aqsa Mosque

HaOphel

Warren's Shaft

Gihon Spring

0   50   100 m

PLACES TO STAY
3 Metropole
4 Rivoli Hotel
7 Jerusalem Golden Walls Hotel
21 Convent of the Sisters of Zion
23 Austrian Hospice
24 Al-Ahram Youth Hostel
26 Armenian Hospice
34 New Hashimi Hostel
36 Al-Arab Hostel
40 Tabasco Hostel & Tearooms
44 New Swedish Hostel
46 Citadel Youth Hostel
47 Lutheran Hospice

PLACES TO EAT
6 Al-Quds Arabic Restaurant; Candy's
13 Jerusalem Star
27 Abu Shukri
35 El-A'elat Restaurant
39 Zalatino's
45 Backpackers Tearooms

OTHER
1 Garden Tomb
2 Mosque
5 Post Office & Police Station
8 Suleyman St Arab Bus Station
9 Entrance to Solomon's Quarries
10 Telephones
11 Entrance to Ramparts Walk
12 Money Changer
14 Ariel Sharon's House
15 Mosque of the Red Dome
16 Pool of Bethesda
17 St Anne's Church
18 Exit from Western Wall Tunnel
19 Chapel of the Flagellation
20 Prison of Christ
22 Ecce Homo Arch
25 Armenian Church
28 Ottoman-era Sabil
29 Ribat Bayram Jawish
30 Palace of the Lady Tunshuq
31 Tomb of the Lady Tunshuq
32 Baidun Shop
33 Aweidah Gallery
37 Ethiopian Monastery
38 Church of the Holy Sepulchre
41 St Alexander's Church
42 Lutheran Church of the Redeemer
43 Butchers' Market
48 Stairs to Rooftop Promenade
49 Stairs to Rooftop Promenade
50 Sabil Suleyman
51 Tomb of Turkan Khatun
52 Tickets & Entrance to Western Wall Tunnel
53 Viewpoint
54 Israelite Tower
55 Rachel Ben-Zvi Centre

HaEmek

The Citadel
(Tower of
David
Museum)

Christian Quarter

Jewish Quarter Road

10

1
2
3
5
6

4

8

9

Habad Street

Public
Toilets

7

Or HaChaim St

11

12

15

14

13

Argat Street

16

Armenian
Garden

17

Jewish
Quarter

18

Armenian
Quarter

Armenian-Patriarchate-Road

Car Park

Batei Mahseh St

To
Western
Wall

20

19

Armenian
Seminary

Hativat Zion Road

Catholic
Cemetery

Armenian
Cemetery

Zion
Gate

Ma'alah-Shalem-Road

Dror Eliel Road

Hativat-Yerushalayim-Road

0   50   100 m

PLACES TO STAY
4 Christ Church Hospice
16 El-Malak Youth Hostel

PLACES TO EAT
6 Armenian Tavern

OTHER
1 Post Office
2 Bank Leumi
3 Zion Walking Tours
5 Armenian Ceramic Shop
7 Police
8 St Mark's Chapel
9 Archaeological Seminars
10 Post Office
11 Hurva Synagogue
12 Ramban Synagogue
13 Jewish Student
    Information Centre
14 Old Yishuv Court Museum
15 Alex de Rothschild
    Craft Centre
17 St James' (Jacques) Cathedral
18 Armenian Art Centre
19 Armenian Museum
20 Disused Mosque

CHRISTINE OSBORNE

The Old City walls and Citadel

MAP 9 – The Old City, Jewish Quarter

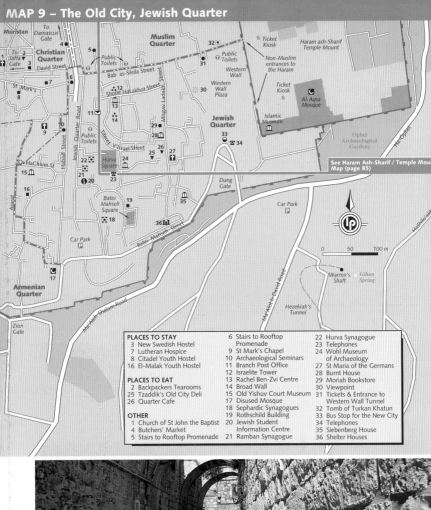

PLACES TO STAY
3 New Swedish Hostel
7 Lutheran Hospice
8 Citadel Youth Hostel
16 El-Malak Youth Hostel

PLACES TO EAT
2 Backpackers Tearooms
25 Tzaddik's Old City Deli
26 Quarter Cafe

OTHER
1 Church of St John the Baptist
4 Butchers' Market
5 Stairs to Rooftop Promenade

6 Stairs to Rooftop Promenade
9 St Mark's Chapel
10 Archaeological Seminars
11 Branch Post Office
12 Israelite Tower
13 Rachel Ben-Zvi Centre
14 Broad Wall
15 Old Yishuv Court Museum
17 Disused Mosque
18 Sephardic Synagogues
19 Rothschild Building
20 Jewish Student Information Centre
21 Ramban Synagogue

22 Hurva Synagogue
23 Telephones
24 Wohl Museum of Archaeology
27 St Maria of the Germans
28 Burnt House
29 Moriah Bookstore
30 Viewpoint
31 Tickets & Entrance to Western Wall Tunnel
32 Tomb of Turkan Khatun
33 Bus Stop for the New City
34 Telephones
35 Siebenberg House
36 Shelter Houses

CHRISTINE OSBORNE

Jewish students exploring the Jewish Quarter's winding alleys.

LEANNE LOGAN

GADI FARFOUR

EDDIE GERALD

For the young and old of Jewish, Muslim and Christian faiths, the Holy Land – especially Jerusalem – has an overwhelming religious significance.

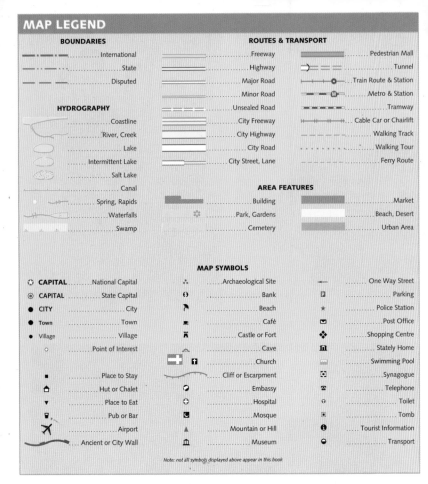

MAP LEGEND

BOUNDARIES
.... International
.... State
.... Disputed

HYDROGRAPHY
.... Coastline
.... River, Creek
.... Lake
.... Intermittent Lake
.... Salt Lake
.... Canal
.... Spring, Rapids
.... Waterfalls
.... Swamp

ROUTES & TRANSPORT
.... Freeway
.... Highway
.... Major Road
.... Minor Road
.... Unsealed Road
.... City Freeway
.... City Highway
.... City Road
.... City Street, Lane
.... Pedestrian Mall
.... Tunnel
.... Train Route & Station
.... Metro & Station
.... Tramway
.... Cable Car or Chairlift
.... Walking Track
.... Walking Tour
.... Ferry Route

AREA FEATURES
.... Building
.... Park, Gardens
.... Cemetery
.... Market
.... Beach, Desert
.... Urban Area

MAP SYMBOLS
⊙ **CAPITAL** .... National Capital
◎ **CAPITAL** .... State Capital
● **CITY** .... City
● **Town** .... Town
● Village .... Village
○ .... Point of Interest

■ .... Place to Stay
△ .... Hut or Chalet
▼ .... Place to Eat
🍺 .... Pub or Bar
✈ .... Airport
.... Ancient or City Wall

.... Archaeological Site
.... Bank
.... Beach
.... Café
.... Castle or Fort
.... Cave
.... Church
.... Cliff or Escarpment
.... Embassy
.... Hospital
.... Mosque
▲ .... Mountain or Hill
🏛 .... Museum

.... One Way Street
.... Parking
★ .... Police Station
.... Post Office
.... Shopping Centre
.... Stately Home
.... Swimming Pool
.... Synagogue
☎ .... Telephone
.... Toilet
.... Tomb
.... Tourist Information
.... Transport

Note: not all symbols displayed above appear in this book

LONELY PLANET OFFICES

Australia
PO Box 617, Hawthorn, Victoria 3122
☎ 03 9819 1877 fax 03 9819 6459
email: talk2us@lonelyplanet.com.au

USA
150 Linden St, Oakland, CA 94607
☎ 510 893 8555 TOLL FREE: 800 275 8555
fax 510 893 8572
email: info@lonelyplanet.com

UK
10a Spring Place, London, NW5 3BH
☎ 0171 428 4800 fax 0171 428 4828
email: go@lonelyplanet.co.uk

France
1 rue du Dahomey, 75011 Paris
☎ 01 55 25 33 00 fax 01 55 25 33 01
email: bip@lonelyplanet.fr
3615 lonelyplanet *(1.29 F TTC/min)*

World Wide Web: www.lonelyplanet.com *or* AOL keyword: lp
Lonely Planet Images: lpi@lonelyplanet.com.au